WHAT DEMOCRACY LOOKS LIKE

WHAT DEMOCRACY LOOKS LIKE

THE RHETORIC OF
SOCIAL MOVEMENTS
AND COUNTERPUBLICS

Christina R. Foust
Amy Pason
Kate Zittlow Rogness

The University of Alabama Press
Tuscaloosa

The University of Alabama Press
Tuscaloosa, Alabama 35487-0380
uapress.ua.edu

Typeface: Caslon and Helvetica

Manufactured in the United States of America
Cover image: Courtesy of Rae Louise Breaux, www.raenorshine.com
Cover design: Michele Myatt Quinn

Cataloging-in-Publication data is available from the Library of Congress.
ISBN: 978-0-8173-5893-8
E-ISBN: 978-0-8173-9118-8

Contents

Acknowledgments

This project began humbly, following a panel at the National Communication Association (NCA) convention in 2010 about agency as it relates to social movements and counterpublics. The three editors of this volume presented and Cate Palczewski responded. As we packed our things, we realized that some of the panelists strongly identified with social movement scholarship while others were more heavily interested in counterpublics. So, we asked ourselves: What is the difference between social movements and counterpublics? The question was significant enough to invite others to help address it, so we organized a preconference at the 2011 NCA convention, "Voicing Connections, Contradictions, and Possibilities in Social Movement and Counterpublic Theories." We are grateful to the original panelists, including contributors in the present volume whose early drafts were shared in New Orleans (Bernadette Calafell, Kevin DeLuca, Christina Foust, Josh Hanan, Ray McKerrow, Cate Palczewski, Amy Pason, and Kate Zittlow Rogness). Given the response to the preconference, we worked to give these important conversations permanence in this volume.

We want to extend a special thanks to Ray and Cate, as well-respected scholars who have supported our editorial vision from the beginning. We are also grateful to the contributors to this volume for signing on and for their diligence and patience throughout the editorial process. Thanks to Dan Waterman, our acquisitions editor at the University of Alabama Press, along with John Lucaites, our series editor. We appreciate the helpful comments from the two anonymous reviewers.

This work is supported by subvention funding from the College of Liberal Arts and the School of Social Research and Justice Studies at the University of Nevada, and we greatly appreciate the assistance to help maintain this as an affordable book. Additional support for finishing costs was provided by the dean's office of the Arts, Humanities, and Social Sciences at the University of Denver.

Christina thanks her family; especially Charles for providing calming perspective and strength in abundance, and Rose and Henry for enduring anesthetizing suppertime discussions for these years. Amy thanks her parents, John and Patty, for educating her in the histories of Students for a Democratic Society, antiwar, and civil rights activists, and for emphasizing the importance of speaking out for what is right. She also wants to acknowledge the support of her University of Nevada colleagues and junior faculty reading group for supporting the project and providing valuable feedback. Kate thanks her family, particularly Colin and Finbar, for their enduring support and shared commitment to social justice; and for being a constant reminder of the value that humor, humility, and compassion play in our efforts toward a more fair and just world.

Introduction

Rhetoric and the Study of Social Change

Amy Pason, Christina R. Foust, and Kate Zittlow Rogness

Communication scholars have a long history of studying social change, but ironically, as protests across the globe capture the public's imagination (evident in *Time*'s 2011 person of the year ["The Protester"]), it is difficult to define what constitutes social change scholarship. Previously, one may have directed students to a canon of scholarship from which to begin their research on social movement rhetoric.[1] Today, however, scholars must select from a plurality of different approaches, with no predominant concept, method, or set of assumptions guiding research. Although we applaud such diversity, the works of different theoretical traditions have been unnecessarily isolated. Such isolation is no clearer than between two prevailing concepts in social change scholarship: social movements and counterpublics.

At various points in disciplinary history, communication scholars have turned to social movements and counterpublics to understand democratic participation, citizenship, advocacy, and performances of social change. Both concepts have expanded what "counts" as legitimate objects of study,[2] broadening how we understand the forms, functions, and influence of rhetoric. However, each reflects a unique theoretical "pedigree" and has developed slightly different accounts of social change in critical practice. Scholars have yet "to systematically interrogate differences" and similarities "between counterpublics and social movements."[3] Hence, our aim in the present volume is to cohere a conversation on social change, positioning rhetorical critics to understand, evaluate, and even join, acts of resistance in the early twenty-first century.

Our focus on counterpublics and social movements to achieve this goal is justified for a number of reasons. These terms have cross-disciplinary (and even broader public) currency. For instance, "social movement" often reflects the kinship between sociology and communication, while "counterpublic" tends to link our field to literary and political theory. Additionally, both terms have inspired robust theoretical debates. For instance, work classified (or classifiable) under the term "social movement" has assumed rhetoric as instrumental, constitutive, and more recently, affective or immediate. "Counterpublic" work has problematized the material origins of discourse, where agent or agency is centered on subaltern identities, texts, or circulation. As these debates continue, social movement and counterpublic theories offer the potential and flexibility to understand and assess social change rhetoric in a variety of contexts.

For simplicity's sake, we posit the relationship between our focal terms metaphorically: counterpublics and social movements are like second or third cousins, members of the same family who are distanced by time and experience. These concepts share an important similarity in their disciplinary development, as rhetorical critics have variously focused on their character as "nouns" or "verbs." In other words, scholars have taken counterpublics and movements as the *things* (agents, collectives of people) behind social change, or have focused on rhetorical processes or *actions* constituting or affecting change.[4]

Yet, each concept guides scholars to ask slightly different questions, with nuances emerging as scholars apply each term to social change discourses. Social movement scholars have tended to focus upon the rhetoric of (or emanating from) noninstitutionalized actors; whereas counterpublic scholars have concentrated upon how discursive norms or processes include and exclude participation. As we elaborate below (within the four problematics animating social change work), social movement and counterpublic scholarship foregrounds different aspects of social change: For instance, counterpublic scholars may view social change outside the dichotomy of the "establishment" versus "the out-group," while social movement work often engages with material conditions.

Given the breadth of studies related to movements and counterpublics, we could write an entire collection parsing the various ways scholars have attempted to define each. Rather than repeat other prominent reviews,[5] we take the remaining introduction to briefly trace a disciplinary history of our focal terms and identify the central problematics emerging from the terms' literatures. This introduction begins to address the research questions animating our volume, including: How have "social movement" and "counterpublic" been taken up by communication scholars? When might each term be more or less appropriate in the study of social change? How might social change scholars augment each other's work by bringing different literatures (e.g., vernacular discourse and resistance) into conversation? What is the future of movement and counterpublic work in light of the economic, political, and cultural climate of the 2000s—particularly related to resistance within a technologized, postindustrial, global context? Through intellectual histories, case studies, and analysis from leading scholars, this book offers trajectories for future research in social change.

The Disciplinary Emergence of Counterpublics and Movements

Reflecting sociological models, early movement scholars placed organizations or leaders in the role of rhetor, and analyzed nondominant actors as they faced challenges in their attempts to influence "the establishment" or state.[6] As Cox and Foust suggest, many communication scholars then joined their colleagues in sociology, focusing on new social movements (NSMs). NSM study demonstrates a shift from previous assumptions, turning away from "old" movement goals directed toward distribution of material goods or political rights. NSMs are oriented toward changing identity, social norms, or challenging the logic governing social systems.[7] Following disciplinary debates in the 1980s concerning the status of social movements as empirically existent entities, scholars concentrated less upon rhetoric's contributions to large, uninstitutionalized collectivities, and more upon changes in meaning over time.[8] Scholars tacitly accepted "social movements" as their broad domain of inquiry, though their work appeared more invested in considering how communication might effect change almost in spite of its association with collective agents.[9]

Early counterpublic scholarship developed in response to Habermas's germinal work on the public sphere.[10] Like social movement scholarship, counterpublic work assumed identifiable actors *producing* discourse, particularly as a response to exclusion from dominant spheres. Fraser, for instance, equates a "counterpublic" with second-wave feminist groups.[11] Asen, however, warned against the reduction of counterpublics to persons, places, or topics, challenging scholars to focus on the communicative aspects of counterpublics. Counterpublic scholars introduced counterpublicity as a way to analyze alternative validity claims and norms of public speech and the formation of oppositional interpretations of identities, interests, and needs.[12]

Within the discipline, scholars warranted their turn to counterpublic theory, in part, due to the rigidity of sociological movement theory. Few scholars have placed social movement and counterpublic explicitly in relationship; those who have tend to assume social movements as grand agents oriented toward policy change and counterpublics as imagined or virtual "agents" or "spaces" circulating discourses that affect localized or subcultural change. For example, Palczewski understands movements to function as counterpublics when they develop oppositional discourse.[13] Warner asserts that counterpublics become social movements when they engage the state and produce discourse in the style of argumentative claims.[14] Counterpublics thus appear similar to a "pre-inception" phase *prior* to movements, or a way to account for abeyance periods in which movement organizations disband or cease engaging in legislative campaigns.[15]

Such distinctions, we argue, are too simplistic and do not account for scholarly attention to social movement in its verb form. As several of our contributors point out, movement scholars followed McGee in prioritizing *meaning* change or analyzing *rhetorical* movement.[16] Movement scholars have also explored how participants can understand themselves as sharing a consciousness without the confines of formal organizations.[17] Movement as verb is understood as "changes in public consciousness with regards to a key issue or issues, measurable through changes in the meanings of key terms in public discourse."[18] Removed from sociological theory's emphasis on the noun form, movements have more affinity with their counterpublic cousin.

The tensions between noun and verb forms are also endemic to counterpublic's disciplinary development. As Asen notes, Fraser defines counterpublics through both the subordinated status of women and material spaces (e.g., women's bookstores) and the circulation of oppositional interpretations and meaning.[19] More recent work has followed the trend in movement scholarship to emphasize the verb form of counterpublic against (or at least over) the noun. Indeed, as Warner articulates, (counter)publics do not exist apart from the discourse that addresses them, and their "counter" status owes to a public's attempts to reimagine sociability and reflexivity.[20] Counterpublic scholarship emphasizes how texts, styles of speaking, and aesthetic choices can mark one's participation in a counterpublic or/and exclude one from wider publics and circulation channels.

Counterpublic work has also expanded the binary of "agitators versus establishment," challenging scholars to attend to the multiple exigencies or competing publics to whom discourse is addressed. For instance, Pezzullo problematizes breast cancer awareness campaigns as they are sponsored by pharmaceutical companies, at the same time that she acknowledges the potential for antitoxics advocates to connect with breast cancer awareness supporters.[21] Differently, Brouwer analyzes HIV/AIDS zines to show how splits within the same movement define what is allowable to say within, and to, wider publics.[22] Although counterpublics might be challenging other publics, Asen and Brouwer remind us that within Habermas's initial theorization, publics are still in relation with the state.[23] Whether directly or indirectly, then, publics or public discourse can influence policy.

As we endeavor to cohere a conversation on social change rhetorics, we view the tension between the noun and verb properties of movements and counterpublics as generative and refuse to privilege verb over noun or noun over verb. Rigid definitions and distinctions are not productive as we consider the changing nature of social issues and communication technologies constituting collectives apart from traditional organizational models. Movement scholars can learn from text-oriented counterpublic scholarship to, for instance, attend to how social media enables networks, operating both on the ground and virtually. Counterpublic scholars can draw from social movement scholarship concerning the ways groups continue to organize instrumentally and constitutively, as message campaigns are oriented toward the "material" ends of policy changes or legal precedents, as well as "symbolic" metamorphosis of dominant meanings. As cases such as the recent campaigns to legalize same-sex marriage demonstrate, overturning bans state by state ("material" change) is woven tightly with symbolic efforts to "normalize" marriage outside of heterosexual partnerships.

A more explicit conversation between counterpublic and movement scholars is warranted as critical theorists identify communication as the general operating principle in a new phase of Empire with power centers no longer defined by the state but more as a confluence of corporations, governments, and media.[24] Just how rhetoric may factor into dominance and resistance within this landscape is currently being written. As we have set forth in this introduction, social movements and counterpublics are valuable resources for scholars advancing social change in the discipline. We turn now to the four major problematics cutting across both concepts, to further explore the affinities and differences between them.

The Main Problematics of Social Change Scholarship

As our brief disciplinary history reveals, precise distinctions between counterpublics and movements are less apparent than similarities. The main distinctions we identify between counterpublic theory and recent work on movements occur as matters of emphasis, or the realization of different possibilities within each term. For instance, while early movement scholars debated whether "coercive" forms of speech should be legitimized through rhetorical study,[25] counterpublic scholars identified a dialectic of retreat and engagement to help explain rhetoric that did not clearly fit within reasoned appeals to the state. Early social movement scholars built typologies of "out-group" persuasion, while counterpublic scholars dilated upon how discursive norms and processes excluded or included advocates from democratic participation. There is nothing precluding social movement critics from exploring, for instance, retreat and engagement, but counterpublic scholars have prioritized such circulatory movement through their analyses.

Though scholars in counterpublics and social movement rhetoric rarely speak with or to each other directly, our review of the literatures found that similar problematics drew scholars' attention. We identified these major research problems as:

1. the clash/ing of discourses;
2. collective identity;
3. rhetorical form and style; and
4. the ends of social change.

We present them in order, from areas in which scholars have found the most common ground, to those areas that have inspired the most difference (and intense debate). We introduce each problematic generally, then consider the ways that counterpublic and movement scholars have rendered similar or different assumptions, approaches, and illustrations within each.

Clash/ing of Discourses

Across various ideologies, exigencies, discursive styles, contexts, and critical stances taken up in the study of social change rhetorics, a common thread exists: scholars concern themselves with *a clash* or *clashing*. While initial social movement theory imagined this contestation as directly oppositional (in the form of citizens against an establishment), counterpublic scholarship recognizes this clashing as existing between multiple publics and directed at a variety of power structures.

To begin with similarities, resistance, as Routledge describes, suggests "some sort of contestation, some juxtaposition of forces."[26] Communication scholars have named this clash/ing in a variety of ways, including the rhetoric of the streets, confrontation, vernacular discourse, outlaw discourse, vernacular rhetoric, agonism, and transgression.[27] In counterpublic studies alone, scholars recognize clash/ing between dominant/wide/mass publics, and marginalized, subordinate, subaltern, emergent, weaker, enclaved, or satellite counterpublics.[28] The clash/ing of forces may respond to an exigent moment, as in perceived or actual exclusion, or resource disparities (e.g., access to funds, media outlets, or organizations).[29] More broadly, rhetoric identifies a limit, typically to what appears as natural, normal, or true. In the process, antagonism opens the possibility not only for questioning ideologies and hegemonic discourses that sustain relations of oppression and marginalization but for beginning to articulate alternatives (that is, speaking forth and setting into relationship new ways of being and acting in the world).[30]

Most scholarship on social change figures clashing as dialectical, where social movement and counterpublic discourse oppose "legitimate" change mechanisms or dominant rational discursive norms for public participation. While social movement scholarship developed from the agitation and control model (in which out-group actors circumvented institutional means to influence policy), counterpublic scholarship was initially conceived as subaltern publics against a dominant or wider public.[31]

Just how much conceptual space separates the dialectical poles in counterpublic and social movement scholarship varies, ranging from Scott and Smith's suggestion that radical, confrontational rhetoric seeks the literal or symbolic death of enemies;[32] to more reformist battles, where debating adversaries define the world in different ways; to more radical challenges that upend the "logic governing the system, and in sum, deconstruct the established naming of the world."[33] However, unlike a debate between equal and consenting opponents, the clash/ing of social change is marked by disparities, and even oppression. Movement and counterpublic scholars assume "that communication structures and practices are politically charged and power-laden."[34] This recognition often guides critics working through both concepts to appreciate or temper their evaluations of rhetoric emerging from the "other" side of dialectics.

The recognition that communication structures and practices are rife with power differences also broadens critics' awareness of antagonism as it might grow from local issues into wider discursive spheres, including (academic) knowledge production. For instance, movement scholars initially turned away from Aristotelian criticism to help explain the "irrational" and "violent" protests that fell outside the scope of "legitimate" persuasion. Similarly, counterpublics allowed critics to come to terms with groups that refused to universalize claims—subcultures whose very appearance seemed to antagonize the "rational" voices and "civil" bodies of the public sphere. Here, counterpublic and movement scholars recognize that institutions or dominant publics may impose their own limits upon "outgroups," deeming the latter illegitimate, irrational, or uncivil. Hence, both movements and counterpublics provide conceptual resources for appreciating antagonism from outside a dominant lens. Fraser's ubiquitous definition of counterpublics as "parallel discursive arenas" represents well the need for scholars to clear space for "counter" discourses to operate concurrently with hegemonic ones.[35] By doing so, critics may identify cracks in dominant discourses, building momentum for the forces of social change through their criticism—in other words, amplifying the clash/ing of forces within scholarly discourse.

Both conceptual paths follow social change as a clash/ing of forces and generally share some version of the in-group/out-group dialectic founded in traditional sociological theories of movements.[36] Clashing, however, does not have to be directly oppositional or limited to collectives that neatly occupy positions outside institutions. This leads to a fine distinction between our focal terms: counterpublic work has considered a clashing of forces as occurring within, and emanating from, *multiple* discursively constituted and discourse-producing collectives. As Fraser recognizes, "not only were there always a plurality of competing publics, but the relations between bourgeois publics and other publics was always conflictual."[37] Further, she describes some publics as being *stronger* (those whose discourse has decision-making power) against *weaker* publics, where stronger publics are not necessarily equated with state or institutional bodies. The possibility for multiple publics to emanate from complex standpoints raises questions concerning the *who* of social change: Who is permitted or excluded from discursive participation? Who initiates social movement? This leads to our second problematic.

Collective Identity

The rhetorical history of movements demonstrates how institutionalized powers create and justify conditions of marginalization by defining the "being" of the oppressed, and oppressors, alike. Furthermore, once dissenters initiate antagonism, the establishment has the power to name them in ways that may limit social change (e.g., as "deviants" or "radicals").[38] Following Warner, one's participation in some publics risks being *marked* in potentially negative ways for that participation.[39] At the same time, Warner's model shows one has agency in *choosing* participation of some publics over others. One's being, then, is at stake in social change.

Accordingly, scholars across disciplines have explored identity. Through the concept of collective identity, sociologists attempted to understand what motivates people to collectively organize, see themselves as part of the same cause, understand and reframe social issues, and risk their own bodies to work against the status quo.[40] For communication scholars studying social change, identity can be synonymous with *agency* (the sense that one is capable of acting, effectively making social change), with *collective consciousness* (as one identifies with shared values, meanings, or/and goals), with *standpoint* (one's positionality within and without different material discourses, such as race, class, gender, sex, sexuality, and nation), and with unique forms of *social relationality* (including the friend-enemy relationship, networks, or figures of collective subjectivity).[41] As such, movement and counterpublic scholars offer diverse perspectives on identity as more than an instrumental means of achieving change. Counterpublic theory introduces the ideas of oscillation and stranger sociability to the study of collective identity.

Most movement and counterpublic scholars assume a connection between voice (a capacity for democratic participation), agency, and identity. Feminist counterpublic scholars underscore how gender categories define and limit who can participate in the public—to the point that not only are female bodies excluded from "the public" but so is anything associated with the "feminine."[42] Further, the ability to speak at all comes from the recognition one has the power to speak. As sociological approaches suggest, agency to engage in change requires a collective or a belief that individuals are not acting on their own. Efficacy often comes in numbers and the perceived esteem of the group.

Counterpublic and movement scholars tend to begin their understanding of agency as constrained by historic relations of dominance and subordination, appreciating how the have-nots come to address the haves. Importantly, then, movement and counterpublic scholars permit a dual-address in the context of social change. Just as Felski describes counterpublic speech as directed *internally* for the purposes of defining identity and consciousness, Gregg identifies the "ego-function" of social movements, redefining essentialist or ascribed social categories to be empowering for members.[43] *Externally* directed discourse for counterpublics is akin to social movement demand making, as both seek to convince society of alternative visions.

Differently, while functionalist movement scholars sympathetically read the identity construction of marginalized groups, they position identity as a means to the end of attaining recognition by a dominant power or achieving agency through the dominant discourse's terms. In other words, rhetoric like "black is beautiful" was not an end in itself, but a means for the black community to rebuild its ego, assuming that a strong ego was necessary to one's ability to function democratically or publicly. Amid the functional paradigm, internal discourses were deemed as "preinception" rhetoric, which assumes that the movement's ability to directly address the state is the proper telos of identity construction.[44]

Critics challenged the functionalist approach to identity, arguing that rhetoric does not merely represent the pregiven identities or concerns of "movement members."[45] Here, we encounter the major distinction between early movement studies and work influenced by NSMs and counterpublic theory: for the latter, identity is assumed as fluid performance, an important rhetorical achievement within social struggle. In comparison to "old" movements clearly defined by identity, class, or homogenized groups, scholars argued that "new" movements emerged from diverse bodies coalescing around values or issues.[46] While most scholars embrace a constructivist view of identity and distance themselves from essentialism,[47] some honor the need to make visible how historically marginalized identities—and the bodies and discourses associated with them—have been and continue to be excluded and oppressed.[48]

Though counterpublic and NSM scholars have generally embraced a flexible approach to understanding identity formation, the former offers unique insights into rhetoric's power in understanding identity. Particularly, counterpublic theory formed as scholars explored subaltern groups' movement between internal and external address as an oscillation of retreat and engagement. Subaltern groups may build oppositional discourses outside the potential threats, censorship, or hegemonic interpretations of dominant publics.[49] For example, Squires identifies how a counterpublic may use "dominant" discourses in the presence of wider publics, but create hidden transcripts to define a group's "true opinions, ideas, and tactics for survival," thus avoiding sanctions or punishment from dominant publics (as with slave spirituals).[50] Such hidden transcripts, counterpublic theory asserts, are not limited to their potential antagonism with dominance nor are they isolated from discourses that confront or engage dominant publics.

Further, counterpublic work pushes scholars to appreciate collective identity outside familiar categories, through the concept of stranger sociability. As Warner posits, publics emerge as discourse is invented and circulated. One's relationship to the discourse and other members of the public is *impersonal*, even when personal relationships precede the public. Publics take on a counter status when oppression or subordinate status is commonly shared.[51] For Warner, stranger relationality is "not just strategic, but constitutive of membership and its affects."[52] Unlike other means of organizing strangers (as through nations or organizations), the (counter)public is a social imaginary, where relationships are "indirect and unspecifiable," while at the same time allowing us to treat others as "belonging to our world."[53]

Stranger sociability contributes to the interdisciplinary theorization of how diverse coalitions come together and advocate for/create change.[54] The rise of social media and transnational discourse circulation (e.g., through the global justice movement) raises questions such as: How do collectives create the appearance (if not the substantial condition) of unity amidst difference? Or, do they have to do so in order to effectively promote change?

From such questions we get the most recent iteration of identity work within movements: the study of "alternative" social configurations, including networks, flash mobs, affinity groups, coalitional and companion subjectivity.[55] Members from a variety of standpoints (e.g., Christians, union workers, anarchists, feminists), and having various degrees of personal attachment to one another, may coalesce temporarily at one protest action. Building upon the claims of NSM theory and counterpublic work, scholars argue that we do not have to formally belong to an organization to appear as viable political agents. Emergent forms of collective subjectivity, along with the diverse histories and experiences helping form the identity of movement and counterpublic participants, bespeak a broad range of rhetorical forms and styles of advocacy.

Rhetorical Form and Social Change

Rhetorics of social change throw into relief taken-for-granted assumptions, particularly related to what we (as critics, activists, people) view as "outsider." "Disorderly" rhetorics—particularly as they may emerge from, or associate with, the feminine, people of color, queer, or other subaltern identities—often present a stylistic "excess." Critics rely on a vocabulary of rhetorical form to understand (and in many cases appreciate) this excess. The notion of form draws attention to *how* rhetoric appears—its shape, structure, and style—rather than *what* is said. Forms may repeat over time, establishing (and satisfying or failing to satisfy) expectations among audiences that direct the tempo, tone, and overall affective experience of rhetoric.[56] Given the different voices and forms emergent in activism, scholars expanded analysis beyond the instrumental effectiveness of arguments, to include a variety of functions rhetoric may serve for agents in social change.

Yet, scholars also explore form's potential impacts apart from (or in combination with) content-level meanings.[57] While the argument that form is itself political invites a richer understanding of the ever-expanding repertoires of social change actors, it also invites debate about the nature of social change. We view here a nuanced difference between movement and counterpublic work, with the latter emphasizing how rhetorical aesthetics contribute to circulation. In some counterpublic theory, style moves from a reflection of subaltern "excess," into a capacity for oppositional discourses to form across time and space. We consider the prospects of circulation later in this subsection, particularly through recent work on the network form.

Common across scholarship on social change is an expansion of what is considered rhetorical. Within social movement work, for instance, scholars moved beyond a single text and traditional argumentation as the proper objects of criticism, to include a "multiplicity of voices," images, places, and events as rhetorical.[58] Critics have analyzed many forms of agitation and organizing, including songs, performance, and consciousness-raising.[59] Critics have warranted their expansion of the object domain, not only as it broadens the empirical catalogue of rhetorical texts but also as it includes the diverse voices overlooked or left out of the scholarly record. As such, movement scholarship expands rhetorical theory writ large beyond its roots in white, heterosexual, propertied, masculine norms.

Social movement and counterpublic critics have posited a consonant relationship between material identity standpoints and rhetorical style. Scholars acknowledge that rhetorical forms reflect the material and/or cultural resources available to different identity-based collectives. For instance, white women's location in the private sphere may have conditioned the form of personal narrative, versus formal argumentation, as women developed a "feminine style" when speaking publicly.[60] Further, identity-based movements strategically use forms as a reflection of their politics or to enhance the message. Feminist movements eschew hierarchy by organizing without single leaders and allow new ideas to come into being through poetry, while civil rights activists used songs to perform the ethos of religious organizations so central to the movement.[61]

Other scholars draw upon rhetoric's formal features to develop new heuristics, introducing a variety of concepts in rhetorical theory. For instance, Ono and Sloop turned to vernacular discourses to develop pastiche and cultural syncretism as the means to value "everyday" and local speech not preserved in historical records.[62] Vernacular criticism does not just entail describing texts but recognizes or even reads against the discourse's power dynamics.[63] Relatedly, concepts like the "public screen" or "image events"[64] allow critics to appreciate formal challenges to clear, rational communication. Amid the fragmented, mediated norms of the "public screen," the "violent" antiglobalization protests of Seattle appear more effective in luring distracted viewers than a well-crafted argument.

The new form-inspired heuristics thus contributed to an expanded understanding of rhetorical effects for, or related to, social movements. Some scholars continued to tie form to function, fostering appreciation for the rhetorical prowess of people of color, women, LGBTQ activists, the poor, and those living outside Western/Northern democracies. Campbell and other feminist critics, for example, theorized consciousness-raising as an activist form that named exigencies, promoted identification, and built coalitions, in fidelity with feminine ways of knowing and being in the world.[65] Lake and others turned to the consummatory rhetoric of American Indian activism, analyzing performances of resistance that were not a means to an instrumental end.[66]

Yet, amid such appreciation for form, critics began to challenge the traditional prescription that movements needed to address establishments and argue convincingly in order to be effective. As the study of NSMs gained momentum across disciplines, rhetoric scholars asserted that form itself challenges dominant ideologies or has powerful effects outside rhetoric's ability to achieve instrumental policy goals. For example, queer public kissing undermines heteronormativity, practicing love and affection in new ways, with the potential to reconfigure social as well as private intimacy.[67]

Counterpublic theory demonstrates the ways that form finds audiences, exploits circulation systems, and conveys political messages through stylistic and lifestyle choices. As Staggenborg and Lang demonstrate, the cultural capital and familiarity of forms such as bookstores or music festivals compel participation and build networks for activists and newcomers alike, allowing exposure to new ideas.[68] Antisuffrage supporters used the ubiquitous form of postcards to spread their message through the postal system, where audiences would read their messages alongside other social and political information.[69] Finally, the DIY (do-it-yourself) aesthetic of zines or the refusal of vegans to wear leather implicates their political arguments without saying a word.[70] Audience familiarity and the common interactional uses of forms allow content to find intentional and new audiences.

Further, style helps constitute publics virtually and discursively, in ways not possible within actually existing organizations or bodies. In particular, Warner positions style as the dimension through which rhetors address (counter)publics that do not yet exist.[71] As Warner writes, "it seems inevitable that the world to which one belongs . . . will be determined at least in part by the way one addresses it. . . . [Writers] want a language that will bring a certain public into being, and they have an idea of what style will work."[72] With no firm connections to time, counterpublic texts may function as placeholders during abeyance periods, when movement organizations or (counter)publics do not actively engage in a policy campaign.[73] Counterpublic scholarship expands our appreciation of form, not only for diverse voices and tactics in resistance but also how circulation constitutes discursive space and publics—contributing to publics' inventive and generative properties.

Counterpublic theory helps account for the effects of social change rhetorics outside their original time and context—a feature becoming increasingly important as figures or practices from movements "past" circulate to bolster counterpublicity in the "present." As Greene postulates, this circulation is potentially infinite as texts move and interact among indefinite strangers and mechanisms for circulation.[74] For example, although Marx ceased to produce new discourses for a Communist public (even waning in popularity for a time following his death), "millennial Marxists" have emerged and circulated Marx's texts in relation to recent movements (Occupy) and publications (Picketty's *Capital in the Twenty-First Century*).[75]

Counterpublic theory's alternative emphasis on circulation leads to a final development concerning style: attention to the "newest" social movement forms, such as networks and flash mobs.[76] As introduced above, a growing interdisciplinary literature extends movement's or counterpublic's formal challenges to standard communication.[77] Networks and flash mobs explain today's rhetorical action or more recognizable movement organizations, where some "movements" straddle the line between the real and virtual. For instance, discourse organized by the #BlackLivesMatter hashtag exists both as a movement of social media followers and protests against racism and police brutality.[78] Understanding these networked forms means both movement and counterpublic scholars need to adopt conceptual vocabularies to attend to the loose, hyperlinked, and immanent logics of recent configurations of activism.[79]

Just as initial movement (and then counterpublic) scholarship recognized that style is intertwined with the substance and effects of social change, networked forms broaden our understanding of how rhetoric works. The efficacy of networks lies in their ability to expand without limits and integrate more nodes, so long as actors share similar communication codes (or follow each other through the same applications, or apps).[80] Networks may manifest new social relationships (such as temporary autonomous zones) rendering the state redundant, and therefore, unnecessary—for the people living within that space feed, clothe, shelter, protect, entertain, and educate, *themselves*.[81] Network represents the newest terrain of social change scholarship, where social movement and counterpublic scholars can build from and inform one another's work. The network form blurs the line between the material and symbolic, leading to our final problematic.

The Ends of Social Change

We have reached the largest and perhaps most divisive concern of social movement and counterpublic scholars: What constitutes social change? What is rhetoric's relationship to it? If most work begins with antagonism as an ontological condition for social change rhetorics, it ends with a wealth of possible outcomes, ranging from the revolutionary to the quotidian practices of daily life; the alteration of material conditions to the recognition of subaltern identities; or changes in policy to transformations in consciousness. Likewise, the different ends of social change position rhetoric in a variety of ways: as a practical tool in the hands of goal-driven subjects, as a malleable glue that articulates new ways of being and acting in the world, or as an immediate force with a capacity to jar witnesses and inspire ethical relationships with others.

As introduced above, counterpublics and social movements have both been considered nouns or organizational forms capable of material change as well as verbs or discursive forms creating symbolic changes at the level of meaning or social norms. In this final problematic, we consider in more depth the debates over material versus symbolic change, acknowledging the blurriness of these two ends and the implications of privileging one outcome over another. We position readers to enter the scholarly conversation of this volume by advocating for a pluralistic view of rhetorics of social change, refusing to follow unnecessary dualisms between the material and symbolic.

As Tilly notes, "in some sense, every position one takes about the desirability, feasibility, or effectiveness of collective action is a political position."[82] Within the discipline, this politics plays out most directly in debates over material versus symbolic change, especially whether scholars should promote rhetoric's achievements or prospects in one vein or the other. Beginning in Marxist theory, materialist change assumes an end to oppressive conditions, immediately and on behalf of (or attained by) those experiencing oppression (e.g., a world in which people are no longer subject to sexual harassment or wage discrimination). From a materialist perspective, the achievement of legal precedents or new legislation provides concrete evidence that an exigent situation has been ameliorated or improved. Symbolic change expands the scope of materialist change, underscoring how "secondary" actors (e.g., voters or "the public") may influence change directly or might yield results over the long term. Symbolic change includes alterations in public opinion, worldviews, ideologies, or subjectivities, manifest largely in the realm of discourse (e.g., television influencing society to accept "femininity" as including both aggressive and nurturing performances, portraying women who are both professionals and parents).

Generally, an instrumental approach to rhetoric has mapped onto materialist change outcomes, as in social movements pursuing policy and/or legal goals with petitions or demonstrations. However, scholars critiqued the reduction of rhetoric to instrumentality, advocating a more constitutive view of rhetoric.[83] Within social movement scholarship, functionalist approaches gave way to the interdisciplinary turn to NSMs, further encouraging communication scholars to explore "movement as meaning" with rhetoric's main effects as symbolic—the articulation of identities and meanings.

Reflecting broader disciplinary trends, the vast majority of recent work in movements and counterpublics adopts a constitutive view of rhetoric, with an accompanying stress on symbolic change. However, the constitutive perspective is not without its critics. As Cloud argues, to concentrate rhetorical efforts on the creation of new identities does little to alleviate the real (material) conditions of poverty and injustice afflicting many people around the world. Cloud further asserts that constitutive rhetorics join neoliberal capitalism in promoting therapeutic approaches, such that individuals problematize their selves and seek solutions in consumption.[84]

The debate over material versus symbolic change has productively advanced our discipline's accounts of rhetoric as more than an instrumental tool to create social change. Yet, we encourage a healthy skepticism toward the trend of scholars promoting "new" conceptual tools or paradigms in stark opposition to materialist, functionalist, and instrumentalist assumptions inherited from early social movement rhetoric work. Rather, we prefer to see such "traditional" assumptions as one end on a spectrum of possibilities, part of a dialectic rather than a dichotomy. The functional approach is not misguided to the extent that people *do* collectively organize and *do* seek recognition, protection, or redress through institutions. Real hunger and poverty *do* motivate people to oust dictators or factory owners.[85] Rhetoric's strategic capacities are still necessary as public problems are still tied to policy solutions. Cox, analyzing climate change, advocates that we continue to view rhetoric as a pragmatic means to analyze the constraints of a situation and act persuasively, in more discretely material ways than the constitution of new identities and meanings.[86]

At the same time, "material" structures and social conditions constraining organizing are also a function of the "symbolic" discourses defining and creating boundaries. As we become more of an "information society," critical theorists recognize increasingly the ways that immaterial, intellectual, and communicative labor dominates other forms of labor.[87] As Castells describes, the Internet coordinates more human activity than the nation-state or its institutions. Though states still make use of coercive power, the latter is less effective than "the construction of meaning in people's minds," which for Castells, is the "more stable source of power."[88] We take Castells, Hardt and Negri, and other critical theorists as supporting a blended approach to the material and symbolic. The structures or mediums through which humans interact (Facebook or a classroom, for instance) become inseparable from the meanings and identities constituted therein. From this perspective, communication is not simply the medium through which power (for and/or against) is expressed but is also how social relationships are constituted and coordinated.

Social change, then, exists as an interaction between various material and symbolic elements defined by and coordinated through communication, where change is about shifting power. Rather than continue to justify scholarly work through interventions within the binary of material versus symbolic change, we encourage scholars to view social change as a blending of these ends. Such a perspective is already developed within counterpublic and social movement scholarship, as with work continuing to theorize direct action, nonviolent civil disobedience (NVCD) and forms of performance including street theater, art, protest, and self-sacrifice.[89]

The plethora of tactics also offers the possibility for any action to function materially and symbolically. For example, critics analyzing NVCD events consider how rhetoric critically interrupts unjust practices, calling witnesses to conscience.[90] NVCD is motivated by the desire to avoid replicating dominant or institutionalized methods for enforcing the social order through violence, while still calling attention to the injustice perpetuated within the order. NVCD relies upon a "playground morality" in which a defenseless party incurs the wrath of a more powerful or violent party: it appears a bully is beating up an innocent or weaker person. Ideally, and out of an ethical imperative, the crowd of witnesses will intervene, either directly (by protecting the innocent) or indirectly (by seeking out aid for the innocent). Recording or circulating viral videos and memes is another way to act as witness, preventing bullying in the future through influencing public opinion. The outcome can be instrumental in calling attention to the injustice but also might work constitutively in constructing an identity of "ethical witnesses."

Unlike a direct call for people to "be more moral," ethical encounters provide a kind of source-code in which to build relations, while permitting us knowledge of the "right" social relations. To underscore our point concerning the need to blend, rather than bifurcate, the material and symbolic: We cannot appreciate NVCD as a tactic outside of its intentionality and material consequence, nor can we assess its ability to move the social outside the symbolic identities and meanings ascribed to the bodies performing it.

The chapters that follow reveal, to varying degrees, rhetoric scholars' preoccupation with social change as a clash/ing of forces, as implicating collective identity and rhetorical form, and as illustrative of material and symbolic effects in the world. They further illustrate the convergences and nuanced differences that have emerged over decades of scholarship on counterpublics and social movements—and, the need to imagine social change outside of standard binaries.

Contributions and Conclusions

This collection is meant for both the seasoned social change scholar as well as a guide for those new to the discipline. Chapters in section I— "Problematizing the Past of Social Movement Rhetoric and Counterpublic Research"—review scholarship with a critical eye toward how disciplinary roots and contemporary practices might provide productive directions for scholars working with social change rhetorics. McKerrow advocates that we understand the critical vocabularies underpinning our approaches and uncovers functionalist "traps" present in social movement scholarship across disciplines. He provides a new interpretation of the formative debate between McGee and Simons (especially as it sets out the possibility for movement as verb, not just noun). Foust performs a critical genealogy of social movement rhetoric scholarship after 1980, demonstrating that preferred concepts (even the rise of counterpublics) relate to neoliberal norms in publication —especially novelty, segmentation, and pleasurable consumption. Taking up McKerrow's call, she revitalizes McGee's work by showing how scholarly conversations may better produce an academic commons pursuing the question of "what *moves* the social?" Finally, Brouwer and Paulesc demonstrate the robustness of counterpublic scholarship as it "goes global." They review counterpublic work as it travels across three distinct lines of inquiry: materialist, ideological, and critical/cultural. They argue that scholars should be attentive to the ways that stretching and applying counterpublic (an Anglo-Saxon concept) to different contexts might reproduce systems of hegemony. In tracing germinal scholarship and key cases of counterpublics in global contexts, they advocate that scholars form alliances with postcolonial theory in an attempt to craft ethical approaches to scholarship.

In the second section, "Distinguishing and Performing Counterpublics and Movements through Case Studies," contributors demonstrate where our two focal concepts may be more or less appropriate (as well as similar and different) in analysis of social change. Pason uses the case of Occupy Homes to show how movements and counterpublics both exist on a phenomenon-meaning continuum. Her chapter performs an experiment to read Occupy Homes through a social movement and then counterpublic lens to tease out nuances in pursuing one line of study or the other. Palczewski and Harr-Largin reconceptualize establishment-conflict models of social movement scholarship through Pledge-A-Picketer Campaigns used by abortion clinics. Along with advocating for a more fluid notion of power, they demonstrate the utility of counterpublic theory as it reveals how competing counterpublics may occupy both dominant and marginal standpoints, as sites of power and targets of protest. In analyzing Slut-Walks, Zittlow Rogness disrupts previous trends in counterpublic theory by exploring the value of the private. She traces how dominant discourses constituting rape culture and slut shaming have limited and impaired women's public subjectivity by coupling the body with property and sex with virtue. She considers how we might parse the personal from the political as it relates to privacy and publicity. Finally, with her collaborators (Nair and Conrad), Chávez reflects upon her work as a scholar-activist with Against Equality (AE), highlighting the influence of public argument action research. Chávez explores how she navigates her roles as academic and activist within AE. For Chávez and collaborators, the politics of AE do not neatly fit within the social movement or counterpublic paradigms, nor within current models of communication activism promoted in the discipline. Chávez advocates for participatory approaches and building coalitional agency for those engaged in activist scholarship.

In the book's final section, "New Directions for Studying Social Movements and Counterpublics Rhetorically," we encouraged contributors to be creative, performative, and even polemical in an effort to diversify the disciplinary conversation on social change. Particularly, our contributors productively link social movement or counterpublic in interdisciplinary or intradisciplinary ways, fostering new connections within changing global dynamics. Calafell and McIntosh show how counterpublic work connects with performance studies and vernacular discourse. They assert a decolonizing approach, addressing Eurocentric biases inherent in counterpublic and social movement work. The authors point scholars to concepts of border crossing, hybridity, and trickster performances, as they may help to understand Other counterpublics. DeLuca and Brunner provocatively call our attention to China to rethink truths about democracy underlying movement and counterpublic research. Highlighting *wild public screens*, they show how Chinese environmental activists have utilized social media and built networks exceeding control of centralized powers. The polemic form of their argument allows DeLuca and Brunner to encourage Western activists and academics alike to avoid domesticating dissent in the name of democracy.

Finally, Chaput and Hanan rethink resistance and agency amid neoliberalism, particularly as market logics are the central organizing principles of society. Using the example of Wikileaks, the authors introduce Foucault's *parrhesia*, exodus, and the common as the new terrain of resistance and transgressive tactics.

In conclusion, we offer the present collection as a means to cohere the disciplinary conversation on social change rhetorics. Refusing to offer prescriptions, or reduce movements and counterpublics to formulaic definitions or simplistic causal models, we hope to inspire future work to revitalize rhetoric's place in understanding and joining social change.

Notes

1. The canon is here defined by textbooks by Charles Stewart, Craig Smith, and Robert Denton, *Persuasion and Social Movements*, 6th ed. (Long Grove, IL: Waveland Press, 2012), and John W. Bowers, Donovan J. Ochs, Richard J. Jensen, and David P. Shulz, *The Rhetoric of Agitation and Control*, 3rd ed. (Long Grove, IL: Waveland Press, 2009).

2. Dilip Parameshwar Gaonkar, "The Forum: Public and Counterpublics," *Quarterly Journal of Speech* 88, no. 4 (2002): 410–12.

3. Daniel C. Brouwer, "Communication as Counterpublic," in *Communication as . . . Perspectives on Theory*, ed. Gregory Shepherd, Jeffrey St. John, and Ted Striphas (Thousand Oaks, CA: SAGE Publications, 2006), 203.

4. Michael Calvin McGee first introduced this distinction, which other scholars have also used to simplify their use of these concepts. See "'Social Movement': Phenomenon or Meaning?" *Central States Speech Journal* 31, no. 4 (1980): 233–44.

5. For social movement disciplinary histories, see Robert Cox and Christina R. Foust, "Social Movement Rhetoric," in *The SAGE Handbook of Rhetorical Studies*, ed. Andrea A. Lunsford, Kirt H. Wilson, and Rosa A. Eberly (Thousand Oaks, CA: SAGE Publications, 2009); Richard Jensen, "Interdisciplinary Perspectives on Rhetorical Criticism: Analyzing Social Movement Rhetoric," *Rhetoric Review* 25, no. 4 (2006): 372–75; Richard Jensen, "Evolving Protest Rhetoric: From the 1960s to the 1990s," *Rhetoric Review* 20, no. 1/2 (2001): 28–32; and Herbert Simons, "On the Rhetoric of Social Movements, Historical Movements, and 'Top-Down' Movements: A Commentary," *Communication Studies* 42, no. 1 (1991): 94–101. For comprehensive bibliographies on movement rhetoric work, see the bibliography in Stewart et al., *Persuasion and Social Movements*; or the landmark essay collection from Charles E. Morris III and Stephen Browne, eds., *Readings on the Rhetoric of Social Protest*, 3rd ed. (State College, PA: Strata Publishing, 2013). For counterpublic scholarship,

see Brouwer, "Communication," introductions in Robert Asen and Daniel C. Brouwer, eds., *Counterpublics and the State* (Albany: State University of New York Press, 2001), and Daniel C. Brouwer and Robert Asen, eds., *Public Modalities: Rhetoric, Culture, Media, and the Shape of Public Life* (Tuscaloosa: University of Alabama Press, 2010).

6. For example, see Leland M. Griffin, "The Rhetoric of Historical Movements," *Quarterly Journal of Speech* 38, no. 2 (1952): 184–88; Herbert Simons, "Requirements, Problems, and Strategies: A Theory of Persuasion for Social Movements," *Quarterly Journal of Speech* 56, no. 1 (1970): 1–11.

7. For a discussion of NSMs and communication studies' uptake, see Kevin DeLuca, *Image Politics: The New Rhetoric of Environmental Activism* (New York: Guilford Press, 1999).

8. James Darsey, "From 'Gay Is Good' to the Scourge of AIDS: The Evolution of Gay Liberation Rhetoric, 1977–1990," *Communication Studies* 42, no. 1 (Spring 1991): 43–66.

9. For instance, Christine Harold and Kevin DeLuca consider the murder of Emmett Till almost as an ontological interruption and call to ethics, rather than a "trigger event" for the civil rights movement (see "Behold the Corpse: Violent Images and the Case of Emmett Till," *Rhetoric and Public Affairs* 8, no. 2 [2005]: 263–86). Likewise, DeLuca's *Image Politics* demonstrates how radical activism of embodied protests creates antagonisms rather than how they fulfill functions for a queer or environmental movement.

10. Jürgen Habermas, *The Structural Transformation of the Public Sphere: An Inquiry into a Category of Bourgeois Society*, trans. Thomas Burger and Frederick Lawrence (Cambridge: Massachusetts Institute of Technology Press, 1989). See also Robert Asen, "Seeking the 'Counter' in Counterpublics," *Communication Theory* 10, no. 4 (2000): 424–46, for tracing of disciplinary uptake of counterpublic work post-Habermas.

11. Nancy Fraser, "Rethinking the Public Sphere: A Contribution to the Critique of Actually Existing Democracy," in *Habermas and the Public Sphere*, ed. Craig Calhoun (Cambridge: Massachusetts Institute of Technology Press, 1992); and Asen, "Seeking the 'Counter.'"

12. Catherine Helen Palczewski, "Cyber-movements, New Social Movements, and Counterpublics," in *Counterpublics and the State*, ed. Robert Asen and Daniel C. Brouwer (Albany: State University of New York Press, 2001).

13. Ibid.

14. Michael Warner, *Publics and Counterpublics* (New York: Zone Books, 2002).

15. Cary R. W. Voss and Robert C. Rowland, "Pre-Inception Rhetoric in the Creation of a Social Movement: The Case of Frances Wright," *Communication Studies* 51, no. 1 (2000): 1–14; Gerard A. Hauser, "Prisoners of Conscience and the Counterpublic Sphere of Prison Writing: The Stones That Start the Ava-

lanche," in *Counterpublics and the State*, ed. Asen and Brouwer; and Kristi Mad-dux, "When Patriots Protest: The Anti-suffrage Discursive Transformation of 1917," *Rhetoric and Public Affairs* 7, no. 3 (2004): 283–310.

16. McGee, "'Social Movement'"; see also McKerrow in this collection for elaboration on this debate. For an example of ideographic analysis related to movements, see James Darsey, "From 'Gay Is Good' to the Scourge of AIDS."

17. Karlyn Kohrs Campbell, "The Rhetoric of Women's Liberation: An Oxy-moron," *Quarterly Journal of Speech* 59, no. 1 (1973): 74–86.

18. DeLuca, *Image Politics*, 36.

19. Asen, "Seeking the 'Counter,'" and Warner, *Publics and Counterpublics*.

20. Warner, *Publics and Counterpublics*, 122.

21. Phaedra Pezzullo, "Resisting 'National Breast Cancer Awareness Month': The Rhetoric of Counterpublics and Their Cultural Performances," *Quarterly Journal of Speech* 89, no. 4 (2003): 345–65.

22. Daniel C. Brouwer, "Counterpublicity and Corporeality in HIV/AIDS Zines," *Critical Studies in Media Communication* 22, no. 5 (2005): 351–71.

23. Robert Asen and Daniel C. Brouwer, "Introduction: Reconfigurations of the Public Sphere," in *Counterpublics and the State*, ed. Asen and Brouwer.

24. Michael Hardt and Antonio Negri, *Empire* (Cambridge, MA: Harvard University Press, 2000).

25. Robert L. Scott and Donald K. Smith, "The Rhetoric of Confrontation," *Quarterly Journal of Speech* 55, no. 1 (1969): 1–8.

26. Paul Routledge, "A Spatiality of Resistances: Theory and Practice in Ne-pal's Revolution of 1990" in *Geographies of Resistance*, ed. Steve Pile and Michael Keith (London: Routledge, 1997), 69.

27. Franklyn S. Haiman, "The Rhetoric of the Streets: Some Legal and Ethi-cal Considerations," *Quarterly Journal of Speech* 53, no. 2 (1967): 99–114; Scott and Smith, "Rhetoric of Confrontation"; Kent A. Ono and John M. Sloop, "The Critique of Vernacular Discourse," *Communication Monographs* 62, no. 1 (1995): 19–46; John M. Sloop and Kent A. Ono, "Out-law Discourse: The Criti-cal Politics of Material Judgment," *Philosophy and Rhetoric* 30, no. 1 (January 1997): 50–69; Gerard Hauser, *Vernacular Voices: The Rhetoric of Publics and Public Spheres* (Colombia: University of South Carolina Press, 1999); Heather Hund-ley and J. Scott Rodriguez, "Transactivism and Postmodernity: An Agonistic Analysis of Transliterature," *Communication Quarterly* 57, no. 1 (2009): 35–50; and Christina R. Foust, *Transgression as a Mode of Resistance: Rethinking So-cial Movement in an Era of Corporate Globalization* (Lanham, MD: Lexington Books, 2010).

28. See Brouwer's "Communication" for a review of many different labels as-cribed to counterpublics.

29. Stewart et al., *Persuasion and Social Movements*; and also Brouwer, "Com-munication"

30. DeLuca, *Image Politics*, chapter 2; and Robert Cox, *Environmental Com-*

munication and the Public Sphere, 3rd ed. (Thousand Oaks, CA: SAGE Publications, 2013).

31. Bowers et al., *Agitation and Control*; for counterpublic approach, see Fraser, "Rethinking."

32. Scott and Smith, "Rhetoric of Confrontation."

33. DeLuca, *Image Politics*, 25.

34. Brouwer, "Communication," 196.

35. Fraser, "Rethinking," 123.

36. See Foust, *Transgression*, for an elaboration of this argument.

37. Fraser, "Rethinking," 116.

38. Bowers et al., *Agitation and Control*, 9.

39. Warner, *Publics and Counterpublics*, 120.

40. Francesa Polletta and James M. Jasper, "Collective Identity and Social Movements," *Annual Review of Sociology* 27, no. 1 (2001): 283–306.

41. See Foust, *Transgression*; and Erin J. Rand, "A Disunited Nation and Legacy of Contradiction: Queer Nation's Construction of Identity," *Journal of Communication Inquiry* 28, no. 4 (2004): 288–306.

42. Rita Felski, *Beyond Feminist Aesthetics: Feminist Literature and Social Change* (Cambridge, MA: Harvard University Press, 1989).

43. Richard B. Gregg, "The Ego-Function of the Rhetoric of Protest," *Philosophy and Rhetoric* 4, no. 2 (1971): 71–91.

44. Voss and Rowland, "Pre-inception Rhetoric."

45. Maurice Charland, "Constitutive Rhetoric: The Case of the *Peuple Quebecois*," *Quarterly Journal of Speech* 73, no. 2 (1987): 133–51; and McGee, "'Social Movement.'"

46. For an overview of NSM work in sociology, see Enrique Laraña, Hank Johnston, and Joseph R. Gusfield, eds., *New Social Movements: From Ideology to Identity* (Philadelphia: Temple University Press, 1994).

47. DeLuca suggests antagonisms are built around how we understand and discursively define material differences (like sex or skin color) that might exclude one's equal participation; not simply upon those bodily differences alone. See *Image Politics*, 41.

48. See Catherine R. Squires, "Rethinking the Black Public Sphere: An Alternative Vocabulary for Multiple Public Spheres," *Communication Theory* 12, no. 4 (2002) 446–68.

49. Karma R. Chávez, "Counter-Public Enclaves and Understanding the Function of Rhetoric in Social Movement Coalition-Building," *Communication Quarterly* 59, no. 1 (2011): 1–18; and Jane Mansbridge, "Using Power/Fighting Power: The Polity," in *Democracy and Difference: Contesting the Boundaries of the Political*, ed. Seyla Benhabib (Princeton, NJ: Princeton University Press, 1996).

50. Squires, "Rethinking the Black Public Sphere," 458.

51. Warner, *Publics and Counterpublics*.

52. Ibid., 122.

53. Ibid., 75.

54. Foust, *Transgression*; and Rand, "A Disunited Nation."

55. Chávez, "Counter-Public Enclaves"; and Foust, *Transgression*.

56. Kenneth Burke, *Attitudes toward History*, 3rd ed. (Berkeley: University of California Press, 1984). Burke's contribution to rhetorical form is also evident in movement criticism inspired by his work, such as Karen A. Foss and Kathy L. Domenici, "Haunting Argentina: Synecdoche in the Protests of the Mothers of the Plaza del Mayo," *Quarterly Journal of Speech* 87, no. 3 (2001): 237–58; and Steven Schwarze, "Environmental Melodrama," *Quarterly Journal of Speech* 92, no. 3 (2006): 239–61.

57. In "Rhetoric of Women's Liberation" Campbell shows how claims made by some bodies are perceived as more radical, demonstrating why strategies of style intertwine with the argument's substance.

58. Griffin, "Rhetoric of Historical Movements."

59. Bowers et al., *Agitation and Control*; Stewart et al., *Persuasion and Social Movements*; and Mohan Dutta, *Communicating Social Change: Structure, Culture, and Agency*, (New York: Routledge, 2011).

60. Karlyn Kohrs Campbell, *Man Cannot Speak for Her: A Critical Study of Early Feminist Rhetoric*, vol. 1 (Santa Barbara, CA: Praeger, 1989).

61. See T. V. Reed, *The Art of Protest: Culture and Activism from the Civil Rights Movement to the Streets of Seattle* (Minneapolis: University of Minnesota Press, 2005).

62. Ono and Sloop suggest that vernacular discourses include texts (such as community newspapers or pamphlets) but also cultural discourses (music, art, architecture, and dance). See "Critique of Vernacular Discourse;" see also Hauser, *Vernacular Voices*.

63. Ono and Sloop, "Critique of Vernacular Discourse"; Bernadette Marie Calafell and Fernando Delgado, "Reading Latina/o images: Interrogating Americanos," *Critical Studies in Media Communication* 21, no. 1 (2004): 1–21; and Hauser, *Vernacular Voices*.

64. See DeLuca, *Images Politics*; and Kevin Michael DeLuca and Jennifer Peeples, "From Public Sphere to Public Screen: Democracy, Activism, and the 'Violence' of Seattle," *Critical Studies in Media Communication* 19, no. 2 (2002): 125–51.

65. Campbell, "Rhetoric of Women's Liberation"; Tasha N. Dubriwny, "Consciousness-Raising as Collective Rhetoric: The Articulation of Experience in the Redstockings' Abortion Speak-Out of 1969," *Quarterly Journal of Speech* 91, no. 4 (2005): 395–422; and Stacey K. Sowards and Valerie R. Renegar, "The Rhetorical Functions of Consciousness-Raising in Third Wave Feminism," *Communication Studies* 55, no. 4 (2004): 535–52.

66. Randall A. Lake, "Enacting Red Power: The Consummatory Function

I

Problematizing the Past of Social Movement Rhetoric and Counterpublic Research

in Native American Protest Rhetoric," *Quarterly Journal of Speech* 69, no. 2 (1983): 127–42.

67. Charles E. Morris, III, and John M. Sloop, "'What Lips These Lips Have Kissed': Refiguring the Politics of Queer Public Kissing," *Communication and Critical/Cultural Studies* 3, no. 1 (2006): 1–26

68. Suzanne Staggenborg and Amy Lang, "Culture and Ritual in the Montreal Women's Movement," *Social Movement Studies* 6, no. 2 (2007): 177–94.

69. Catherine Helen Palczewski, "The Male Madonna and the Feminine Uncle Sam: Visual Argument, Icons, and Ideographs in 1909 Anti-woman Suffrage Postcards," *Quarterly Journal of Speech* 91, no. 4 (2005): 365–94.

70. Jason Del Gandio, *Rhetoric for Radicals: A Handbook for the 21st Century Activists* (Gabriola Island, BC, Canada: New Society Publishers, 2008).

71. Warner, *Publics and Counterpublics*, 130.

72. Ibid., 129.

73. Maddux, "When Patriots Protest"; also Palczewski, "The Male Madonna."

74. Ronald Walter Greene, "Rhetorical Pedagogy as a Postal System: Circulating Subjects through Michael Warner's 'Publics and Counterpublics,'" *Quarterly Journal of Speech* 88, no. 4 (2002): 434–43.

75. Ross Douthat, "Marx Rises Again," *New York Times*, April 19, 2014, accessed July 11, 2014, www.nytimes.com/2014/04/20/opinion/sunday/douthat-marx-rises-again.html. Thomas Picketty, *Capital in the Twenty-First Century*, trans. Arthur Goldhammer (Cambridge, MA: Harvard University Press, 2014).

76. Rebecca A. Walker, "Fill/Flash/Memory: A History of Flash Mobs," *Text and Performance Quarterly* 33, no. 2 (2013): 115–32.

77. Following Hardt and Negri's *Empire* thesis, where communication is inflected by a consumerist logic, the form of communication becomes a primary site for antagonism: resisting neoliberalism through cooperation and the commons.

78. See Black Lives Matter, accessed March 14, 2015, http://blacklivesmatter.com/.

79. Cox and Foust, "Social Movement Rhetoric." For network theory, see Mario Diani, "Introduction: Social Movements, Contentious Actions, and Social Networks: 'From Metaphor to Substance,'" in *Social Movements and Networks: Relational Approaches to Collective Action*, ed. Mario Diani and Doug McAdam (New York: Oxford University Press, 2003).

80. Alexander R. Galloway and Eugene Thacker, *The Exploit: A Theory of Networks* (Minneapolis: University of Minnesota Press, 2007).

81. Richard J. F. Day, "From Hegemony to Affinity: The Political Logic of the Newest Social Movements," *Cultural Studies* 18, no. 5 (2004): 716–48.

82. Charles Tilly, *From Mobilization to Revolution* (Reading, MA: Addison-Wesley Publishing, 1978), 6.

83. McGee, "'Social Movement;'" and Malcolm O. Sillars, "Defining Movements Rhetorically: Casting the Widest Net," *Southern Speech Communication Journal* 46, (1980): 17–32.

84. See Dana L. Cloud, *Control and Consolation in American Culture: Rhetorics of Therapy* (Thousand Oaks, CA: SAGE Publications, 1998); Dana L. Cloud, "*The Matrix* and Critical Theory's Desertion of the Real," *Communication and Critical/Cultural Studies* 3, no. 4 (2006): 329–54.

85. Dana L. Cloud, "Doing Away With Suharto—and the Twin Myths of Globalization and New Social Movements," in *Counterpublics and the State*, ed. Robert Asen and Daniel C. Brouwer (Albany: State University of New York Press, 2001).

86. J. Robert Cox, "Beyond Frames: Recovering the Strategic in Climate Communication," *Environmental Communication* 4, no. 1 (2010): 122–33.

87. Hardt and Negri, *Empire*.

88. Manuel Castells, *Networks of Outrage and Hope: Social Movements in the Internet Age* (Malden, MA: Polity, 2012), 5.

89. See Dutta, *Communicating Social Change*, chapter 7.

90. Phaedra C. Pezzullo, "Performing Critical Interruptions: Stories, Rhetorical Invention, and the Environmental Justice Movement," *Western Journal of Communication* 65, no. 1 (2001): 1–25.

Social Movement Scholarship

A Retrospective/Prospective Review

Raymie E. McKerrow

This collection aims to address the question about the connections and differences between social movement and counterpublic scholarship; more importantly it aims to understand what one critical approach yields that another does not.[1] My goal in this essay is to provide a context for responding to the questions and ideas that current scholarship raises about the nature and direction of a *functional* versus a *meaning-centered* perspective on how best to understand and evaluate the success or failure of a movement to achieve social change. My purpose is to use prior history as a framework for a review of contemporary approaches. In particular, my concern is that we recognize that these are not either-or perspectives, as both have value. A functionalist perspective may incorporate a meaning-centered analysis, while a meaning-centered perspective may be most useful in those cases where a social movement or protest action does not fit within the confines of a functionalist orientation.

Framing Social Movement's Identity as Functionalist or Meaning-Centered

These contrary positions are represented in Simons's functional approach to social movements and what might be termed a minority "rhetorical movement" or meaning-centered position articulated by McGee in 1980 and again in 1983.[2] Because Simons initiated the break from a modernist Aristotelian approach to analyzing protest rhetoric and established a major orientation toward social movement research, his perspective will serve as a "representative anecdote,"[3] standing in for similar orientations during the debate in the early 1980s. McGee's approach is the oppositional "representative anecdote" as it moves us from a positivist to a postmodern orientation grounded in the contingency of language in generating social change.[4]

Understanding the implications of what was treated as an oppositional divide is critical in assessing what might be gained in recognizing the respective strengths of both in contemporary scholarship.

Within a functionalist perspective, the focus is on a social movement as a unique thing; thus, studying movements lends itself to identifying their unique organizational and instrumental features. As such, it focuses on a movement's trajectory through time. It addresses the rhetorical goals of spokespersons in each stage (as if they were discrete) and predicts outcomes according to the movement's reputed success in managing the "constraints" within the limits of their abilities (to employ an equally positivist orientation recommended by Bitzer's sense of a "rhetorical situation").[5] What Simons/functionalists provide is a critical vocabulary—a grammar of sorts that allows the critic to "ticket and label" a social movement as one kind or another, with the presumption that in "labeling" one has said something. That something implies that a social movement by another name would not be the same, even though each could be analyzed in terms of the strategic response to the requirements and problems faced. Thinking about movements in this manner, with clearly specified goals, audiences, and organizational structure, allows functionalists to employ a variety of classificatory typologies. For example, in the movement typology (Reformist, Expressivist, etc.) Simons situates rhetoric as an instrumental activity within the structure of the organization's functional orientation: the movement acts (typically through or with rhetoric) and things happen.[6] He provides very extensive and clear instructions for approaching movement analysis from the tripartite perspective of his 1970 orientation: The analysis of *Requirements* asks the analyst to figure out how the movement came into being and notes the role of the "leader" charged with multiple tasks. *Problems* relates to the structural impediments (e.g., internal bickering and lack of societal legitimacy). *Strategies* allows one to bifurcate those who agitate into militants and moderates, with specific predictable consequences of the rhetorical success, or lack thereof, by each in terms of audience receptivity.[7]

From this formal perspective, "a social movement is an uninstitutionalized collectivity that operates on a sustained basis to exert external influence in behalf of a cause."[8] While this seems an iron-clad definition with clear boundaries, Simons allows that "a collectivity may be partially institutionalized and still be a movement," thus showing a limit to understanding movements even in his own definition.[9] He provides, as the prime examples of such a situation, the National Organization for Women and the National Rifle Association, as both are ostensibly mainstream organizations complicit with institutional norms. At the same time, they function outside the mainstream to the extent that their respective agitation for feminist causes or antigun control belongs to *the movement* as an, in Simons's terms, un-institutionalized collectivity.

Although Simons's main focus is on organizational forms, he connects to meaning making, whether counter to or in support of institutions, in noting that they "are engaged most fundamentally in struggles over meaning."[10] While meaning is an important component in what is otherwise a highly functional, organizationally focused examination of who does what to whom under what social conditions, the link to "meaning" or rhetorical action is not a central focus in the analysis. There is a distinct reluctance to privilege rhetoric in its guise as a constitutive force impacting one's sense of social events. It is true that, ostensibly, a social movement somehow comes into being, and once identifiable as such ("movements select from a reper-toire of possibilities"), a critic can engage in an understanding of how the rhetoric unfolds.[11] Keep in mind that, from Simons's perspective, it is *the movement* that selects what rhetorical action might be advanced on behalf of a cause. It is the case that the key term for Simons is "agent"—"what movement actors (and the forces they oppose) say and do to make a differ-ence in the world."[12] However, the agent is an effect of the organization of which s/he is a part, and the emphasis is on the relationship between what the agent does on behalf of the organization and what impact the rhetori-cal action has on the audience it engages.

Thus, Simons's RPS (Requirements, Problems, Strategies) strategy to label and analyze movements becomes part of the functionalist approach. However, the primary weakness of the highly structured approach lies in its inadequacy in analyzing social protests that remain impervious to the de-mands a functionalist approach makes on what a "successful" social movement should be and do. The trap that exists in following a formulaic or cookie-cutter approach is that it precludes the possibility of engaging rhetoric in terms outside the formula. If Simons's perspective were styled as "here's a way of thinking in broad terms," without presuming that one actually writes with a tripartite organizational structure as the governing model, it might be a more acceptable gloss on how one might approach analysis. As is, DeLuca is correct in noting that Simons's view of social movement rheto-ric is organizational or managerial to a fault.[13]

Simons was not the only one writing about movements at this time; other scholars also offered their own perspective on social movement analy-sis.[14] McGee dismisses all of the alternative perspectives in arguing that "social movement" was a chimera, and that the focus should be on the crea-tion of meaning between people.[15] A sense of the conversation that ensued might best be represented by Simons's observation that, among the reasons for rejecting McGee was that he "offers questionable charges, innuendos, and fallacious arguments."[16] Gronbeck provides a clear sense of the division between Simons's position and that advanced by McGee: "Simons (1970) had urged that movement leaders had to manage the physical resources available to the group to succeed; McGee said, no, what must be managed are beliefs, attitudes, values, and especially self-identities."[17] This neatly categorizes the split between a functionalist and meaning-centered orientation: a critic approaches movements as real things *or* focuses attention on the people and their expression. My rereading of this debate leaves me with the uneasy sense that McGee was simply misunderstood. That may be too simple a claim, but I want to start with this thought as a beginning observation.

By unpacking McGee's argument, we can better understand the criticism it engendered. McGee begins with the assertion that "social movement is a set of meanings and not a phenomenon."[18] McGee also notes Simons's usage of social movement is "an almost organic presence" in referring continually to features as "*their . . . their . . . they . . . them . . . animate them.*"[19] In arguing "(they) are not phenomena *as a matter of fact,*" McGee is taking a precisely contrary position.[20] In his view, the term "movement" "is an interpretation of phenomenal data controlled *less by what happens in the real world than by what a particular user . . . wants to see in the real world.*"[21] Another key statement advances this same perspective: "The whole notion of 'movement' is mythical, a trick of the mind which must be understood *as an illusion* and not as a fact."[22] McGee's earlier argument on the fictional status of "the people" further exemplifies his position on social movements: "The people" do not exist in real time until called into being by a rhetoric that constructs their momentary existence—even here, the particularity of "the people" is illusory—a photo of a mass rally depicts a slice of "the people" but by no means captures the entirety of those who find a particular discourse or event resonates with their own personal comfort or discomfort.[23]

The distinction that follows from these recollections is to constitute an analysis of the rhetoric *of* "movement" rather than a study of the rhetoric *in a* "movement" as a viable enterprise.[24] Chávez explains McGee's distinction thusly: "When *social movements* is used as a noun, it suggests that a movement is a phenomenon. Using *social movement* in its verb form . . . reduces the possibility of limiting social movement studies to the investigation of things."[25] Another way of construing the distinction is to recall bell hooks's references to "women's movement" rather than to *the* women's movement.[26] While she is writing within the historical milieu that was/is considered a social movement, she seldom references it as a "thing." Restating McGee's main premise: Movements do not act. You will not see "the movement" walking down the street sipping a drink and waving a sign in protest. Rather, you will see a person or persons acting. Your description of their action is the meaning.

Before going further, it may be useful to briefly consider the objections to McGee as a means of shoring up a claim that his position was misunderstood. Lucas took the position that "serious flaws" in McGee's critique culminated in an "oversimplified" approach. In rejecting McGee's distinction between phenomena and meaning, Lucas argues that social movements are "no different from most other phenomena."[27] If you accept his rejection of the distinction, this follows; but unless you accept the fact that McGee is *not* talking about *the* movement or phenomena you miss the point entirely.

Cathcart's position is closer to McGee's in noting that "social movements are a special type of collective behavior characterized by a unique rhetorical form"; consequently, we should "focus our movement studies on . . . languaging strategies."[28] McGee agrees with the focus on language but rejects the sense that there is a "unique rhetorical form" that constitutes "collective behavior" as a social movement. This returns the emphasis to understanding the meaning of "movement" as "an ideological state and rhetoric as constitutive or representative of that state."[29] To name a rhetorical event is, to use Burke, to take an attitude toward the nature of the event, whether it is social movement or some other change.[30]

What I have attempted to isolate above delineates what is at stake in focusing attention on *the movement* as opposed to focusing attention on *social movement*. The binary itself is a "convenient fiction" in that it promotes seeing phenomena and meaning as mutually exclusive orientations; in practice, the critic may focus on both, with either orientation as the primary. There is a cost to this "both/and" approach, as it contravenes McGee's original argument that the functional orientation was incapable of responding to the critical question of "meaning." Foust argues "to take McGee's challenge seriously, one would have to relinquish the assumption that movements are built by rational actors or effective persuaders—but one would also have to relinquish the ability to attribute 'constitutive communication' to a coherent, collective agent."[31] As a critical rhetorician, that move is not as difficult as it may seem; it recognizes that an agent, qua agent, is not the author of her own words—but rather her words reflect a conversation within which she is immersed. In particular, in taking the approach inspired by McGee, one must abandon Simons's tripartite approach to social movement analysis if one's goal is to understand the relationship between rhetoric and movement.

This is not to say that McGee's position destroys the possibility of understanding the history of *a movement*; it is to say that both can exist as strategies, while noting that the questions they answer belong to different orders. McGee's orientation does not preclude an analysis of the dialectical tension between the opposition and those in power, should that be a determining focus that captures the discourse. Nor does it necessarily preclude a "Simonesque" functional analysis, if the primary purpose is to ground the analysis in a specific historical context and analyze what the rhetorical *and* organizational constraints are, either from the perspective of those focused on change, or from those resisting the call for action. Furthermore, one might focus on "meaning" as the primary aim, from McGee's perspective, while taking into account the manner in which the organizational structure inhibits or permits particular meanings. A pluralist approach allows both perspectives, granted viability as aims with different goals, to coexist within the critic's repertoire.

With this in mind, one should not be confused about what one is doing with either analysis. This may have been McGee's fundamental objection— a formulaic "inception-agitation-demise" orientation to the movement of ideas may not always be helpful in unpacking symbolic meaning. It may underscore who did what when, but does not, in itself, force a focus on issues of power difference, on the potential for symbolic change that culminates in a new power configuration or, in Foucault's terms, on the creation of a new game of truth.[32]

In transitioning to a review of contemporary approaches, I want to make certain my position is clear. Just as Hauser and McClellan suggest their purpose was not to dismiss leader-centered movements while encouraging a focus on the role of vernacular rhetoric in protest actions,[33] my purpose is not to dismiss a structural/functionalist approach. Rather it is to suggest that a sole reliance on this perspective limits the possibility of enjoining a rhetorical orientation toward meaning: what a social movement *does* in contrast to what it *is*.

Contemporary Approaches: Implications for Social Movement Analysis

A question that emerges from the foregoing historical review is "how does the above review of our past history and the argument for a pluralist approach play out in contemporary approaches to social movements?" In responding to this question, it is useful to contextualize current social movement research more broadly, especially in relation to resource mobilization (RM) and new social movement (NSM) research, largely conducted outside our discipline. This research provides a frame for approaching critical components such as identity, collectivity, and instrumentality in relation to our own analysis of social change. Scholars, primarily from sociology, have approached social movements from an RM perspective in the United States and from an NSM perspective in Europe. It can be argued that both traditions privilege a functional perspective in analyzing the nature of collective protest action. In particular, identity and collectivity are concepts around which analysis often revolves in both arenas.[34] While NSM research is not confined a singular approach, there is merit in seeing within NSM research a set of common assumptions that generate a sense of sameness across analyses. Barker and Dale provide this argument in advancing several challenges to the distinctions assumed to exist between "new and old social movements," including such questions as to whether NSMs are really "new."[35] In particular, functionalist NSM scholarship provides further illustrations of the utility in adopting alternative approaches in the analysis of contemporary movements. There are occasions where the functionalist approach is not as useful in analyzing movements that do not answer well to structural or resource demands. The following discussion focuses attention on the limits of utilizing identity and/or collectivity as the primary themes in social movement analysis. In moving beyond these limitations, I argue for what I term a "new instrumentality" that demands alternative approaches, especially in relation to reclaiming the utility of a meaning-centered orientation.

The Limits of Identity

In and of itself, a focus on identity does not produce defensible interpretations of meaning in movements. Even if we do not want to reduce movements to "phenomenon," identity cannot also be reduced to essentialist or phenomenal versions of understanding the nature of a movement. A focus on a broader conception of social movements avoids the reductionist tendencies of earlier research that highlighted issues such as NSMs.[36] As Johnston, Laraña, and Gusfield indicate, NSMs "often involve the emergence of new or formerly weak dimensions of identity."[37] This focus on identity, however, comes at a price, in that it risks replicating the same phenomenal status of social movements within RM work. Reiter reminds us that the concepts we use are "not of the world but about the world" and warns against reifying terms in "making us believe that, for example, 'race,' 'class,' or 'social movement' really exists."[38] McGee would applaud, as this orientation suggests that these terms are social constructions—they are not "real" in the sense of having an existence apart from their use in language. This is not an attempt to erase the significance of the hurt they may impart—they feel real, irrespective of their status as constructed artifacts. As noted above, in a manner reminiscent of McGee's argument, Reiter notes that scholars "seem to assume that new social movements are genuine things of this world—phenomena that somehow produce their own definitions and establish borders for themselves (which, needless to say, they do not)."[39] He goes on to specify ways in which the European model of NSM and its "identity focus" provides a "misleading" account of what actually occurs. Labeling a movement as "new" may overlook its actual history: "Black organizing in Brazil is a crucial case of identity-based organizing, and there is evidence for its reaching back to the early times of slavery."[40] The point to be made here is that aligning ourselves with NSM's sense of identity may not produce a defensible interpretation of the meaning of social movement.

The Limits of Collective Organization

Just as identity is problematic as a focus on movements, the reliance on the "collective" as an entry point suggests that social movements are, always and only, about specific issues around which like-minded people coalesce. To the contrary, some contemporary movements challenge previous notions of associations and coalitions that have defined movement studies.

Like functionalist scholars, sociologists have attended to organizational structure as part of their understanding of movements. Tilly and Wood operate from a general principle of "contentious collective action" whereby social movements express views in myriad forms of action: the "creation of special-purpose associations and coalitions, public meetings, solemn processions, vigils, rallies, demonstrations, petition drives, statements to and in public media, and pamphleteering" giving rise to what is termed a "*social movement repertoire*."[41] They do, however, note that scholars may often "confuse a movement's collective action with the organizations and networks that support the action,"[42] thereby placing the emphasis on the act not the resources that brought it into being. Tarrow concurs with the general emphasis on collective action, noting that a social movement occurs when there are "*collective challenges, based on common purposes and social solidarities, in sustained interaction with elites, opponents, and authorities*."[43] While there is recognition of the importance of context, the emphasis on sustained interaction belies a more traditional perspective. To the contrary, collective action may be a flash in the pan—a one-time occurrence that, while it generates publicity and some pressure on its target to consider action, it may die aborning in failing to move beyond the initial act.

In sum, then, neither a reliance on identity nor a reliance on collectivity will resonate well with the respective examples used as counters to that perspective. These illustrations serve as a framework for addressing additional illustrations, specifically focusing on movements that are even more pronounced in their distanciation from traditional approaches to movement studies.

The "New Instrumentality"

What constitutes a social movement, or facilitates movement, may not depend on identity or a collective unity. While functionalists tend to examine a single organization with a coherent/effective message with a defined instrumental goal, there are movements that function neither with a preformed sense of identity, nor a precisely formed collectivity. Instead, they may have a chaotic or imprecise organizational "identity"; in addition, their existence may be as an unorganized "critical mass" that allows for multiple messages, goals, aims, actions, and so on, all loosely collected under a complex or multiply defined theme that aims toward a similar target or addresses different targets. This is what I am describing as the "new instrumentality." In particular, it resonates well with a primary focus on what McGee asserted was the goal of analyzing "movement" in the sense of the meaning of rhetorical messages.

As a beginning example, recent communication scholarship has focused on the kind of flash events noted earlier. For example, Sprain, Endres, and Peterson analyze the "Step It Up (SIU) Congress" movement begun by six college students from Middlebury College in Vermont.[44] SIU focused on a single day in 2007 and, via the web and email, sent out a call across the nation asking for involvement in a national "climate change" protest. The approach was not one of sustained interaction but rather an attempt to engage citizens where they lived and ask that they construct their own means of challenging Congress to act on climate change. SIU differed from those defined with either traditional or NSM orientations; it was a do-it-yourself orientation to social change, leaving people free to interpret the central message as their local needs dictated or their imaginations created. In a balanced review of this national protest day, Cox notes that while "unresolved tensions in SIU's design, and the strategic requirements set forth by the scale and complexity of the change, may have limited" the movement's influence, it also represented "strategic potential: *the ability of a loosely coordinated network of agents, opportunities, and practices at multiple local sites of decision to 'signal' in critically important ways within our energy system.*"[45] The last blog entry on SIU's website was in 2008; the movement has transformed into a global climate change orientation.[46]

The story does not end here, however, as there are numerous action groups aimed, not only at climate change, but also a wide range of environmental, social justice causes. For example, the Energy Action Coalition comprises fifty youth/student groups across the country, all engaged in a variety of activities that aim to change the way we manage our environment.[47] Such loosely collaborative networks[48] may be the wave of the future; as opposed to focusing on traditional forms of social action, we may find it appropriate to examine broader coalitions and networks, however defined, especially in the context of how they frame messages both internally and externally.[49] Functionalism, and a focus on what is "new," has its place in responding to questions related to structure and tactics writ large. But reliance on these orientations alone may not do justice to what may be said about the role of rhetoric in fostering change.

"Critical Mass" movements are another case in point; while loosely collective, they also coexist within a broad array of social actions, without, as in the case of the Energy Coalition, necessarily having a common theme. The emphasis on "mass" is clear in the name itself—the collective action suggests a well-known truism: there can be strength in numbers. As a more precise illustration of what is intended, consider the treatment of a single Senegalese woman objecting to genital cutting and being ostracized versus a change action that engaged entire villages in Senegal and elsewhere in Africa as a means of reducing the incidence of this practice.[50] As another example, what is clear from a perusal of the Thrive Movement website[51] is that any number of actions can be taken to generate specific, if sporadic, pressure on those targeted for change. One can sign up to "End the Federal Reserve," create a "Genetically Modified Organism Free Zone," participate in a mass protest at Monsanto Headquarters and boycott Monsanto products, or any number of other socially desired acts to end undesirable activities on the part of government, corporations, or individual/corporate farming practices. While the goal is to achieve critical mass, the actions undertaken remain at the local level—it is just that thousands are engaged in the same activity across multiple sites, potentially influencing change in their respective locales. The solutions hub lists current actions by residents in various communities who have signed on to engage in local activities destined to improve their communal existence. In both cases, the meaning of the activity is central, and the strategies employed require a discursive approach to enacting collaborative change.[52]

As another illustration, the recent Occupy Wall Street movement operates much more loosely than a functional approach would suggest, while furthering the sense of movement that McGee privileged. The initial act of occupying Wall Street went viral in terms of multiple sites engaging the refrain "We are the 99%." Following the initial occupation of Zucotti Park in New York City, the movement spread internationally, "involving hundreds of thousands of people."[53] Seen as a response to the collapse of the economy at the hands of the greedy denizens of Wall Street, the Occupy Movement might be claimed to have failed.[54] However, a perusal of the Occupy "infotent" suggests that, while the initial focus on Wall Street has diminished, the central values underlying the initial activity are very much in place and support a range of social protest actions similar to those promoted by Thrive.

A similar orientation to movement as a series of fragments of social action would recognize techno-mobs as potential players in the game of change. Jessica Ketcham Weber suggests that the "creative use of *techno*logy to *mobi*lize citizens (e.g., techno-mob) in public performances" enables those who may not have political power to gain attention through "raising awareness and disrupting dominant ideologies." As she notes, such groups have a "rhizomal structure" in that "there are no leaders, organizer meetings, or memberships."[55] Whereas Simons's approach to social movements remains mired in a modernist world where structure, leadership, and vision are central, postmodern rhizomic groups move beyond even the commitment Occupy Wall Street makes to a leaderless "structure." In fact, the sense of an identity or collective group associated with NSMs may disappear. A technomob may come into being and disappear just as quickly following its attempt to move citizens to action. Flash mobs provide another instance of a group that embraces a temporary existence.[56] Distancing ourselves from a sole reliance on a collective action format, especially when that suggests sustained organizational action focused on a coherent goal, allows us to focus on "movement" as differentiated from "the" organization.

A wide variety of groups disengage from organizationally directed collective action on the part of a specific movement. Food Not Bombs describes itself as a charity and a grassroots movement active across the world in aiming to eradicate hunger, among other goals. It "works in coalition with groups like Earth First!, The Leonard Peltier Defense Committee, Anarchist Black Cross, the IWW, Homes Not Jails, Anti Racist Action,

Farm Animal Rights Movement, In Defense of Animals, the Free Radio Movement."[57] Anarchist Black Cross works to free political prisoners; the Farm Animal Rights movement is an institutionalized nonprofit, which seeks to end the use of animals as food. Free Radio focuses on civil disobedience and links its efforts to various protests against the World Trade Organization, the World Bank, and other similar economic agents. Neighborhood assemblies, both as discrete units and as part of a network, are not oriented toward policy change, but rather toward changing the role of citizens, activating them to make a difference in their communities. As Day suggests, "all of these tactics consciously defy the logic of reform/revolution by refusing to work through the state, party, or corporate forms. Instead, they are driven by an orientation to meeting individual/group/community needs by *direct action*."[58]

In this sense, the approach taken challenges a Simonesque functionalism that argues from a strict typology in focusing attention on "the" social movement. More to the point, it means we need to move beyond the oppositionality in the Simons/McGee debate, as well as beyond the limitations provided by extant NSM work. The "new instrumentality" impacts how identity and collectivity may function within the kind of protest actions noted above. The ways in which movements might engage us, especially in their instrumental approach to change, may be far less functional while remaining vital and vibrant protests. They may not be successful from a functionalist perspective, but may nonetheless move change forward.

Conclusion

The return to the Simons/McGee debate over a functional versus meaning-centered approach presented the primary arguments on both sides. The purpose of the review was to provide a framework for moving beyond that controversy into an analysis of contemporary approaches. The focus on NSM permitted an examination of the limits of identity and collectivity as primary frames for the analysis of current social change. The discussion of the new instrumentality orientation to movements provides evidence that further illustrates the value inherent in reconsidering the role of identity and collectivity within social movements. In extending our analysis beyond traditional approaches to these concepts by attending to what has been termed the "new instrumentality," we will be in a stronger position to adapt to unique formats within which protest is expressed. In this connection, attending, as McGee suggests, to what is seen and perceived to be the rhetoricality of a movement will further advance our scholarship.

What has been said does not detract from the potential inherent within a functionalist approach, provided it is utilized to answer questions that only a focus on structure and organization, for example, might produce. At the same time, we are not left only with a structuralist or a "meaning-centered approach." There are other perspectives that may also be considered in merging our critical questions with tools that may be best equipped to provide insights.[59] For example, Foust articulates a different approach that also fits within the discussion of a focus on "movement" rather than organizational matrices: "The shift from rhetorical agent to agency may help reinvigorate the study of social movement rhetoric to include resistance in all its guises: sanctioned and spontaneous, organizational and individual, mediated and immediate, hegemonic and transgressive."[60] Ott offers a more far-reaching proposal, in rejecting the focus on social movement as such. He argues that "treating the discourses of dissension on a given social issue as a 'movement' dangerously risks homogenizing a diverse set of voices, viewpoints, and volitions under a single label, motive, and purpose." He proposes *rhetorics of social resistance* as the alternative and outlines key heuristics, including "materiality, visuality, corporeality, performativity, and publicity."[61] While I see the inherent value in "resistance" as a key term, it may be useful to keep in mind that the key terms he advances are not unique to the study of movements or counterpublics nor to resistance itself. One or more can be engaged in virtually any study of rhetoric's engagement with the world.

Irrespective of the questions we ask or the critical tools we employ in analysis, we need to let our work speak as we engage protest on its own grounds, in its own terms. Such is the never-ending task of a critic's engagement with discursive events.

Notes

1. Previous versions of this paper were presented at the 2011 NCA Pre-Conference Seminar: Voicing Connections, Contradictions, and Possibilities in Social Movement and Counterpublic Theories and as the Gravlee Lecture at Colorado State University, September 2012. I am indebted to Christina Foust and Amy Pason for their assistance and advice in sharpening the original argument.

2. See the following: Herbert W. Simons, "Requirements, Problems, and Strategies: A Theory of Persuasion for Social Movements," *Quarterly Journal of Speech* 56 (1970): 1–11. Herbert W. Simons, "On Terms, Definitions, and Theoretical Distinctiveness: Comments on Papers by McGee and Zarefsky," *Central States Speech Journal* 31, no. 4 (1980): 306–15; Herbert W. Simons, Elizabeth

W. Mechling, and Howard N. Schreier, "Functions of Communication in Mobilizing for Collective Action from the Bottom Up: The Rhetoric of Social Movements," in *The Handbook on Rhetorical and Communication Theory*, ed. Carroll C. Arnold and John Waite Bowers (Boston: Allyn and Bacon, 1984), 792–868; Herbert W. Simons, "Social Movements," in *Encyclopedia of Rhetoric*, ed. Thomas O. Sloane (New York: Oxford University Press, 2001), 724–32; Michael Calvin McGee, "'Social Movement': Phenomenon or Meaning?" *Central States Speech Journal* 31 no. 4 (1980): 233–44; Michael Calvin McGee, "Social Movement as Meaning," *Central States Speech Journal* 34 (1983): 74–77.

 3. Kenneth Burke, *A Grammar of Motives*, (Berkeley: University of California Press, 1962), 59–61.

 4. See McGee, "'Social Movement'" and "Social Movement as Meaning."

 5. Lloyd Bitzer, "The Rhetorical Situation," *Philosophy and Rhetoric* 1 (1968): 1–14.

 6. Simons, "Social Movements," 725–26. The key terms are as follows: "reformist," "resistance," "restorative," and "expressivist." While noting that these are not entirely mutually exclusive, Simons nonetheless is committed to an approach that sees the typology as an important part of the process of demarcating the rhetorical function of a movement.

 7. Simons, "Requirements, Problems, and Strategies."

 8. Simons, "Social Movements," 724.

 9. Ibid., 725.

 10. Ibid.

 11. Ibid., 726.

 12. Ibid, 725.

 13. Kevin M. DeLuca, *Image Politics: The New Rhetoric of Environmental Activism* (New York: Guilford Press, 1999), 27–31.

 14. Special issues of *Central States Speech Journal* were devoted to the status of social movement research in 1980 and 1983. In addition to Simons and McGee, see Leland M. Griffin, "On Studying Movements," *Central States Speech Journal* 31, no. 4 (1980): 225–32; David Zarefsky, "A Skeptical View of Movement Studies," *Central States Speech Journal* 31, no. 4 (1980): 245–54; Stephen E. Lucas, "Coming to Terms with Movement Studies," *Central States Speech Journal* 31, no. 4 (1980): 255–66; Robert S. Cathcart, "Defining Social Movements by Their Rhetorical Form," *Central States Speech Journal* 31, no. 4 (1980): 267–73; James R. Andrews, "History and Theory in the Study of the Rhetoric of Social Movements," *Central States Speech Journal* 31 no. 4 (1980): 274–81; Carol J. Jablonski, "Promoting Radical Change in the Roman Catholic Church: Rhetorical Requirements, Problems and Strategies of the American Bishops," *Central States Speech Journal* 31, no. 4 (1980): 282–89; Ralph R. Smith, "The Historical Criticism of Social Movements," *Central States Speech Journal* 31, no. 4 (1980): 290–97; Charles J. Stewart, "A Functional Approach to the Rhetoric of Social Movements," *Central States Speech Journal* 31, no. 4 (1980): 298–305; Charles J. Stewart, "A Functional Perspective on the Study of Social Move-

ments," *Central States Speech Journal* 34, no. 1 (1983): 77–80; James R. Andrews, "An Historical Perspective on the Study of Social Movements," *Central States Speech Journal* 34, no. 1 (1983): 67–69; Robert S. Cathcart, "A Confrontation Perspective on the Study of Social Movements," *Central States Speech Journal* 34, no. 1 (1983): 69–74; Bernard L. Brock, "Editor's Commentary," *Central States Speech Journal* 34, no. 1 (1983): 80–82.

15. McGee, "'Social Movement'" and "Social Movement as Meaning."

16. Simons, "On Terms," 309.

17. Bruce Gronbeck, "The Rhetoric of Agitation and Control Confronts Movement Theory and Practice," *Poroi: An Interdisciplinary Journal of Rhetorical Analysis and Invention* 9, no. 2 (2013): 2.

18. McGee, "'Social Movement,'" 233.

19. Ibid., 235 (italics in original).

20. Ibid., 236 (italics in original).

21. Ibid., 237 (italics added).

22. Ibid., 242–43 (italics in original).

23. Michael Calvin McGee, "In Search of the 'People': A Rhetorical Alternative," *Quarterly Journal of Speech* 61, no. 3 (1975): 235–49.

24. McGee, "'Social Movement,'" 243.

25. Karma R. Chávez, "Counter-Public Enclaves and Understanding the Function of Rhetoric in Social Movement Coalition-Building," *Communication Quarterly* 59, no. 1 (January–March 2011): 14.

26. bell hooks, *Feminist Theory: From Margin to Center*. (Cambridge, MA: South End Press, 2000).

27. Lucas "Coming to Terms," 256, 258.

28. Cathcart, "A Confrontation Perspective," 70, 73.

29. McGee, "Social Movement as Meaning," 76.

30. Kenneth Burke, *Permanence and Change* (Berkeley: University of California Press, 1984), 177.

31. Christina R. Foust, *Transgression as a Mode of Resistance: Rethinking Social Movement in an Era of Corporate Globalization* (Lanham, MD: Lexington Books, 2010), 64.

32. Michel Foucault, "Truth and Juridical Forms," in *Power/Essential Works of Foucault*, vol. 3, ed. by James D. Faubion (New York: New Press, 2000).

33. Gerard Hauser and Erin Daina McClellan, "Vernacular Rhetoric and Social Movements: Performances of Resistance in the Rhetoric of the Everyday," in *Active Voices: Composing a Rhetoric of Social Movements*, ed. by Sharon McKenzie Stevens and Patricia M. Malesh (New York: State University of New York Press, 2010), 25.

34. As representative examples, see Nancy Whittier, "Meaning and Structure in Social Movements," in *Social Movements: Identity, Culture, and the State*, ed. David S. Meyer, Nancy Whittier, Belinda Robnett (New York: Oxford University Press, 2002), 289–307; Christian Fuchs, "The Self-Organization of Social Movements," *Systemic Practice and Action Research* 19 (2006); Robert Huesca,

"Conceptual Contributions of New Social Movements to Development Communication Research," *Communication Theory* 11, no. 4 (2006): 415–33; Bernd Reiter, "What's New in Brazil's 'New Social Movements'?" *Latin American Perspectives 38, no.* 1 (2011): 153–68; Hank Johnston, Enrique Laraña, and Joseph R. Gusfield, "Identities, Grievances, and New Social Movements," in *New Social Movements: From Ideology to Identity*, ed. Enrique Laraña, Hank Johnston, and Joseph R. Gusfield (Philadelphia: Temple University Press, 1994), 3–35; Colin Barker and Gareth Dale, "Protest Waves in Central Europe: A Critique of 'New Social Movement' Theory," *Critical Sociology* 24 (1998): 65–104; Charles Tilly and Lesley J. Wood, *Social Movements: 1768–2012*, 3rd ed. (Boulder, CO: Paradigm Publishers, 2012); Sydney G. Tarrow, *Power in Movement: Social Movements and Contentious Politics* (New York: Cambridge University Press, 2011).

35. Colin Barker and Gareth Dale, "Protest Waves in Central Europe," 73.

36. See Huesca, "Conceptual Contributions" for a concise review of NSM as part of the broader analysis of movements.

37. Johnston, Laraña, and Gusfield, "Identities, Grievances, and New Social Movements," 7.

38. Reiter, "What's New?" 153.

39. Ibid., 154

40. Ibid.

41. Tilly and Wood, *Social Movements*, 4, italics in original.

42. Ibid., 7.

43. Tarrow, *Power in Movement*, 9, italics in original.

44. Leah Sprain, Danielle Endres, and Tarla Rai Peterson, "Introduction: A National Day of Climate Change," in *Social Movement to Address Climate Change*, ed. Danielle Endres, Leah Sprain, and Tarla Rai Peterson (Amherst, NY: Cambria Press, 2009), 1–13.

45. Robbie Cox, "SID SIU and Beyond: Challenges of Scale and the Strategic," in *Social Movement to Address Climate Change*, ed. Danielle Endres, Leah Sprain and Tarla Rai Peterson (Amherst, NY: Cambria Press, 2009), 394. Italics in original.

46. Step It Up, accessed July 16, 2012, www.stepitup2007.org/; also see new website: www.350.org. accessed January 1, 2016.

47. Environment Energy Action Coalition, accessed July 16, 2012, www.energyactioncoalition.org/partners.

48. Cox, "SID SIU and Beyond," 415.

49. Foust, *Transgression as a Mode of Resistance*. As Foust suggests, "network organizing also reflects the use of new communication technologies, which allow for more spontaneous and potentially impacting protest: activists may adapt to changing street conditions through the use of cell phones and the Internet" (2).

50. "This is the practice employed in Malicounda Bambara, Senegal for young women who wanted to stop the traditional practice of female genital cutting,"

Critical Mass Movements, accessed February 20, 2015, www.thrivemovement
.com/has-been-done-before.

51. Thrive Movement, accessed July 16, 2012, www.thrivemovement.com/.
The Thrive Movement website introduces Foster Gamble's documentary, Thrive,
and focuses on the general theme "what will it take for humans to thrive on
planet earth?"

52. Thrive Movement, www.thrivemovement.com/.

53. Sarah Van Gelder, "Introduction: How Occupy Wall Street Changes
Everything," in *This Changes Every Thing: Occupy Wall Street and the 99% Movement*, ed. Sarah Van Gelder (San Francisco: Barrett-Koehler, 2011), 2.

54. Kyle Scott, "Guest Commentary," *Mercury News*, accessed May 6, 2013,
www.mercurynews.com/top-stories/ci_21072133/guest-commentary-whither
-occupy-movement-these-days.

55. Jessica Ketcham Weber, "Techno-Mob Movements: Public Performances
and the Collective Voices of Outsiders," in *Agency in the Margins: Stories of Outsider Rhetoric*, ed. Anne Meade Stockdell-Giesler (Teaneck NJ: Farleigh Dick-
inson University Press, 2010), 262.

56. I'm indebted to Christina Foust for this observation.

57. "The Story of Food Not Bombs," accessed July 16, 2012, www.foodnotbombs
.net/story.html.

58. Richard J. F. Day, *Gramsci Is Dead: Anarchist Currents in the Newest Social Movements* (Ann Arbor, MI: Pluto Press, 2005), 44–45. As another example
of neighborhood assemblies, see Benjamin Dangl, "Argentina to Wall Street:
Latin American Social Movements and the Occupation of Everything," Truth-
out, accessed May 15, 2013, www.truth-out.org/news/item/3978:argentina-to-wall
-street-latin-american-social-movements-and-the-occupation-of-everything.

59. Schutten argues that "social movement scholars need to consider the
active interpretation and incorporation of media by social movement actors,
not only the interpretation and incorporation of the movement by the media."
Julie K. Schutten, "Invoking *Practical Magic*: New Social Movements, Hidden Populations, and the Public Screen," *Western Journal of Communication* 70
(2006): 331; Givan, Roberts, and Soule's edited text examines the relationship
between diffusion of innovations theory and social movements. Rebecca K. Givan, Kenneth M. Roberts, and Sarah A. Soule, eds. *The Diffusion of Social Movements: Actors, Mechanisms, and Political Effects* (New York: Cambridge University Press, 2010); Fox and Frye provide a model that utilizes dimensions of
praxis as another alternative approach. Rebekah L. Fox and Joshua J. Frye,
"Tensions of Praxis: A New Taxonomy for Social Movements," *Environmental
Communication: A Journal of Nature and Culture* 4, no. 4 (2010): 422–40.

60. Foust, *Transgression as a Mode of Resistance*, 216.

61. Brian L. Ott, "Assessing Rhetorics of Social Resistance," *Quarterly Journal of Speech* 97 (2011): 335, 336.

2

"Social Movement Rhetoric"

A Critical Genealogy, Post-1980

Christina R. Foust

The year 1980 provides a convenient point of departure for this chapter, which offers an alternative disciplinary history of social movement rhetoric and counterpublics—a critical genealogy that follows the withering of the former and the proliferation of affiliated concepts like the latter.[1] Pres. Ronald Reagan began his first term in office one year after Margaret Thatcher became prime minister. The election of these two prominent conservatives helped realize politically a neoliberal economic regime that had been brewing since the end of World War II, when international financial institutions (like the World Bank) were crafted to facilitate economic recovery and integrate nations through the free market. Reagan and Thatcher represented well the ideologies that would become common sense for many, including "supply-side" economics, deregulation and decreased tariffs, policies designed to "shrink" government and privatize state-run industry, and a crack-down on opposition to such policies (e.g., organized labor). Neoliberal policies advanced a libertarian morality, celebrating as progress the individual's free activities in and through the market.

Though much could be (and has been) said of the opposition and localized alternatives to neoliberal globalization, I want to feature another element of this context. Social movement rhetoric's falling out of fashion, and counterpublic theory's coming into vogue, has taken place within the alienating and alienated knowledge work of the contemporary US academy. At least since 1980 we have witnessed the rising hegemony of postindustrial production, the circulation of "knowledge, communication, and affects."[2] Particularly for those who can afford it, postindustrial capitalism thrives on the fluidity or fragmentation of identity and the promise of consumption and lifestyle experiences to (re)constitute subjectivity temporarily.[3] Such broad trends affect scholars. As universities become increasingly marketized, faculty are goaded to do more with less, such as teach more students with less compensation or job security. For those fortunate to be on the tenure track, expectations to "publish or perish" are complicated by the privatization and segmentation of academic journals. As Striphas suggests, for authors who sign away their copyrights to large, multinational publishers, intellectual labor feels increasingly *"entrepreneurial."*[4] Joined by increased surveillance from administrators and rabid calls for efficiency, the dignified, comfortable autonomy of professorial life seems as quaint as the robotronic Teddy Ruxpin doll popular in the 1980s.

The year 1980 also represents a watershed moment in the disciplinary study of social change, with the publication of the special issue on social movement rhetoric in the *Central States Speech Journal.* Therein, McGee responds to the query, "does 'social movement rhetoric' constitute a unique domain of study?," by forwarding a greater question: What moves the social?[5] As I elaborate in the essay's first section, McGee's rather cryptic answer begins with a bifurcation between social scientific and humanistic approaches. The former treats social movements as phenomenon: empirical entities that are directly experienced in the world, prior to ascriptions of meaning. The hermeneutic alternative posits movement as meaning, or "an analogue comparing the flow of social facts to physical movement."[6] The latter, McGee asserts, provides a more productive avenue for understanding social change and rhetoric's relationship to it.

McGee's essay inspired important interventions in rhetorical scholarship on social movement.[7] As Cox and Foust note, the essay helps scholars feature rhetoric's contributions to social movement, particularly beyond sorting rhetoric into typological classifications (as is the purview of functional movement theory).[8] Building upon McKerrow's essay in the present volume, McGee's naming of phenomenon and meaning provides a convenient shorthand from which we might cohere a conversation on rhetorics of social change.

In the genealogical spirit, I approach McGee's essay more as a forgotten resource than canonical prescription for studying movement—for McGee did not develop, or clearly answer, the question of what moves the social. Indeed, direct responses to it are the exception rather than the rule. In spite of (or perhaps because of?) the essay's polemic against the functional approach, the majority of movement and counterpublic work of the last thirty-plus years does not explicitly orient itself to McGee's argument. Moreover, the keyword "social movement" fades from the disciplinary record, while a constellation of related theoretical, methodological, and critical pursuits (including counterpublics) occupy the scholarly agenda. I undertake in the remaining chapter a critical genealogy, inspired by the questions: What happened to social movement rhetoric? How have scholars of social change responded to the central question of what moves the social, since McGee articulated it in 1980?

Casting a wide net, I explore, in the chapter's second section, movement scholarship from 1980 through late 2013. I describe this period as "nomadic." Nomadic work has productively expanded "rhetorics of social resistance," legitimating a range of texts, identities, and tactics against the universalizing tendencies of functional theory.[9] Yet, as I critically assess, the introduction of "novel" concepts appears particularly productive amid the entrepreneurial and consumerist norms of the neoliberal academy. Unfortunately, nomadic work misses an opportunity to advocate for rhetoric's power of moving the social—save, perhaps, for its ability to effect social change by responding to contingencies through "original" concepts.[10] I thus conclude the chapter by advancing an alternative: the cultivation of a scholarly commons, as a broadly accessible, abundant garden that grows more fertile with contributions from each other's work. Crucial to this cultivation is a return to the forgotten possibilities of McGee's movement as meaning; greater reflexivity in developing and deploying concepts in rhetorical criticism; and the recovery of the term "social movement" itself.

The Significance of McGee's Essay for Social Movement Rhetoric

In this section, I position McGee's essay as a foil from which to view the last thirty-plus years of scholarly production (and preparing to advance it as a forgotten resource to aid in the recovery of social movement rhetoric). McGee revisits the etymology of "social movement," remarking that the term reflected a growing "historical consciousness, an awareness of the ways prior human activity constrain[s] immediate choice."[11] To name a "movement" provided legitimacy for groups operating outside of the status quo, while providing the status quo a means to control excessive behavior. The notion of movement lent narrative sequence and causality to empirical facts and the common sense derived from them—as though some force drove history to unfold in a way that confirmed the meaning philosophers attributed to it. McGee concludes, however, that grand thinkers could not agree on "*what* 'moves' in history—the material things which are our physical environment or the human ideas which mediate and interpret the facts of our experience."[12] Unfortunately, the materialism-idealism debate that grew out of the fundamental questions of social change was subverted, as social scientists converted historical movement into the empirical fact (or phenomenon) of a social movement.

McGee's answer to the question he raises (what moves the social?) is rather cryptic; and perhaps owing to the dualistic structure of his original critique, it is easier to discern what movement as meaning is *not*. Social movement is not a living, breathing thing that uses rhetoric to achieve its goals. It has little to do with ordering members in larger groups like "organizations, industries, or sectors."[13] Social movement is not a deterministic pulse that beats on, impervious to the contingent moment or humans' rhetorical responses to it. McGee suggests that movement as meaning is found not only in the constitutive effects of rhetoric but also in desire: "Whether one is caught up in political agitation, fascinated by the appearance of pattern and meaning in history, or desirous of being no more than a detached witness to endemic social change, 'movement' is our fondest wish, our dream, a reason to keep living in human society, for it contains an affirmation of human significance."[14] Hence, McGee retains the term "movement," honoring not only its history and potential effects but also its imbrication within democratic discourse and the possibility of meaning itself.

Yet, readers may well ask after reading McGee's essay: What is the relationship between meaning, interpretation, and desire? How does rhetoric or/and desire move the social? And what of phenomenal movements? Must we excommunicate persuasion from the study of social change, in favor of McGee's cryptic "movement as meaning?"

Direct responses to McGee's essay (though few in number) have begun to develop such questions. Scholars allied with McGee focus on the constructionist implications of movement as meaning. They treat the constitution of a collective agent as a key rhetorical effect, rather than the source, of an antagonism.[15] Scholars opposing McGee position him as an idealist. Because McGee advocates for dispersing (if not fully decoupling) rhetoric's potential for social change from the hands of "a social movement," McGee has been charged with obscuring the necessary material circumstances constraining actors in a rhetorical situation.[16]

While the constitutive implications of McGee's argument have been taken up directly by a handful of scholars—either in favor of, or opposed to, movement as meaning—the central question of what moves the social remains implicit in scholarship over the last three decades. Indeed, as I elaborate in the next section, scholars largely abandon the term "social movement" (however conceived), and practice four moves that I read as productive within the neoliberal academy: advancing an array of concepts, expanding the object domain or historical record, focusing upon particular causes, or situating social change in a new terrain of struggle.

The Nomad Period of Social Movement Rhetoric

Genealogical analysis typically consists of gathering and revisiting discursive fragments, with an eye toward how the past conditioned possibilities that were (and were not) realized. In the Foucauldian tradition, genealogy helps explain how certain regimes of power/knowledge came to be—not through an "objective" historical narrative but rather through a subjective critical account.[17] Genealogy highlights the *productive capacities* of power: how subjects (scholars) within discourses (like academic disciplines, constituted, in part, through their journals) are constrained and afforded particular agency (achieving publication, "doing criticism," etc.). Foucault famously avoided explicit evaluations of such agency as "furthering oppression" or "resisting dominance," leaving readers to create alternative discourses themselves. In this spirit, I approach the work of my colleagues (and myself) with care. For instance, I endeavor to avoid isolating or attributing responsibility to individuals. Instead, I highlight systemic capacities and trends.

Imagining how a novice researcher might approach movements in communication studies, I began with the EBSCO Communication and Mass Media Complete (CMMC) database as a commonly available interface that typically indexes national disciplinary journals, along with many important international, regional, and rhetoric-specific outlets. I found only twenty-four articles published in mainstream disciplinary journals tagged with the keywords "social movement" and "rhetoric" by their authors. So robust a term that it occasioned special issues in journals and its own section in a popular graduate text on rhetorical criticism,[18] social movement rhetoric (or its variants) apparently lost utility as a keyword for authors publishing after 1980. However, the term retained its significance for EBSCO, which delivered over 150 articles published on "social movement" and "rhetoric" (when these terms were followed without restriction).[19] After reviewing these two sets of publications, I returned with more keywords, allowing me to create a broader terrain in which social movement rhetoric could appear[20] and a citational trail following key works from prominent scholars that permitted me greater depth in understanding what happened after 1980.[21]

Given this set of articles, I characterize movement work following 1980 as *nomadic*, in the sense that communication, rhetoric, and cultural studies scholars wandered an expansive terrain of discourse broadly related to social change (including texts, events, and practices, as well as concepts and theories). Naming this time as nomadic also accounts for the influence of continental theory, particularly the uptake of French poststructuralism and postmodern philosophy.[22] Lastly, it speaks to the isolation of discourse communities organized around particular concepts—almost as though social movement, counterpublic, "vernacular discourse," "vernacular rhetoric," "outlaw discourse," or "minor rhetoric" scholars were affinity groups, wandering proverbially through a desert. Occasionally, they may have hit upon each other, but they likely did not continue their relationships beyond very brief, happenstance encounters. Though the very notion of the nomad resists generalizations, I turn to describe four prevailing trajectories following 1980.

Proliferation of Concepts

After 1980, scholars introduce an array of concepts informed by a variety of intellectual traditions.[23] A basic pattern for nomad scholarship is as follows: critics focus upon a rhetorical "object" that is related to a social movement and advocate for its resistant potential, typically in conversation with rhetorical theory or/and continental philosophy. From a genealogical perspective, this move appears productive in its addition of "new" interpretive heuristics. It appears less productive to relate new concepts to "old" conversations (chief among them, social movement rhetoric).

For instance, Dubriwny advances a theory of "collective rhetoric" through her exploration of the Redstockings' 1969 abortion speak-out (a panel discussion in which twelve women shared personal testimonies of abortion). Dubriwny situates the essay, published in 2005, amid "an energetic expansion in the theorization" of collective persuasion, including vernacular discourse.[24] Dubriwny differentiates collective rhetoric from leader-centered movements, in the same way that Campbell ascribes formal differences in women's consciousness-raising.[25] However, Dubriwny subverts almost entirely a discussion of social movement, save for citing Simons's influence in helping to fashion a "collaborative creation of rhetoric"[26]—shorthand, it would seem, for many people speaking together in the same place, at the same time. Distanced from the standard terms of social movements, collective rhetoric appears to advance a fresh reading derived from the unique rhetorical case of the Redstockings' speak-out. Collective rhetoric bears striking resemblance to the classic function of naming an exigency, or in

Stewart's words, "alter[ing] the ways audiences perceive the past, the present, and the future to convince them that an intolerable situation exists and that it warrants urgent action."[27] Nomadic work introduces seemingly novel terms to explain social change, in part, by foregoing conceptual connections with movement work of the past.

Similarly, Greene and Kuswa provide a timely analysis of "the occupation of such places as Tahrir Square, Zuccotti Park, Syntagma Square, and *La Puerta del Sol*," following how "a rhetoric of protest re-draws . . . maps of power by exposing their present configuration to the potential that another world (another map) is possible."[28] The essay foregrounds its novel approach to a neoliberal cartography of regionalism, accents, and subjectivities, though it does not directly relate the rhetorical work of protests to movement. Waisenan illustrates "glocal recursion" as "a rhetorical strategy that invites social change by imitating global methods of resistance, with slight variations, in local contexts," through the rhetoric of *Otpor*, the Serbian resistance movement critical to ousting Slobodan Milosevic in 2000.[29] In the context of immigration reform, Cisneros draws readers' focus not to La Gran Marcha's contributions to social movements per se but to how the concepts of hybridity and citizenship as performance explain this event.[30]

Like other work from the nomad period, Dubriwny's, Greene and Kuswa's, Waisenan's, and Cisneros's essays share an intuitive relationship to social movement rhetoric, for their objects of focus are traceable to what others might take as phenomenal movements. That nomad work situates itself within the context of social change rhetorics (by analyzing such rhetorical acts as protests or campaigns) supports the view emergent through this critical genealogy. Though I doubt that any scholar cited herein (including myself) intentionally chose to introduce a new concept instead of replicating "old" work, the genealogical perspective encourages us to meditate upon the lost possibility of naming our work in relationship to social movement.

Since scholars draw upon different intellectual traditions, it is perhaps not surprising that their essays develop conceptual resources outside a social movement vocabulary (especially derived from sociology). Yet, we might consider the affinities between nomadic concepts and social movements. The novel concepts often perform work similar to the rhetorical effects attributed to movements, as in Cisneros's essay, where "the hybrid position of migrants can challenge sedimented cultural forms by crafting new, diverse, and multi-positional forms of political identity."[31] Cisneros's attention to sociality adds great depth to either the classic functional view that rhetoric transforms perceptions of self or McGee's assertion that rhetoric itself moves the social. Readers are left to infer rhetoric's relationship to movement. Rather than attribute the effects of moving the social to a collective agent, critics suggest that new concepts (e.g., collective rhetoric, hybridity, protestor subjectivity, or glocal recursion) are the engines of social change.

Expanding the Object Domain and Historical Record

Critics also convey their work's significance as taking up new objects and historical figures for study. These twin trajectories reflect movement work of the past, in that early scholars expanded the purview of rhetoric to include a multiplicity of voices or body rhetoric, as well as lesser-studied identities. When viewed in a neoliberal context, the expansion of what or who counts as rhetorical also appears productive for its novelty and segmentation.

A number of scholars publishing in the nomad phase claim that more texts or events are, themselves, rhetorical. This expansion includes mainstays of social movements past and present and accounts for social change in a mediated world.[32] It also reflects trends in rhetorical scholarship more broadly, including rhetorics of place/space, visual or material rhetoric, the body, memory, and performance.[33]

For instance, Endres and Senda-Cook mark an expansion of social movement rhetoric, by considering "how words and bodies interact in and with place."[34] Though the essay's exploration of space/place in relationship to movements is novel, the underlying view of social change is quite traditional. The essay's conclusions reinforce a functional logic that treats place as a constraint to be navigated instrumentally by movement agents. Certain sites may become normalized as "protest places," like the National Mall; likewise, free speech zones threaten to normalize the protest that takes place within them, by their official, sanctioned nature. Contrarily, by holding protests in unpermitted, unexpected places, protestors may "disrupt a dominant meaning of a particular place."[35]

Here, place begins to sound like a *means* for *a movement* to meet the requirements of confronting an establishment or drawing broader public attention to its cause. Endres and Senda-Cook expand Stewart's original taxonomy of the demands movements face and the breadth of rhetorical tactics available to meet such demands. They offer readers a clear analytic framework for approaching the rhetorical significance of place, a much-needed contribution in the contemporary landscape including Occupy Wall Street and Tahrir Square. However, such contributions are not explicated, and the piece joins the nomadic production of novelty in broadening what counts as rhetorical.

Nomad scholarship also introduces lesser studied movements or identities to the disciplinary record.[36] Such studies may approach their object as historically misunderstood, advocating for a renewed appreciation of rhetoric's resistant potential. For instance, Parker deploys different notions of irony to understand the Black Manifesto and advances an alternative to literal interpretations that reduce James Forman's text to "hypocritical, extortionary, and retributive statements" countering white violence.[37] The Black Manifesto's contributions to social change are not as focused as the new perspective afforded through irony. Expanding the object domain and historical record, as well as forwarding an original reading on a movement text, proves productive within neoliberal scholarly norms.

Specifying Contributions to Particular Movements

Third, nomad phase work tends to contextualize itself within specific causes (notably, environmentalism, feminism, global justice, LGBTQ activism, or Chicano/a and Latina/o movements) rather than generalizing contributions to social movement rhetoric. For instance, Morris and Sloop consider the resistant potential of man-on-man kissing as "a juggernaut in a broader project of queer world making."[38] Morris and Sloop perform the twin moves of critical rhetoric, identifying the heteronormative logics that depoliticize queer performances and advocating new ways of witnessing the many "tumultuous destabilization[s]" occurring when two men kiss publicly.[39] Readers are likely to learn much about social change, though in keeping with the conceptual position of the nomad, the lessons offered are smaller scale, situated conclusions.

   Here, some work of the nomad period foregrounds the politics of knowledge production, as critics question the canonical status of social movement rhetoric itself (particularly prior to 1980), wary that interpretive methods replicate white, patriarchal dominance.[40] DeLaure's analysis of Ella Baker as an understudied figure in the civil rights movement, for instance, follows Campbell in advancing beyond leader-centered criticism: the "classic model of rhetorical persuasion—one speaker seeking to mobilize audiences capable of taking action on a specific exigence—doesn't fit [women's] liberation discourse."[41] Similarly, Hundley and Rodriguez, and Endres, turn to consummatory rhetoric in analyzing transgender and American Indian activism;[42] Henry advocates Afrocentric methods to explore protests like the Million Man March, as does Holmes in revisiting the sermonic rhetoric of Ralph Abernathy.[43] Such work defies the "rootlessness" of other nomadic work, as it encourages critics to embrace their subjectivity and position rhetorical criticism as a means to advance particular movements' "identity politics" within academic discourse.[44]

Following the more general pattern of nomad scholarship, though, such work tends to isolate its contribution to particular causes (not always identified through the terms of social movements). From the incongruous perspective on scholarship that I adopt in writing this essay, "siloing" could also be read as productive for its market segmentation, as different constituencies develop unique constructs suited to particular movements—so consciousness-raising is valued for its relationship to feminism or women, versus social movement more generally. Regardless of whether "siloing" supports contingency, identity politics, or/and neoliberal segmentation, it appears as a nomadic move that may relieve scholars of the burden of responding to an "old," but nonetheless unresolved (and, at least as I argue, productive) debate over how rhetoric moves the social.

Resistance and a New Terrain of Struggle

Finally, nomad period authors concentrate on the shifting terrain of power within a postindustrial, globalized, fragmented, mediated, neoliberal scene, characterized by "impure politics."[45] As dominance and resistance become less distinguishable, rhetorical criticism may discern how hegemony maintains itself in the guise of resistance. For instance, critics identify how patriarchal forces maintain themselves through postfeminist discourses that control the perception and development of feminist alternatives. As Johnson concludes, "the categories of agitator and establishment are . . . identities constructed discursively through the successful use of the rhetoric of protest or control."[46] Postfeminist discourses are effective, in large part, by positioning hegemonic masculinity as an act of resistance (as in *The Man Show*) to a feminist "establishment" and by reducing agency to a woman's ability to make personal choices (often to consume media or lifestyle products).[47]

Building upon impure politics, nomadic critics also honor how people "make do" or resist through tools commonly associated with dominance. Harold, for instance, develops different means of pranking in conversation with French poststructuralism, situationist activism, and contemporary culture jamming efforts. Though such tactics as throwing pies in the faces of Bill Gates or Milton Friedman may not immediately appear effective—for they do not participate in standard argumentative forms—Harold reads them as resistant through their responsiveness to neoliberalism. By appro-

priating, turning, or folding marketing discourses upon themselves, pranking infects the communicative environment, demonstrating that daily life
in late capitalism does not have to be as it appears.[48] Pranking allows critics to appreciate the resistant potential of culture jamming as effective amid
the public screen.

Even within this "new" scene of power, however, critics typically do not
stray far from phenomenal movements in their choice of resistant tactics
and in their attribution of resistant effects. So while DeLuca and Peeples
incisively map a new terrain of struggle with the public screen, their evaluation of anarchist "violence" supports a fairly traditional, functional view of
rhetoric's ability to attract "the attention of the distracted media," presum-
ably for the global justice movement.[49]

In summary, following 1980, scholars largely abandoned the term "social movement" (however defined) in characterizing their work. I have described this nomad phase through four moves, as scholars asserted their
work's value in terms of generating concepts, diversifying what counts as
worthy of rhetorical criticism, advancing particular movements, and positioning critics (and their readers) to navigate a new terrain of impure
politics. Productively, the nomadic orientation encourages critics to explore
a wide range of interests (from the textual through the conceptual) and
advocate for rhetoric's effects in any number of contingent moments. As
underscored in the third move, nomad work also supports a metacritique
on scholarship that replicates dominance through claims to universality or
generality.

Yet, by foregoing productive engagements with its disciplinary past (and
the synchronic relationships between "new" concepts), the nomadic orientation also heightens the originality or/and singularity of scholarly production. Without a more explicit account of rhetoric's relationship to social
change, readers are left to infer that concepts, or the ghosts of phenomenal
movements, do the heavy lifting. As a final illustration, I consider a piece
that has greatly influenced my own thinking on social change: Bruner's account of global justice protests via the carnivalesque.[50] Bruner highlights
how an event like the "Turtle people's" protest in Seattle confounds state
logic and thus draws out the state's violence. The Turtles' nonviolent presence advances the global justice cause by drawing the attention of the press
(and the reading public, by extension). Carnivalesque protests are meeting with decreased success because the state has become adept at controlling the immediate and discursive context through heightened security and
free speech zones. Thus, haunting the conclusions is a functionalist premise: movements (as entities represented by carnivalesque protestors) must

navigate an increasingly complicated rhetorical situation in order to achieve their goals (e.g., promoting a cleaner, healthier environment for endangered species and the people who live near, or care for, them).

Here, as in other examples analyzed above, we may question how well concept generation measures up to the neoliberal criteria of novelty. But, more importantly, we may ask: How does the carnivalesque (or any other concept) link rhetoric to movement? Unfortunately, what is lost in a nomadic orientation is the very relationality that could reveal similar challenges and possible responses to those challenges. In other words, and as I explore in the chapter's conclusion, lost in the turn toward originality and segmentation is an opportunity to cultivate a commons that may support work on social change, particularly in terms of rhetoric's relationship to social movement.

Reading Nomad Work in Response to McGee

My alternative disciplinary history of social movement rhetoric proceeds with a critical assessment of nomad work, concentrating on its fidelity to the central question articulated by McGee in 1980: What moves the social? The last three to four decades of scholarly production tends to advance originality, novelty, contingency, and differentiation, leaving this question largely implicit. McGee's phenomenon versus meaning distinction provides a convenient way to begin addressing the rather large question of what moves the social. While the constitutive implications of McGee's position have been productively advanced, the full possibilities of rhetoric's ability to "move the social" as well as the prospects of a phenomenal orientation to movement, remain to be articulated. Before turning to the fertility of McGee's essay for developing a scholarly commons, I read nomadic work in terms of its responsiveness to the essay, beginning with a failure to engage McGee's critique on the part of functionalist critics. I then consider the reduction of movements to phenomenon in developing alternative heuristics (namely, counterpublics) and the latent assumptions that could help realize movement as meaning.

Perpetuating a "Nonresponse": The Persistence of Functionalism after 1980

Initially, the functional paradigm is alive and well in communication studies. Between 1980 and today, scholars have explored "a movement's" in/effective use of rhetoric to mobilize audiences; vilify opponents in social struggle; navigate ideological tensions in confronting the establishment; adapt to moderate or militant styles; or aid a movement in advocating for

"Others."[51] Reflecting the fourth move of the nomad phase, functional critics conclude that more "established" movements (like environmentalism)
must adapt rhetorically to remain effective, as a neoliberal, mediated world
demands new tactics.[52]

Other advances within functional scholarship question the defining mark-
ers of movements as uninstitutionalized collectivities, existing materially
prior to rhetoric—thus raising questions remarkably similar to those McGee
articulated in 1980. For instance, Nelson problematizes the in-group/out-
group distinction through Mussolini's rise to power, concluding that the
dictator relied upon the trope of struggle before and after he headed the
Italian state.[53] Nelson also questions the ability of critics to posit a discrete
ending to movements, echoing McGee's concerns that functional critics
treated movements as empirically existent prior to rhetoric. Relatedly, functionalist scholars suggest that rhetoric gives birth to a movement during the
"preinception" phase, as people who have been denied agency must create a
capacity to speak publicly.[54] If movements cannot be defined as inherently
oppositional to institutions, how can we continue to assert that movements
are unique, a priori agents, the subjects responsible for social change?

There is a strong case to be made for retaining some idea of movements
as indelible collective agents—and even recovering rhetoric as a pragmatic
tool responsive to the contingent moment in the hands of those identifying
with such movements. But such a case cannot be made simply by throwing
around the weight of positivist certainty. Nor can it be made by carrying
along as though serious challenges to one's conception of movement had
not been raised repeatedly over the last thirty years. I elaborate in the conclusion on how social movement rhetoric scholars may productively situate
the functional paradigm post-McGee.

Situating the "Counterpublic Turn" in Nomad Work

Scholars conducting work generally related to social change would do well
to revisit McGee's criticisms of the functional paradigm to avoid replicating the same problems he identified in 1980 and to develop more directly
the connection between rhetoric and movement. Building upon the idea
that novelty is productive within the neoliberal academy, I consider here
the introduction of counterpublics as a "fresh" way to approach rhetorics
of social change. In the nomad period, there is an unclear relationship between movements and counterpublics, such that the two terms are often
conflated or, when they are explicitly compared, movements are reduced
to a functionalist paradigm, while counterpublics are positioned as a more
"flexible" analytic.

As we note in the introduction to this volume (and following Chávez), it is, in some ways, expected that the two terms could be synonymous, as both ideas access publicity and resistance.[55] As Eltantawy describes in the case of Argentinian women's resistance to globalization: "Women make their private concerns more public through their counterpublic discourses; they do so through means such as creating and participating in social movements and civil societies. In many cases, women not only gain access to the public sphere, but impose government and global policy changes."[56] Unfortunately, by detouring past the 1980 debate, Eltantawy presents a functional movement analysis in the guise of counterpublics. Specifically, her work reads as an extension of the preinception phase and ego-function literature, where loud, pot-and-pan-banging protests (*cacerolazos*) "allowed women to access the public sphere and shame policymakers for their suffering" and "endowed women with a new identity—namely, a powerful, autonomous, and fearless" agency for social change.[57] Reflecting the productivity of nomad work, this piece advances a more-or-less novel concept (counterpublics) to approach the unconventional protest of an understudied movement and, by foregoing "old" debates, advances conclusions that critics might have arrived at through a functionalist lens.

The few pieces placing movements and counterpublics into relationship tend to sequester the former in a resource mobilization paradigm, either a larger-scale revolutionary result of discursive activism at the smaller counterpublic level[58] or an instrumental relic incapable of explaining the new identities and oppositional tactics produced in counterpublics. As Maddux characterizes it, movement appears very much like Simons's 1970 configuration, identifiable by "leadership, membership, [and] organizational structure."[59] As Maddux's analysis proceeds, the National Association Opposing Women's Suffrage evolved from a narrowly focused, instrumental social movement to a broadly oppositional, constitutive counterpublic. Counterpublic theory appears particularly advantageous for rhetorical critics against the backdrop of functionalism ascribed to social movements, for movement theory is overly attendant to "the state and modernists' limited understandings of political participation."[60] By eschewing a full engagement with McGee's essay, counterpublic work may reduce social movements to phenomenal agents.

In fairness, because functional critics continue to simply ignore McGee's (and others') criticisms, it is easy to dismiss social movements as an outdated, sociological concept, justifying the turn to "newer" analytics, such as counterpublics. Would scholars' turn away from movements be as persuasive without a functional reduction of the latter? More pertinently, is counterpublic a "phenomenon" as McGee describes it or would it be closer to "meaning"? What is rhetoric's role in counterpublics: instrumental, constitutive, both, neither? Asen raises similar questions, as he warns scholars of harmful reductions along the axes of people (as in the conflation of counterpublics with "the identity of their participants" rather than as "social, discursive entities"), place (which reduces counterpublics to their discursive form, as in a television talk show), and topics (which define counterpublics by their oppositional status alone).[61] Revisiting McGee's work could help counterpublic scholars avoid replicating functionalist reductions.

Reading Movement as Meaning into Nomad Work

Though I have been critical in my assessment of nomadic work, implications from McGee's cryptic movement-as-meaning approach have emerged in the last thirty years. These are especially worth considering for advancing a scholarly commons, as I elaborate in the final section. Initially, an important outcome of McGee's critique is the idea that *rhetoric* (with our without a phenomenal movement) moves the social. Thus, the focus on leaders as the origin, or movements as the ends, of rhetorical production fade. Likewise, scholars become less concerned with intentionality as the principle means to assess rhetorical effects. For instance, Boor Tonn considers the visuality in early labor advocacy as, itself, moving the social.[62] While the phenomenal movement remains, in the relationship between the object of a critic's focus (in this case, Mother Jones's visual activism) and well-known collectivities (like the labor movement), it does not dictate rhetoric's effects.

Another key implication derived from McGee suggests that movements are rhetorical constructions "all the way down." There is no preexistent agent (individual or collective) using rhetoric. So the deterministic configuration of movements based on stable identities (such as out-groups), with rhetoric as reflective of those identities, no longer holds. As critics of postfeminism, postracism, and postidentity politics discourses advocate, dominant practices may appear resistant by taking on the style of movements and associating movements with the establishment.[63] Thus, the status of dominant and/or resistant are not determined prior to rhetorical struggle.

Further, "dominant discourses" compete with movements to frame or control the meanings/perceptions of social change (in the form of phenomenal movements, or otherwise). Stewart and Anderson's analysis of the *Sex in the City* voter campaign, for instance, posits that a collective whose members identify as "third wave feminists" is struggling with postfeminist discourses for the ability to define and channel women's agency. The postmodern blurring of in-group and out-group makes sophisticated ideological criticism more imperative, as audiences are confronted with a scene in which "personal agency replaces social activism, empowerment comes through individual consumption rather than political participation, and each woman is responsible for the enhancement of her own life."[64] Assuming that the very idea of movement and its effects are now in contest, scholars have identified that battles over the meanings of social change take place through memory or are fought over the history of movements.[65] As Griffin concludes, "it is hardly inevitable that we should remember as a social movement every group that wished to call itself such. Rather, movement as memory is itself a conviction, a consciousness, the end result of a process of persuasion."[66]

A final implication derived from McGee suggests that not only are movements rhetorical "all the way down." Their rhetoricity reveals desire, on the part of those identifying with movements or/and those engaged in their study. Thus, while McGee's perspective encourages us to see movements as verbs, he acknowledges the possibility for movement to be, even temporarily, a noun. The term itself, McGee concludes, "causes us to order social and historical facts such that we can maintain the illusion of 'morality,' 'purpose,' and 'destiny.'"[67] Social movement in its phenomenal/noun form connotes a certain legitimacy (particularly within a democratic context), as the collective outcome of struggle. A movement is a fictitious, but nonetheless significant, manifestation of struggle, a name to which people attach their desires, through which they enact their power for change.

Nowhere is the affective attachment to phenomenal movements more apparent than in battles over the perceptions of movements past and present. For instance, Dow's analysis of *Women's Liberation* (a television documentary airing in 1970) demonstrates how the rhetorical action intrinsic to the film fixes, or "stabilize[s] and repair[s]" meanings of second-wave feminism.[68] More particularly, the documentary legitimizes the feminist movement "by analogizing it to civil rights, by emphasizing its benefits for men, and by highlighting its possibilities for individual opportunity and self-improvement."[69] While Dow adopts a traditional stance toward rhetorical criticism by attributing the textual action to the documentarian's intentions, she does not assume second-wave feminism as a static, pregiven agent. Rather, "it" is the unstable manifestation of a rhetorical struggle still in process. The movement created in *Women's Liberation* indexes peoples' desires for social change in a more palatable form than radical feminism.

In summary, the scholarly conversation post-1980 considers less how a text or event advances "a social movement," while also deferring a full development of how rhetoric moves the social. Instead, nomadic work medi-

ates rhetorical effects through conceptual innovation. While we may read
the implications of McGee's movement as meaning into nomad period
work, the majority of scholarship over the last three decades deflects engagement with different ideas of "movement." Returning to the neoliberal
context in which this critical genealogy is situated, we encounter the underlying question of why: What did the move away from social movement
rhetoric, and/or the turn toward the nomad's four moves, afford scholars?
And how might we promote alternatives to the critical entrepreneurship
that has come to inflect the disciplinary study of social change—perhaps
radicalizing the democratic possibility of critique endemic to social movement rhetoric work?

Conclusion: Situating and Challenging the Nomad Phase within the Neoliberal Academy

In 1980, McGee posed the fundamental question: What is rhetoric's relationship to social change? Scholars branding themselves as critics of social
movement did not answer the question, so much as clung to the very positivist categories that (as McGee argued) served as a red herring. In other
words, functional critics emphasized that preexistent agents used rhetoric
to create social change. Alternative critical approaches to dissident rhetoric have developed since 1980—a few of which articulate themselves to
movement as meaning. As this chapter's genealogy reveals, though, scholars
largely detour past the phenomenon-meaning division. Instead, their work
implies that rhetoric moves the social, through an array of mediating concepts; or, it takes as its primary contribution the expansion of what counts
as legitimate rhetoric, particularly within a new political scene.

The four moves of nomad work heighten the originality of scholarly
contributions and further segment the study of social change. Throughout
this chapter's genealogy, I have suggested that novelty and segmentation
fit the prevailing mode of knowledge production within (and beyond) the
academy. Taking Striphas's observations concerning the structural changes
of academic publishing one step further,[70] we may consider how the *content* of scholarship is shaped by entrepreneurialism. The introduction of
counterpublics, "outlaw discourse," and the like, heightens scholars' original labor in a way that simply studying social movement rhetoric would
not. With nearly every aspect of human life "freed" for trade (or otherwise
structured through the norms of the market), it should be no surprise that,
as Thoburn describes, humanities publishing is prone to "a boom and bust
cycle of consumption," driven by "the intense but ephemeral passion and

simultaneous delimitation of the critical field."[71] Indeed, the traits Sedwick ascribes to consumerism—"a search for novelty and pleasure" fueled by "creativity and personal imagination"—reflect the norms of scholarly production in the nomad phase.[72]

While concept proliferation is not an ill in and of itself, when it is coupled with the neoliberal imperative toward singular, original readings, it threatens to dilute rhetoric's critical project. Scholars become conceptual entrepreneurs, unable to connect to a disciplinary conversation for fear of replicating previous work. Readers are left to infer rhetoric's relationship to social change, while consuming new constructs, forms of resistance, or/and cartographies of power.

Obviously, critical entrepreneurship has its advantages, even apart from its productive contributions within neoliberal discourse. The imperative toward novelty has helped critics avoid methodic formalism. Introducing new concepts, in conversation with a wide range of social change rhetorics, has permitted critics to speak to broader conceptual issues without reducing their art to a scientistic enterprise.[73] Furthermore, as the third move of nomad work illustrates, the turn toward more particular movements disrupts the discipline's canonical or domineering tendencies. Such work honors the contributions of activists and discourses that had been excluded from mainstream academic production, including women, people of color, and those identifying as lesbian, gay, bisexual, trans, and queer. To develop conceptual resources in close conversation with rhetorics of resistance also calls attention to how rhetors respond to, and create, contingencies in moments of social change. Is it possible to retain such advantages, while diminishing the neoliberal tendencies of scholarly production?

At the risk of appearing entrepreneurial or nomadic myself, I believe that scholars of social change may find a useful metaphor for fashioning future work: the commons. A number of contemporary thinkers, especially within neo-Marxist and autonomist circles, have revisited the commons as an alternative to neoliberalism. Particularly, the commons refers to an undifferentiated reality openly available and accessible to humans.[74] The commons is comprised of resources that form a "*pre-individual reality*," including modes of production, thought, and language. The wealth of the commons "belongs to everybody and to nobody"[75] and is rendered more bountiful with each creative act that springs forth from it—acts of artistry that are only possible through the commons' shared wealth.

While the forces of capitalism are actively privatizing the commons, as the work of Hardt and Negri considers, the potentiality of the commons helps fuel resistance.[76] Such resistance appears not in its ability to represent some principle, identity, or ideology against capitalism but in the commons' *resonances*, its moves toward self-perpetuation. Privatization and consumption may weaken (though not totally destroy) the commons, by cutting off fecund potentialities. In other words, as people are excluded from the commons (because they are denied rights of access or because they are conditioned to passively siphon its "resources"), the commons wither. As people are invited to the commons (permitted access, but also situated as contributors, members, or stewards—not simply consumers), the potentialities available to all expand.[77]

The metaphor of the commons provides critics with alternative norms to guide research. Here, novelty—particularly as it is supported by privatization, entrepreneurship, segmentation, and the pleasures of consumption—does not denote "top-shelf" scholarship. Instead, an essay's artful transformation of shared resources, its abundance for others in the network (now, or in the future), warrants its contribution.

To help ground this rather ephemeral discussion, I believe we foster a commons by returning to "the rich legacy of studies that is available" to us.[78] Specifically, as I have demonstrated in this chapter, the central question of what moves the social and the relationship between rhetoric and different visions of movement are places to begin. How does a protest, event, text, person, group, or so on relate to movement? How does rhetoric move, or fail to move, the social in a given moment?

We may create a more interconnected, responsive, reflexive scholarly conversation by actively orienting toward, and rendering more vibrant, the network of concepts available for social change work. Rather than view relationships with ideas like vernacular discourse as "replicating old work," for instance, we may come to a better understanding of social change through such terms. Relatedly, when introduced with a "new" concept, tactic, or identity in social change scholarship, we may begin from a suspicious stance: What does the introduction of novel concepts or unique combinations—however pleasurable reading (or writing) an essay on affect, for instance, might be—teach us about social movement?

Revisiting the colloquial question with which I began, I also want to position the recovery of the term "social movement" as a key part of constituting a scholarly commons. Arguably, the greatest difference between counterpublics and movements (or other related concepts) is terminological. In public discourse, we do not hear "counterpublic" circulating as often, outside of groups literate in counterpublic theory, or the occasional reference to terrorism. The term "movement" remains so strongly integrated in the public imaginary that it now refers to protests (along the lines of the

Tea Party or Occupy Wall Street) and even in-group efforts (as in the ubiquitous emails I received during both of President Obama's campaigns).

Contributing to a more robust scholarly conversation on social movement in its myriad forms has potential to bring our voices into conversation with those outside academia. Thus, rather than abandon the term as a relic of some idealized democratic past—in favor of a term like "resistance," as Ott and McCormick have separately advocated[79]—I prefer, with McGee, to see the polyvocal possibilities within movement itself.

This leads to the specific potentialities within McGee's 1980 essay that remain for articulation, of which I explore but one: elaborating on the relationship of phenomenon and meaning as ends on a spectrum of possibilities, rather than an either-or binary. Just as Burke advocates viewing identification *and* persuasion as rhetorical, critics could infuse the commons with relationships across meaning- and phenomenon-centered vocabularies. Peeples, for instance, comfortably connects articulation as an ability to "make 'connections, establish associations, or build links between different things—different events, . . . social movements, . . . ideas, . . . people'" with the functional imperative for movement actors to "make connections between themselves and other entities" or "resonat[e] with audiences."[80] Finding common ground along the spectrum of phenomenal and meaning-centered movements is also possible, as critics consider the constitution of movements as a key rhetorical effect. Perhaps the midpoint on the spectrum of movement is the idea that movements are fictions to which people attach their sense of agency or identity in public struggle.

The commons could also be fertilized through critique that pushes further toward the phenomenal or meaning ends. Toward the former, for instance, critics could feature rhetoric's capacities for crafting responses to pressing public problems, in situ. Cox's analysis of campaigns to address climate change is an excellent model for a revised functional critique.[81] Cox advocates for "the strategic as an heuristic for identifying openings within networks of contingent relationships and the potential of certain communicative efforts to interrupt or leverage change within systems of power."[82] Rather than focus upon rhetoric's contributions to building the necessary agent for social change, Cox highlights rhetoric's pragmatic capacities to aid those identifying with movements to achieve tangible effects. Key to such an effort, though, is refusing to legitimate one's work via positivist categories or standards (like typologies or predictions).

In the other direction, pushing scholarship even further away from phenomenal movements, a more "radical" interpretation of movement as meaning would refuse the nomenclature of establishment versus movement. Nomad scholarship has fully realized the rhetorical qualities of movements and further problematized the in-group/out-group distinction as a fixed basis upon which social change occurs. Yet, it could go further in opening the terrain of struggle to any number of collectives in contest. As contributions to this volume demonstrate, to fully embrace movement as meaning suggests that the antagonisms driving social change do not have to manifest in a conflict between the state and movements. Likewise, the history of anarchist agitation reveals possibilities beyond friend-enemy sociality.[83] Here, counterpublic work very productively infuses the scholarly commons, as multiple publics (whether dominant or counter) may be battling discursively at any given moment.

In conclusion, by turning to a polyvocal understanding of movement, we may nourish a commons whose values are "discerned, assessed, and modulated through a critical immanence" with particular struggles, rather than "through concepts abstracted from [struggles] and generalized as idea-commodities" in scholarly publishing.[84] While the reaffirmation of social movement rhetoric risks failing to produce more "new" ideas, it may contribute to a richer, deeper knowledge of social change. At the risk of sounding hokey or imperialistic we may not only perpetuate our disciplinary narrative but constitute a scholarly community, in contrast to (and in spite of) the neoliberal forces affecting us.

Notes

1. I appreciate the feedback from my coeditors, Amy and Kate, as well as reviewers from the University of Alabama Press, throughout the editorial process. Hearty gratitude to Darrin Hicks and Kate Willink for their instrumental feedback on early drafts. I also credit the 2011 Rhetoric Society of America Summer Institute Seminar (Rhetoric's Critical Genealogies, led by Chuck Morris, Vanessa Beasley, James Jasinski, and Kirt Wilson), and Robert Cox's Publics Seminar at the University of North Carolina for originally inspiring my approach and arguments here.

2. Michael Hardt and Antonio Negri, *Empire* (Cambridge, MA: Harvard University Press, 2000), 407.

3. Zygmunt Bauman, *Liquid Modernity* (Cambridge, UK: Polity Press, 2000).

4. Ted Striphas, "Acknowledged Goods: Cultural Studies and the Politics of Academic Journal Publishing," *Communication and Critical/Cultural Studies* 7, no. 1 (2010): 8.

5. Michael Calvin McGee, "'Social Movement': Phenomenon or Meaning?" *Central States Speech Journal*, 31, no. 4 (1980): 233–44.

6. Ibid., 236–37.

7. See Kevin Michael DeLuca, *Image Politics: The New Rhetoric of Environmental Activism* (New York: Guilford Press, 1999); Darrel Enck-Wanzer, "Trashing the System: Social Movement, Intersectional Rhetoric, and Collective Agency in the Young Lords Organization's Garbage Offensive," *Quarterly Journal of Speech* 92, no. 2 (2006): 174–201; and Christina R. Foust, *Transgression as a Mode of Resistance: Rethinking Social Movement in an Era of Corporate Globalization* (Lanham, MD: Lexington Books, 2010).

8. Robert Cox and Christina R. Foust, "Social Movement Rhetoric," in *The SAGE Handbook of Rhetorical Studies*, ed. Andrea A. Lunsford, Kirt H. Wilson, and Rosa A. Eberly (Thousand Oaks, CA: SAGE Publications, 2009).

9. Brian J. Ott, "Review Essay: Assessing Rhetorics of Social Resistance," *Quarterly Journal of Speech* 97, no. 3 (2011): 334–47.

10. My critique of nomad scholarship relates to a trend in critical work: the "singular 'theory of the case,'" whereby scholars hone in on "the lived rhetorical experience of protestors" while offering theoretical generalizations. Charles E. Morris III and Stephen Howard Browne, eds., *Readings on the Rhetoric of Social Protest*, 1st ed. (State College, PA: Strata Publishing, 2001), 175.

11. McGee, "'Social Movement,'" 238.

12. Ibid.

13. Ibid., 240.

14. Ibid., 242.

15. See Maurice Charland, "Constitutive Rhetoric: The Case of the *Peuple Quebecois*," *Quarterly Journal of Speech* 73, no. 2 (1987): 133–51.

16. For instance, Cloud asserts that the majority of work on social change focuses on "symbolic, rhetorical features," at the expense of concrete relations of oppression. Dana L. Cloud, "The Null Persona: Race and the Rhetoric of Silence in the Uprising of '34," *Rhetoric and Public Affairs* 2, no. 2 (1999): 201. Murphy argues that "by focusing almost exclusively on the 'collective consciousness,'" critics may erase the subjective agency of rhetors. John M. Murphy, "Domesticating Dissent: The Kennedys and the Freedom Rides," *Communication Monographs* 59, no. 1 (1992): 63. Such critiques echo Lucas, who advises against a "rhetorical determinism" that would erase the ways "objective material conditions" constrain rhetors' ability to move the social. Stephen E. Lucas, "Coming to Terms with Movement Studies," *Central States Speech Journal* 31, no. 4 (1980): 263.

17. Michel Foucault, "Nietzsche, Genealogy, History," in *Language, Counter-Memory, Practice: Selected Essays and Interviews*, ed. D. F. Bouchard (Ithaca: Cornell University Press, 1977), 139–64.

18. Carl R. Burgchardt, ed., *Readings in Rhetorical Criticism*, 4th ed. (State College, PA: Strata, 2010).

19. When I searched the University of Denver library's EBSCO CMMC database for "social movement" as a subject term, the database yielded 133 peer-reviewed journal articles published since 1980 (if "rhetoric" is added as a subject

term, the results dropped to 44). When I searched for "social movement" anywhere in the database, along with "rhetoric," the database returned 171 articles.

20. These terms were "social movement," "resistance," "protest," "activism," and "network."

21. I searched the University of Denver library's Social Sciences Citation Index for publications citing the following key works: McGee, "'Social Movement'"; DeLuca, *Image Politics*; Enck-Wanzer, "Trashing the System"; Phaedra C. Pezzullo, "Resisting 'National Breast Cancer Awareness Month': The Rhetoric of Counterpublics and Their Cultural Performances," *Quarterly Journal of Speech* 89, no. 4 (2003): 345–65; and Danielle Endres and Samantha Senda-Cook, "Location Matters: The Rhetoric of Place in Protest," *Quarterly Journal of Speech* 97, no. 3 (2011): 257–82.

22. I do not want to be read as suggesting that Deleuze and Guattari, as the origins of the "nomad," are "representative" of French poststructuralism or postmodernism. Rather, the term honors the significance of nomadic thought, with a distinctly nonmodern approach to criticism.

23. The concepts named and developed are too great to detail in this chapter. For the curious, though, examples included ideas from social movement rhetoric's (SMR's) past, such as confrontation. See Robert J. Brulle, "From Environmental Campaigns to Advancing the Public Dialog: Environmental Communication for Civic Engagement," *Environmental Communication* 4, no. 1 (2010): 82–98. Other work develops concepts from contemporary rhetorical theory within a social movement context, including agency, citizenship, constitutive rhetoric, and the ideograph. See Robert D. Dechaine, "Bordering the Civic Imaginary: Alienization, Fence Logic, and the Minuteman Civil Defense Corps," *Quarterly Journal of Speech* 95, no. 1 (2009): 43–65; Erin J. Rand, "An Inflammatory Fag and a Queer Form: Larry Kramer, Polemics, and Rhetorical Agency," *Quarterly Journal of Speech* 94, no. 3 (2008): 297–319; Helen Tate, "The Ideological Effects of a Failed Constitutive Rhetoric: The Co-option of the Rhetoric of White Lesbian Feminism," *Women's Studies in Communication* 28, no. 1 (2005): 1–31; Kate Zittlow Rogness and Christina R. Foust, "Beyond Rights and Virtues as the Foundation for Women's Agency: Emma Goldman's Rhetoric of Free Love," *Western Journal of Communication* 75, no. 2 (2011): 148–67. Others explore different tactical forms affiliated with movements, as well as forms of collective action, such as: coalition building, personal testimony, and vernacular. See Karma R. Chávez, "Counter-Public Enclaves and Understanding the Function of Rhetoric in Social Movement Coalition-Building," *Communication Quarterly* 59, no. 1 (2011): 1–18; Billie Murray, "For What Noble Cause: Cindy Sheehan and the Politics of Grief in Public Spheres of Argument," *Argumentation and Advocacy* 49, no. 1 (2012): 1–15; Christina M. Smith and Kelly M. McDonald, "The Mundane to the Memorial: Circulating and Deliberating the War in Iraq through Vernacular Soldier-Produced Videos," *Critical Studies in Media Communication* 28, no. 4 (2011): 292–313.

24. Tasha N. Dubriwny, "Consciousness-Raising as Collective Rhetoric: The Articulation of Experience in the Redstockings' Abortion Speak-out of 1969," *Quarterly Journal of Speech* 91, no. 4 (2005): 396.

25. Karlyn Kohrs Campbell, "The Rhetoric of Women's Liberation: An Oxymoron," *Quarterly Journal of Speech* 59, no. 1 (1973): 74–86.

26. Dubriwny, "Consciousness-Raising," 398.

27. Charles J. Stewart, "A Functional Approach to the Rhetoric of Social Movements," *Central States Speech Journal* 31, no. 4 (1980): 302.

28. Ronald Walter Greene and Kevin Douglas Kuswa, "From the Arab Spring to Athens, from Occupy Wall Street to Moscow: Regional Accents and the Cartography of Power," *Rhetoric Society Quarterly* 42, no. 3 (2012): 272, 273.

29. Don J. Waisanen, "(Trans)national Advocacy in the Ousting of Milosevic: The Otpor Movement's Glocal Recursions," *Communication Studies* 64, no. 2 (2013): 160.

30. Josue Cisneros, "(Re)Bordering the Civic Imaginary: Rhetoric, Hybridity, and Citizenship in *La Gran Marcha*," *Quarterly Journal of Speech* 97, no. 1 (2011): 26–49.

31. Ibid., 33.

32. Such acts include pop culture representations of movements and songs. See Kristen Hoerl, "Burning Mississippi into Memory? Cinematic Amnesia as a Resource for Remembering Civil Rights," *Critical Studies in Media Communication* 26, no. 1 (2009): 54–79; Sheryl Hurner, "Discursive Identity Formation of Suffrage Women: Reframing the 'Cult of True Womanhood' through Song," *Western Journal of Communication* 70, no. 3 (2006): 234–60.

33. See Wendy Atkins-Sayre, "Articulating Identity: People for the Ethical Treatment of Animals and the Animal/Human Divide," *Western Journal of Communication* 74, no. 3 (2010): 309–28; Kevin Michael DeLuca, "Unruly Arguments: The Body Rhetoric of Earth First!, ACT UP, and Queer Nation," *Argumentation and Advocacy* 36, no. 1 (1999): 9–21; Endres and Senda-Cook, "Location Matters"; Foust, *Transgression as a Mode of Resistance*; Charles J. G. Griffin, "Movement as Memory: Significant Form in *Eyes on the Prize*," *Communication Studies* 54, no. 2 (2003): 196–210.

34. Endres and Senda-Cook, "Location Matters," 258.

35. Ibid., 277.

36. For instance, Sowards considers Dolores Huerta's leadership in the United Farmworkers movement. Stacey K. Sowards, "Rhetorical Functions of Letter Writing: Dialogic Collaboration, Affirmation, and Catharsis in Dolores Huerta's Letters," *Communication Quarterly* 60, no. 2 (2012): 295–315. Similarly, some scholars focus on lesser-known figures in the civil rights movement, like Muhammad Ali. See Ellen W. Gorseveski and Michael L. Butterworth, "Muhammad Ali's Fighting Words: The Paradox of Violence in Nonviolent Rhetoric," *Quarterly Journal of Speech* 97, no. 1 (2011): 50–73. Rhetoric scholars also studied American Indian resistance and Chicana/o movement poetry. See, for

instance, Jason Edward Black, "Native Resistive Rhetoric and the Decolonization of American Indian Removal Discourse," *Quarterly Journal of Speech*
95, no. 1 (2009): 66–88; Michael Victor Sedano, "Chicanismo: A Rhetorical
Analysis of Themes and Images of Selected Poetry from the Chicano Movement," *Western Journal of Communication* 44, no. 3 (1980): 177–90.

37. Maegan Parker, "Ironic Openings: The Interpretive Challenge of the
'Black Manifesto,'" *Quarterly Journal of Speech* 94, no. 3 (2008): 322.

38. Charles E. Morris III and John M. Sloop, "'What Lips These Lips Have
Kissed:' Refiguring the Politics of Queer Public Kissing," *Communication and
Critical/Cultural Studies* 3, no. 1 (2006): 3.

39. Ibid., 12.

40. See Sonja K. Foss and Cindy L. Griffin, "A Feminist Perspective on
Rhetorical Theory: Toward a Clarification of Boundaries," *Western Journal of
Communication* 56, no. 4 (1992): 330–49.

41. Marilyn Bordwell DeLaure, "Planting Seeds of Change: Ella Baker's
Radical Rhetoric," *Women's Studies in Communication* 31, no. 1 (2008): 5; citing
Campbell, "Rhetoric of Women's Liberation."

42. Danielle Endres, "American Indian Activism and Audience: Rhetorical
Analysis of Leonard Peltier's Response to Denial of Clemency," *Communication Reports* 24, no. 1 (2011): 1–11; citing Randall A. Lake, "Enacting Red Power:
The Consummatory Function in Native American Protest Rhetoric," *Quarterly
Journal of Speech* 69, no. 2 (1983): 127–42. Heather L. Hundley and J. Scott Rodriguez, "Transactivism and Postmodernity: An Agonistic Analysis of Transliterature," *Communication Quarterly* 57, no. 1 (2009): 35–50.

43. Jessica M. Henry, "An Africalogical Analysis of the Million Man March:
A Look at the Response to the March as a Measure of its Effectiveness," *Howard
Journal of Communications* 9, no. 2 (1998): 157–68; David C. Holmes, "Speaking
of Moses and the Messiah: Ralph Abernathy's Rhetoric for and by the People,"
Journal of Communication and Religion 35, no. 1 (2012): 1–11.

44. In this context, the turn toward "engaged" or "activist" scholarship bears
special mention. Critics may study movements in situ, crafting ethnographic
criticism in order to better understand and reinforce protest efforts as they unfold. See Danielle Endres, Leah Sprain, and Tarla Rai Peterson, "The Imperative of Praxis-Based Environmental Research: Suggestions from the Step It
Up 2007 National Research Project," *Environmental Communication: Journal
of Nature and Culture* 2, no. 2 (2008): 237–45. Others retain rhetorical criticism
as a means to influence current issues, such as climate change communication
and academic labor. See Kathryn M. Olson, "Rhetorical Leadership and Trans-
ferable Lessons for Successful Social Advocacy in Al Gore's *An Inconvenient
Truth*," *Argumentation and Advocacy* 44, no. 2 (2007): 90–109; Amy M. Pason,
"We Are All Workers: A Class Analysis of University Labour Strikes," *Ephemera* 8, no. 3 (2008): 322–30.

45. Phaedra C. Pezzullo, "Contextualizing Boycotts and Buycotts: The Im-

pure Politics of Consumer-Based Advocacy in an Age of Global Ecological Crises," *Communication and Critical/Cultural Studies* 8, no. 2 (2011): 124–45; citing Lawrence Grossberg, *We Gotta Get Out of this Place: Popular Conservatism and Postmodern Culture* (London: Routledge, 1992).

46. Ann Johnson, "The Subtleties of Blatant Sexism," *Communication and Critical/Cultural Studies* 4, no. 2 (2007): 179.

47. Karrin Vasby Anderson and Jessie Stewart, "Politics and the Single Woman: The 'Sex and the City Voter' in Campaign 2004," *Rhetoric and Public Affairs* 8, no. 4 (2005): 595–616.

48. Christine Harold, "Pranking Rhetoric: 'Culture Jamming' as Media Activism," *Critical Studies in Media Communication* 21, no. 3 (2004): 208.

49. Kevin Michael DeLuca and Jennifer A. Peeples, "From Public Sphere to Public Screen: Democracy, Activism, and the 'Violence' of Seattle," *Critical Studies in Media Communication* 19, no. 2 (2002): 144.

50. M. Lane Bruner, "Carnivalesque Protest and the Humorless State," *Text and Performance Quarterly* 25, no. 2 (2005): 136–55.

51. See William E. Jurma, "Moderate Movement Leadership and the Vietnam Moratorium Committee," *Quarterly Journal of Speech* 68, no. 3 (1982): 262–72; Elizabeth Walker Mechling and Gale Auletta, "Beyond War: A Socio-Rhetorical Analysis of a New Class Revitalization Movement," *Western Journal of Speech Communication* 50, no. 4 (1986): 388–404; Sara Ann Mehltretter, "Dorothy Day, the Catholic Workers, and Moderation in Protest during the Vietnam War," *Journal of Communication and Religion* 32, no. 1 (2009): 1–32; Gary S. Selby, "Framing Social Protest: The Exodus Narrative in Martin Luther King's Montgomery Bus Boycott Rhetoric," *Journal of Communication and Religion* 24, no. 1 (2001): 68–93; Charles J. Stewart, "Championing the Rights of Others and Challenging Evil: The Ego Function in the Rhetoric of Other-Directed Social Movements," *Southern Communication Journal* 64, no. 2 (1999): 91–105; Marsha L. Vanderford, "Vilification and Social Movements: A Case Study of Pro-life and Pro-choice Rhetoric," *Quarterly Journal of Speech* 75, no. 2 (1989): 166–82.

52. Rebekah L. Fox and Joshua J. Frye, "Tensions of Praxis: A New Taxonomy for Social Movements," *Environmental Communication: A Journal of Nature and Culture* 4, no. 4 (2010): 422–40.

53. Elizabeth Jean Nelson, "'Nothing Ever Goes Well Enough': Mussolini and the Rhetoric of Perpetual Struggle," *Communication Studies* 42, no. 1 (1991): 22–42.

54. Richard J. Jensen and Cara J. Abeyta, "The Minority in the Middle: Asian-American Dissent in the 1960s and 1970s," *Western Journal of Speech Communication* 51, no. 4 (1987): 402–16; Richard J. Jensen and John C. Hammerback, "Working in 'Quiet Places': The Community Organizing Rhetoric of Robert Parris Moses," *Howard Journal of Communications* 11, no. 1 (2000): 1–18; Anne F. Mattina, "'Rights as Well as Duties'"The Rhetoric of Leonora O'Reilly," *Com-*

munication Quarterly 42, no. 2 (1994): 196–205; and Cary R. W. Voss and Robert C. Rowland, "Pre-inception Rhetoric in the Creation of a Social Movement: The Case of Frances Wright," *Communication Studies* 51, no. 1 (2000): 1–14.

55. Chávez, "Counter-Public Enclaves," 1–2.

56. Nahed Eltantawy, "Pots, Pans, and Protests: Women's Strategies for Resisting Globalization in Argentina," *Communication and Critical/Cultural Studies* 5, no. 1 (2008): 47.

57. Ibid., 55.

58. See, for instance, Dana L. Cloud, "Doing Away With Suharto—and the Twin Myths of Globalization and New Social Movements," in *Counterpublics and the State*, ed. Robert Asen and Daniel C. Brouwer (New York: State University of New York Press, 2001), 235–64.

59. Kristy Maddux, "When Patriots Protest: The Anti-suffrage Discursive Transformation of 1917," *Rhetoric and Public Affairs* 7, no. 3 (2004): 301.

60. Catherine Helen Palczewski, "Cyber-movements, New Social Movements, and Counter-publics," in *Counterpublics and the State*, ed. Robert Asen and Daniel C. Brouwer (Albany: State University of New York Press, 2001), 162.

61. Robert Asen, "Seeking the 'Counter' in Counterpublics," *Communication Theory* 10, no. 4 (2000): 431.

62. Mari Boor Tonn, "'From the Eye to the Soul': Industrial Labor's Mary Harris 'Mother' Jones and the Rhetorics of Display," *Rhetoric Society Quarterly* 41, no. 3 (2011): 231–49.

63. Johnson, "The Subtleties of Blatant Sexism." See also Naomi R. Rockler, "*Friends*, Judaism, and the Holiday Armadillo: Mapping a Rhetoric of Post-identity Politics," *Communication Theory* 16, no. 4 (2006): 453–73.

64. Anderson and Stewart, "Politics and the Single Woman," 609.

65. Christina R. Foust and Jenni Marie Simon, "Memories of Movement in a Postfeminist Context: Conservative Fusion in the Rhetoric of Tammy Bruce and 'Dr. Laura' Schlessinger," *Western Journal of Communication* 79, no. 1 (2015): 1–21.

66. Griffin, "Movement as Memory," 207.

67. McGee, "'Social Movement,'" 237.

68. Bonnie J. Dow, "Fixing Feminism: Women's Liberation and the Rhetoric of Television Documentary," *Quarterly Journal of Speech* 90, no. 1 (2004): 54.

69. Ibid., 74.

70. Striphas, "Acknowledged Goods."

71. Nicholas Thoburn, "Is There an Autonomist Model of Political Communication?" *Journal of Communication Inquiry* 35, no. 4 (2011): 338.

72. Peter H. Sedgwick, *The Market Economy and Christian Ethics* (Cambridge: Cambridge University Press, 1999), 101–2.

73. Dilip Parameshwar Gaonkar, "The Forum: Publics and Counterpublics," *Quarterly Journal of Speech* 88, no. 4 (2002): 410–12; William L. Nothstine, Carole Blair, and Gary A. Copeland, *Critical Questions: Invention, Creativity,*

and the Criticism of Discourse and Media (New York: St. Martin's Press, 1994). Others have challenged the rise of concept-driven criticism as threatening the venerable place of history or as flattening humanistic knowledge with theoretical discourse that "is common and can be regularized." James Jasinski, "The Status of Theory and Method in Rhetorical Criticism," *Western Journal of Communication* 65, no. 3 (2001): 254; citing James Darsey, "Must We All Be Rhetorical Theorists?: An Anti-democratic Inquiry," *Western Journal of Communication* 58, no. 3 (1994): 165–81. I am less concerned about returning movement criticism to an idealized past and more concerned with shaping resources for the future, as much as possible outside the norms of neoliberal production and consumerism.

74. A neo-Marxist turn toward the commons resonates with Arendt's distinction between the private and the public, the latter of which refers to "a world of things . . . between those who have it in common" that "relates and separates [people] at the same time." Hannah Arendt, *The Human Condition*, 2nd ed. (Chicago: University of Chicago Press, 1958), 52. Arendt continues: the common "stuff" that humans fabricate relates people synchronically and diachronically, providing a "sameness" that nonetheless becomes infinitely differentiable (and differentiated) through the singular perspectives of individuals (58).

75. Paolo Virno, *A Grammar of the Multitude: For an Analysis of Contemporary Forms of Life* (Los Angeles: Semiotext[e], 2004), 76, 77.

76. Cesare Casarino and Antonio Negri, *In Praise of the Common: A Conversation on Philosophy and Rhetoric* (Minneapolis: University of Minnesota Press, 2008).

77. The "tragedy of the commons" suggests that the environment of potentialities is a finite resource that will be exploited by consumers. However, if we consider the commons more as an infinite resource (as in communication, language, and intellectual or/and artistic activity), or if we view it more as a living environment of which we are an integral part, the "tragedy of the commons" loses its potency as an argument against communal relations. The ecological approach to the commons, though, suggests a need for balance when one considers herself or himself as part of the networked ecosystem.

78. Jensen, "Interdisciplinary Perspectives," 374. I present two caveats, however, in making better use of the past's resources. First, we should guard against disciplinarity, as in editorial *requirements* to cite certain authors or frame one's work in terms of SMR. Second, we must be wary of holding so tightly to the past that we miss necessary, progressive interventions. For instance, in 1980, Hahn and Gonchar chided rhetoricians for poaching definitions and concepts from sociology, declaring that movements are not significantly different "from other kinds of collective and individual behavior." Pining for classical methods through which to conduct criticism, they rejected the basic premise of functional theory—that movements are "unique entities, demanding a unique rhetorical theory." Dan F. Hahn and Ruth M. Gonchar, "Social Movement Theory:

A Dead End," *Communication Quarterly* 28, no. 1 (1980): 61. I suspect that most readers would concur that dissident rhetoric presents fundamental challenges to Aristotelian theory; but Hahn and Gonchar's dismissal of "social movement rhetoric" reminds us that the term itself came into vogue alongside free trade, globalization, and an economy of communication. Social movements may represent as much of an idea commodity as counterpublics, so any return to SMR cannot be had without acknowledging the same possibilities of academic consumerism to which all concepts are subject. Moreover, though, the commons may grow substantially through progressive innovation.

79. Ott, "Review Essay"; Samuel McCormick, "The Political Identity of the Philosopher: Resistance, Relative Power, and the Endurance of Potential," *Philosophy and Rhetoric* 42, no. 1 (2009): 72–91.

80. Jennifer A. Peeples, "Downwind: Articulation and Appropriation of Social Movement Discourse," *Southern Communication Journal* 76, no. 3 (2011): 251. Quoting James Jasinski, *Sourcebook on Rhetoric: Key Concepts in Contemporary Rhetorical Studies* (Thousand Oaks, CA: SAGE Publications, 2001), 65.

81. J. Robert Cox, "Beyond Frames: Recovering the Strategic in Climate Communication," *Environmental Communication* 4, no. 1 (2010): 122–33.

82. Ibid., 122 (abstract).

83. Foust, *Transgression as a Mode of Resistance*.

84. Thoburn, "Is There an Autonomist Model," 340.

3

Counterpublic Theory Goes Global

A Chronicle of a Concept's Emergences and Mobilities

Daniel C. Brouwer and Marie-Louise Paulesc

Communication scholars in the United States have fashioned studies of the counterpublic sphere[1] into an industrious line of inquiry over the last several decades.[2] Overwhelmingly focused on the United States, they have interrogated the promises and perils of its conceptual counterpart, the *public* sphere, exercising a skeptical disposition toward the public sphere's dramatic imaginings of freedom of expression, informed reason giving, and rational-critical debate, while exposing its spectacular shortcomings of explicit or implicit exclusions, preference for certain forms or styles of communication, and failure to resolve social stratifications.[3] Theorizing the conditions for and analyzing the practices of opposition and resistance within the United States have constituted the primary commitments of such studies.[4] At the same time, scholarship from numerous disciplines demonstrates that the counterpublic sphere has been living a robustly cosmopolitan life. Scholars have located counterpublics or counterpublic spheres in Poland, Japan, Indonesia, the Philippines, Taiwan, South Korea, Thailand, Mexico, Bolivia, Brazil, Lebanon, Egypt, Uganda, and Ghana, nation-states seemingly distant from—geographically, historically, economically, politically, culturally—the contexts and conditions of the counterpublic sphere's conceptual emergence in western Europe.[5]

In important ways, the empirical question of the counterpublic sphere's global mobility is thus settled. Further, in the face of calls for more studies of non-Western expressions of social and political protest and opposition, counterpublic's mobility should be encouraged and applauded.[6] Unsettled about the counterpublic sphere's mobility, however, are key questions about the ethical dynamics of such mobility and the broader politics of scholarship. While a spirit of intellectual generativity typically drives the mobilizations of counterpublic theory to make sense of social change across the globe, we anticipate that such mobilizations risk committing "conceptual neo-colonialism."[7] Scholars perform conceptual neocolonialism when presuming the fitness of one's beloved or familiar theories and concepts for any sort of communication phenomena, when imagining the use of beloved or familiar theories and concepts as a gift to Others, or when forcing local data to take the shape of theories and concepts from elsewhere, theories and concepts that have particular histories and formations (even if those histories and formations are hidden or ignored). Vigilance about conceptual neocolonialism recognizes that the global mobility of counterpublic theory and other concepts exposes "the difficulties of translating such notions across linguistic and cultural boundaries."[8] Because of its Western roots and because of its connection to specific Western communicative practices and structures, counterpublic risks contributing to what Chakrabarty calls "asymmetric ignorance."[9] He argues, primarily in reference to historians, that while Western scholars work in "relative ignorance of non-Western histories," their non-Western counterparts can never afford to ignore the knowledge produced in the West.[10] These asymmetries require us to be more alert to the ways in which our conceptual choices might participate in and reproduce Western (especially Anglo-Saxon) hegemony. In short, a focus on counterpublic sphere theory's circulation beyond its originary contexts captivatingly illustrates the normative, ethical, and material dynamics of theorizing communication structures and practices in our accounts of social change.

In the next several sections, we make the following broad moves: First, we attend to scholars' efforts to circulate the concept of *the public sphere* on a global basis. This pathway through the public sphere is warranted by the fact that in most accounts of the counterpublic, it is the public sphere—through its exclusions and norms—that produces the need for the counterpublic. As a result, the public sphere always travels as a shadow figure to the counterpublic. Further, one of the dynamics that facilitates the circulation of a counterpublic is its seemingly diminished commitment to the normativities of the public sphere. Indeed, oftentimes authors explain their move to counterpublic as following naturally from the idea that the public sphere is inadequate for their particular study. By featuring the distinction between public and counterpublic spheres, we are better able to demonstrate how and why the latter circulates so well.

Second, we narrate three distinct versions of the *counterpublic* sphere, marking the significance of some of its Western/Anglo origins. Broadly, we follow the concept of the counterpublic sphere—a theory and a concept that comes into being as an immanent critique of a specifically Western/Anglo theory of the public sphere—as it travels to places, contexts, and registers beyond a European–Anglo geography, where it is made to explain and assess social change. More specifically, we investigate the dynamics of counterpublic's travels by distilling the strategies and "motives" that scholars employ as they mobilize the concept.

Finally, we engage and newly inflect an important conversation between counterpublic theory and postcolonial theory. Contact with postcolonial theories exposes empirical and ethical dilemmas that haunt the work of mobilizing the concept on a global level. Further, postcolonial theories sensitize us to questions about the potential for empirically flawed and/or normatively arrogant misreadings of local communication structures and practices, the potential reinscription of Western epistemologies and ontologies through circulation of concepts, and the challenge of decolonization through use of a concept whose conceptual counterpart, the public sphere, historically depended upon actual colonization. We move through this discussion invested primarily in unearthing and explicating the risks, rewards, and ambivalent commitments produced when counterpublic goes global.

On the Public Sphere and Its Circulation

A deceptively simple phrase, "public sphere" names a concept that relies upon or invokes theories of democracy and democratic engagement, structures and practices of communication, theories of the nation-state, and more. The generally recurring components of these theories can be summarized as follows: the public sphere is a communicative realm distinct from but related to the state and to the private sphere, where reason-using, self-sovereign citizens enact critical discourse on issues of common or collective concern and where the force of the better argument wins the day.[11] To some critics, this is a democratic ideal type toward which we must strive. Exemplifying this spirit of criticism is Fraser's admonition that "something like Habermas's idea of the public sphere is indispensable to critical social theory and to democratic political practice."[12] This spirit generates various forms of immanent critique that goad the concept and its undergirding theories toward better actualizations of their imaginings. Thompson summarizes four prominent lines of such critique: theories of the public sphere neglect proletarian collective mobilizations that contribute to the conditions of public life, undervalue sex as a central structuring element of public life, dismiss popular cultural and new communication technologies as constitutive forces of public life, and fail to offer a concrete project for better public discourse.[13] Additional lines of critique have problematized the public sphere in terms of citizenship status, race and ethnicity, sexuality, and urbanity/provinciality, in terms of the logocentricity and textcentricity of the public sphere and in terms of its reliance upon the nation-state as a grounding structural entity.[14]

Revisions forged through immanent critique have made the public sphere pliable for analyzing social change across the globe. International political developments dramatize the appeal of the public sphere. Indeed, treaties such as the Universal Declaration of Human Rights and organizations such as the European Union require, as conditions of signing or entry, the democratic vistas that undergird the public sphere.[15] Ikegami observes: "The emergence of new democracies in the post-Soviet bloc has encouraged the transfer of the Habermasian model eastward to help explain the fragility of the traditions of civic engagement in these new states."[16] In conjunction with this eastward mobility, in 2009, the twentieth anniversary of the fall of the Berlin Wall and the ostensible collapse of Communism occasioned reassessments of the vitality of public life in former central and eastern European Communist countries. The 2010 and subsequent popular protests in Tunisia, Egypt, Libya, Syria, and other countries in North Africa and the Middle East have especially galvanized interest among Western commentators in the Arabic public sphere in conditions of emergent or rejuvenated democracy; too, local activists and analysts on the Arab Spring have taken up vocabularies of public opinion and the public sphere to make protest activities intelligible both to themselves and to Western audiences. In sum, these sorts of conversations, employing these sorts of vocabularies, seem to confirm Lee and LiPuma's claim that the public sphere, along with the citizen-state (their terminology for a notional "we the people") and the market, circulates in the world as easily as capital does; in doing so, it serves as a key component of the "social imaginary of modernity."[17] The public sphere's charisma as a repository of democratic visions and aspirations compels its global circulation.

Global circulation, however, engenders empirical and ethical complications. Notwithstanding Habermas's own explicit warning against "idealtypically generalized" transfer of the public sphere as a category of society, the fact that distinct norms undergird the public sphere means that as the concept circulates globally, it carries—and thus at least suggests, if not demands—its norms wherever it goes.[18] Thus, extending the public sphere beyond its originating contexts threatens to commit normative arrogance. That is, if we retain the normative dimensions of germinal theories of the liberal public sphere (such as Habermas's), we posit Western democratic governance and democratic culture as the primary forms or *teloi* of communal life. Garnham offers perhaps an extreme example of loyalty to the normativities of the public sphere; in the face of diverse contemporary challenges such as the global market, the global media, and identity politics, he calls for the universal adoption of the public sphere and its normativities.[19] To defend this call, Garnham argues that global democratic life is impossible without universally accepted norms; thus, he voids the issue of cultural particulars of any practical consequences.[20] In contrast, Chari and Verdery caution against the entailments of such loyalty by explicating the political functions of dominant, preferred theories. They recount that dominant theories of modernization and development (a family of theories in which public sphere theory is a member) were explicitly crafted in response to Cold War ideologies.[21] These theories were explicitly anti-Communist and typically included reference to "stages" of sociopolitical development (with the US and European models, of course, having entered or possibly achieved the end stage).[22]

Tempering the circulation of the public sphere on both empirical and normative grounds, Eder tersely notes that the public sphere is "historically bound and culturally specific," with the distinction between public and private realms describing the experience of a small portion of the globe's peoples during a short period of human sociality.[23] Along these lines, Somers stresses the historical baggage of the public sphere, a concept that is rooted in a "metanarrative of Anglo-American citizenship theory."[24] In her complex analysis, Somers demonstrates that together with the political culture concept, the concept of the public sphere is a "narrative political fiction" that, in time, has become "naturalized."[25] In other words, the public sphere and its normativities have become part of our underlying assumptions about the world. Their appearance as "natural" also makes them approachable as "universal." Because counterpublic is forged as a direct, explicit critique of the public sphere, some of the concerns that we locate in the circulation of the public sphere are transferred to the circulation of counterpublic. We must ask of counterpublic, then: Does counterpublic further extend its critique to the Western/Anglo roots of the public sphere?

On Key Theorizations of Counterpublic Theory

Habermas has celebrated the public sphere as a new kind of publicity, whose discrete function was to defend the freedom of the private realm against the domination of the state. Most accounts of the counterpublic, in turn, dwell on the hegemonic aspects of the public sphere; in a way, they turn the public sphere on its head to show not merely that the ideal is untenable or that the project is imperfect but to highlight the ways in which it becomes exclusionary and threatens to produce domination. Thus, the counterpublic is first and foremost a manifesto against the public sphere as both a normative ideal and an empirical entity. The public sphere seeks social change via rational debate in which differences between participants are supposed to be bracketed. Counterpublics, on the other hand, affirm and punctuate these differences. On a theoretical level, the concept denounces the public sphere as imperfect, incomplete, or, more fatally, delusional; on an empirical level, counterpublics denounce the taken-for-granted societal arrangements, challenge current normativities, and push the social imagination to conjure up new political possibilities.

In our chronicle of the concept's emergence we discern three versions of counterpublic theory: materialist, ideological, and critical/cultural. Recognizing others' efforts to craft genealogies of counterpublic across the chapters of this book, we circumscribe our labor to the production of précis regarding each germinal version's account of social change and the accompanying modalities of critique. While distinct, they represent differences in emphases rather than discrete, mutually exclusive commitments.[26] The existence of these versions helps the concept circulate, for this diversity makes counterpublic supple enough for a wide range of scholarly inquiries. These plural modes of critique also promise to perform a de-essentializing or denaturalizing function, thus mitigating against conceptual neocolonialism when counterpublic is made to travel. Nevertheless, each version of counterpublic retains characteristics of "Westernness," particularly an agonistic and public orientation in liberal-democratic processes, thereby engendering challenges to its global circulation.

Responding directly to Habermas, Negt and Kluge offer as the first version of counterpublic theory a powerfully materialist critique. They offer a vivid account of the public sphere's absorption of all critiques, its viral mutability, and its temporal location of its perfection always on the future horizon:

The public sphere as an illusory synthesis of the totality of society has the tendency to modernize itself more rapidly than the actual tempo of historical development. In this respect, the public sphere is bound to a rule: it must sustain the claim that it represents the totality of society. On account of its mechanisms of exclusion, it cannot, however, fulfill this claim. It disintegrates rapidly because at no time does it possess the substance it purports to have. The public sphere must overcome this disintegration through permanent variation. One of its specific forms of expression is thus the attempt to reach out into the future, the long-term program, the replacement of its present by the anticipation of its future.[27]

While extoling a materialist critique that demands of the public sphere the realizations of its normative imagination, Negt and Kluge distrust the public sphere's capacity to match its self-description. Thus, they do not aspire to recuperate the public sphere through immanent critique so that it better supports incremental liberalization or emancipation; they wish to discard its false dreams altogether—(Marxist) revolution, not evolution. Counterpublic, then, names a critical and oppositional orientation that foregrounds a proletarian "context of living" as a counterpart to the exclusions exercised in a bourgeois context.[28] A counterpublic achieves social change not by ameliorating currently existing conditions but by founding new conditions altogether; Negt and Kluge require that we read any sort of social transformation that falls short of revolution (such as liberalization of civil rights for some) as incomplete or failed.

While Negt and Kluge's materialist critique foregrounds class, Felski's and Fraser's ideological critique foregrounds gender to open up possibilities for oppositional, progressive-liberal political expansion. Both scholars feature feminist aesthetics and feminist politics as exemplars of counterpublics. A key difference between these theorists is their focus on different feminist modalities—aesthetics for Felski and politics for Fraser. Of course, aesthetics and politics are distinct but inseparable, yet Felski asks us to attend to the politics of aesthetics (e.g., what sorts of political work can modernist feminist aesthetics accomplish), while Fraser invites us to heed the aesthetics of politics (e.g., what exclusions and inequalities do the masculinist norms of rational-critical debate commit). For both scholars social change is achieved through oppositional acts that expose the structures and practices of patriarchy in socially stratified societies. Access to and participation in both wider, dominant publics and the state is necessary but insufficient; critique of the very conditions for access and participation must accompany.[29] Through advocacy on behalf of new or different topics using new or different modes of address, new or different public agents expand discursive space. Broadened to account for multiple "differences that make a difference,"[30] counterpublic names conscious, explicit self-fashioning as alternatives to dominant discursive norms or arenas.

Distinct from *materialist* and *ideological* modes of counterpublic critique is a *critical/cultural* mode exemplified by Warner. Similar to Felski and Fraser, he affirms counterpublics' consciousness of their position as an oppositional alternative to other publics. Notably, Warner's innovative inflection is his focus on modalities such as "corporeal expressivity," or the staging of opposition on or through the human body.[31] His version of counterpublic is more amenable to cultural performance (including "low art" in comparison to Felski's "high art") and broadens scholars' senses of how and where social change can happen. In Warner's account, counterpublics possess an imaginary and a logic of expression that is radically different from the mainstream, dominant public. It is in this radical difference that the hope for transforming the public life resides.

In distinguishing these three versions, we seek to demonstrate the different ways that counterpublic can be and has been used to account for social change. To a certain degree, this variety in its modes of critique facilitates its circulation; such variety expands and multiplies the fields and registers of its conceptual and analytic activities. Yet these different versions do not circulate with equal ease. While being the "first," Negt and Kluge's materialist version has circulated the least perhaps because it most aggressively accuses the public sphere of being a delusion, and its version of counterpublicity unwaveringly centers the proletariat as its standpoint. The ideological and critical/cultural modes have a larger circulation perhaps because neither requires the overthrow of liberal democracy or the promises of liberal-democratic aspirations.

Differences notwithstanding, each version operates in direct response to, and thus on the key terms of, the public sphere—each is a Western critique launched on Western terms and grounds. This Westernness is evidenced by the very privileging of the public as a primary or especially valued scene for forging social life (over the private or altogether different demarcations of social life); the assumption of agonistics as preferred ways of achieving social change; and, in its two most prominent versions, a commitment to liberal democracies' self-understanding and/or self-improvement. Hirschkind, cognizant of this heritage in his study of suppressed Islamist discourses under the presidency of Hosni Mubarak in Egypt, obligingly clarifies: "I use the term 'counterpublic' to interrogate a set of discursive practices founded on a very different conceptual articulation of the public than that provided by liberal-democratic traditions."[32] Even if not fully conscious of, or actively committed to, these aspects of liberal democracy and public agonistics, any uptake of counterpublic necessarily recalls these qualities as part of the concept's ontological, axiological, and epistemological heritage.

Its Western heritage, however, does not deter scholars from using counterpublic to understand and explain social change beyond Western contexts. Why? Broadly, it is situated alongside the public sphere, a transdisciplinary, globally dispersed, and particularly industrious research project. Contemporary conditions of knowledge production in the academy render it a prominent way of categorizing and theorizing—popular, perhaps even necessary, to use in order to participate in broad academic conversations (particularly in English, which is increasingly the language of the academy as much as the market).[33] Additionally, its usage broadcasts a general, multidisciplinary interest in public life and public culture.

Moreover, when it forwards a "discursive arena" as its locus of inquiry and foregrounds alternative or oppositional discourses, counterpublic is appealing because it is not reducible to organizations or social movements understood as phenomena.[34] As a result, it is helpful in narrating civil society activities in, for example, authoritarian conditions where a more open, luxurious version of a public sphere is officially prohibited. And finally, as we have been emphasizing, its appeal and circulation in non-Western contexts derives from its seeming diminished commitment to normativities, a move that permits scholars to discern social change without recourse to a Western liberal-democratic horizon. As Lee and LiPuma note about the public sphere, the idea of counterpublic has become an important part of the social imaginary of modernity—better, of "alternative modernities."[35] As such, it is important to offer an account of the global circulation of counterpublic before we (re)stage its encounter with postcolonial theory.

On the Circulation of Counterpublic Theory

Scholars have mobilized counterpublic to frame and assess social change at a number of different geopolitical scales. A familiar gesture is to assess collective action *within* the boundaries of a nation-state. Even then, sometimes, intranational agitation is often imagined or practiced in *transnational* ways or in ways that show how the *nation* exceeds the *state*.[36] Morton, for example, argues that Canada's national narrative of official multiculturalism, which promises to expand discursive space, actually commits various forms of "historical amnesia."[37] These forms of amnesia elide the racialized bodies and racialized labor that helped produce the nation and threaten to depoliticize and dehistoricize cultural productions of diasporic peoples associated with Canada. Focusing on specific cultural texts, he defines a "diasporic counterpublic" as "a rhetorical site for articulating histories of migration and racialization."[38]

Other scholars have discerned transnational or global counterpublics.[39] Increasingly, scholars amplify the roles that new communication technologies play in the constitution of counterpublics and the circulation of their discourses, as in the transnational counterpublicity of Romani activists and the

transnational circulation of anticopyright activism originating in Aotearoa/
New Zealand.[40] The translation and circulation of cultural texts in global
markets also offer a productive context for examination of transnational
counterpublicity. For instance, Wood chooses the concept of "counterpublic" to analyze pop-culture texts from Japan as they circulate beyond
their sites of origin. Here, counterpublic is open to the multiplicity of processes through which individuals engage texts and constitute a dispersed
global readership.[41] In a different hemisphere, Noel theorizes a "diasporic
counterpublic" that accounts for the simultaneous movement of people and
cultural forms between Puerto Rico and the US mainland, specifically New
York City. Counterpublic helps him investigate what the specific cultural
form of Nuyorican poetry can do across generations and thus across changed
material and symbolic contexts.[42]

In one sense, scholars' myriad sitings of counterpublics or counterpublic
spheres at regional and global scales (and in the list of nation-states that
we featured in the chapter's opening) evidence the concept's mobilization
in non-Western contexts. In another sense, these sitings, with their rapid
careening across the globe, "prove" the achievement of the counterpublic
sphere—of its having gone global and having become naturalized as a flexible, fungible concept. These aspects open up space for us to discuss the
significance of the concept's Western origins, to discern what counterpublic accomplishes or is imagined to accomplish in non-Western places
and contexts and to navigate mindfully through a dialectic of intellectual
generativity (or, a spirit of openness to heuristic or analytic possibilities)
and conceptual neocolonialism (or, a spirit of anxiety about asymmetrical
knowledges).

We acknowledge outright that the very categories of "West" and "non-
West," figured as mutually exclusive or stable and distinct counterparts, are
corrupt; so, too, is the notion of a pristine, authentic homeland that her-
metically or independently produces knowledges for use at home and distribution elsewhere. As Said and others have powerfully argued, the categories of East, West, Western, and non-Western are historically specific
discursive formations rather than natural, given, and stable entities.[43] Further, the very vocabulary that centers the West and decenters the "elsewhere"
iterates asymmetries. Nevertheless, use of these vocabularies throughout
this chapter functions strategically to recognize the symbolic and material forces that have been constituted by—and that recursively constitute—
these nonessential but meaningful distinctions.

At first glance, moving the counterpublic from the West toward the
non-West seems like a logical and uncomplicated thing to do. Counter-

public is seemingly easier to transport as it does not have the normative baggage of the public sphere.[44] Often times, when public sphere is pressed against non-Western contexts, the concept ends up being deemed inadequate to account for political, social, economic, and cultural realities different from the ones that occasioned its initial theorization in Habermas's *Structural Transformation*. Theorists pay careful attention to the specific historical circumstances that allow one to speak or not of a public sphere. For instance, Garcelon performs a detailed and nuanced analysis, specifying which of the Western conceptual meanings of the public sphere fit Soviet-type societies.[45] Calhoun stresses the problems of transferring the public sphere from "its European context to that of 'modern,' especially early twentieth-century China."[46] In order to talk about a public sphere in the Muslim world, Eisenstadt and Schluchter have to first eliminate the requirement of a certain type of civil society as a markedly European tradition.[47] These scholars show the limitations of the concept and caution against too hastily adopting a Western concept for non-Western contexts. Generally, the public sphere is not dismissed altogether; scholars appreciate the value of the concept to account for public life in non-Western contexts but insist on carefully nuancing the conditions of this narration.

Counterpublic, on the other hand, seems to circulate in the world more freely—that is, without so many qualms about its Western provenance. This apparent easiness is justified by the fact that counterpublic does not carry the same normative constraints as the public sphere. In fact, counterpublic is constructed as a sort of rebuttal to the public sphere. For Negt and Kluge, the proletarian counterpublic should produce the remedy for an indefensible bourgeois public sphere;[48] for Fraser, counterpublics have always "contested the exclusionary norms of the bourgeois public."[49] For Warner, counterpublic disputes not only ideas and political issues, but also the "speech genres and modes of address."[50] Thus, the counterpublic is an antagonist to the mode of publicity imagined by Habermas—an antagonist that is not, however, a villain. On the contrary, the counterpublic, defined perpetually by its "friction against the dominant public," is celebrated for its transformative potential, for the promise it holds to correct, overcome, and deeply transfigure the public sphere and, more importantly, democracy.[51]

While many scrutinize the Western roots of the public sphere, few seem to mark the equally Western ancestries of counterpublic. Loehwing and Motter rightfully argue that in scholarship about public sphere and counterpublic, "what remains relatively underarticulated" is "in what relationship to a specific characterization of democracy publics and counterpublics operate."[52] Without articulating the background theorizations of democracy against which public sphere and counterpublic are asked to do their work, both concepts remain implicitly, silently anchored in their Western heritage. If counterpublic is to be useful for critiquing communicative practices more generally, then a more careful narration of the counter and of that which it counters is necessary. What is the dominant public and the domination that a counterpublic contests? What are the conditions that produce this dominant public and its domination? What are the philosophical, historical, cultural, and political traditions that account for the rise of this dominant public?

Attending to these types of questions requires careful attention to the interplay between the global circulation of ideas and structures and local histories. This includes seriously considering the uneven histories of capitalism and colonialism and their contribution to local discursive practices. Hence, we consider that an alliance with postcolonial theory helps negotiate the global circulation of the counterpublic.

Postcolonial and Counterpublic Theories: Engaging and Inflecting a Conversation

We have argued that within Anglo-European contexts of their emergences, the public sphere *produces* the need for the counterpublic; counterpublic, in turn, perpetually shadows the public sphere as both its offspring and its gadfly, generating and constituting alternative practices, contexts, and conditions for communication. In a different register, postcolonial theory performs homologous functions against the Western intellectual project itself. As communication scholars Shome and Hegde argue, postcoloniality is "the underside of Anglo-Euro history, casting a long shadow on its self-proclaimed enlightenment and teleology of progress."[53] Scholars such as Said, Spivak, and Mohanty have crafted a complex, diverse, and interventionist body of scholarship that proceeds under the name of postcolonial studies. This body of scholarship demands reflexivity about the conditions of being, knowing, and doing that shape our scholarship, politics, and everyday interactions.[54] In comparison to other lines of critical inquiry, the postcolonial critique is heavily invested in recognizing "the mutual operations (and erasures) of history, geography, geopolitics, and international division of labor, through which institutionalized knowledge in the West (but not only) has been performed."[55]

For communication studies, Hegde discerns several critical contributions from postcolonial theory: "Postcolonial discourses contribute to our critical scope by (a) offering a way of situating and historicizing difference by studying the systematic manner in which exclusions have been legitimized in Western scholarship, (b) dismantling binaries of West-rest, tradition-modernity, and showing how the colonizer-colonized are in fact dialectically related and constituted, and (c) problematizing culture as a 'pure,' homogenous entity and providing the analytical construct of hybridity."[56] Given its commitments, postcolonial theory has been mobilized to illuminate transnational communication, communication structures and practices of globally dispersed people (in the form of diaspora, migration, etc.), new communication technologies, and the production of cultural and political "difference."

As we have argued in the previous pages, counterpublic studies focus attention on publics and communicative modalities that are articulated in response to exclusion and domination. More often than not, projects foregrounding counterpublics in liberal democracies interrogate political, social, and/or cultural inequities that make possible such domination and, consequently, exclusion; ultimately, these works hope to obtain an ever more inclusive public sphere. Generally speaking, the agenda of postcolonial studies, in turn, focuses attention on the modes in which we perceive, produce, and make sense of cultures. In very broad terms, these two critical agendas converge at the points where they examine, expose, and challenge domination. The former is concerned with the domination of certain discursive-material arrangements that privilege certain publics; the latter is concerned with the domination of a certain way of knowing and acting in the world. Beyond this convergence of general critical commitments, if counterpublic continues to go global, it will be well served by inviting the sensitizing questions and concerns of postcolonial theory; doing so will mitigate the risk of counterpublic being just a part of what Said called "the limited vocabulary and imagery" of the West.[57]

Scholars have already staged a number of arguments for joining counterpublic and postcolonial theory and, in what follows, we turn our attention to some specific case studies. In discussing these examples, we are interested in (1) the *warrants* scholars provide for this move; (2) the claims they make about what is *generated* in the process; and (3) the *risks* that are in turn engendered by this convergence.

Warrants

In this section, we focus on the justifications that scholars provide for their decision to combine counterpublic and postcolonial theories in their analyses. For scholars examining social change and the dynamics of political action in non-Western contexts, the process of choosing the best explanatory tool is often staged as a choice between counterpublic and the public sphere. As theory, public sphere is a valuable "conceptual resource"[58] but not a necessity; the public sphere demonstrates the gravity of the situation (incipient democracies, contestation), but too many of its requirements do not appear in actually existing cases. Counterpublic thus becomes the preferred conceptual framework because of its capacity to capture social change without having to evaluate normatively the concrete communicative modalities that are enacted in each context. One key move is to pair counterpublic with *indigenous*; another key move is to supplement counterpublic with *specific local terms*. Both moves express postcolonial sensibilities.

Dube offers a vigorous and recent effort to place counterpublic in contact with postcolonial theory. Noting that Habermas uses the language of colonization but only in a figurative and ahistorical sense, Dube joins Gopinath, de la Dehesa, and others in amplifying Habermas's silence about the material and symbolic conditions of colonialism and imperialism that structured and enabled the specific emergences of French, British, and German public spheres.[59] Public sphere theory needs postcolonial theory, Dube argues, because the latter "introduces a necessary dystopian moment from the very inception in the relationship between the liberal bourgeois public sphere and the nation-state that has a number of significant interrelated theoretical consequences."[60] These consequences are: amplification of collective identity as a central topic for analysis; explanation for the public sphere's repeated failure to live up to its normative ideals; and exposure of the Western bourgeois public sphere as inadequate to theorizing justice movements, whose primary focus is material redistribution.[61]

In Stephenson's study of an indigenous Aymara counterpublic in Bolivia, she advances carefully through the public sphere of Habermas, the counterpublic of Fraser, and the decolonial project of Mohanty.[62] Not unlike Dube, Stephenson stops to evaluate the Habermasian public sphere before deciding on the use of counterpublic. The public sphere appears as a "conceptual resource" (in Fraser's phrasing), one that is "particularly apt" to explain practices of protest, opposition, struggle, citizenship, self-organization, identity formation, and calls for rights in "incipient democracies."[63] However, to apprehend Aymara politics requires attention to multiply-scaled publics (including a transnational indigenous public) that exceed the nation, indigenous "citizenship" that is marginal or second-class, nonownership by indigenous people, the role of native bodies as themselves sites of struggle, and the force of the *allyu* indigenous kinship structure of relationship that operates in a different register from family, village, polis, or nation.[64]

Similarly, Matar carefully performs a series of theoretical moves in her characterization of the Lebanese Heya TV as a feminist counterpublic.

Like Dube and Stephenson, she first approaches Habermas's public sphere but finds it inadequate; she then engages Fraser's version of counterpublic as helpful in discussing the relationship between media and feminist activism.[65] Finally, Mohanty's postcolonial theory proves instrumental as it discerns how patriarchy operates differently across the globe and how "third-world" women simultaneously confront "racism, sexism, colonialism, imperialism and monopoly capital."[66] It is only by intersecting Fraser's counterpublic with Mohanty's postcoloniality that Matar can build an astute analysis of the ways in which Lebanese satellite television Heya constitutes a feminist counterpublic for Arab women.

If one's primary interest is in oppositional or dissenting communication in non-Western or post- or neocolonial contexts, then counterpublic is warranted as a conceptual lens because it helps us to understand opposition in these contexts. It does so in part by carrying some of the substance and tone of its shadow counterpart—the public sphere—but without the public sphere's demanding normativities. That postcolonial theory poses a set of questions about materiality, historicity, and alternative modernities that are *imaginable within* but not *inherent to* counterpublic warrants their pairing. Together, the case studies we feature suggest that postcolonial theory enables the circulation of counterpublic in ways that are mindful of concrete local resources and histories. More importantly, the encounter with postcolonial theory not only nuances but reinvents counterpublic.

Generativities

We name in this section the ostensible insights that are gained through the double lens of counterpublic and postcoloniality. These generativities take the form of situating and historicizing difference, dismantling binaries, and problematizing culture (to return to Hegde's outline). In Dube's case study, we witness the texturing of counterpublic with the qualifiers Oaxacan, feminist, and (recovered from Fraser's flattening) subaltern; we also witness elaboration of *guelaguestza* ("from a Zapotec word, mean[ing] mutual aid and . . . the symbol of solidarity") and *tequio* ("a tradition of unpaid community work") as indigenous concepts that help us to understand the particularities of the social justice work under scrutiny.[67] In this sense, counterpublic's estrangement from, or its active denaturalizing of, the ideal norms of the public sphere, enables us to seek out or stay alert for "native" concepts. Stephenson's argument about theory includes two important moves—a shift from "public sphere" to "counterpublic sphere" and supplementation of "counterpublic" with "indigenous." The latter move, distilled as a call to read Fraser together with Mohanty, amplifies the importance of territorial demands and the struggle to achieve autonomy by the Aymara.[68] This supplementation signals that geopolitical autonomy is a goal rather than a precondition for political action.

Both Dube and Stephenson bring counterpublic in contact with postcolonial theory to examine social movements. Noel's use of counterpublic is motivated by the oppositional nature of the performance discourses he is probing. Noel moves through Fraser's theorization to arrive at Warner's distinction between *counter-* and *mass* publics; the difference in these types of publics captures the difference between the poetry's emergence as a predominately oppositional, anticolonialist performance form, and the later, more recent circulation of the form as a multicultural commodity that cultivates broader, mass appeal.[69] For Noel, Warner's version is more appealing because it is more open to myriad sites, scenes, and modalities of cultural performance. In his reading of specific performance texts and enactments, Noel features Mayda del Valle as an exemplary mediator of several key tensions: between historically specific and multiculturally expansive notions of "Nuyorican"; between anticolonial oppositionality and pragmatic commodification; between counter- and mass modalities of address; and between crafting and using Nuyorican poetry "as a movement" and "as a strategy deployable outside of its geographic home."[70]

Placing counterpublic theory in conversation with postcolonial theory generates several productive outcomes. Most notably, doing so demonstrates that while certain communication practices might be generically apprehended as "oppositional," those oppositional practices take shape in relation to their colonial, neocolonial, or diasporic contexts; compels us to investigate the historically situated material conditions for the production of discursive, visual, aesthetic, and other modes of opposition and resistance; calls for us to attend carefully to both the empirical and ethical dynamics of circulating theories and concepts; and more broadly, forces recognition of scholarship as a mode of power that operates in a field of unequal power relations.[71] Through rich descriptions of local communication structures and practices and through the treatment of the indigenous as an epistemological site, these case studies suggest that counterpublic can be, perhaps must be, reinvented as part of its circulation.

Risks

The circulation of counterpublic is both a fact and a conundrum. On the one hand, in the studies under our scrutiny postcolonial theory functions as a supplement that facilitates such circulation; that is, once sensitized to a set of postcolonial topics and questions, counterpublic is enhanced and enabled to do critically nuanced work in non-Western contexts. On the other hand, postcolonial theory organizes a set of metatheoretical questions regarding ontology, epistemology, and axiology and a set of urgent topics, particularly regarding nation, empire, geopolitical relations, and flows of people and capital, that dramatize the risk of such circulation. Having addressed the warrants and generativities of the counterpublic/postcolonial pairing, we now focus on the risks of this pairing.

Even as Matar provides a dense description of the Lebanese media landscape and demonstrates the uniqueness of Heya's position among its competitors, her narration misses the sophisticated concurrent action of the varied oppressions and forces that are at play in this case. For instance, she ignores the implications of the Western journalistic model used by the station and the ways in which the reproduction of this model, while maybe contributing to the contestation of patriarchal dynamics of Arab society, might be further questioned as a factor of domination. Without this questioning, key problematics raised by postcolonial theory remain unaddressed and, what is more, social change via the Heya TV counterpublic is imagined as a consequence of external forces: globalization, capitalism, Western media models. In this instance, excessive excitement over counterpublic's capacity to name and substantiate oppositional practices hinders the sharpness of postcolonial critical obligations.

Of special interest to us is that Stephenson frames both the work of Aymara activists in Bolivia and her own scholarship as part of a broader project of *decolonization*. Balagangadhara and Keppens see decolonization as an important direction for postcolonial critique that proceeds in part by starting with local, indigenous versions of accounting for cultural difference; recognizing histories of words, ideas, and stories; and recognizing "alternative modernities" that do not abide by the "political cosmology" of a monolithic Western modernity.[72] In this regard, a refusal to use the conceptual tools of public and counterpublic sphere theories beyond their originating contexts contributes to the decolonization of scholarship.

That Stephenson both advocates decolonization and conducts her work through the counterpublic sphere illustrates the tensions inherent in associating counterpublic and postcolonial theory. Material vestiges of colonization function as enduring obstacles to contemporary democratic reform; the work of the indigenous counterpublic sphere in Bolivia, then, is decolonization.[73] Decolonization necessitates critique of Western epistemologies, with activist work "expressing profound commitment to an alternate form of historical consciousness"; indeed, recovery of the *allyu* as an indigenous alternative form of social organization exemplifies such decolonization.[74]

Describing efforts by Leftists to facilitate political inclusion of indigenous people through their interpellation as workers or mestiza/os, Stephenson argues that these strategies demonstrated a neocolonial logic that only homogenized and further diminished Aymara indigeneity.[75] At the level of political activity, then, logics of hybridity fail to produce conditions for decolonization.

This raises for us a set of questions at the level of scholarly inquiry: If criolization failed to achieve material benefits in political practice, then how can we expect a mode of critique modeled after it—via hybridization of *indigenous* and *counterpublic*—to achieve critical insights in scholarly practice? More broadly, does analysis of indigenous resistance in Bolivia routed through the Western "conceptual resources" of public sphere and counterpublic sphere recolonize ways of knowing? More, in what meaningful ways are Aymara people benefited by the scholar's use of counterpublic theory to explain and assess communication structures and practices? Stephenson offers several compelling responses: First, this hybrid mode of critique performs decolonization as it foregrounds *allyu* as an indigenous structure, as a way of being in and knowing one's relations to others, and by centering the *allyu's* self-understanding. Second, by elaborating the reasons for the publication of Aymara texts in both Quechua and Spanish languages and by practicing her own language politics through inclusion of untranslated passages, Stephenson demonstrates that bilingualism accomplishes a simultaneous self-affirmation and a cultivation of wider publics that might audience the recovered histories of indigenous people. Third, to the grave question of how Aymara people are benefited through the use of counterpublic, she enfolds the concept into her account of the concrete ways in which, beyond valuing indigenous knowledges, activists and scholars succeeded in returning those knowledges to the Aymara, thereby illustrating "how the recovery and decolonization of native historical knowledge can empower a community to reclaim its identity."[76]

Conclusions

As scholars mobilize the concept of counterpublic to account for social change in a significant number of non-Western contexts across the globe, we want to recognize the notion's transferability and its benefits, but we also address some of the epistemological and ethical issues raised by counterpublic's journeys. We critically survey the concept's trajectory from its inception as a strong critique targeting the Western theorization of the public sphere to its deployment as a "conceptual resource," which is apt to effectively explain various communicative dynamics around the globe. Along the way, we discern the warrants invoked for the mobilization of the counterpublic; this exploration sheds light on the reasons why the concept is useful and appealing.

We also draw attention to the complicated relationships that emerge when we theorize about non-Western contexts with the help of counterpublic, a term imbued by Western philosophy and history. When we transfer "counterpublic" to non-Western contexts, we might extol its circulation; we might presume this circulation evidences its explanatory power; and we might get excited that travel to these "new" contexts presents us with opportunities to nuance and refine the concept. However, this happy conceptual exploration continues to reproduce the West as the theoretical center of the world; it also seeks to make these new, "other" contexts intelligible to *us*, in *our* terms; more importantly, we risk using "marginal" territories to confirm, celebrate, and perfect *our* theories.

Importantly, to recognize the *risk* of conceptual neocolonialism in the circulation of Western concepts is to hedge against the *inevitability* of such an outcome. Chakrabarty has noted that in spite of Western theories' ignorances of Others' lives and the distinct conditions of Others' discursive activities, *Others* may find Western theories useful in understanding *their own* societies.[77] Further, Others may feel motivated to use Western theories as a way of producing more nuanced and accurate characterizations of their world in response to exogenous mischaracterizations and distortions. The frequent use of the syntagma "Arab street" to account for Arab public life with the occasion of multiple protests in 2010 is a case that mediates some tensions between exogenous imposition and indigenous uptake and revision. Several scholars labored to demonstrate that the use of the Arab street metaphor, in conjunction with the refusal to use such concepts as "public opinion" or "public sphere," severely misinterprets the Arab world and its political activities.[78] The impetus for this labor is a deep concern with how the Arab world is represented by the concepts used; the arguments problematize precisely the conventional assumptions of the Western concepts.

Cognizant that reductive dichotomizing in terms of "West" and "non-West" does injustice to the fluidities, fragmentations, diversities, and nuances that constitute both members of the binary, we nevertheless have employed this distinction to think through the epistemological, ethical, and political issues brought forth when we do theory. That is why we regard the fusion between counterpublic studies and postcolonial theory as conducive to theorizing in ways that carefully consider the genealogy of concepts, their unequal circulation, the power relationships that cause them to take center stage in disciplinary debates, and, ultimately, how concepts might perpetuate colonization in more insidious manners. Thus, we hope we have contributed to a larger discussion about *how* we do theory and what the consequences of our theorization might be.

If we want to use counterpublic as a concept that is able to account for social change for territories where the political arrangements, the communicative practices, and the cultural contexts are vastly different from the ones that occasioned its emergences via Negt and Kluge, Fraser, Warner, and others, then how do we do it in a way that remains sensitive to the work that it both hopes and threatens to achieve?

From our examination, a few gestures surface as possible answers: First, scholars should practice careful reflexivity about what it means to use counterpublic as an analytic. As we noted, one of postcolonial theory's major interventions has been its demand for greater reflexivity about the epistemological and axiological conditions that shape our scholarship. Our own use of terminology that distinguishes between West and non-West registers both the troubling, imperfect work performed by those vocabularies and a conscious positioning of ourselves in particular conversations about the conduct of scholarship. As Stephenson's example suggests, while the very fact of using counterpublic risks centering the West, reflexivity about its uses coupled with conceptual supplementation can mitigate and transform that risk.[79]

Second, inspired by Dube, we should more avidly consider colonialism's role in the production of Anglo/European public spheres and extend that consideration to the role of colonialism in the production of counterpublics. About the emergence of public spheres like those theorized by Habermas, key questions are often left unasked: What resources, plundered or exploited from where, helped to generate wealth for a growing merchant class? Whose labor, forced or indentured, paid or unpaid, enabled the time and space for a merchant class to read and deliberate? In what ways are contemporary conditions of discourse historically shaped by colonial or neocolonial relations? Dube is certainly right in drawing attention to the fact that the Habermasian public sphere is but one of the possible variants of theorizing.[80] Counterpublic, too, is but one of the possible variants of theorizing communication in non-Western contexts, a variant that shares genetic material with the Habermasian conceptualization of the public sphere. Thus, alongside Dube, we argue for a serious engagement between counterpublic studies and postcolonial theory.[81] Even as the counterpublic is not bound up by the strict normativities of the public sphere, its emergence as the concept meant to demonstrate the vices of the public sphere cannot be neglected.

Consequently, scholars might want to carefully account for the ways that domination occurs in each case or context and, ultimately, to attentively examine the particular conditions of discourse. Without this careful accounting, counterpublic risks becoming a catchall notion for any oppositional activity. And while counterpublics are oppositional, we might want to remain attuned to the ways in which they constitute a particular kind of publicity.

Next, it is also equally important not to regard the dominating conditions that create counterpublics, or "domination" more generally, as self-explanatory. Globalization, transnationalism, and neocolonialism do not warrant us to regard domination as a homogenous force guilty of introducing exclusions in an identical manner everywhere. Domination is produced by conditions that depend on both "supranational" phenomena and specific cultural and historical processes. Along these lines, for instance, before providing an account of the diasporic counterpublic under his scrutiny, Morton examines the conditions of the "dominant public sphere" and the qualities of its particular emergence (legislation, "habits," etc.) and is thus able to narrate how it performs its particular exclusions and elisions.[82] Morton's account carefully examines the ways in which both the Canadian public sphere *and* the global economy marginalize diasporic subjects.

Finally, along with careful attention to the specific conditions of domination for each case, scholars might also consider the incorporation of "local" ways of theorizing. Including in our scholarly discussion local conceptual resources will allow the relativization of Western scholarship; the decentering of English as *the* language for academia; and a more equitable flow of knowledge. This gesture, we think, has the potential to restrict the troublesome asymmetric ignorance and promote a generative conversation relying on a polyconceptual approach.

As scholars increasingly fly the flag of counterpublic across the globe (in Britain, Germany, France, and the United States as well as in Japan, the Philippines, Bolivia, Lebanon, Ghana, and elsewhere), we are mindful of Massey's warning about the potential to produce "an imaginative geography which still knows which is 'the exotic' and which 'the banal.'"[83] The banal—counterpublic theory, familiar to and in Western contexts—brought as a gift to make sense—for us—of the difference of Others. We have labored in this chapter to heed Lowenhaupt Tsing in her call for an ethic of care in exploring "how scholars might immerse themselves in cultures, nations, and regions without reifying their units of analysis."[84] As counterpublic theory goes global, we are challenged to craft ethical ways of using without reifying the concept of counterpublic; critical attention to the conditions of its emergences and its mobilities aids us in the service of that cause.

Notes

1. Habermas's *Öffentlichkeit* has been translated and stabilized into English as "public sphere" (although many have noted that "publicness" or "publicity" would be better translations). See the introductory materials in Jürgen Habermas, *The Structural Transformation of the Public Sphere: An Inquiry into a Category of Bourgeois Society*, trans. Thomas Burger and Frederick Lawrence (Cambridge: Massachusetts Institute of Technology Press, 1989). Negt and Kluge's *Gegenöffentlichkeit* has similarly been translated as "counterpublic sphere." See Oskar Negt and Alexander Kluge, *Public Sphere and Experience: Toward an Analysis of the Bourgeois and Proletarian Public Sphere*, trans. Peter Labanyi, Jamie Owen Daniel, and Assenka Oksiloff (Minneapolis: University of Minnesota Press, 1993). We use the phrase "counterpublic sphere" here to recognize this emergence and common translation. However, throughout we vary our language to recognize differences among counterpublic sphere as a theory or concept, "counterpublics" as particular instantiations or sets of action and "counterpublic studies" as a loosely organized line of inquiry.

2. E.g., Robert Asen, "Seeking the 'Counter' in Counterpublics," *Communication Theory* 10, no. 4 (2000): 424–46; Robert Asen and Daniel C. Brouwer, eds. *Counterpublics and the State* (Albany: State University of New York Press, 2001); Daniel C. Brouwer, "Communication as Counterpublic," in *Communication as . . . : Perspectives on Theory*, ed. Gregory J. Shepherd, Jeffrey St. John, and Ted Striphas (Thousand Oaks, CA: SAGE Publications, 2006), 195–208; Daniel C. Brouwer, "Counterpublicity and Corporeality in HIV/AIDS Zines," *Critical Studies in Media Communication* 22 (2005): 351–71; Melissa Deem, "Stranger Sociability, Public Hope, and the Limits of Political Transformation," *Quarterly Journal of Speech* 88, no. 4 (2002): 444–54; Thomas R. Dunn, "Remembering 'A Great Fag': Visualizing Public Memory and the Construction of Queer Space," *Quarterly Journal of Speech* 97 (2011): 435–60; Ronald Walter Greene, "Rhetorical Pedagogy as a Postal System: Circulating Subjects through Michael Warner's 'Publics and Counterpublics,'" *Quarterly Journal of Speech* 88, no. 4 (2002): 434–43; Lisa M. Gring-Premble, "'It's We the People . . ., Not We the Illegals': Extreme Speech in Prince William County, Virginia's Immigration Debate," *Communication Quarterly* 60 (2012): 624–48; Gerard A. Hauser, *Vernacular Voices: The Rhetoric of Publics and Public Spheres* (Columbia: University of South Carolina Press, 1999); Catherine H. Palczewski, "Argument in an Off Key: Playing with the Productive Limits of Argument," in *Arguing Communication and Culture*, vol. 1, ed. G. Thomas Goodnight (Washington, DC: National Communication Association, 2002), 1–23; Mark Porrovecchio, "Lost in the WTO Shuffle: Publics, Counterpublics, and the Individual," *Western Journal of Communication* 71 (2007): 235–56; Stacey K. Sowards and Valerie Renegar, "Reconceptualizing Rhetorical Activism in Contemporary Feminist Contexts," *Howard Journal of Communications* 17, no. 1 (2006): 57–74; Catherine R. Squires,

"Rethinking the Black Public Sphere: An Alternative Vocabulary for Multiple Public Spheres," *Communication Theory* 12, no. 4 (2002): 446–68.

3. Notable exceptions to this focus on the United States include Hauser, *Vernacular Voices* and "Prisoners of Conscience and the Counterpublic Sphere of Prison Writing: The Stones That Start the Avalanche," in *Counterpublics and the State*, ed. Robert Asen and Daniel C. Brouwer (Albany: State University of New York Press, 2001), 35–58; and Dana L. Cloud, "Doing Away With Suharto—and the Twins Myths of Globalization and the New Social Movements," in *Counterpublics and the State*, ed. Robert Asen and Daniel C. Brouwer (Albany: State University of New York Press, 2001), 235–63.

4. The authors wish to thank Robert Asen, Elizabeth Richard, and the book coeditors for their generous and helpful critique at various stages of this chapter project.

5. See, consecutively, Hauser, "Prisoners of Conscience"; Katsuhiko Suganuma, "Ways of Speaking about Queer Space in Tokyo: Disorientated Knowledge and Counter-Public Space," *Japanese Studies* 31 (2011): 345–58; Cloud, "Doing Away With Suharto"; Jazmin Badong Llana, "Pilgrimage as Utopian Performative for a Post-colonial Counterpublic," *Performance Research* 16 (2011): 91–96; Fran Martin, "From Citizenship to Queer Counterpublic: Reading Taipei's New Park," *Communal/Plural* 8 (2000): 81–94; Jeongmin Kim, "Queer Cultural Movements and Local Counterpublics of Sexuality: A Case of Seoul Queer Films and Videos Festival," trans. Sunghee Hong, *Inter-Asia Cultural Studies* 8 (2007): 617–33; Constance Chay-Nemeth, "Revisiting Publics: A Critical Archaeology of Publics in the Thai HIV/AIDS Issue," *Journal of Public Relations Research* 13 (2001): 127–61; Reena Dube, "Making Your Own Media: The Oaxacan Feminist Subaltern Counterpublic Sphere," *Works and Days* 29 (2011): 217–40; Josée Johnston, "Pedagogical Guerrillas, Armed Democrats, and Revolutionary Counterpublics: Examining Paradox in the Zapatista Uprising," *Theory and Society* 29 (2000): 463–505; Marcia Stephenson, "Forging an Indigenous Counterpublic Sphere: The Taller de Historia Oral Andina in Bolivia," *Latin American Research Review* 37 (2002): 99–118; Esther Hernández-Medina, "Social Inclusion through Participation: The Case of the Participatory Budget in São Paulo," *International Journal of Urban and Regional Research* 34 (2010): 512–32; Dina Matar, "Heya TV: A Feminist Counterpublic for Arab Women?" *Comparative Studies of South Asia, Africa and the Middle East* 27 (2007): 513–24; Charles Hirschkind, "Civic Virtue and Religious Reason: An Islamic Counterpublic," *Cultural Anthropology* 16 (2001): 3–34; Stephen A. Bell and Peter Aggleton, "Time to Invest in a 'Counterpublic Health' Approach: Promoting Sexual Health Amongst Sexually Active Young People in Rural Uganda," *Children's Geographies* 10 (2012): 385–97; Glorya Cho, "Hiplife, Cultural Agency and the Youth Counter-Public in the Ghanaian Public Sphere," *Journal of Asian and African Studies* 45 (2010): 406–23.

6. See Robert Cox and Christina R. Foust, "Social Movement Rhetoric,"

in *The SAGE Handbook of Rhetorical Studies*, ed. Andrea A. Lunsford, Kirt H. Wilson, and Rosa A. Eberly (Thousand Oaks, CA: SAGE Publications, 2009), 605–27; and Don J. Waisanen, "(Trans)national Advocacy in the Ousting of Milošević: The Otpor Movement's Global Recursions," *Communication Studies* 64 (2013): 158–77.

7. See Cathy A. Rakowski, "The Ugly Scholar: Neocolonialism and Ethical Issues in International Research," *American Sociologist* 24 (1993): 77. More importantly, for public sphere theory, see Daniel C. Brouwer and Robert Asen, "Introduction: Public Modalities, or the Metaphors We Theorize By," in *Public Modalities: Rhetoric, Culture, Media, and the Shape of Public Life*, ed. Daniel C. Brouwer Robert Asen (Tuscaloosa: University of Alabama Press, 2010), 15.

8. Mehdi Abedi and Michael M. J. Fischer, "Thinking a Public Sphere in Arabic and Persian," *Public Culture* 6 (1993): 220.

9. Dipesh Chakrabarty, *Provincializing Europe: Postcolonial Thought and Historical Difference* (new ed.) (Princeton, NJ: Princeton University Press, 2009), 28–29.

10. Ibid.

11. See, e.g., Habermas, *Structural Transformation*; and John Dewey, *The Public and Its Problems*, rev. ed. (1927; repr., Athens, OH: Swallow Press, 1954).

12. Nancy Fraser, "Rethinking the Public Sphere: A Contribution to the Critique of Actually Existing Democracy," *Social Text* 25/26 (1990): 57.

13. Cited in Jim McGuigan, "Cultural Policy Studies," in *Culture and the Public Sphere* (London: Routledge, 1996), 27.

14. See, consecutively, Asen "Seeking the 'Counter'"; Squires "Rethinking the Black Public Sphere"; The Black Public Sphere Collective, *The Black Public Sphere* (Chicago: University of Chicago Press, 1995); Lauren Berlant and Michael Warner, "Sex in Public," *Critical Inquiry* 24 (1998): 547–66; Michael Warner, "Publics and Counterpublics," *Public Culture* 14 (2002): 49–90; Cara A. Finnegan and Jiyeon Kang, "'Sighting' the Public: Iconoclasm and Public Sphere Theory," *Quarterly Journal of Speech* 90 (2004): 377–402. Vikki Bell, "The Potential of an 'Unfolding Constellation': Imagining Fraser's Transnational Public Sphere," *Theory, Culture and Society* 24 (2007): 1–5; Nancy Fraser, "Transnationalizing the Public Sphere: On the Legitimacy and Efficacy of Public Opinion in a Post-Westphalian World," *Theory, Culture and Society* 24 (2007): 7–30; Kate Nash and Vikki Bell, "The Politics of Framing: An Interview with Nancy Fraser," *Theory, Culture and Society* 24 (2007): 73–86; Shalini Randeria, "De-Politicization of Democracy and Judicialization of Politics," *Theory, Culture and Society* 24 (2007): 38–44.

15. Abedi and Fischer, 220; European Commission, "Conditions for Membership," *European Neighbourhood Policy and Englargement Negotiations*, December 10, 2015, http://ec.europa.eu/enlargement/policy/conditions-membership/index_en.htm.

16. Eiko Ikegami, "A Sociological Theory of Publics: Identity and Culture as Emergent Properties in Networks," *Social Research* 67 (2000): 989.

17. Benjamin Lee and Edward LiPuma, "Cultures of Circulation: The Imaginations of Modernity," *Public Culture* 14 (2002): 194.

18. Habermas, *Structural Transformation*, xvii.

19. Nicholas Garnham, "The Mass Media, Cultural Identity, and the Public Sphere in the Modern World," *Public Culture* 5 (1993): 251–65.

20. Ibid., 262.

21. Sharad Chari and Katherine Verdery, "Thinking between the Posts: Postcolonialism, Postsocialism, and Ethnography after the Cold War," *Comparative Studies in Society and History* 51 (2009): 19.

22. Ibid., 18–20. Chari and Verdery do not discuss it directly, but it is obvious that at least a Habermasian version of public sphere theory, with its preference for reason and rationality, shares key assumptions with modernization and development theories.

23. Klaus Eder, "The Public Sphere," *Theory, Culture and Society* 23 (2006): 607.

24. Somers argues that this metanarrative was first outlined by John Locke, subsequently articulated by the eighteenth-century Scottish moralists, later integrated into "the foundations of nineteenth-century modern sociological theory," and persisted as "the basic core of liberal political thought today." Margaret R. Somers, "Narrating and Naturalizing Civil Society and Citizenship Theory: The Place of Political Culture and Public Sphere," *Sociological Theory* 13 (1995): 232.

25. According to Somers, the story "of the necessary conditions for popular sovereignty" is "a Manichean one." The narrative stages a struggle between "the public realm of the administrative state" and the "invented capacity of the people to be self-organized and harmonious as a *people*." Once it was "grafted to the epistemology of *social naturalism*," this narrative "became 'naturalized.'" Ibid., 233–34.

26. Differences in emphases do not necessarily constitute exclusions. For example, an emphasis on earnest political discourse does not constitute Fraser's failure to attend to a wider variety of discursive forms. Similarly, Warner's emphasis on critical/cultural critique does not mean that he fails to attend to materiality or ideology.

27. Negt and Kluge, *Public Sphere*, 79.

28. See Miriam Hansen, foreword to Negt and Kluge's *Public Sphere and Experience*, ix-xli.

29. See Fraser, "Rethinking;" and Rita Felski, "Politics, Aesthetics, and the Feminist Public Sphere," in *Beyond Feminist Aesthetics: Feminist Literature and Social Change* (Cambridge, MA: Harvard University Press, 1989), 154–82.

30. We borrow this phrase from G. Thomas Goodnight, "Opening Up 'the Spaces of Public Dissension,'" *Communication Monographs* 64 (1997): 270.

31. Warner, "Publics and Counterpublics," 82.

32. Charles Hirschkind, *The Ethical Soundscape: Cassette Sermons and Islamic Counterpublics* (New York: Columbia University Press, 2006), 232n3, ebrary.

33. For a discussion of English as the "hypercentral" language of scientific research, see Rainer Enrique Hamel, "The Dominance of English in the International Scientific Periodical Literature and the Future of Language Use in Science," *AILA Review* 20 (2007): 54.

34. For the significance to rhetorical criticism of the difference between social movements understood as phenomena and social movements understood as meaning, see Michael Calvin McGee, "'Social Movement': Phenomenon or Meaning?," *Central States Speech Journal* 31 (1980): 233–44. See also Raymie McKerrow's chapter elsewhere in this volume.

35. Dilip Parameshwar Gaonkar, "On Alternative Modernities," in *Alternative Modernities*, ed. Dilip Parameshwar Gaonkar (Durham, NC: Duke University Press, 2001), 8–9, 14.

36. See Tessa J. Houghton, "'Land of the Long Black Cloud': Copyright Globalization and Viral Counterpublicity in Aotearoa New Zealand," *Journal of Broadcasting and Electronic Media* 56 (2012): 511–28; Stephen Morton, "Multiculturalism and the Formation of a Diasporic Counterpublic in Roy K. Kiyooka's StoneDGloves," *Canadian Literature* 201 (2009): 89–109; Urayoán Noel, "Counter/Public Address: Nuyorican Poetries in the Slam Era," *Latino Studies* 9 (2011): 38–61; and Kristin M. Sziarto and Helga Leitner, "Immigrants Riding for Justice: Space-Time and Emotions in the Construction of a Counterpublic," *Political Geography* 29 (2010): 381–91.

37. See Morton, "Multiculturalism," 96, for "historical amnesia."

38. Ibid., 90.

39. See Houghton, "'Land of the Long Black Cloud'"; Nikita Dhawan, "Transnational Justice, Counterpublic Spheres and Alter-Globalization," *Localities* 2 (2012): 79–116; Andrea Wood, "'Straight' Women, Queer Texts: Boy-Love Manga and the Rise of a Global Counterpublic," *Women's Studies Quarterly* 34 (2006): 394–414; Shayna Plaut, "Expelling the Victim by Demanding Voice: The Counterframing of Transnational Romani Activism," *Alternatives: Global, Local, Political* 37 (2012): 52–65.

40. Plaut, "Expelling the Victim"; Houghton, "'Land of the Long Black Cloud.'"

41. Wood, "'Straight' Women," 404.

42. Noel, "Counter/Public Address," 56–60.

43. Edward W. Said, *Orientalism*, 25th anniv. ed. (1978; repr., New York: Vintage Books, 2003).

44. Often times, authors explain their option for the counterpublic as a move that follows "naturally" from evaluating the public sphere as inadequate for their particular study. This inadequacy comes generally from the impossibility to meet all the conditions articulated by Habermas. This is, among oth-

ers, how Stephenson and Hirschkind proceed (although Hirschkind does not formally engage counterpublic as it has been theorized).

45. Marc Garcelon, "The Shadow of the Leviathan: Public and Private in Communist and Post-Communist Society," in *Public and Private in Thought and Practice: Perspectives on a Grand Dichotomy*, ed. Jeff Weintraub and Krishan Kumar (Chicago: University of Chicago Press, 1997), 303–32.

46. Craig Calhoun, "Civil Society and the Public Sphere," *Public Culture* 5 (1993): 269.

47. Shmuel N. Eisenstadt and Wolfgang Schluchter, "Introduction: Paths to Early Modernities: A Comparative View," *Daedalus* 127 (1998): 12.

48. Negt and Kluge, *Public Sphere*, 54, 79–80.

49. Fraser, "Rethinking;" 61.

50. Warner, "Publics and Counterpublics," 86.

51. Ibid., 86.

52. Melanie Loehwing and Jeff Motter. "Publics, Counterpublics, and the Promise of Democracy," *Philosophy and Rhetoric* 42, no. 3 (2009): 230, 231.

53. Raka Shome and Radha S. Hegde, "Postcolonial Approaches to Communication: Charting the Terrain, Engaging the Intersections," *Communication Theory* 12 (2002): 254.

54. Ibid., 250.

55. Ibid., 251.

56. Radha S. Hegde, "A View from Elsewhere: Locating Difference and the Politics of Representation from a Transnational Feminist Perspective," *Communication Theory* 8 (1998): 283.

57. Said, *Orientalism*, 60.

58. Stephenson, "Forging an Indigenous Counterpublic Sphere," 100.

59. Reena Dube, "Making Your Own Media: The Oaxacan Feminist Subaltern Counterpublic Sphere," *Works and Days* 29 (2011): 223. See also Gayatri Gopinath, *Impossible Desires: Queer Diasporas and South Asian Public Cultures* (Durham, NC: Duke University Press, 2005); and Rafael de la Dehesa, *Queering the Public Sphere in Mexico and Brazil: Sexual Rights Movements in Emerging Democracies* (Durham, NC: Duke University Press, 2010).

60. Dube, "Making Your Own Media," 219.

61. Ibid., 219–20.

62. Marcia Stephenson, "Forging an Indigenous Counterpublic Sphere," 99–118.

63. Ibid., 103, 100.

64. Ibid., 103–4.

65. Dina Matar, "Heya TV: A Feminist Counterpublic for Arab Women?" *Comparative Studies of South Asia, Africa and the Middle East* 27 (2007): 515.

66. Ibid., 516.

67. Dube, "Making Your Own Media," 230.

68. Stephenson, "Forging an Indigenous Counterpublic Sphere," 101.

69. Noel, "Counter/Public Address," especially 59–60.

70. Ibid., 55.

71. One might surmise that global circulation promises to reactivate the subaltern of Fraser's subaltern counterpublic. Although a charismatic adjective (via Gayatri Spivak), subaltern has generally been dropped, as it names a set of material or symbolic conditions that do not match the abject conditions about which Spivak and other scholars have written. Some have noted the quiet dropping of subaltern, the ease of its elision suggesting either its nonnecessity or its nonutility (e.g., Warner, "Publics and Counterpublics," 85–86; Dube, "Making Your Own Media," 224–25; Brouwer, "Communication as Counterpublic," 205–6). Recent efforts to activate the subaltern as a salient qualifier for counterpublics have directly engaged Spivak's famous discussion of discursive agency in the context of postcolonial Canadian subjects (Morton, "Multiculturalism," 89–109) or have marked the material conditions that constitute political, social, and cultural alterity for geographically dispersed Roma people (Plaut, "Expelling the Victim," 52–65). This reactivation of subaltern through global circulation reminds us of counterpublic's Western dynamics. As Prakash narrates, some subaltern studies exposed the inability of a Marxist framework to aptly account for "the oppressed's 'lived experience' of religion and social customs." See Gyan Prakash, "Subaltern Studies as Postcolonial Criticism," *American Historical Review* 99 (1994): 1477. More importantly, Prakash notes that the Marxist perspective on history can work alongside colonialism and nationalism to deny the subaltern's agency (ibid., 1478). In this context, the gesture toward postcolonial reanimation of subalternity helps but does not itself "solve" the problem of counterpublic's Western dynamics.

72. S. N. Balagangadhara and Marianne Keppens, "Reconceptualizing the Postcolonial Project: Beyond the Strictures and Structures of Orientalism," *Interventions* 11 (2009): 50–68. We borrow the language of "alternative modernities" from Dilip Parameshwar Gaonkar and the language of "political cosmology" from Doreen Massey. See Gaonkar, "On Alternative Modernities," 8–9; and Doreen Massey, *For Space* (London: SAGE Publications, 2005), 122.

73. Stephenson, "Forging an Indigenous Counterpublic Sphere," 105–6.

74. Ibid., 103.

75. Ibid., 103–5.

76. Ibid., 106.

77. Chakrabarty, *Provincializing Europe*, 29.

78. See, among others, Marc Lynch, "Beyond the Arab Street: Iraq and the Arab Public Sphere," *Politics and Society* 31 (2003): 55–91; and Terry Regier and Muhammad Ali Khalidi, "The *Arab Street*: Tracking a Political Metaphor," *Middle East Journal* 63 (2009): 11–29.

79. We thank the book editors for guiding us toward this implication.

80. Dube, "Making Your Own Media," 220.

81. Ibid., 218. She wants public sphere studies to engage postcolonial theory,

but part of what we argue here is that although intimately connected through their history, doing research under the banner of the public sphere is a related but distinct critical project from exploring communicative engagements via the notion of counterpublic.

82. Morton, "Multiculturalism," 90–92.

83. Massey, *For Space*, 81.

84. Anna Lowenhaupt Tsing, "Worlds in Motion," in *Words in Motion: Toward a Global Lexicon*, ed. Carol Gluck and Anna Lowenhaupt Tsing (Durham, NC: Duke University Press, 2009), 11.

II

Distinguishing and Performing Counterpublics and Movements through Case Studies

4

Phenomenon or Meaning?
A Tale of Two Occupies

Amy Pason

The 2008 recession spurred a home mortgage/foreclosure crisis where over two million homes were in the process of or were being foreclosed.[1] Movements for housing justice have been around for decades, taking the form of tenant unions, community organizing around public housing, or affordable housing campaigns. However, what makes the latest housing rights fight different is that foreclosures in this recession are double those in any previous recession, largely due to nationwide job loss coinciding with housing market crashes.[2] Some of the victims of this latest recession are those considered housing secure: middle class, with skilled labor, union, or public service jobs. Instead of fighting "slumlords," these victims are fighting banks that committed fraudulent mortgage practices, turning one's "home" into an abstract investment. To cover their fraud, banks falsified paperwork (if any was created at all); some provided loans to prospective homeowners intending for the homeowner to default. In some cases, banks erroneously foreclosed on an owner even when they no longer owned the loan, having traded it to another bank.[3] As more fraudulent practices are uncovered, some states are taking action with passing homeowner bills of rights and policies to make lending practices fair and transparent. However, these macrolevel changes do not immediately help those who are at risk of being evicted. This is where efforts of Occupy Our Homes, an outgrowth of the Occupy Wall Street Movement of 2011, come in.

Occupy Our Homes groups such as Occupy Homes Minnesota (OHMN)[4] work with homeowners facing evictions by assisting with refinance paperwork, providing legal assistance or resources for housing court hearings, or, like other housing rights movements, demonstrating, petitioning, or occupying foreclosed homes to help owners stay in their homes. OHMN have also taken advantage of operating in a Web 2.0 world, producing their own media including videos of homeowner narratives or demonstrations, photos of events, and re/posting news of the home foreclosure crisis. The self-produced media expose unfair bank practices, emphasize housing as a right, and show houses as "homes"—not some abstract bank investment.

Given the range of OHMN's tactics, OHMN could be analyzed as a "social movement" creating advocacy campaigns and utilizing direct action to save homes *or* analyzed as a counterpublic by tracing discourses countering misconceptions of the foreclosure crisis. Both direct action and counterdiscourse create discursive space in which foreclosure is portrayed as a systematic issue—not an individual failure. I use McGee as a theoretical starting point and understand OHMN as both phenomenon (as a defined organization) as well as meaning (as the label used to categorize foreclosure discourse in virtual or material discursive spaces).[5] If McGee's phenomenon and meaning are understood as mutually exclusive categories, then OHMN complicates these distinctions. For example, both OHMN's direct action demonstrations *and* social media campaigns threaten the reputation and business as usual of banks. Instead of treating McGee's categories as mutually exclusive, scholars should instead follow McGee's argument to trace meaning change, including how meaning might influence policy change. This challenges scholars to capture both the material and symbolic effects of discourse—especially in cases where they occur simultaneously.

This chapter proceeds as an analytical experiment, beginning with one reading of OHMN from a "social movement" perspective: How do we account for the "function" of direct action in achieving material or immediate goals? How do we evaluate the interpretations of direct actions as they contribute to symbolic change or constituting the significance of the action? To understand the success of home occupations, we have to also understand how meanings of "home" and "occupation" are part of the contested ground to achieve social change.[6] Secondarily, the experiment reads OHMN from a counterpublic perspective: How does creating the physical and virtual spaces to circulate narratives of homeowners and the mortgage crisis constitute a counterpublic that shifts dominant discourses about the economic crisis?[7] How do shifting discourses correlate to material changes in financial laws or increases in direct action to save homes? To understand the significance of counterpublic discourse is also to trace its circulation as influencing (however indirectly) material or policy change. To understand and analyze social change, scholars should attend both to the material change as well as the symbolic change enacted through activist discourses, attending to both the phenomenon and meaning of dissent.

Social Movements as Phenomenon; Counterpublics as Meaning (?)

One question underlining this collection is: what is the relationship between movements and counterpublics? McGee challenges scholars to resist thinking about movements as a *phenomenon* defined by historically recognized organizations, leaders, or coalitions demanding instrumental policy change. Rather, McGee argues that we think of "movement" as a theory of human consciousness and change in meaning. By extension, the key question for scholars is to whom or what does a critic ascribe agency, and how does that "agent" affect what kind of social change is sought or accomplished? McGee argues the figure of movement should not be the starting premise of research (i.e., here's a movement; let's understand what it says). Instead, McGee understands movement as the conclusion to research (i.e., here's a change in what something means that happened; what accounts for it?). McGee allows the critic to be an agent in determining and defining a movement from historical facts and discursive fragments, suggesting people find meaning and develop shared consciousness of social change events. Similarly, critics determine whether they are approaching an event as a movement or counterpublic by how they identify speaking agents (as people or texts) and what the social change outcomes are (as instrumental demands met or constituting new subjectivities or public consciousness). At the same time, as both McKerrow and Foust argue independently in this collection, phenomenon and meaning should not be understood as mutually exclusive categories and rather exist on a continuum of where a scholar focuses analysis. Counterpublics and social movements can be thought of both as noun and verb, tangible *thing* and *process*, and this orientation has implications for text selection and analysis. Moreover, to understand social change or what has *moved* from rhetorical efforts, scholars might address the interplay of phenomenon and meaning as they are mutually constitutive of how we interpret and experience a given social change event.

On the social movement end of the continuum, functionalist scholars followed other social sciences, focusing upon an organization's or leader's resources and requirements to persuade movement members or establishments.[8] The movement is represented by human or organizational agents making rhetorical choices to address a particular exigency. Contextual analysis, then, outlines historical and political conditions to present the possibilities and constraints for movements to speak and make claims to those in power. It may also demonstrate what challenges movements might face when the establishment physically or verbally quells or controls dissent.[9] This type of contextual analysis can be seen in Cloud's analysis of the 1998 revolution in Indonesia where she focuses on global trade agreement policy, rigged elections, army invasions, and ultimately the literal hunger motivating people to rise up and take action.[10] Accounting for the phenomenon is important as structural and material conditions do affect what kind of dissent is chosen by human agents and whether humans have agency to address hardships at all.[11] Material consequences do pose real limitations to agency. For example, Cloud argues cotton mill workers literally could not speak on their own behalf because of power structures,[12] and Murphy shows changes in meaning (such as changes of vocabulary in public discourse about African Americans) do not necessarily correlate with actual human behavior or law enforcement regarding constitutional rights.[13] Although McGee's call to meaning has led some scholars to only focus on what was said, it would be in error to divorce meaning completely from the phenomenon of people and social structures. Actual lives are at stake in movement action.

However, the functionalist/materialist approach is incomplete without including meaning making or how "the people" interpret advocacy strategies. DeLuca highlights the political responsibility of critical rhetoricians to assemble a "con/text" in which to read acts of resistance, in an effort to make activist tactics intelligible to audiences.[14] For example, Enck-Wanzer describes the con/text of the lived conditions of the barrio to establish why constituting agency was an important outcome of the Young Lords' direct action and how direct action participation is part of the discourse constituting empowered identities.[15] Part of "instrumental" speech and action, then, is meaning change. Meaning change can also work materially to constitute and influence how we interact with people and places, as with Endres and Senda-Cook's theorization of place as rhetoric.[16] Focusing on meaning making also pushes scholars to look beyond human agents and consider other material objects as part of the communication systems implicated in movement work, as Feigenbaum demonstrates with the tents and tear gas of the Occupy movement.[17]

Movements, then, cannot only be thought of as material phenomena. Human agents and organizations constitute, and/or are constituted by, the meaning making of the societal networks of which those actors take part. In terms of OHMN, a social movement analysis would address why and how the direct action of occupation works to saves homes. It would also seek to understand how the meaning of "homes" and "occupation" contributes to why homeowners are fighting with banks in the first place. Additionally, the physical home "speaks" and makes arguments about the fore-closure crisis in ways humans cannot, and the visuals of the homes at stake disrupt our understanding of what is being lost in foreclosure.

On the counterpublic side of the spectrum, for scholars following War-ner's direction to identify counterpublics by discourse (as I do here), con-textual analysis is centered more on text type (e.g., zine, postcard) and com-peting discourses. Warner argues counterpublics come into being by the circulation of texts alone,[18] and although human agents and material con-ditions are implicated, the focus prioritizes texts. Importantly, this move al-lows counterpublics to not be conflated with social movements or attached to specific organizations or individuals. Unlike humans, who can be killed or scared into silence, texts have freedom to circulate and address domi-nant ideas or the ability to invent new worlds outside the view of dominant publics. Further, individuals have agency to *choose* identities/publics through mere attention. The agency of texts, defined by the discursive spaces in which texts circulate,[19] also has more range than human agents, where texts can find audiences beyond the temporality of their initial creation or be put to use in ways the original author did not intend.[20]

Scholars contextualize counterpublics by defining particular styles of speech, mediums of communication or the dominant discourse against which counter-publics speak as these texts constitute our consciousness of a given issue, event, or social group. Similar to DeLuca's con/text, readers become know-ing audiences: to understand the interpretation and effects of counterpublic discourse, audiences have to understand its form and stylistic norms.[21] So-cial change sought by these texts is described as shifting public discourse or calling attention to exclusions and marginalization of the groups repre-sented in the texts, where making space for new beliefs, identities, and ex-periences (poetic world making for Warner) is an end in itself. At the same time, shifting public discourse or creating critical space can directly or in-directly influence policy.[22]

The focus of text as agent and discursive change does not mean counter-publics are removed from material considerations; Asen advocates for counter-public scholars to address issues of resources, power, and circulation as part of analyses.[23] As much freedom as there might be to exist in text only, texts still need human producers, audiences, and physical systems of cir-culation.[24] However, a different materialist turn for counterpublic scholar-ship might be necessary given how "real" our informational worlds have be-come. Following Greene, communication does not just articulate demands but rather assembles and coordinates networks and social knowledge de-fining our realities.[25] Beyond constituting identities empowered to engage with dominant publics, counterpublic speech transcends identities allowed to exist in the real world or constructs the very boundaries of public and private enabling speech and action. A threat to the reputation of those in power by a social media campaign is just as damaging as protests outside their door—with oppositional discourse, rather than direct action, being the tool for material change.

Counterpublics, then, cannot just be thought of as meaning or existing in discursive spaces only. Materially existent people make meaning and constitute the real world, and in an information age, communication wields power.[26] In analyzing OHMN, this means understanding the functions and use of social media networks in shifting dominant understandings of the foreclosure crisis. Shifts in meaning empower individuals to take direct action as well as threaten banks, influence policy makers, and protect communities against banks.

"Whose House? Our House!" Occupying Foreclosed Homes as Direct Action

"Foreclosures powerfully represent the hypocrisy of our current system in which the orchestrators of the bubble received trillion-dollar bailouts, and the victims of its burst receive eviction notices. . . . Homes are both the symbolic and the real site of Wall Street's injustice, as well as an opportunity for collective intervention."[27] In occupying foreclosed homes, OHMN took direct action to prevent police from physically evicting an owner, but as a demonstration, occupations also provided an image of the crisis to urge others to confront the system's hypocrisy. Cathcart asserts movements are defined by the "*dialectical tension growing out of moral conflict*,"[28] where critics can locate movements by the rhetoric and reciprocating counterrhetoric by the establishment. With OHMN's direct action, the conflict was both physical, as an occupation of a home, and symbolic, as the justification for preventing eviction turns on how we understand "homes" and how homeownership functions for whole communities.

Monique White was one of the first to seek help from OHMN after finding out from the gas company the bank foreclosed on her in January 2011. White lost her job at a nonprofit due to funding cuts and was attempting to modify her loan with US Bank, although the loan had since changed hands to Freddie Mac—Freddie Mac proceeded with foreclosure without notifying White. White allowed OHMN to occupy her home, transforming her private space to a community center with tents in her yard, signs on her windows, and activists holding meetings, talking with press, or chant-ing slogans.[29] After a seven-month campaign, White was able to get a new loan and stay in her home.

The campaign to save White's home included traditional tactics where activists went *to* sources of power: demonstrating at banks, filling hous-ing courtrooms, and even having White become a shareholder to attend US Bank meetings to confront CEO Richard Davis in person. However, it is the home occupations that carried more leverage for the group to pre-vent home eviction. Given the context of lending policies, where banks benefit by foreclosures, activists realized negotiating with banks through loan policies would not create change; the home had to become the center of the conflict. Occupation of a home, then, was direct action taking place in the location where one experiences the trauma of foreclosure, where one has power to change situations, and that carries with it the meaning of "home."[30] The home's symbolism also influenced the type of activism OHMN engaged in, as they utilize the structure and meaning of what typi-cally happens at a home to frame their actions.

Thus, for the social movement analysis of OHMN, I provide the context of foreclosure policies creating the conflict and explain OHMN's direct ac-tion tactics. Following Fox Piven, we must examine the disruptive effects of a direct action and its political reverberations, and, as I am adding here, the meaning change implicated from those actions. In short, analyzing direct action accepts movement as simultaneously phenomenon and meaning.

OHMN activists attending one of White's housing court hearings em-phasized homes are sacred places—not commodities,[31] an understanding lost under current mortgage practices. Home mortgages used to be a simple process: you worked with a local commercial bank who owned your loan for its entire life—if you needed modifications, you would work with your lo-cal representative to change your payments as it was better for the bank to have the loan paid some rather than not at all. Prior to the Great Depres-sion, banks limited their loan risk by requiring lendees to provide sizable down payments of nearly half the home's value. This policy limited who could purchase houses but provided incentive for banks to keep people in their home.[32] However, in an effort to make ownership possible for more families, the federal government established secondary markets to subsidize loans: one could buy a home with as little as a 20 percent down payment. These secondary markets expanded from subsidizing homes to opening space for investment housing purchases, and by 1965, the government-sponsored Freddie Mac and Fannie Mae became a force in buying mortgages, creating mortgage-backed securities and a system where loans are bundled together to be sold on the public stock market.[33] Subsidized loans allowed for lower down payments, longer repayment, and eventually included the variable interest subprime loans typical of the latest housing bubble.[34] By 1970, nearly 70 percent of all mortgages were part of this secondary market process, and with capital gains taxes eliminated in 1997, the housing market favored those looking to profit from housing investments. The shift was cemented in 1999 when parts of the Glass-Steagall Act were repealed; investment banks (not just commercial banks) were able to play with houses as abstract investments.[35] Instead of being understood as someone's home in the care of a single bank, houses were transposed to bundles of stock bought and sold back and forth for investors to make money—regardless if homeowners defaulted or not.

The meaning of "home" is a product of both lived practices and governmental/banking policies to promote ownership. Arguably, "home" has always been considered an investment. For the rich, houses are one piece of one's estate or overall worth. For the less wealthy, investing in a house was investing in the well-being of a community by having stable residents or an investment to pass on to your offspring.[36] In these cases, a house investment presumes *living* and using a home, where one is not looking to profit in their own lifetime by flipping or reselling. The change to an *abstract* investment on the part of banks, I am arguing, presumes a house only for profit. Those profiting do not live in the home and do not consider impacts on communities where the house is physically.

Once banks transformed the home from being a place where someone lives to an investment option, fraudulent mortgage practices became common policy in order to maximize profits. Lenders approved as many loans as possible, often omitting or purposefully limiting paper trails on loans not meeting qualification standards, as the initial lender could profit on defaulted loans by selling them to another lender beforehand.[37] During the bubble, so many mortgage applications were made that banks hired temporary workers as due diligence officers to evaluate loans. These officers would discover fraud—such as embellished income statements where elementary school teachers earned ten thousand dollars a month—but were often persuaded to approve the loan anyway.[38] Given these practices, banks lacked most paperwork required to prove ownership, so when they foreclosed on a home, they would need to create fraudulent paperwork, often processing so many foreclosures they needed "robosigners" to complete the paperwork without fully reviewing the case.[39] For anyone attempting refinancing, prime and subprime loans were bundled together and could potentially be lost in the system.

Subprime or predatory loans were first introduced to minority or low-income neighborhoods "redlined" as too risky for most mortgages but then expanded to include variable rate and other creative lending practices used during the bubble.[40] Those living in historically redlined areas, however, faced the most resistance when trying to re/negotiate any type of home loan. OHMN has been active in North Minneapolis where Monique White lives, a predominantly African American neighborhood disproportionately hit by the foreclosure crisis. Hennepin County (where Minneapolis is) had over two thousand "sheriff sales" (foreclosure auctions organized by law enforcement) in the first seven months of 2012, with 263 in North Minneapolis—the second highest total in the city.[41] Supported by a recent University of Minnesota study, OHMN organizers claim banks are less responsive to residents in minority neighborhoods.[42] Perhaps thinking these neighborhoods lack resources to fight back, banks will foreclose and often leave properties vacant, decreasing property values for the entire neighborhood.[43] With banks and mortgage servicers "passing the buck" around various offices, and with little incentive to negotiate with homeowners, the only recourse is direct action and utilizing the "people power" of entire neighborhoods against banks using (police) force to evict families.[44]

"Home" is also the interpretive frame to understand OHMN's tactics. Following OHMN's Facebook posts, you might mistake the protest movement as any other community group. Organizational meetings are held at homes (often the ones being occupied to prevent eviction), barbeques serve for eviction defense strategy meetings, and Facebook events are posted for fundraisers, phone call campaigns, or demonstrations. One general assembly meeting held at Bobby Hull's home let guests know Bobby was making gumbo. Photos of homeowners and events dot the page's timeline, along with news articles and videos covering OHMN and foreclosure issues nationwide. When homeowners are able to modify their loans, celebration events occur at the home. OHMN has also helped owners fix their homes, clean up trees after major storms, plant gardens, and offer yard work in neighborhoods where they occupy. Read through this lens, OHMN is not a radical protest organization but rather community coffee clutch. Eviction strategy meetings are akin to having a house party and home occupations (sometimes complete with "house rules" for occupiers) are akin to mass sleepovers—protest actions are otherwise normal and legal uses of one's own private property. Although the material direct action of occupation emphasizes the stakes of losing one's home, it also transforms one's "private" residence into public or community space, symbolizing how individuals (and their homes) are part of communities.

OHMN also utilizes the private homes of bank CEOs as part of their actions. Documented in a YouTube video, OHMN marched to US Bank CEO Richard Davis's home in the more affluent Loring Park neighborhood, demanding he meet to negotiate new loans with White and others, threatening to come back to his home if he did not show.[45] In terms of material change, protesters at Davis's door threatened his reputation with his neighbors and reflected poorly on his business reputation—and US Bank, by extension.[46] With occupiers at his door, Davis might be more compelled to fix the issue and prevent another invasion to *his* home. In terms of meaning change, OHMN's presence at Davis's home may allow Davis to identify with eviction victims whose privacy is invaded with illegal eviction notices. As Pezzullo argues, "critical interruptions" by activists are necessary for those in power to start "seeing people" as part of their decision-making processes.[47]

OHMN's video of this event, however, shows something more. Davis was not physically at home and had body guards stationed outside his doors—underscoring the haves's privileges and their ability to keep out the havenots. One of Davis's neighbors had an Occupy Homes sign in the window, and activists chanted how a relative of this neighbor was fighting foreclosure. Visually, we can compare Davis's larger house to White's more modest home and are forced to make sense of why banks (and their CEOs) would fight so hard for something of less monetary value than where they live. The answer, in part, comes from the video's soundtrack: Bruce Springsteen's *Death to My Hometown*. Foreclosing on homes literally brings death to neighborhoods by turning "public" spaces into "privately" bank-owned properties. Foreclosure becomes a fight over who *owns* and has the right to a neighborhood. OHMN frames housing as a "right" and not a privilege, showing CEOs as taking rights away from lawful homeowners. OHMN's rhetoric exposes contradictions that open up a space for the public to question bank practices and exert their own pressure on banks and lawmakers.

More contradictions are exposed in the reaction of those in power. Alinsky notes, sometimes the "real action is the enemy's reaction."[48] As an example, in May 2012 when police attempted to evict the Cruz home five times in south Minneapolis, OHMN made sure to inform neighbors of their occupation plans and attempted to gain neighbor support. After weeks of occupation, police came with battering rams and jackhammers to remove activists, arresting many occupiers. The use of police force and subsequent media coverage of the arrests forced the Minneapolis community to reconcile why so many police were needed to clear one home and whether the police or the occupiers were aggressors.[49]

Although not all neighbors were supportive of the Cruz home occupation, the sense making on the OHMN Facebook page shows support for occupiers and not the banks.[50] Occupation at one home reverberates and influences larger public policy. Public opinion shifted even more when reports of how much police force cost the city—over forty thousand dollars. The ensuing outcry prompted the city council to declare that PNC Bank and Freddie Mac should pick up the bill because the city should not be in the foreclosure business.[51] The occupation eventually led lawmakers to question the bank policy of using public police. Materially, the cost to taxpayers is reason enough to stop bank evictions. The use of police to carry out evictions also disrupts our understanding of who police serve, who has the right to exert ownership, and who controls the daily life in neighborhoods. Symbolically, "occupation" reminds us claims of ownership can be manipulated to dispossess the less powerful, as "occupy" connotes a place is already owned. In many cases, when the have-nots occupy, they are taking back what was rightfully theirs.[52]

Finally, at the heart of OHMN's success is the physical house: the object articulating Occupy's politics, "sticky" with meaning and feeling.[53] Through videos and personal narratives accompanying online petitions, owners articulate what the home means to them as they advocate why they should be allowed to stay. The home is a site of occupation: for activists to expose banks as illegitimate owners and with banks asserting force and lawlessness to vacate and control neighborhoods. With the case of OHMN direct action, the collision of phenomenon and meaning exemplifies how actions can have immediate, material effects, but also opens the space for indirect material and symbolic change as people make sense of the action.

The Power of Truth: The Counterpublicity of Occupy Homes

Whereas direct action via social movements relies on "people power," counterpublics build the power of public opinion through oppositional discourse. Alejandra Cruz, commenting on efforts to save her home, may have articulated it best: the group does not have money, but they have love, and they have "the power of truth, power of justice" on their side.[54] Dominant discourses blaming subprime borrowers for foreclosure, promoting homes as part of the American Dream, and neoliberal logics asserting individual responsibility as remedies have obscured the real causes of the foreclosure crisis: fraudulent lending practices. These discourses have, as Cruz puts it, made families afraid to stand up when they are mistreated by banks.[55] By shedding light on homeowners' stories and confronting bank practices, banks have been quicker to negotiate with homeowners.[56] In this, OHMN offers their own truth, constituting discursive space allowing homeowners to recognize their individual struggle as part of systematic practices. Counterpublic discourse makes public the otherwise private interactions between banks and owners, exposing exclusions and fraudulent practices otherwise hidden. OHMN creates and circulates counterpublicity through virtual and physical spaces, thus my analysis will contrast counterdiscourses against dominant discourses,[57] as well as the interaction of publics through online forums. Finally, as virtual networks are embedded with real life practices, the constitution of counterpublic spaces is also the assemblage networks for social change.

OHMN as organization has identifiable activist members and homeowners, but for counterpublic analysis, the focus shifts to texts representing "OHMN." OHMN as counterpublic is evident with Facebook and websites linked to videos and news articles, with OHMN-produced news circulating through other online and traditional news forums. The most direct news coverage of OHMN has come from the *Uptake*, a nonprofit online news organization that is "citizen fueled" rather than corporate controlled.[58] OHMN stories are distributed through progressive and alternative media such as: *Minneapolis City Pages*, *TC Daily Planet*, the *Nation*, the *Huffington Post*, *Think Progress*, and *Democracy Now*. Mainstream local news such as the *Star Tribune* attend to OHMN actions mostly when occupiers are arrested or when government officials took up the Homeowners Bill of Rights, and some news of the foreclosure crisis and of individual homeowners have been reported in national outlets (even in *Fox Business News*).

Physical spaces have also produced and enabled the circulation of counterpublicity: for example, Connie Gretsch joined OHMN to help save her home after attending a meeting at the Cruz home, and Ruby Brown decided to "come out" of "the foreclosure closet" after seeing the support Bobby Hull received to save his home.[59] Whereas dominant discourses cause homeowners to feel shame or assume individual responsibility for foreclosure, individuals are empowered to act when exposed to alternative validity claims supporting systematic causes of foreclosure. The circulation of alternative understandings of the foreclosure crisis is both symbolic and material as it changes belief and shifts dominant discourses but also enables and constitutes networks of people discussing and acting together as the wider Occupy Homes movement.[60]

Homeownership articulates to national prosperity, as both Democratic and Republican presidents have tied homeownership to the ethic of hard work, growth of the economy, civil rights, and lifestyle expectations.[61] Policies to deregulate mortgage lending were to help all achieve the homeownership dream, but with deregulation and financialization of the mortgage market, houses became tied to investments and abstract financial equations rather than understood as a physical structure stabilizing communities and family life.[62] More problematically, home ownership was framed as an investment without risk, and one all should start saving for.[63] Given this discourse, OHMN homeowners *were* being responsible citizens in buying homes, and many note how their home was a place for them to raise families, care for elderly parents or extended family, and promote their stability and standing in the community for over a decade.[64]

Personal and individual responsibility is interwoven into dominant foreclosure discourse with personal failing and irresponsibility cited as the cause of the crisis. Public discourse placed blame on subprime borrowers, using language of "troubled borrowers," "troubled urban communities," and "delinquents" to argue borrowers bought outside their means and should pay up.[65] Banks similarly shifted blame to individual owners, with JP Morgan CEO, Jamie Dimon, rationalizing, "We're not evicting people who deserve to stay in their home."[66] Comments on OHMN's Facebook and on *Star Tribune* articles echo the individual responsibility mantra, with one individual noting the group could stop foreclosures if people just paid their mortgages. Another wondered why one would protest a contract made by consenting adults. Further emphasizing personal culpability, experts argued financial literacy was the proposed remedy, and that those competent at math are less likely to default on their mortgage.[67]

However, subprime loans were *not* disbursed to fully informed, consenting, or knowledgeable adults. From the 1990s to 2004, news discourses described lending practices as "predatory loans," but this term was determined to be too broad for Congress to regulate.[68] "Subprime" became the new term used by banks, legislators, and news alike, but then "subprime" was spun positively, championed by the *Wall Street Journal* and Congress for equalizing housing opportunity. Risky subprime loans gave more opportunity to lenders to profit, and so even those who qualified for prime loans were persuaded toward subprime loans.[69] Individuals were expected to weigh the costs and risks of loans as mortgage experts, regardless of the advice they were being given by lenders.[70] Experts writing about subprime loans for news outlets did not recognize the danger these practices posed to communities, yet individuals without financial background were meant to foresee these consequences. More problematically, naming loans "subprime" instead of "predatory" "removes all reference to aggressor and victim;" when subprime started to be recognized as bad, subprime *borrowers* also appeared irresponsible, while lenders were "just doing their job."[71] When an owner is foreclosed on, they have to navigate the even more complicated maze of bank policy and modification processes. Thus, dominant discourses obscured the real risk and consequences, as well as systemic causes and exigencies.

To counter personal irresponsibility claims, OHMN owners emphasized their agency in attempting to modify their loans and emphasized their employment (or loss of employment due to the recession). In fact, most emphasized how they were willing and able to pay, had jumped through the numerous paperwork hoops and changes requested by banks, and explained their lender's faulty advice in the process to modify their loans. In response to commenters who told homeowners to pay their mortgages, OHMN members posted news stories of individuals who had paid and were erroneously foreclosed on, or linked stories of banks foreclosing on individuals even when the bank no longer owned the loan. Further, homeowners countered irresponsibility claims by showing how they followed banks' advice to pursue modification, even when banks told them to be delinquent and stop paying in order to qualify for new policies.[72] OHMN activists were able to correct misinformation and provide alternative explanations in these online spaces. Counterpublicity symbolically changes the truth of foreclosure and materially empowers owners by exposing fraud and enabling collective action.

Counterpublic politics of making these stories *public* matters for social change. Financial matters are relegated to the *private* sphere, with most wanting to keep money matters secret, allowing banking practices to also remain hidden. Public records of fraudulent practices are especially threatening to bank profits, so publicizing homeowner stories is a potent weapon to change public opinion and as evidence for legal proceedings. Individual homeowners' stories become public record through online news sites, forcing the otherwise private issue into public knowledge, so that it may become political. Similarly, Doxtader argues counterpublicity recovers a public's capacity for both *speech* and *action* by calling critical awareness to the practices limiting participation or agency.[73]

For legal challenges to foreclosure, it often becomes a bank's word against a homeowner's, with banks limiting their liability through limiting a paper trail. Caylin Crawford was diligent in keeping all emails and recording calls with US Bank during her renegotiation process—especially when she was told to be delinquent on payments. However, to keep things "private," US Bank discontinued emailing Crawford and ended calls when Crawford recorded them.[74] Collectively, similar stories of these banking practices lend weight to homeowners' words, and publicizing the issue allows for legal investigation or legislation against these practices. Making bank fraud public has enabled direct action by fostering a climate to destabilize power.

Moreover, text spaces are becoming more material with advancing technology. Viewing OHMN's events on Facebook is like checking any other friend's feed. Social media is now part of organizational structure, providing groups the same instrumental functions advocated by early social movement scholars: it combats media inaccuracies, public misconceptions, or allows others to show support through liking or sharing content.[75] Similarly, social media is used to plan, and in conjunction with, direct action.[76] By extension, counterpublicity has similar functions: to name enemies and allies, offer arguments, craft oppositional interpretations of events, or constitute a public attending to the text.[77] We *participate* in a public through our attention to social media. For OHMN, the network constituted through online discourse is attached to real life action, with those coming to *know* homeowners online being compelled to take action even states away.[78]

Counterpublics can also influence policy, sometimes as directly as social movement actions. Today, one tweet can damage brand reputation; oppositional discourse has as much weight as protests outside bank offices. In fact, OHMN's use of social media and publicity has been instrumental in getting banks' attention, with banks now creating "customer-related escalation groups" to deal with social media (and bad publicity).[79] Relatedly, exposing bank practices influenced the Minnesota attorney general to investigate banks on behalf of OHMN homeowners. In this, counterpublics are not just capable of Warner's poetic world making, but also leveraging discourse as an "ontological mode of constitutive power . . . capable of remaking the world."[80] Counterpublicity constitutes networks that direct and coordinate participation, interaction, and activist recruitment as much as they define reality to enable change. Meaning making is necessitated by discourses constituting material conditions, and shifting meaning creates the possibility of instrumental action to change those constitutions.

Conclusions

Occupy has pushed scholars to rethink what they know about theories of social change. With OHMN, I have attempted to show how, regardless of approaching the analysis as a social movement or counterpublic, phenomenon and meaning elements exist on a continuum and add to our understanding of how social change occurs. Both *structural systems* of policy and practices, as well as *dominant meaning systems* prevent humans from taking action. Both *direct action* pressuring those in power, as well as *counterdiscourses* exposing power, are responsible for policy change. As my analysis details, OHMN effectively combined phenomenon and meaning to save individual homes and build communities. This is not to say all OHMN efforts have been successful. OHMN has encountered resistance from other Occupy activists worried about their publicity tactics and promotion of private homeownership.[81] However, examining both material and symbolic actions, through the vocabularies of movements and counterpublics, enables us to understand possibilities and constraints of social change. Understanding these complexities better illuminates how activists might successfully grapple with them each day.

Notes

1. The author would like to acknowledge the College of Liberal Arts at the University of Nevada for the Junior Faculty Summer Research grant in support of completing this project.

2. Thomas F. Cooley, "The Great Housing Recession Continues," *Forbes*, April 21, 2010, accessed August 12, 2013, www.forbes.com/2010/04/20/housing -foreclosure-unemployment-opinions-columnists-thomas-cooley-peter-rupert .html.

3. See John W. Schoen, "Inside the Foreclosure Factory, They're Working Overtime," *NBC News*, April 19, 2012, accessed August 12, 2013, http:// economywatch.nbcnews.com/_news/2012/04/19/11269115-inside-the-foreclosure -factory-theyre-working-overtime?lite.

4. I focus on OHMN because I knew some of the activists when I was a graduate student at the University of Minnesota, and OHMN has purposefully built a social media and publicity presence. My data comes from the OHMN main organizational website, www.occupyhomesmn.org/, and their community organization Facebook page, www.facebook.com/OccupyHomesMN.

5. Michael Calvin McGee, "'Social Movement': Phenomenon or Meaning"? *Central States Speech Journal*, 31, no. 4 (1980): 233–44.

6. Analyses from a social movement perspective can utilize paradigmatic functional/instrumental approaches such as Charles Stewart, Craig Smith, and Robert Denton, *Persuasion and Social Movements*, 5th ed. (Long Grove, IL: Waveland Press, 2007), as well as those working from a symbolic/meaning-making perspective such as Kevin DeLuca, *Image Politics: The New Rhetoric of Environmental Activism* (New York: Guilford Press, 1999).

7. In terms of understanding counterpublic goals of challenging discourse

or creating alternative validity claims, I follow Catherine Helen Palczewski, "Cyber-movements, New Social Movements, and Counterpublics," in *Counterpublics and the State*, ed. Robert Asen and Daniel C. Brouwer (Albany: State University of New York Press, 2001). I am also working from Michael Warner's approach to counterpublics as being self-organized by discourse and not requiring copresence of participants. See *Publics and Counterpublics* (New York: Zone Books, 2002).

8. Stewart, Smith, and Denton, *Persuasion and Social Movements*.

9. John W. Bowers, Donovan J. Ochs, Richard J. Jensen, and David P. Schulz, *The Rhetoric of Agitation and Control*, 3rd ed. (Long Grove, IL: Waveland Press, 2009).

10. Dana Cloud, "Doing Away With Suharto—and the Twin Myths of Globalization and New Social Movements," in *Counterpublics and the State*, ed. Robert Asen and Daniel Brouwer (Albany: State University of New York Press, 2001), 235–63.

11. Frances Fox Piven, "The Structuring of Protest," in *Who's Afraid of Frances Fox Piven: The Essential Writings of the Professor Glenn Beck Loves to Hate* (New York: New Press, 2011), 67–102.

12. Dana L. Cloud, "The Null Persona: Race and the Rhetoric of Silence in the Uprising of '34," *Rhetoric and Public Affairs* 2, no. 2 (1999): 177–209.

13. John Murphy, "Domesticating Dissent: The Kennedys and the Freedom Rides," *Communication Monographs* 59, no. 1 (1992): 61–78.

14. DeLuca, *Image Politics*.

15. Darrel Enck-Wanzer, "Trashing the System: Social Movement, Intersectional Rhetoric, and Collective Agency in the Young Lords Organization's Garbage Offensive," *Quarterly Journal of Speech* 92, no. 2 (2006): 174–201.

16. Danielle Endres and Samantha Senda-Cook, "Location Matters: The Rhetoric of Place in Protest," *Quarterly Journal of Speech* 97, no. 3 (2011): 257–82.

17. Anna Feigenbaum, "Resistant Matters: Tents, Tear Gas, and the 'Other Media' of Occupy," *Communication and Critical/Cultural Studies* 11, no. 1 (2014): 15–24.

18. Warner, *Publics and Counterpublics*.

19. Following Daniel C. Brouwer's definition, discursive spaces are understood broadly to include face-to-face exchanges, visuals, performances, and nonverbal forms. See "Communication as Counterpublic," in *Communication as . . . Perspectives on Theory*, ed. Gregory Shepherd, Jeffrey St. John, and Ted Striphas (Thousand Oaks, CA: SAGE Publications, 2006), 195–208.

20. Ronald Walter Greene, "Rhetorical Pedagogy as a Postal System: Circulating Subjects through Michael Warner's 'Publics and Counterpublics,'" *Quarterly Journal of Speech* 88, no. 4 (2002): 434–43.

21. For example, Catherine Palczewski provides the context of sharing postcards for public discussion as well as arguing the necessity to understand anti-Catholic sentiment of the time to understand the visuals and arguments made

on antisuffrage postcards. See "The Male Madonna and the Feminine Uncle Sam: Visual Argument, Icons, and Ideographs in 1909 Anti-woman Suffrage Postcards," *Quarterly Journal of Speech* 91, no. 4 (2005): 365–94.

22. Working from Fraser's understanding of strong and weak publics, Daniel C. Brouwer argues counterpublic groups gain access to stronger publics (e.g., Congressional hearings), to influence decision making directly, but they also perform critical publicity to expose exclusion and make discursive spaces more inclusive. See "ACT-ing UP in Congressional Hearings," in *Counterpublics and the State*, ed. Robert Asen and Daniel C. Brouwer (Albany: State University of New York Press, 2001), 87–109.

23. Robert Asen, "Ideology, Materiality, and Counterpublicity: William E. Simon and the Rise of a Conservative Counterintelligentsia," *Quarterly Journal of Speech* 95, no. 3 (2009): 263–88.

24. Daniel C. Brouwer notes one HIV/AIDS zine stopped publication due to editor burn out and other frustrations with distributors. See "Counterpublicity and Corporeality in HIV/AIDS Zines," *Critical Studies in Media Communication* 22, no. 5 (2005): 351–71.

25. Ronald Walter Greene, "Orator Communist," *Philosophy and Rhetoric* 39, no. 1 (2006): 85–95.

26. Manuel Castells, *Networks of Outrage and Hope: Social Movements in the Internet Age* (Malden, MA: Polity, 2012).

27. Laura Gottesdiener, "We Win When We Live Here: Occupying Homes in Detroit and Beyond," *Waging Nonviolence*, March 28, 2012, accessed August 5, 2013, http://wagingnonviolence.org/feature/we-win-when-we-live-here -occupying-homes-in-detroit-and-beyond/.

28. Robert Cathcart, "New Approaches to the Study of Movements: Defining Movements Rhetorically," *Western Speech* 36, no. 2 (1972): 87.

29. See "Occupy MN Moves into Foreclosed Home in North Minneapolis," YouTube video, 1:57, November 10, 2011, accessed April 8, 2012, www.youtube .com/watch?v=scW8oByzYsk.

30. I am using "home" and "house" purposefully. House signifies the abstract investment, whereas "home" signifies the place embedded with meaning where one lives. In most of OHMN's discourse, they use "home."

31. Jacob Wheeler, "Occupy Homes Buys Time, Gets Jury Trial for Foreclosure Case," *The Uptake*, March 6, 2012, accessed August 14, 2013, http://theuptake .org/2012/03/06/occupy-homes-buys-time-gets-jury-trial-for-foreclosure-case/.

32. Crystal Colombini, "Rhetorics of Risk in American Homeownership," PhD dissertation, University of Nevada, Reno, 2012, *ProQuest Dissertations and Theses*.

33. Joshua Hanan, "Home Is Where the Capital Is: The Culture of Real Estate in an Era of Control Societies," *Communication and Critical/Cultural Studies* 7, no. 2 (2010): 176–201.

34. Lending standards for subprime loans are lower than other loans (for those with bad credit or lower incomes) and often made expecting the borrower to default. See Elinore Longobardi, "How 'Subprime' Killed 'Predatory': And What It Tells Us About Language, Business Journalism, and the Way We Think about the Economic Crisis," *Columbia Journalism Review*, September/October 2009, 45–49.

35. Colombini, "Rhetorics of Risk"; and also Hanan, "Home Is Where the Capital Is."

36. See Colombini, "Rhetorics of Risk."

37. Mortgage broker Mark Goldman noted servicers received increased servicing fees when loans are in default. See Al Lewis, "Wrongfully Foreclosed Woman Must Battle Giants," *Fox Business*, January 11, 2013, accessed August 5, 2013, www.foxbusiness.com/industries/2013/01/11/wrongfully-foreclosed-woman -must-battle-giants/.

38. "The Untouchables," *Frontline*, written and produced by Martin Smith, PBS, January 22, 2013.

39. Matt Taibbi, "Invasion of the Home Snatchers: How Foreclosure Courts Are Helping Big Banks Screw Over Homeowners," *Rolling Stone*, November 10, 2010, accessed August 5, 2013, www.rollingstone.com/politics/news/matt -taibbi-courts-helping-banks-screw-over-homeowners-20101110.

40. Lenders do not use the term "predatory"; this term has been taken up and used by journalists and government leaders. Subprime can also refer to variable interest loans heavily (deceptively) marketed during the bubble: a low teaser interest rate was offered for the first two to three years, with the interest rate (and monthly payments) increasing exponentially after that period. Thus, borrowers might be able to afford the teaser rates but unable to pay the higher rates later on. See Longobardi, "How 'Subprime' Killed 'Predatory.'"

41. Zach Avre, "Map of the Week: Submarkets Shape Foreclosure Crisis," Minnesota 2020 (Nonpartisan Think Tank), accessed August 14, 2013, www.mn2020 .org/issues-that-matter/economic-development/map-of-the-week-submarkets -shape-foreclosure-crisis.

42. Jennifer Bjorhus, "U of M Study Sees Signs of Mortgage Redlining in Twin Cities," *Star Tribune*, April 8, 2014, accessed April 18, 2014, www.startribune .com/business/254464331.html.

43. Ben Austen, "The Death and Life of Chicago," *New York Times*, May 29, 2013, accessed May 29, 2013, www.nytimes.com/2013/06/02/magazine/how -chicagos-housing-crisis-ignited-a-new-form-of-activism.html?pagewanted=all &_r=0.

44. Activists must keep the pressure on the "haves" wielding bureaucratic infrastructures as a means to frustrate and wear out activists. See Saul Alinsky, *Rules for Radicals: A Practical Primer for Realistic Radicals* (New York: Vintage Books, 1971).

45. See "Occupy Homes MN Marches on the Home of US Bank CEO Richard Davis," YouTube video, 4:09, March 15, 2012, accessed April 8, 2012, www.youtube.com/watch?v=d8W-FKF4lV0. Davis did not make this negotiation meeting, and Occupy Homes organized another march to Davis's house on April 7, 2012.

46. See Phaedra C. Pezzullo, "Contextualizing Boycotts and Buycotts: The Impure Politics of Consumer-Based Advocacy in an Age of Global Ecological Crises," *Communication and Critical/Cultural Studies* 8, no. 2 (2011): 124–45.

47. Phaedra C. Pezzullo, "Performing Critical Interruptions: Stories, Rhetorical Invention, and the Environmental Justice Movement," *Western Journal of Communication* 65, no. 1 (2001): 14.

48. Alinsky, *Rules*, 136.

49. See Eric Roper and Nicole Norfleet, "Foreclosure Protest Puts Minneapolis Officials in a Tight Spot," *Star Tribune*, May 31, 2012, accessed August 12, 2013, www.startribune.com/local/minneapolis/156108395.html.

50. Neighbor Sasha posted on Facebook (June 3, 2012) that the occupiers, who had been in the Cruz home for almost a month before the first police eviction raid, were "quiet as mice" unlike police who used jackhammers to break up the concrete blocks used by protesters to resist eviction.

51. Aaron Rupar, "Gary Schiff Wants City of Minneapolis to Send Cruz Home Police Bill to PNC Bank," *City Pages*, June 15, 2012, accessed August 14, 2013, http://blogs.citypages.com/blotter/2012/06/gary_schiff_wants_city_of _minneapolis_to_send_cruz_home_police_bill_to_pnc_bank.php.

52. Jenny Pickerill and John Krinsky, "Why Does Occupy Matter?" *Social Movement Studies* 11, nos. 3–4 (2012): 279–87.

53. Feigenbaum, "Resistant Matters."

54. "Alejandra and David—Facing Foreclosure," YouTube video, 7:11, posted by Peter Leeman, June 15, 2012, accessed August 14, 2013, www.youtube.com/watch?v=c_6Kz8MIpns.

55. "Cruz's Home," *Occupy Homes MN*, accessed July 22, 2013, www.occupyhomesmn.org/cruz_s_home/.

56. See Democracy Now! "Occupy Homes: New Coalition Links Homeowners, Activists in Direct Action to Halt Foreclosures," November 11, 2011, accessed August 5, 2013, www.democracynow.org/2011/11/11/occupy_homes_new _coalition_links_homeowners.

57. I am using "dominant discourse" here to represent the views expressed through mainstream media (often representing banks or other institutional voices) taken up as "common sense" or "the" public understanding of the foreclosure crisis.

58. The Uptake, http://theuptake.org/.

59. Warner addresses the issue of "the closet" and notes people do not create closets for themselves; closets are produced in everyday assumptions of public talk. See *Publics and Counterpublics*.

60. Warner, *Publics and Counterpublics*, contends circulation is why [counter] publics are referenced both notionally and materially in the literature.

61. See Colombini, "Rhetorics of Risk."

62. Hanan, "Home Is Where the Capital Is."

63. Colombini, "Rhetorics of Risk."

64. OHMN encourages homeowners to write personal narratives about their situations to accompany online petitions linked on Facebook.

65. Megan Foley, "From Infantile Citizens to Infantile Institutions: The Metaphoric Transformation of Political Economy in the 2008 Housing Market Crisis," *Quarterly Journal of Speech* 98, no. 4 (2012): 386–410. Foley notes that in 2006, only 12 percent of delinquent loans were subprime.

66. Cited in Taibbi, "Invasion of the Home Snatchers."

67. See Helain Olen, "What Caused the Subprime Mortgage Crisis? Not our Math Skills," *Guardian*, June 27, 2013, accessed July 19, 2013, http://helaineolen .com/2013/07/03/what-caused-the-subprime-mortgage-crisis-not-our-math -skills/.

68. Longobardi, "How 'Subprime' Killed 'Predatory'."

69. Foley, "From Infantile Citizens," notes even higher-income minorities were pushed to subprime loans.

70. Colombini, "Rhetorics of Risk," cites a 1995 HUD study arguing lower-income individuals should balance the risk of home loans.

71. Longobardi," How 'Subprime' Killed 'Predatory'," 46.

72. Lewis, "Wrongfully Foreclosed."

73. Erik Doxtader, "In the Name of Reconciliation: The Faith Works of Counterpublicity," in *Counterpublics and the State*, ed. Robert Asen and Daniel Brouwer (Albany: State University of New York Press, 2001), 65.

74. Bill Sorem, "Homeowner Wins Twice against Freddie Mac," Uptake, November 18, 2012, accessed August 12, 2013, http://theuptake.org/2012/11/18/ homeowner-wins-twice-against-freddie-mac/.

75. Sarah Gaby and Neal Caren, "Occupy Online: How Cute Old Men and Malcolm X Recruited 400,000 US Users to OWS on Facebook," *Social Movement Studies* 11, no. 3/4 (2012): 367–74.

76. Joel Penney and Caroline Dadas, "(Re)Tweeting in the Service of Protest: Digital Composition and Circulation in the Occupy Wall Street Movement," *New Media and Society*, 16,no. 1 (2014): 74–90.

77. Brouwer, "Counterpublicity and Corporeality."

78. For example, activists in Pittsburgh demonstrated on behalf of the Cruz family outside PNC Bank headquarters.

79. When OHMN launched its Minnesota 5 campaign and posted a video to YouTube, it was a social media liaison from Bank of America that contacted homeowners. See Jacob Wheeler, "Occupy Minnesota Fights the Banks," *City Pages*, October 31, 2012, accessed August 12, 2013, www.citypages.com/2012–10 –31/news/occupy-minnesota-fights-the-banks/.

80. Greene, "Orator Communist," 87.

81. See Olivia LaVecchia, "Occupy MN Cuts Ties with Occupy Homes MN, Calls the Group 'Commercial' and 'Classist,'" *City Pages*, March 26, 2013, accessed August 12, 2013, http://blogs.citypages.com/blotter/2013/03/occupy_mn _cuts_ties_with_occupy_homes_mn_calling_the_group_commercial_classist _hierarchical.php.

5

Pledge-a-Picketer, Power, Protest, and Publicity

Explaining Protest When the State/Establishment Is Not the Opposition

Catherine Helen Palczewski and Kelsey Harr-Lagin

Antiabortion protests, and the responses to them, are prime examples of protest rhetoric that is not always directed toward the established power of the state. Condit explains that, after the 1970s, antiabortion protestors shifted their attention away from the courts and toward women's health clinics.[1] The clinics initially appealed to the state, seeking legal protection from these protests in the form of buffer zones. However, as the judiciary upheld protestors' free speech rights (finding floating buffer zones to be unconstitutional and limiting the size of fixed buffer zones), the clinics were forced to craft rhetorical responses directed not at the establishment in the form of the state, but toward the antiabortion picketers.

As early as 1985, the Emma Goldman Clinic of Iowa City, Iowa, developed an intriguing response to antiabortion picketers at their clinic: "Pledge-A-Picketer" campaigns.[2] Other clinics followed suit. These fund-raising campaigns are structured similarly to benefit walks and races, but with the dual (yet seemingly conflicting) goals of deterring picketers *and* raising money. Individual clinics using this tactic ask donors to pledge a certain amount of money for each picketer who appears at the clinic during a pledge period (usually tied to a particular antiabortion group's campaign such as the "40 Days for Life" rally). The Emma Goldman Clinic website describes the campaign as a way to "turn the picketer's negative energy into positive community support for the clinic."[3] Either the picketers would stop protesting to avoid raising money for the clinics or the picketers would continue and the clinic would raise money to increase access to reproductive healthcare.

As Palczewski points out regarding the relationship between the pro-choice and reproductive freedom movements, "not only may counterpublics oscillate toward the public, but also toward other (more dominant) counterpublics. In other words, social movements may seek to *move* other movements, not just the establishment."[4] However, in the case of the abortion protests studied here, the issue is not that a more dominant counterpublic is marginalizing the demands of another but that two opposing counterpublics bypass the state as they seek to work through their demands. Sometimes the social is moved not because the establishment reacts, but because of interactions between nonestablishment agents. Existing social movement frameworks that read protest as always directed toward establishment policy makers assume a unitary public and seem to ignore the important interactions between competing publics.

Pledge-a-picketer campaigns provide a powerful case with which to chart, and redraw, theories of social movement, social protest, and counterpublicity. Although social movement models that foreground confrontation with the establishment are unable to explain protest that is not directed at the state, counterpublic theory, supplemented with a fluid conception of power, can. We use the pledge-a-picketer campaigns to illustrate why counterpublic theory is necessary to study how the social is moved.[5] We emphasize a conception of power that is not contained within a single entity but, rather, exists in multiple locations simultaneously. Operating from a conception of a multiplicity of publics, and a multiplicity of power relations, one may track rhetorical movement that otherwise would be unintelligible in a model that assumes a unitary public and top-down power relations.

To develop this argument, we first review early social movement studies' understanding of the establishment primarily as the institutionalized power of the state. Recognizing the limits of a model relying on a top-down conception of power, we identify a more fluid understanding of power, making the case that counterpublic theory appears to be more nimble in its ability to account for complex relations of power. With this theoretical framework, we then analyze the case of pledge-a-picketer campaigns and identify how they represent a form of social protest that operates in a world of dispersed power, where the target of protest action is not the establishment but another group that also sees itself as countering a dominant public.

Reconceiving Social Movement and Protest

Even as approaches to the study of social movements have evolved, the main theories canonized in textbooks remain overly focused on protest against the institutions representing establishment power and continue to presume power exists in a top-down dynamic. The complex dynamics of the abortion controversy, and in particular the pledge-a-picketer campaigns, cannot be explained fully by these approaches. Although appeals to the state still occur, the importance of protestors responding directly to each other cannot be underestimated.

The Establishment-Conflict Model and Its Limits

Communication studies scholars have long highlighted the agonistic relationship between protestors and the establishment, a relationship premised on a top-down conception of power. The "establishment" is defined narrowly as the state, larger structures, or an established order with decision-making power, even as scholars recognize that who is, or is not, a member of the establishment is "relative."[6] This establishment-conflict model for analyzing social movements is foregrounded in the main textbooks and readings used to teach the rhetoric of social movement.

Bowers and colleagues' *The Rhetoric of Agitation and Control*, initially published in 1971, reissued in 1991, and with new editions in 1992 and 2009, organizes its analysis around a dyadic relationship between protest and establishment response.[7] They describe the establishment as "a small group of decision makers who hold the legitimate power of the organization" including the power to decide policy (legislate) and enforce policy (discipline).[8] Just as in their 1971 version, in the third edition, they define agitation (and control) as occurring when: "(1) *people outside the normal decision-making establishment* (2) *advocate significant social change* and (3) *encounter a degree of resistance within the establishment such as to require more than the normal discursive means of persuasion.* Control refers to *the response of the decision-making establishment to agitation.*"[9] Given that *establishment* is modified by *decision making* and holds "legitimate" power, it seems clear the establishment is usually represented by the state with its legislative and enforcement powers. This definition limits protest to that which triggers establishment resistance and institutional responses.

Morris and Browne's *Readings on the Rhetoric of Social Protest* opens with "Chapter 1: Theoretical Foundations and New Directions."[10] In this section, six of the nine foundational essays focus on conflict with an establishment structure and conceive of power as operating from the top down. Essays emphasizing a state focus and linear power include: Griffin's stages of inception/crisis/consummation;[11] Simons's leader-focused movements that seek "adoption of their product . . . and must react to resistance generated by the larger structure";[12] and Cathcart's[13] and Scott and Smith's[14] analysis of confrontational rhetoric.

Although Griffin recognizes the existence of "pro" and "anti" movements, they are not pro and anti in relation to each other but in relation to "an existing institution or idea."[15] Scott and Smith focus on the relationship between the haves and have-nots in their description of the "rhetoric of confrontation."[16] For them, "radical confrontation reflects a dramatic sense of division" between the "'haves' and the 'have nots'" and thus focuses on an agonistic relationship between protestors and those with "established power."[17] The have-nots challenge the institutions of the haves and seek to create a different establishment.

Cathcart's work defining movements through the prism of confrontation also limits the analytic lens. Within this theory, "a social movement is an extremely complex human experience involving as it does dynamic interactive and overlapping group relationships with an equally dynamic established social order."[18] Although Cathcart's description of protest as "'agonistics', i.e. pertaining to ritual conflicts" does seem to speak to the nature of the conflict between prochoice and antiabortion groups, his description falls short in that he sees those agonistics as "dramatiz[ing] the symbolic separation of the individual from the existing order."[19] Cathcart again foregrounds the idea of a unitary, central order against which protest occurs.

Murphy includes most of the essays just described as part of the "'Establishment-Conflict' theory" of social movements.[20] Murphy argues, "This theoretical perspective accounts for only a narrow range of confrontative rhetoric. Some critics provide excellent analysis of social movements from this perspective, but they do so in spite of their theoretical framework, not with assistance from it."[21] While Murphy focuses on the model's failure to explain social control, we highlight the model's failure to account for protest in a world of multiple publics and fluid power relations. Theories of movement need to be able to explain protest that is not directed at the established, institutionalized order, yet still moves the social.

Foust's deployment of Day's work to analyze anarchist social protest offers a promising rethinking of power and the relationship to the state. Instead of thinking of contemporary movements as *counter*hegemonic, Foust urges scholars to see them as *non*hegemonic, as attempting to operate outside of controlling logics of power. Thus, contemporary movements direct protest not at state locations of power but instead seek to enact the social change they want by operating outside of existing power structures.[22]

Although neither group studied in this essay employed transgressive, instead of hegemonic, techniques as described by Foust, her insight into the changing forms, methods, modes, and goals of movements is a stellar example of theorizing that stretches scholars beyond the confines of early rhetorical movement work. This chapter offers a slightly different insight. Even for those protest groups operating within hegemonic (or counterhegemonic) logics, theories of protest and social movement that assume a top-down, institutionalized power against which protest occurs may miss some of the more interesting dynamics of contemporary protest rhetoric.

Abortion protests are a prime example of confrontation that is not always directed toward the establishment, especially in the form of state institutions composed of groups of people with the power to legislate. The shift away from the establishment followed the Supreme Court's 1973 *Roe v. Wade* decision recognizing a woman's right to an abortion as constitutionally protected.[23] When the Supreme Court declared that the ability to choose abortion is a constitutional right, antiabortion activists shifted their attention away from the courts and toward women's health clinics, seeking to limit access to abortion both through direct action protest and state-level nuisance laws—the goal of which is to close clinics. Thus, although access to abortion remains a right in principle, antiabortion activists seek to deny it in practice. While state-level nuisance laws have successfully led to the closure of many clinics,[24] the protests have not.

Since the 1980s, protests targeting clinics have become a staple tactic of antiabortion groups,[25] with the most visible incident being Operation Rescue's 1991 "Summer of Mercy" in Wichita, Kansas. This is not to say that protests against establishment institutions such as the judiciary and legislatures suddenly came to a halt but rather that many antiabortion activists began dividing their attention between centralized establishment institutions and decentralized clinics. In turn, when clinics' appeals to the state for protection (in the form of buffer zones or an application of antiracketeering laws to some antiabortion groups) failed, prochoice activists sought out direct action means to limit the power of antiabortion picketers. Two groups who both saw themselves as outside an institutionalized, established order countered each other.

Counterpublic versus Counterpublic, Social Movement, and Protest

Challenging the Habermasian notion of a unitary public sphere, Fraser and Felski independently offer a conception of multiple publics, some of which countered the dominant public.[26] For them, this multiplicity of publics was not a sign of decline but a reasonable response to unequal power relations. Fraser defines counterpublics as "parallel discursive arenas where members of subordinated social groups invent and circulate counterdiscourse to formulate oppositional interpretations of their identities, interests, and needs."[27]

Early work on counterpublics seems to have replicated the establishment-conflict model's focus on the relationships between those on the margin and structures at the center, with early definitions of counterpublics often emphasizing that what made them counter was their rejection of the dominant public's definition of their identity, interests, and needs.[28] The first significant collection of counterpublic essays in communication studies also focused on the relationship between counterpublics and the state, replicating the focus on agitation-establishment relations.[29]

Early articulations of counterpublic rhetoric explored how, as parallel discursive arenas, counterpublics often engage in enclaved rhetorical action and, how, to function productively, counterpublics need to oscillate outward and actually counter a dominant public. Brouwer's study of ACT UP and its participation in congressional AIDS hearings identifies a number of reasons why those seeking to move the social might oscillate outward from their enclaved discussions and toward a strong public, an institutionalized decision-making entity. Oscillation (1) garners attention and enhances a group's credibility, (2) opens a forum for the repetition and recognition of the group's message, (3) can demand institutional support for the implementation of the group's recommendations, and (4) enables the counterpublic to "push for access to strong publics."[30] Yet, it also seems possible that a counterpublic may oscillate to counter another counterpublic.

Pezzullo is right to demand that scholars "pay attention to power relations and to the various types of publics that form in one's society,"[31] and Asen is right to warn scholars to not oversimplify the relations *between* counterpublics.[32] Chávez makes clear it is important to examine not only oppositional counterpublic interactions but also those enclaved interactions that result in coalition building.[33] Implicit within these calls is a reconceptualization of power. If the only target of protest that matters is the establishment, then the unspoken assumption is that power resides in the establishment. But, if power is more dispersed, it becomes possible to move the social while bypassing the establishment.

Just as early rhetorical social movement work reminded scholars to attend to the dialectical relationship between the pro- and antirhetoric of opposing movements,[34] counterpublic theory opened scholars' eyes to the possibility of multiple sites of rejoinder. The groundwork has been laid to consider rhetorics of social movement and protest as occurring within horizontal power relations, where each group sees itself as both dominant and marginal, and where the target of protest is not a singular establishment or public but a complex of protests within multiple modes of power.

Reconceiving Power

Implicit in the establishment-conflict models of social movement and protest is a conception of power as unidirectional and hierarchical. Protestors target establishment publics because they have power *over* law. Have-nots challenge the haves because the haves possess power *over* the have-nots.

Alternate conceptions of power are available. Foucault highlights that power neither resides in only one location nor moves in only one direction: "Power is everywhere; not because it embraces everything, but because it comes from everywhere. . . . Power is not an institution, and not a structure; neither is it a certain strength we are endowed with; it is the name that one attributes to a complex strategical situation in a particular society."[35] This does not mean that power does not exist. Instead it exists everywhere, diffused throughout the apparatus of language, knowledge structures, and institutions. Power does not reside in establishment structures or institutions but in a dominant ideology that individuals accept and fortify in their quotidian daily relations. Because power is everywhere, there is an opportunity for individuals to exert pressure against those who exercise disciplinary and sovereign power. Even in the paradigmatic example of linear, possessed power—the panopticon—opportunity for opposition exists. As Dutton writes, "the prisoner in the cell has 'all the time in the world' to map the cracks in the wall that offer the opportunity to escape, for, as Catherine Ingraham notes, even panoptic power must blink."[36] Therefore, even those who are seemingly powerless can find power by exploiting the cracks and fissures within power relations and structures. This does not mean that power is dispersed equally. The state does represent one place in which relations of power are codified. Similarly, particular discourses come to represent regimes of truth that structure people's understanding of the world and their place in it.

Our point here is to make clear that power is far more complicated than establishment-conflict models would presume. If one only looks for protest against power by looking for protest against establishment institutions, then one misses the more diffused conflicts that populate contemporary life.

In an analysis of digital Zapatistas, global studies scholar Lane describes power as "nomadic," implying that the location of power moves and changes.[37] She argues that in order to resist power one must find ways of *disturbing* it: "The only viable avenue for oppositional practice is to produce calculated 'disturbance' in the rhizomatic or 'liquid' networks of power itself."[38] If power moves through networks, then focus on a single establishment location misses opportunities for protest. One may counter not only the dominant public but also other publics through which power moves.

Pezzullo's work on buycotts and boycotts provides an example of an analysis guided by a fluid conception of power and a commitment "to clarify which power relations are at stake in a given struggle."[39] She attends to the "contingent and pragmatic practices of social change," modes of rhetorical action that participate in a system even as they attempt to challenge it—an "impure politics" that she describes as the norm for contemporary social protest.[40]

This dispersed conception of power also appears in more recent counterpublic theorizing. Brouwer and Asen critique existing metaphors for publics, including the spatial metaphor of *sphere*. In sphere's stead, they offer *modalities*, a concept that is consistent with our argument about dispersed power.[41] They argue modality "entails a focus on multiplicity, movement and activity," the very things that linear power relations of establishment-conflict models elide.[42] For Brouwer and Asen, "modality illuminates the diverse range of processes through which individuals and groups engage each other, institutions, and their environment in creating, reformulating, and understanding social worlds."[43] In the pledge-a-picketer campaigns, it is important to recognize that, as counterpublics, distinctive modalities are involved in direct action protest *and* direct action response as the groups engage each other.

Clinic Pickets and Pledge-a-Picketer Campaigns

In 1973 the US Supreme Court delivered its official ruling on abortion in *Roe v. Wade*, the primary effect of which was the elimination of numerous, and often contradictory, state laws over abortion. However, the Supreme Court decision on abortion did little to quiet the public debate. Condit describes the period after the *Roe v. Wade* ruling as "resolute schizophrenia."[44]

After *Roe v. Wade* made it clear that a federal-level ban on abortion was not probable, antiabortion activists shifted toward a two-pronged approach: (1) develop state-level regulations that resulted in fewer clinics, thus limiting access to abortion, and (2) direct protests at reproductive health clinics in the hopes of deterring women from seeking their services. The direct action protests, mounted in the late 1980s, sought (and continue to seek) to block access to clinics.[45] These tactics span a continuum of violence, from murder to property crime to physical interference to clinic blockades to clinic pickets.[46] To be clear, direct action does not necessarily entail violence against people. Direct action generally refers to those strategic actions whose immediate effect is to achieve the goal sought. However, in this case, some antiabortion activists believe the most direct way to stop abortions is to murder abortion providers.

Antiabortion direct actions used against clinics include the use of "outright thugs who physically assaulted the women and the clinic escorts and barricaded the doors," to engaging in "forcible harassment, like shoving patients and staff and blocking entrances, to the most violent of crimes, such as bombings, arson, and kidnappings" and instances where "glue was poured into door locks, and clinics were bombed, set on fire, and polluted with butyric acid."[47] The use of physically violent tactics "definitively put the protest 'over the line' from public persuasion to violent coercion."[48] The most extreme form of direct action is the assassination of doctors who perform abortions and their allies, such as the 1993 murder of Dr. David Gunn; the 1994 murders of Dr. John Britton, James Barrett, Shannon Lowney, and Lee Ann Nichols; the 1998 murders of Robert Sanderson and Dr. Barnett Slepian; and the 2009 murder of Dr. George Tiller.

The focus of this essay is on those picketers who sought to make their presence visibly known without engaging in physical violence, including lawful protestors and those who engaged in civil disobedience. Lawful protesters range from those who "prayed, sang, and passed out leaflets, to lawful but obnoxious protesters who screamed 'murderer' and 'baby-killer.'"[49] Some protestors also engaged in unlawful, but not physically violent, protest, trespassing on private property, and following patients and doctors to their homes and protesting there in an effort to intimidate them further. Antiabortion activists describe these unlawful tactics as nonviolent civil disobedience that many people "viewed as legitimate as long as protesters [were] willing to serve their sentences."[50]

As antiabortion activists used blockades and direct pickets against women's health clinics, clinics responded to picketers through juridical channels,[51] appealing to the establishment to control the antiabortion pickets. Clinics initially responded by seeking control from the establishment using anticonspiracy laws (e.g., the Ku Klux Klan Act and RICO), court-ordered injunctions, and temporary restraining orders to stop protests at the clinics.

When judicially tested, it became clear that state-based protection of clinics would be quite limited. In *Bray v. Alexandria Women's Health Clinic* (1993), the Supreme Court held that the Ku Klux Klan Act provided no federal protection against the activities of obstructive protestors.[52] In *Scheidler v. National Organization for Women* (2003), the Court ruled that federal RICO laws could only be used to stop antiabortion activists if there was proof of an underlying crime.[53] Numerous courts upheld picketers' constitutional rights to protest at the clinics, although buffer zones between protests and the clinics were allowed.[54] However, both injunctions and statutes were subject to the toughest constitutional test—strict scrutiny—if they were to survive constitutional challenge.[55]

In *Madsen v. Women's Health Center, Inc.* (1994), the Supreme Court ruled that the vast majority of the protests were constitutionally protected speech. When clinics worked through established legal structures to stop protest actions, they were unsuccessful in prohibiting protestors from gathering outside clinics. Because the clinics found the available legal protections to be inadequate, they needed to develop responses to the antiabortion pickets that did not require governmental/establishment interventions.

The Emma Goldman Clinic website asks "for your support against pick-eters" and describes their pledge-a-picketer campaign as a way to co-opt the energy and power of the picketers.[56] The Planned Parenthood of Western Pennsylvania (PPWP) website describes pledge-a-picketer as the ultimate example of "turn[ing] lemons into lemonade" because clinic pick-eters actually make money for the clinic.[57] Each campaign then takes the money raised and uses it to make reproductive healthcare more accessible to women who might otherwise not be able to afford it. The crucial last step of these campaigns is to report back to the picketers so that they understand how much money their protests have raised for each clinic. The Emma Goldman Clinic reports back to the picketers by displaying a large sign in front of the building indicating how much money has been pledged due to protest activities. The power of picketers is not interrupted, taken, or inverted; instead, it is disturbed.

Pledge-a-Picket through the Lens of Counterpublicity and Rhizomatic Power

As antiabortion picketers shifted their attention to women's health clinics instead of state entities, clinics have had to respond without the help of state power. What most would consider the establishment is bypassed in these protest actions and responses. Rhetorical collectives confront each other, seeing each other as sites of power. This does not mean the issue lacks a public orientation. Instead, one can track modalities of protest across multiple publics. In the case of antiabortion picketers, they seek to use the power of their bodies and voices to block access to clinics. Responding along a different modality, clinics seek to transform the power of protesting bodies into money for the clinic. We offer an analysis that recognizes the ways that pledge-a-picketer campaigns function as counterpublics countering each other rather than the establishment.

The very possibility of a stable notion of establishment is disrupted, with both sides positioning themselves as inside and outside what could be considered the establishment. Antiabortion activists could be said to represent (and sometimes represent themselves as) the establishment insofar as they embrace dominant Christian values, proclaim they are upholding the constitutional right to life, position themselves as acting under the norms of the First Amendment and the legacy of civil rights protests, and claim to be speaking for a majority of people in the United States; at the same time, they position themselves as outsiders, fighting for what is right and true in a society that has forsaken the sanctity of life. Concomitantly, prochoice activists could be said to represent (and sometimes represent themselves as) the establishment insofar as they provide a legal and constitutionally sanctioned service and represent a majority of people in the United States; at the same time, they position themselves as outsiders, fighting for what is right and true in a society that has never really valued the full humanity of women.

Clinics using pledge-a-picketer campaigns, and the picket campaigns themselves, provide evidence that those involved in protests are attentive to dispersed power and that the establishment is not their only target of protest. This becomes clear when clinics describe the pledge-a-picketer campaigns. First, the direct response to the antiabortion picketers is necessary because an establishment-based protest is inadequate; the antiabortion picketers are the target of the clinic protests. Second, pledge campaigns are being reinvigorated because antiabortion pickets are increasing; the power of the protest response is proportional to the power of the pickets. Third, a disturbance of power is sought rather than a seizing of it; instead of using direct confrontation as counterprotest, clinics seek to redirect the power of pickets to productive ends.

Countering Other Publics

Clinics' descriptions of the pledge-a-picketer tactic make clear that the target of their counterprotests are the pickets, not the establishment or state. Although the antiabortion movement is not a strong public in the sense that it can engage in legislative decision making, it is more than a weak public seeking only to influence opinion formation. The direct action of pickets creates conditions of decision making, where the pickets seek to make decisions for others (through blockades) and to influence others' decision making (through deterring women seeking reproductive health services, including abortions).

When appeals to the establishment failed, an alternative form of engagement became necessary. Judicially sanctioned legal restrictions on, and punishments of, blockades and pickets were inadequate to provide protection for the clinics' employees and patients; this called for a direct response to the pickets. Preterm, a Cleveland, Ohio, based clinic, describes its campaign this way:

> Imagine going to a clinic for a legal medical procedure. As you approach, the street is lined with huge, gruesome photos. Someone is carrying a poster that says you're committing murder. Someone else might be taking your picture. A man comes up to your car and thrusts a brochure through your open window. It contains outrageous lies about the procedure you're about to have. As you park your car and walk to the door, people yell terrible things at you.
>
> This is what it's like at most abortion clinics, where picketers try to deter women from getting abortions and clinic workers from providing abortions. You can't stop them because the law says that they're exercising their right to free speech. But you can make them work for a good cause. Sign up for our Pledge-A-Picketer campaign, and we'll use your tax-deductible donations to keep abortion accessible to low-income women.[58]

Given court protections of freedom of speech, clinic supporters cannot force antiabortion picketers to go away. Thus, an alternative response is needed—a response not channeled toward the state but directly against an opposing, nonestablishment agent. In their descriptions of the pledge-a-picketer campaigns, clinics make clear that picketers are the target of their counterprotest.

Clinics describe the picketers as the key agents denying women's reproductive rights. On its website, the Mountain Country Women's Clinic of Montana indicates that "these anti-choice demonstrators want to take away women's reproductive rights and women's right to make healthy decisions about their bodies and their families."[59] These messages demonstrate how the clinics see antiabortion picketers as the key entity to oppose.

Clinics using pledge-a-picketer campaigns explicitly inform the picketers of the results of their actions: increased money raised for the clinic. The Abortion Access Project, an organization that is focused on ensuring that all women have access to safe abortions, declares on its "How to Run a 'Pledge a Picketer' Campaign" website that one of the most important parts of the campaign is to make sure that the picketers know how much money they have raised for the clinic by protesting.[60] Preterm's site explains, "We display our own poster in front of Preterm to let our picketers know how much money their presence raised."[61] Many of the clinics explicitly say that they make sure to tell the picketers about the campaign and provide updates on the total amount raised.

The pledge-a-picketer campaigns function as a response to the activities of antiabortion counterpublics on two levels: (1) they attempt to deter picketers and (2) they attempt to raise funds should pickets continue. The money raised by the campaigns is reinvested into the clinic in order to make reproductive healthcare more affordable for women who might not otherwise be able to afford it. The Cedar River Clinics in Washington state outline exactly what they can do with the money they raise. For every $500 they raise, they are able to cover the entire cost of a first-trimester abortion. General anesthesia for a sexual assault victim requires a $125 donation. Smaller amounts ranging from $15 to $75 can provide services such as a motel room for an overnight patient who must stay close to the clinic, contraception, postabortion antibiotics, or gift cards to buy food at a grocery store to take with medications.[62] The detailing of these costs functions as more than an expense report. It also makes real the true costs of reproductive freedom for poor women: food, medicine, hotel rooms. It reminds donors that an abortion is not just a surgical process. It is a procedure experienced by a woman with human needs.

Despite the fund-raising, picketers continue to return to protest at the clinics. Emma Goldman Clinic officials explain that despite having initiated the campaign more than twenty-five years earlier, the clinic is still visited by thirty to forty picketers per month.[63] Keith Synder, a reverend and chair of an antiabortion organization, explains that he has no plans to stop protesting during the pledge-a-picket campaign: "We're doing what we feel we need to be doing."[64] When questioned about the money that he might be raising for the clinic he is protesting, Synder responds that any money raised is "absolutely irrelevant" because he is not competing with the clinic for donations.[65]

Both prochoice and antiabortion activists see themselves as responding to the other, not to the establishment. And, the nature of the response need not be of the same kind as the action that initiates the response. The antiabortion picketers respond to the clinics' provision of reproductive services by seeking to block peoples' access to the clinic or to dissuade them from accessing the clinic. The clinics' primary response is to co-opt the power of the picketers into a fund-raising mechanism. Even if they fail to stop the protests, the clinic benefits.

Rethinking Power

Those able to impact women's reproductive health decisions are not only those with legislative, decision-making power but also those who use pickets to interrupt a woman's decision and actions to terminate her pregnancy. And, as the power of the pickets intensifies so must the response.

The Mountain Country Women's Clinic ties its use of pledge-a-picketer to "increasingly active" demonstrators,[66] demonstrators that began even before the clinic opened in 2009.[67] Planned Parenthood of Western Pennsylvania, which has used pledge-a-picketer since 2002, notes on its current pledge website that "protestor activity has steadily increased at our downtown Pittsburgh office over the past year, and we are beginning to see protestors at our Bridgeville, Greensburg and Johnstown health centers as well."[68] The Abortion Access Fund hosts a national website that funnels pledges to clinics of the donor's choice. It frames its appeal in relation to the 2008 election of Pres. Barack Obama, explaining, "with the election of President Obama, anti-choice protestors, as well as fundamentalist religious terrorists, have stepped up their activities of protesting."[69]

Pledges are framed as a direct response to the action of picketers and the urgency to pledge is heightened as a result of the intensifying actions of the picketers. Because the picketers' actions are legal, and counterprotest would be inadequate, pledging becomes the most productive response. The power of the state cannot be used to constrain the protests and counterprotest would not dissipate the power of the clinic blockaders, but pledging is a way to transform the power of the protests against the clinic into monetary power that can be used for the benefit of the clinic.

Women's health clinics around the United States are able to provide services as a result of the money raised from pledge-a-picketer campaigns. A National Network of Abortion Funds website proclaims that a clinic in Kansas has raised over $10,000, which has all been used to make women's healthcare more affordable.[70] Over the years, Planned Parenthood of the Rochester/Syracuse Region (PPRSR) has raised over $282,000.[71] The Cedar River Clinics' website lists their monthly fundraising totals between June 2006 and March 2007 as $8,688.[72] In 2010, Planned Parenthood of Delaware raised over $11,000.[73] Planned Parenthood of Southeastern Pennsylvania raised more than $25,000 in 2012.[74] The clinics have created a method for turning protest against the clinic into support for the clinic.

Although pledge-a-picketer clearly is a fund-raising mechanism, it is more than that. In addition to the antiabortion picketers, clinics also see their staff and patients as a key audience. Planned Parenthood of Collier County, Florida, exhorts: "Your donation—*no matter the size*—will send a message to our patients and health center staff that the community supports them, and that the protestors' tactics don't work."[75] Kerry Koonce, of Planned Parenthood of Greater Iowa, explains that in addition to the ten thousand dollars raised during a forty-five-day drive, there is an emotional impact on clinic users: "It brings a peace of mind to the patients."[76] Donors have the power to help the staff and clinic users' resist being enervated by the actions of the picketers.

Here, it is not that power existed or did not exist but whether relations of power were exercised. Once the power to picket was exercised, it opens up a relation that can be exploited for clinic ends. You cannot fund-raise through pledging a picketer if no pickets exist.

Redefining Confrontation

Foucault's notion of the fluidity of power and its ability to exist everywhere at once makes clear it is no longer useful to conceptualize confrontation as a battle between the "'haves' and the 'have nots.'"[77] Indeed, everyone is part of the haves because everyone participates in the exercise of power in some form. The "dramatic sense of division" described by Scott and Smith does not occur between protestors and the state but instead between any two locations of power.[78] Scott and Smith, as well as Cathcart, would claim that confrontational protestors seek the attention of the establishment. Instead, we suggest that confrontational strategies target any group or individual that is a location of power.

In the case of antiabortion picketers, individual women have the power to decide whether they will have an abortion and thus they are a location of power. Because the establishment will not outlaw abortion, antiabortion activists direct their attention to another location of power: women. In the case of the clinics, antiabortion picketers have the power to limit access to the clinic as a result of legal protest. Because the state will not restrict the picketers' actions, prochoice groups direct their attention to another location of power: antiabortion picketers.

PPRSR echoes this explanation, indicating to donors: "We can't keep [picketers] from coming here, but supporters like you have been putting a positive spin on their actions since 1987 by making a donation to Planned Parenthood in response to their demonstration."[79] In the case of PPRSR, they also recognize that simply counterprotesting would not be a solution, explaining: "We certainly won't make our clients more uncomfortable seeking health care by counter-protesting. But we can make their presence count!"[80] A directly agonistic response against pickets would not enable women to access reproductive health care. Instead, a monetary donation would. Here, traditional confrontational responses are eschewed. The choice is not to engage in an agonistic response—a pure refutation scream for scream, poster for poster, body for body—in an attempt to stop the exercise of picketer power. Instead, the power is diverted to the clinics' own productive ends.

Because power exists everywhere, confrontational strategies are not limited to those who confront the state. Social protest scholars must study confrontation as protest that ebbs and flows in multiple directions, sometimes all at once. In the case of the pledge-a-picketer campaigns, both groups constantly respond to each other. As the antiabortion activists direct their attention toward clinics, the clinics are forced to respond to the new picketers, who are literally at their doorsteps. And, even though the two sides are in an agonistic battle, this does not mean all their responses to each other manifest in agonistic confrontation. Sometimes, the response is to divert the power to one's own ends.

Pledges' ability to divert the power of the pickets does not necessarily mean that the antiabortion picketers have stopped. One picketer's blog indicated: "As for the 'Pledge a Picketer' campaign, I don't care about their dumb sign or their wicked pledge program."[81] Life Decisions International declared in *The Caleb Report* that even though pledges had raised money, "the plan to discourage protesters . . . has been a total failure."[82]

However, in other cases, even the threat of the tactic has worked. In 1990, the Christian Action Coalition (CAC) threatened a boycott of Patagonia clothing company because of its support for Planned Parenthood. Patagonia wrote a letter to the CAC indicating it would donate an amount of money to Planned Parenthood for every person who showed up at a store to protest. CAC backed down.[83]

Conclusion

The controversy over reproductive rights illustrates why a framework with a more fluid understanding of power—especially one that assumes multiple publics rather than a single establishment—is necessary to fully understand the rhetoric of social protest and movement. This analysis serves both as a corrective to social movement research that has centered attention on the establishment and as a reminder of the potential of counterpublic theory to challenge scholars to attend to the multiplicity of power relations at work in contemporary protest rhetoric.

Bowers, Ochs, Jensen, and Schulz explain that agitation confronts the "decision-making establishment."[84] Unfortunately, their description of the establishment makes it coextensive with the state and government agencies. Yet, the power to make decisions resides in more than just the establishment. Recognition that power exists everywhere enables social protest scholars to identify the ways in which protestors confront multiple locations of power. Even in a world where the Supreme Court has declared that women have the constitutional right to elect to have an abortion, some protestors realize that individual women have the power to not invoke that right.

Antiabortion picketers adjusted their tactics out of necessity because they perceived directing their message toward the government was insufficiently productive. Antiabortion picketers refocused their efforts on a different locus of power: the individual. The *Roe v. Wade* decision did not convince antiabortion activists to admit defeat; instead, they needed to create new methods of protest and direct their message toward a new audience. Similarly, when the Supreme Court repeatedly refused to prohibit antiabortion activists from protesting at women's health clinics, clinic officials had to create new strategies for coping with the picketers. Both groups recognized that the government is not the sole location of power and attempted to move the social without the help of the government. They represent publics confronting each other, without having to pass through the modes of interaction dictated by the dominant public.

The pledge-a-picketer tactic is not limited to the abortion controversy. For instance, some have used the pledge tactic as a response to Westboro Baptist Church.[85] Thus, to study contemporary social movement and protest, scholars would be wise to recognize that protestors do not always confront the state. This tactic makes clear that social change occurs not only via conflict with an establishment and that the determination of who is, and is not, the establishment is itself a rhetorical construction.

Finally, the clinics' pledge-a-picketer response also highlights the fluid form of power. After seeking to cut off the power through legal maneuvers failed, both picketers and clinics sought to disrupt the others' power. Picketers sought to deploy interpersonal coercive power. The clinic response did not cut off a linear flow of power but redirected it to the end of helping the clinic. As this example makes clear, a framework with a more fluid understanding of power and that assumes multiple publics rather than a single establishment is necessary to fully understand the rhetoric of social protest and movement.

Notes

1. Celeste M. Condit, *Decoding Abortion Rhetoric: Communicating Social Change* (Urbana: University of Illinois Press, 1990). As Condit (and others) make clear, all language is suasive. We recognize that terms such as "prochoice" and "antiabortion" do not reflect the full diversity of positions in the controversies over (women's) reproduction and that they may not be accepted by those to whom we use them to refer. However, we use these terms to more easily

reference protestors who generally seek to either keep abortions legal so that they are an option for women (prochoice) or to make abortions illegal (antiabortion).

2. Dan Valentine, "Abortion Protesters Raise Funds for Emma," *Daily Iowan*, July 28, 2005, 3A.

3. "Pledge-A-Picketer! Let Them Work for Us!" Emma Goldman Clinic, accessed May 27, 2013, www.emmagoldman.com/contributions/pledgepicket .html.

4. Catherine H. Palczewski, "Reproductive Freedom: Transforming Discourses of Choice," in *Contemplating Maternity: Discourses of Choice and Control*, ed. Sara Hayden and Lynn O'Brien Hallstein (Rowman and Littlefield, 2010), 77.

5. Like McGee, we do not consider a social movement to be a discrete phenomenon but rather an instance in which the social is moved as a result of rhetorical action. Michael Calvin McGee, "'Social Movement': Phenomenon or Meaning?" *Central States Speech Journal* 31, no. 4 (1980): 233–44, "Social *Movement* as Meaning," *Central States Speech Journal* 34 (Spring 1983): 74–77. For a discussion of the evolution from movement studies to new social movements to counterpublics and the role McGee's insight played in this evolution, see Robert Cox and Christina R. Foust, "Social Movement Rhetoric," in *The SAGE Handbook of Rhetorical Studies*, ed. Andrea A. Lunsford, Kirt H. Wilson, and Rosa A. Eberly (Thousand Oaks, CA: SAGE Publications, 2009), 605–27.

6. John W. Bowers et al., *The Rhetoric of Agitation and Control*, 3rd ed. (Long Grove, IL: Waveland Press, 2009), 4. For a discussion of how the establishment can be part of a movement, see David Zarefsky, "President Johnson's War on Poverty: The Rhetoric of Three 'Establishment' Movements," *Communication Monographs* 44, no. 4 (1977): 352–73. For an analysis of how a movement may become the establishment, see Elizabeth Jean Nelson, "'Nothing Ever Goes Well Enough': Mussolini and the Rhetoric of Perpetual Struggle," *Communication Studies* 42, no. 1 (Spring 1991): 22–42, 37.

7. Bowers et al., *Rhetoric*.

8. Ibid.

9. Ibid., 3–4.

10. Charles E. Morris III and Stephen Howard Browne, eds., *Readings on the Rhetoric of Social Protest*, 3rd ed. (State College, PA: Strata, 2013). The next chapter is "Competing Perspectives." Yet, students' introduction to the study of social protest is through essays that use an establishment-conflict model.

11. Leland M. Griffin, "The Rhetoric of Historical Movements," *Quarterly Journal of Speech* 38, no. 2 (April 1952): 184–88, "A Dramatistic Theory of the Rhetoric of Movements," in *Critical Responses to Kenneth Burke*, ed. William H. Reuckert, 456–78 (Minneapolis: University of Minnesota Press, 1969).

12. Herbert W. Simons, "Requirements, Problems, and Strategies: A Theory

of Persuasion for Social Movements," *Quarterly Journal of Speech* 56, no. 1 (1970): 1–11, 3–4.

13. Robert S. Cathcart, "Movements: Confrontation as Rhetorical Form," *Southern Speech Communication Journal* 43, no. 3 (1978): 233–47, "Defining Social Movements by Their Rhetorical Form," *Central States Speech Journal* 31, no. 4 (1980): 267–73, "A Confrontation Perspective on the Study of Social Movements," *Central States Speech Journal* 34 (Spring 1983): 69–74.

14. Robert L. Scott and Donald K. Smith, "The Rhetoric of Confrontation," *Quarterly Journal of Speech* 55, no. 1 (1969): 1–8.

15. Griffin, "Rhetoric," 185.

16. Scott and Smith, "Rhetoric." See also Richard B. Gregg, "The Ego-Function of the Rhetoric of Protest," *Philosophy and Rhetoric* 4, no. 2 (1971): 71–91.

17. Scott and Smith, "Rhetoric," 2–3.

18. Cathcart, "Confrontation Perspective," 70.

19. Cathcart, "Movements," 235.

20. John M. Murphy, "Domesticating Dissent: The Kennedys and the Freedom Rides," *Communication Monographs* 59, no. 1 (1992): 62.

21. Ibid.

22. Christina R. Foust, *Transgression as a Mode of Rethinking: Rethinking Social Movement in an Era of Corporate Globalization* (Lanham, MD: Lexington Books, 2010).

23. Roe v. Wade, 410 U.S. 113 (1973).

24. Laura Bassett, "Anti-abortion Laws Take Dramatic Toll on Clinics Nationwide," *Huffington Post*, August 26, 2013, accessed October 14, 2015, www .huffingtonpost.com/2013/08/26/abortion-clinic-closures_n_3804529.html. Bassett notes over fifty clinics have closed since 2010.

25. A sit-in by antiabortion protestors at a clinic occurred in early 1970 at a Planned Parenthood office in Dallas, but these early actions "were isolated incidents that were quickly forgotten." Christopher P. Keleher, "Double Standards: The Suppression of Abortion Protesters' Free Speech Rights," *DePaul Law Review* 51 (2002): 836. It is important to note that the use of civil disobedience was not initially universally accepted by antiabortion activists. Despite early debates about direct action civil disobedience, and some antiabortion groups' prohibition against it, it eventually became a staple of antiabortion protest. See James Risen and Judy L. Thomas, *Wrath of Angels: The American Abortion War* (New York: Basic Books, 1998).

26. Nancy Fraser, "Rethinking the Public Sphere," in *Habermas and the Public Sphere*, ed. Craig Calhoun (Cambridge: Massachusetts Institute of Technology Press, 1992), 109–142; Rita Felski, *Beyond Feminist Aesthetics* (Cambridge, MA: Harvard University Press, 1989).

27. Fraser, "Rethinking," 123.

28. Fraser, "Rethinking"; Felski, *Beyond Feminist Aesthetics*. For a discussion of what is counter about counterpublics, see Robert Asen, "Seeking the 'Counter' in Counterpublics," *Communication Theory* 10, no. 4 (November 2000): 424–46.

29. Robert Asen and Daniel C. Brouwer, eds., *Counterpublics and the State* (Albany: State University of New York Press, 2001).

30. Daniel C. Brouwer, "ACT-ing UP in Congressional Hearings," in *Counterpublics and the State*, ed. Robert Asen and Daniel C. Brouwer (Albany: State University of New York Press, 2001), 100. See also Catherine Squires, "The Black Press and the State: Attracting Unwanted (?) Attention," in *Counterpublics and the State*, ed. Robert Asen and Daniel C. Brouwer (Albany: State University of New York Press, 2001), 132n1, italics added. In addition to enclave and oscillating, she offers two additional levels of distinction: a counterpublic "engages in mass actions to assert its needs . . . utilizing disruptive social movement tactics to make demands on the state" and parallel publics "work[ ] in conjunction with others [publics] on equal footing."

31. Pheadra C. Pezzullo, "Resisting 'National Breast Cancer Awareness Month': The Rhetoric of Counterpublics and Their Cultural Performances," *Quarterly Journal of Speech* 89, no. 4 (2003): 348.

32. Asen, "Seeking the 'Counter.'"

33. Karma R. Chávez, "Counter-Public Enclaves and Understanding the Function of Rhetoric in Social Movement Coalition-Building," *Communication Quarterly* 59, no. 1 (2011): 1–18.

34. Griffin, "Rhetoric."

35. Michel Foucault, *The History of Sexuality* (New York: Vintage, 1980), 93.

36. Michael Dutton, "Street Scenes of Subalternity: China, Globalization, and Rights," *Social Text* 60 (1999): 65.

37. For a discussion of power fluidity in protest, see Jill Lane, "Digital Zapatistas," *Drama Review* 47, no. 2 (2003): 134.

38. Ibid., 134.

39. Phaedra C. Pezzullo, "Contextualizing Boycotts and Buycotts: The Impure Politics of Consumer-Based Advocacy in an Age of Global Ecological Crises," *Communication and Critical/Cultural Studies* 8, no. 2 (2011): 128.

40. Ibid., 126–27.

41. Daniel C. Brouwer and Robert Asen, "Introduction: Public Modalities, or the Metaphors We Theorize By," in *Public Modalities*, ed. Daniel C. Brouwer and Robert Asen (Tuscaloosa: University of Alabama Press, 2010), 1–32.

42. Ibid., 3.

43. Ibid., 16.

44. Condit, *Decoding*, 147.

45. David S. Meyer and Suzanne Staggenborg, "Opposing Movement Strategies in U.S. Abortion Politics," *Research in Social Movements, Conflicts, and Change* 28 (2008): 207–38.

46. In including violence as a form of direct action, we are not making

a moral judgment about its use. Instead, we recognize that, throughout so-cial protest history, direct action has included the use of violence against both people and property. For example, anarchist and labor activist Lucy Parsons, in her circa 1886 pamphlet "To Tramps," exhorted them to *Learn the use of explosives!*" (accessed October 14, 2015, www.chicagohistory.org/dramas/act1/fromTheArchive/wordToTramps_f.htm). British suffragettes targeted both build-ings and politicians. In addition, DeLuca and Peeples make a compelling case for the productive role of direct action violence against property in the 1999 Seattle WTO protests. Kevin Michael DeLuca and Jennifer Peeples, "From Public Sphere to Public Screen: Democracy, Activism, and the 'Violence' of Se-attle," *Critical Studies in Media Communication* 19, no. 2 (2002): 125–51.

47. Fay Clayton and Sara N. Love, "NOW v. Scheidler: Protecting Wom-en's Access to Reproductive Health Services," *Albany Law Review* 62 (1999): 970–71.

48. Condit, *Decoding*, 153.

49. Clayton and Love, "NOW v. Scheidler," 971.

50. Condit, *Decoding*, 153.

51. Rachel L. Braunstein, "A Remedy for Abortion Seekers under the Inva-sion of Privacy Tort," *Brooklyn Law Review* 68 (2002): 309–50; Tiffany Keast, "Injunction Junction: Enjoining Free Speech after Madsen, Schenck, and Hill," *American University Journal of Gender, Social Policy and the Law* 12 (2004): 273–307.

52. Bray v. Alexandria Women's Health Clinic, 506 U.S. 263 (1993).

53. Scheidler v. National Organization for Women, 537 U.S. 393 (2003).

54. Courts have found buffer zones between clinics and protestors are not infringements on protestors' free speech rights. In Schenck v. Pro-Choice Net-work, the Supreme Court found that a fixed fifteen-foot buffer was constitu-tional but a moving fifteen-foot bubble around those entering and leaving a clinic is not. Schenck v. Pro-Choice Network, 519 U.S. 357 (1997). Other states have enacted larger buffers that have survived judicial scrutiny (e.g., a 2007 Massachusetts law prohibits antiabortion protests within thirty-five feet of a clinic, Martin Funicane, "Appellate Court Upholds Mass. Abortion Protest Law," *Boston Globe*, January 9, 2013, accessed July 28, 2016, *www.bostonglobe.com/metro/2013/01/09/federal-appeals-court-again-upholds-mass-abortion-buffer-clinic-zone-law/h8B40j5A1I6GVy1NqfB6IO/story.html*.

55. Madsen et al. v. Women's Health Center, Inc., et al., 512 U.S. 753 (1994).

56. Emma Goldman Clinic, "Pledge-a-Picketer."

57. Planned Parenthood of Western Pennsylvania, "Help Planned Parent-hood Turn Lemons into Lemonade," accessed February 1, 2007, www.ppwp.org/pledgeapick1-2.html. The idea of lemons also appears in the Planned Parent-hood Advocacy Fund of Delaware's 2013 fund-raising efforts, both on their web-site (see www.plannedparenthood.org/about-us/newsroom/local-press-releases/press-release-03-07-13-planned-parenthood-stands-up-protestors-turning

-lemons-into-lemonade-41052.htm) and Facebook account (see www.facebook.com/prochoicedelaware).

58. Preterm, "Pledge-a-Picketer," accessed January 20, 2016,www.preterm.org/donate/pledge-a-picketer.htm.

59. Trust Women Fund, "Pledge-a-Picketer," accessed January 26, 2013, http://trustwomenfund.org/Pledge-a-Picketer.html. This clinic closed on October 1, 2013.

60. Abortion Access Project, "How to Run a 'Pledge a Picketer' Campaign," accessed February 1, 2007, www.abortionaccess.org/viewpages.php.

61. Preterm, "Pledge a Picketer."

62. Cedar River Clinics, "Pledge a Picket: Help Picketing Make Dollars and Sense," accessed February 1, 2007, www.cedarriverclinics.org/pledge-a-picket/pledgeform.pdf. See also "Pledge a Picket Counts for Cedar River Clinics," accessed February 1, 2007, www.cedarriverclinics.org/pledge-a-picket/picketcounts2.html.

63. "Abortion Protesters Raise Funds for Emma," *Daily Iowan*, July 28, 2005, media.www.dailyiowan.com/media/storage/paper599/news/2005/07/28/Metro/Abortion.Protesters.Raise.Funds.For.Emma-964742.shtml?sourcedomain=www.dailyiowan.com&MIIHost=media.collegepublisher.com.

64. Quoted in Claire Churchley, "Pledge a Picket Campaign to Make Money off Protesters," *Michigan Tech University Online Lode*, accessed February 1, 2007, www.mtulodearchives.com/index.php?issuedate=&section=12&artid=1150.

65. Ibid.

66. Trust Women Fund, "Pledge-a-Picketer."

67. Katha Pollitt, "From My Inbox: Pledge-a-Picket for New Clinic in Montana," *Nation*, February 4, 2009, www.thenation.com/blog/my-inbox-pledge-picket-new-clinic-montana#.

68. Planned Parenthood of Western Pennsylvania, "Pledge-a-Picketer," accessed January 26, 2013, www.plannedparenthood.org/western-pennsylvania/pledge-picketer-37642.htm.

69. Abortion Access Fund, "Pledge-a-Picket," accessed January 26, 2013, www.pledge-a-picket.org.

70. National Network of Abortion Funds, "Pledge a Picketer Campaign a Huge Success: Over $10,000 Raised for Low-income Women's Access!" accessed February 1, 2007, www.nnaf.org/pledge.html.

71. Planned Parenthood of Rochester/Syracuse Region, "Pledge-a-Picket," accessed January 26, 2013, www.plannedparenthood.org/rochester-syracuse/pledge-a-picket-23972.htm.

72. Cedar River Clinics, "Pledge a Picket Counts."

73. Planned Parenthood of Delaware, "Pledge a Picket Campaign Exceeds Initial Goal," June 24, 2010, press release, www.plannedparenthood.org/about-us/newsroom/local-press-releases/press-release-06–24–10-pledge-picket-campaign-exceeds-initial-goal-33028.htm.

74. Planned Parenthood of Southeastern Pennsylvania, "Pledge-a-Picket," accessed January 27, 2013, www.plannedparenthood.org/ppsp/pledge-picket -39092.htm.

75. Planned Parenthood of Collier County, "Pledge-a-Picket," accessed January 26, 2013, http://ppcolliercounty.wordpress.com/2012/02/23/pledge-a-picket/.

76. Jeffrey Dubner, "Money in Their Pickets," *American Prospect*, February 2005, 8.

77. Scott and Smith, "Rhetoric," 2.

78. Ibid., 2.

79. Planned Parenthood of Rochester/Syracuse Region, "Pledge-a-Picket."

80. Planned Parenthood of Rochester/Syracuse Region, "Planned Parenthood: Pledge a Picket," *Democratic Underground*, accessed January 26, 2013, www.democraticunderground.com/discuss/duboard.php?az=view_all&address =389x562165.

81. Out of the Miry Clay, "Pledge a Picketer," February 15, 2008, accessed January 26, 2013, http://outofthemiryclay.wordpress.com/tag/pledge-a-picketer/.

82. "Variation on a Theme: '40 Days of Harassment' New Version of 'Pledge-a-Picket' Serves Dual Purpose," *The Caleb Report*, September/October 2009, 1, accessed January 26, 2013, https://docs.google.com/viewer?a=v&q=cache :2doMzoyO78AJ:www.fightpp.org/downloads/pubs/September-October2.pdf+ &hl=en&gl=us&pid=bl&srcid=ADGEESg4ufOevrMUuCQmn7wMoIHaoo OKRa5SRPqMY-fYIwchUCFWljw36meajOj-59IEkBriolD5ozzeY_6sy6syR2kBf _ygVYakhecfWPRlZWvjolMFSckdoKLTGZ9OdkItHO6oJMmz&sig=AHI EtbTrr-3NFdNTyWMiiAJrTwQReU_RWQ.

83. Dawn MacKeen, "Pro-choice Activism is Reactivated," *Salon*, February 9, 2001, accessed January 26, 2013, www.salon.com/2001/02/09/donations/.

84. Bowers et al., *Rhetoric*, 4.

85. William McGuinness, "Vassar College Students Raise Thousands in Response to Westboro Protest Threat," *Huffington Post*, February 12, 2013, accessed January 26, 2013, www.huffingtonpost.com/2013/02/12/vassar-westboro -protest_n_2671924.html.

6

(Re)turning to the Private Sphere

SlutWalks' Public Negotiation of Privacy

Kate Zittlow Rogness

On April 6, 2013, the campus of a small, liberal arts college in a rural, mid-western community transformed into a space for social protest.[1] A bedsheet proclaiming "SLUTWALK" hung from a residence hall. Students passing the sign signaled curiosity, disdain, and delight through gestures and facial expressions. Their varied reactions foretold the event's attendance of SlutWalk defenders and cynics. Shortly before two o'clock, a crowd of students and professors collected in the courtyard. Women and men in various states of undress adjusted to their nakedness, their anxious embarrassment evolving into brazen confidence. Holding a microphone, I interrupted the crowd's anticipation, signaling the event's start.[2] As I spoke, a group of students stationed on the balcony above the courtyard in protest of the event lowered their signs. As bagpipers began to play "Scotland the Brave," the crowd shifted forward energized with purpose. Carrying signs that read "Yes means yes!" and "Consent is sexy," the group trekked through campus chanting: "Blame the system not the victim!"

To appropriate Heather Jarvis and Sonya JF Barnett's claim from their TED talk, "The Spread of Infected Language," the SlutWalk phenomenon has gone viral.[3] It has infected personal, public, political, and professional conversations, while outbreaks of the protest continue to crop up. Recent actions by the federal government and major organizations like the National Football League (NFL) demonstrate the efficacy of SlutWalk publicity, indicating a growing awareness of the public impacts of sexual violence and rape.[4] According to outspoken feminist author, Jessica Valenti, "SlutWalks have become the most successful feminist action of the past 20 years."[5]

SlutWalks harness the vernacular of public and private to characterize rape (as an act of violence) and sex (as an act of desire) as mutually exclusive. Recasting the body as person instead of property, SlutWalks define rape as an act of violence on one's personhood for which the perpetrator should be held solely responsible. Rape is a *public* concern; it injures the person, impairing their civic subjectivity. While both sex and rape are *personal*, rape is public and political whereas sex is *private*. Thus, walkers also promote an argument of sexual positivity. (Women's) sexuality is not an indicator of (their) civic virtue and therefore not of public concern.

SlutWalks' antirape/prosex argument reveals a problematic tension generated by conflating the personal with the political in the progress toward gender equality. During the walks, SlutWalkers' bodies present a collage of images conveying idealized and deviant female sexuality (sometimes simultaneously). The illogic that women bear responsibility for being sexually harassed, assaulted, or raped—because their personal is political—is rendered explicit by the performative juxtaposition between an erotic feminine "other" and the proper "pure" woman. Bystanders are thus prompted to confront their own complicity in perpetuating rape culture by associating the body with property and women's sexuality with virtue.

It seems fitting to turn to counterpublic studies to explore the rhetoric of SlutWalks. Counterpublic studies provide a useful theoretical framework to describe public advocacy that attempts to transform the public sphere by altering the balance between the public and the private. According to Asen and Brouwer, "'Public' and 'private' are not fixed, content-specific categories that structure the public sphere prior to discourse. Rather, 'public' and 'private' emerge in social action and dialogue even as collectively held conceptions of each shape the conditions of their emergence."[6] Reflecting the trend within feminist advocacy, many counterpublic scholars have expanded and transformed the conditions of the public sphere to address an imbalance of power. However, SlutWalks appear to deviate from this tradition by narrowing the public while transforming the conditions of the private. SlutWalks seek to make apparent how distinctions between "public" and "private" have bolstered rape culture and offer an alterative conceptualization of privacy that recognizes and values individual difference to further progress gender equality.

To develop these claims, I first present a history of SlutWalks that includes an overview of rape culture, a brief history of the word "slut," and explanation for how slut shaming and victim blaming bolster an environment where sexual violence has become normalized. I then provide an overview of counterpublic studies, focusing specifically on the role of the private and its relation to the public sphere. Third, I argue that SlutWalks decouple the body from property and sexuality from morality by calling for an alternative model of privacy. I conclude with some considerations for how this analysis contributes to counterpublic studies.

History of SlutWalks and Rape Culture

In January 2011, a law enforcement officer in Toronto suggested women might "avoid dressing like sluts in order to not be victimized" during a crime prevention assembly at York University.[7] The comments especially resonated with Jarvis, a queer feminist activist, who stated: "We had just had enough. . . . It isn't about just one idea or one police officer who practices victim blaming, it's about changing the system and doing something constructive with anger and frustration."[8] Four months later, in April 2011, marchers protested the officer's statements in what would become the first "SlutWalk." Since then, SlutWalks have become an international phenomenon, with walks taking place on nearly every continent.

SlutWalks follow in the tradition of Take Back the Night rallies, which began as local protests in the 1970s and have since evolved into a formal organization.[9] Take Back the Night rallies work to bring public awareness and transform the national conversation around sexual violence by offering safe spaces for survivors to share their stories.[10] The tone is typically serious and reverent. In contrast, SlutWalks are inherently irreverent, and advocate positive sexuality in concert with contesting rape culture.[11] Further, unlike Take Back the Night, SlutWalks are "popping up in organic and often impromptu fashion in several countries, with no central office or network to help coordinate."[12] SlutWalks protest what is referred to colloquially as "rape culture" or "environments that support beliefs conducive to rape and increase[d] risk factors related to sexual violence."[13]

Rape culture is informed by gendered norms, and is evidenced by sexual assaults, the cultural phenomena of victim blaming and slut shaming, and institutional forms such as laws and policies that serve to impair women's agency in order to sustain their "morality." Constituted by conflating women's sexuality with civic virtue in an economic logic that treats the body as property, rape culture justifies the public policing of women's bodies through threats and violence.

Rape Culture: The Cyclical Nature of Slut Shaming and Victim Blaming

The use of "slut" as an indication of women's virtue has remained constant, even as the dominant meaning of the term has evolved. According to the Oxford English Dictionary, "slut" was first used in the fifteenth century to identify "a woman of dirty, slovenly, or untidy habits or appearance." In the sixteenth century, slut was coupled with sexuality, reflecting the cultural perception that women's (lack of) sexuality determined their virtue. But the term did not become part of the general vernacular until the twentieth century.[14] Today, a slut's dirty appearance is merely symbolic; any apparent sign of promiscuity may indicate a woman's deviant sexuality. Because promiscuity is dependent on cultural norms, it is highly variable and inconsistent between and among communities, cultures, and countries. However, coupling women's *civic* virtue with the *appearance of* her (a)sexuality is a consistent norm throughout most of the world's cultures.[15]

As a natural extension of this etymology, "slut shaming" refers to "the act of criticizing or insulting individuals for their perceived sexual availability, behavior, or history as a way to shame or degrade them."[16] This perception is shaped by norms that govern appearance and "normal" gender performance or "the mundane way in which the bodily gestures, movements, and styles of various kinds constitute the illusion of an abiding gendered self."[17] To be a woman is to perform societal expectations of femininity, two of which are dress and speech.

As a primary indicator of one's gender identity, dress has historically been a marker of one's social standing. In the United States during the nineteenth century, Torrens explains that fashion not only conveyed one's status but those characteristics associated with bourgeois gentility: manners, refinement, *virtue*.[18] This had particular resonance for women, as those qualities of "true womanhood"—submissiveness, domesticity, purity, piety— "were represented, reinforced, and enabled by fashionable dress."[19] As Ray points out, suffragists used their appearance, particularly dress, to engender their citizenship as particularly virtuous. In so doing, suffragists built their civic ethos upon norms governing feminine virtue.[20]

Conversely, appearance also signals a deficiency of virtue, warranting exclusion from participation in democratic publics. Where white middle-class women are pressured to adhere to a specific image of femininity, the bodies of women of color, working-class women, and some immigrant women are perceived to be always already impure because of their very appearance. According to Rogness and Foust, at the turn of the twentieth century, "feminine virtue was thus defined in the context of masculinity and Whiteness. The eugenics movement reinforced this relationship: the more pale and delicate a woman appeared, the more fit she was to produce healthy, moral children. Working-class, Black, and immigrant women, with their calluses and (naturally or suntanned) dark(ened) skin, conveyed degeneracy. They were the 'hypersexual' and 'feeble-minded' individuals targeted for (voluntary and involuntary) sterilization."[21] The image of the seducing black woman, or "jezebel," has expanded into a cacophony of slurs against black women, each reflecting deviant sexuality: welfare queen, gold digger, hoochie.[22] These slurs continue to be used to justify intimate, medical, and public violations of black women's bodies.[23] Thus, while white women may become sluts, women of color are always already sluts, determined solely by the appearance of their nonwhite skin. As a result, slut shaming is not uniformly experienced by all women but rather nuanced by race, class, sexuality, and nationality.

In addition to dress, voice has also been used as an indicator of woman's virtue, in ways that extend from the private to public and political spheres.[24] Gendered assumptions about speech have been grounded in the body. While men were affiliated with the mind and rationality, women were more closely associated with the body and emotion.[25] From its position outside of reason and civility, nineteenth-century women's public speech could be dismissed as promiscuous—deviant and potentially out of control.[26] Today, women's speech continues to be guided by narrow parameters determined by intersecting norms of gender, class, race, sexuality, and nationality. Women of color risk being stereotyped as the "angry black woman" or "spicy Latina" when expressing emotion. These stereotypes serve to warrant intimate partner violence in African American communities.[27]

Both speech and dress are tools for women to produce their gender and signal their (feminine) virtue. It matters not that she be sexually promiscuous, but that she has a *tendency* for promiscuity, evidenced through appearance (speech, dress, race, or ethnicity). Her virtue, then, is not determined by what she does but what she does not do (arouse man's desire).

Calling a woman's morality into question continues to have symbolic implications for her civic agency, as demonstrated by the Limbaugh/Fluke controversy. In the 2012 public debate around whether insurance companies should be mandated to cover prescription contraception, Rush Limbaugh attempted to undermine Sandra Fluke's congressional testimony, insinuating she was ethically impaired.[28] Limbaugh labeled Fluke a "slut" and "prostitute" and insisted that she broadcast herself having sex in exchange for the public paying for her contraception.[29] Fluke's guilt was in arguing for contraception coverage in a political forum. By simply uttering the word contraception, Fluke conjured up the idea of premeditated sexual intercourse, personifying sexual deviance.

In addition to damaging one's civic personhood, slut shaming can be characterized as bullying, particularly in a culture that associates women's sexuality with moral worth.[30] Vrangalova, Bukburg, and Rieger have found slut to be a form of social leprosy, as women are less likely to associate with a woman who has a reputation of being a slut.[31] Slut shaming thus encourages women to become hypervigilant about their bodies—who they associate with, how they use space, and how they appear outside the confines of their private spaces.

Slut shaming leads to victim blaming; it draws attention to a woman's indecent appearance or behavior, encouraging her to discipline herself before making further transgressions. As a form of cultural policing, slut shaming perpetuates the idea that a woman can protect herself against sexual assault if she dresses, acts, and speaks in a certain way. As a result, when a woman is assaulted, she is perceived as somehow complicit, or in some cases completely responsible, for the assault or rape because she did not take appropriate precautions.

Victim blaming captures the idea that victims should be held responsible for their oppression, rather than the perpetrator and/or the cultural and political institutions that facilitate that oppression.[32] Feminists have appropriated the term to refer to the act of blaming survivors for the sexual violence they experienced. As in slut shaming, victim blaming evokes gendered norms to assess whether or not the survivor is at fault and absolve the perpetrator of guilt. For example, in a recent Article 32 proceeding, the military equivalent of a civilian grand jury, a woman alleging sexual assault was interrogated to determine her complicity in the attack. She was asked whether she was wearing a bra or underwear and how wide she opened her mouth to perform oral sex.[33] The woman's choice in undergarments suggests *appearance* of *premeditated* intercourse while her oral sex technique conveys sexual proficiency. In other words, she provoked the attack because her previous actions led the perpetrator to think she was sexually promiscuous, and her apparent promiscuity indicated her standing invitation for sex. Such questions served to revictimize her, as defense counsel simultaneously questioned her sexual *and* discursive purity—her credibility as a sexual actor and as someone reporting a crime/seeking justice.

While feminine gender norms are used to assign guilt to victims, masculine gender norms are used to excuse or valorize men's sexual transgressions. Masculinity is associated with aggression, force, competition, and conquest.[34] Within this context, a man who pursues sex aggressively and persists even when the woman says "no" may be seen as merely following his masculine scripts, whereas a woman who says "no" is "playing hard to get."[35] For instance, a judge in a recent trial for the rape of a fourteen-year-old by her former teacher held the victim as responsible for her rape. The judge commented that the victim appeared "older than her chronological age" and was "as much in control of the situation" as the perpetrator.[36] Because portraying oneself as more "mature" transgresses the image of the young pure female, the judge wrongly assumed the young girl's apparent sexuality was synonymous with agency. Further, it is only *natural* for a grown man to desire and pursue a sexually active young woman. As evidence of the trauma victim blaming may have on survivors of sexual assault, the young woman committed suicide shortly after the trial.

Outside the courtroom, however, public opinion may prevail, even in cases where the rapist is convicted. For instance, in an interview for *Rolling Stone*, Serena Williams offered her thoughts on the Steubenville rape case, when a high school girl was gratuitously raped by two football players while their classmates looked on:[37] "I'm not blaming the girl, but . . . why was she that drunk where she doesn't remember? It could have been much worse. She's lucky."[38] Williams's comments reflect Valenti's criticisms of the purity myth. Valenti argues that "women and girls are the ones expected to carry the shame of the sexual crimes perpetuated against them. And that shame is a tremendous load to bear; because once you're labeled a slut, empathy and compassion go out the window. The word is more than a slur— it's a designation."[39] A woman may innocently lead a man on, but a slut is always already guilty. From the actual courtroom, to the "courtroom of public opinion," rape culture places the burden of proof upon victims.

Because boys and men are unable to check their virulent sexual drive, women must monitor their own bodies in order to avoid being assaulted.[40] Consequently, females are assumed to be complicit in those acts of sexual assault or rape that take place in private (what is typically referred to as "date or acquaintance rape") because of decisions they made regarding dress, speech, or physical location.[41] For example, while Mike Tyson was convicted for the rape of Desiree Washington, the public has continued to doubt whether Washington was legitimately raped and has held Washington publically accountable for the assault. Washington should have known better than to accompany Tyson to his hotel room at two o'clock in the morning because it was within Tyson's *nature* to be sexually aggressive.[42]

Combined, slut shaming and victim blaming constitute the rape culture protested by SlutWalks. Slut shaming conveys the evaluation of a woman's civic subjectivity by coupling her body (appearance, action) with moral virtue. A virtuous woman does not dress and act in ways that arouse a man's desire. If she does, she should be held accountable for the ensuing events. Victim blaming brings closure to slut shaming and evidences that women's deviant sexuality is, in fact, the catalyst for sexual assault and rape. As a result, women's sexuality becomes the public issue to police, and the cycle repeats.

From Public to Private: Where Counterpublic Studies and Feminist Advocacy Intersect

SlutWalks focus on the tension between the public and the private as a foundation of patriarchal logic. In this section, I review legal and colloquial uses of public and private as related to feminist advocacy then describe how this advocacy intersects with counterpublic studies. As I demonstrate, Slut-Walks harness the spirit of feminist advocacy and counterpublicity yet deviate from past trends that sought to widen the public sphere by making the personal political. SlutWalks instead argue that the scope of the public sphere should be narrowed and the conditions of the private sphere should be transformed.

Privacy is a repeated theme within US law and feminist public advocacy. In 1965, the Supreme Court determined that a married couple's choice to use contraception fell within a "zone of privacy" and declared Connecticut's ban on contraception for married couples unconstitutional.[43] Zone of privacy refers to recognizing citizens' decisional autonomy or the ability of an individual to make decisions without unjustified intrusion from the state.[44] This decision provided the foundation for the Supreme Court's decision in *Roe v. Wade* (1973). In both cases, privacy was attributed to decision making, suggesting "the Court seems to conceive of intimate relationships as entirely the product of personal choice, instead of as constitutive of the persons who participate in them."[45] So individuals are treated as self-contained agents, ascribed with freedom of choice in "private" matters (though history demonstrates how denying one's personhood led to denials of their right to privacy).

Outside law, colloquial uses of public and private have peppered arguments for and against women's equality for centuries. Feminist advocates have sought recognition for the ways that the "private" spaces of the home or workplace are publically and politically charged. Most recognized is the anthem "the personal is political" that resonated through the mid-twentieth-century surge for women's rights. The move to politicize the personal paved the way for legislation against sexual harassment and the recognition of marital rape. Politicizing the personal also drew attention to the varied ways women's experiences in the home and workplace were not separate and distinct from the public culture or the political gaze.[46]

The anthem recalled similar articulations of the public and private uttered in the rhetorics of free love at the turn of the twentieth century, when free love advocates drew attention to the ways that public, religious and political institutions infected women's private and intimate lives.[47] The mythical divide between the private and public has also been a long-standing focus in the advocacy of the working class and feminists of color who argue that privacy is both the cause and effect of privilege.[48] As middle- and upper-class white families portray the "American Dream" by cordoning off the home and workplace from intrusion by the public or state, privacy becomes a "right" to be protected. But if we peek behind the curtains, we find that the American Dream is only made possible by standing on the backs of working-class people and people of color.

The general trend in feminist advocacy, as evidenced by the above examples, is to *publicize* women's experiences and the ways that *public* (institutional and cultural) forces serve to impair or injure women, often in places hidden from shared scrutiny. By making them public, women's issues become *common* interest, rather than particular, generating opportunities for cultural or institutional change. To make the personal political responds to the historical discrediting, degrading, and delimiting of women's subjectivity via privacy or the private sphere (e.g., by articulating civic virtue to sexual purity).

Mainstream feminist advocacy in the United States shares public sphere theory's drive toward realizing democracy. Feminist groups have called attention to how the private has served as a tool for suppressing women's voices and justified violence against them. These groups have functioned as *counterpublics* or "parallel discursive arenas where members of subordinated social groups invent and circulate counter discourses to formulate oppositional interpretations of their identities, interests and needs."[49] Counterpublics emerge in response to perceived exclusionary discursive norms, like slut shaming and victim blaming, which result in some combination of subordination, marginalization, and resource disparities.[50]

Fraser argues that there are multiple, overlapping publics as opposed to one singular public sphere.[51] Pezzullo and Brouwer (writing separately) further demonstrate that multiple complementary and contradictory counterpublics may exist in relationship to dominant publics.[52] This nuanced lens reflects the variance across feminist advocacy. There is not, nor has there ever been, one singular feminist movement with a unified goal. Instead we may find associations of individuals who collect around a common issue, identity, location, or otherwise. For instance, Butler highlights both difference and commonality in her experience participating in a SlutWalk in Turkey: "I was on a march with a group of transgender women, queer activists, human rights workers and feminists, people who were both Muslim and secular, everyone objected to the fact that transgender women were being killed regularly on the streets of Ankara. So, what's the alliance that emerged? Feminists who had also been dealing with sexual violence on the street. Gay, lesbian, queer people, who are not transgender, but are allied because they experience a similar sense of vulnerability or injurability on the streets."[53] Butler articulates a common experience of vulnerability and threat, and the desire to protest those forces that generate those feelings—feelings that serve to delimit or punish access and use of public spaces, as much as they harm individuals in private.

Scholars generally agree that the progression toward equality in the public sphere relies on expanding the scope of what may be considered public or at least engaged and deliberated by the public. This suggests that inclusivity is contingent upon and evidenced by publicity. As per Benhabib, "All struggles against oppression in the modern world begin by redefining what had previously been considered private, nonpublic, and nonpolitical issues as matters of public concern, as issues of justice, as sites of power that need discursive legitimation."[54] Fraser similarly advocates for widening discursive contestation.[55] Even Asen values the expansion of discursive space, as it "would entail recognizing the potential for value conflicts in a pluralist society, and welcoming the adjudication of these conflicts through public engagement."[56]

The advocacy of SlutWalks contrasts this ideal. SlutWalks argue to *privatize* women's sexuality, reducing the scope of the public sphere. In so doing, they engage in a public negotiation of privacy. This prompts a turn to better understand the role that privacy may hold in the quest toward a better democracy.

In Habermas's explanation of the rise and fall of the bourgeois public sphere in the eighteenth and nineteenth centuries, he describes what appears to be an ideal democratic public: one composed of private citizens who collectively debate issues of common concern, generating public opinion, which influences political transactions.[57] The public sphere was made possible by bracketing one's singularities and identifying with the collective, public body. In order for one to bracket his or her singularities, however, one must first develop them. Habermas poses subjectivity as the prerequisite of the public and "subjectivity as the inner-most core of the private."[58]

Habermas describes two types of privacy. One related to private, economic interests, the other to the domestic and intimate functions of the home. Both were necessary for a well-functioning bourgeois public sphere. In the private intimate sphere, individuals generated their subjectivity by addressing each other through the medium of the letter. One became a subject in the act of the address, as both author and reader. Letters were written as private conversation and a public performance of that private conversation. The world of letters evolved into a literary outlet for people to experience private enjoyment but also the means to educate the masses on the appropriate and necessary conditions of the private, intimate sphere of the conjugal family *and* the private economy of property ownership. The private sphere thus reflected one's capacity to develop (proper) intimate relationships and consumption practices and conveyed the illusion that these relationships were immune from public or state interference.

Yet, Habermas never describes the private sphere as exclusive of the public. Instead, the public and the private relate more as a dialectic. The public stood in relation to the private, relying on certain conditions being met to ensure the democratic potential of the community. Balance was paramount.

Fraser and Warner offer more critical orientations of the private, underscoring how oppression is justified and maintained through distinctions between public and private. For instance, Fraser scrutinizes Habermas's focus on the private as "pertaining to private property in a market economy, and pertaining to intimate domestic or personal life, including sexual life."[59] Privacy is associated with the personal and/or familial; that which is personal or related to the family *may be* declared outside the scope of public concern, if one has the power to do so. For instance, during the Clarence Thomas confirmation hearings, "Thomas was enabled to declare key areas of his life 'private' and therefore off-limits," while Anita Hill was not afforded that same privilege.[60] As explained by Fraser, "the labeling of some issues and interests as 'private' limits the range of problems, and of approaches to problems, that can be widely contested in contemporary societies."[61] The private, thus, may be wielded as a patriarchal hammer to substantiate a person's status, character, and cultural currency.[62] Fraser's account of the use of public and private in the Thomas confirmation hearings demonstrate that what is "private" is constructed through public talk and served to reinforce Thomas's patriarchal privilege.[63]

Warner discusses how evocations of the public and private reflect and reinforce norms of gender and sexuality. The public and private are more than "abstract categories for thinking about law, politics, and economics. . . . They seem to be preconceptual, almost instinctual, rooted in the orientation of the body and common speech."[64] What is public is not only reflective of dominant interests but also evidences rules of decorum: "Just as feminists since Fanny Wright have found that to challenge male domination in public is to change both femininity and the norms of public behavior, lesbians and gay men have found that to challenge the norms of straight culture in public is to disturb deep and unwritten rules about the kinds of behavior and eroticism that are appropriate to the public."[65] Distinctions between the public and the private are felt viscerally and evoked to police that which is "aberrant." Even Habermas relays a normalized private sphere scripted by the dominant interests of the public sphere. Fraser and Warner echo feminist criticisms that the public/private divide has been a mere myth; it may exist as a privilege for certain classes, but for many, there has never been a sense of private. Women's bodies, for instance, are never really their own.[66]

Building from Fraser and Warner, Squires suggests that counterpublics may secure safe spaces in the form of enclaves where they may cultivate their public subjectivity. While counterpublics reflect those moments when the marginalized public engages with the public sphere, enclave publics hide "counterhegemonic ideas and strategies in order to survive or avoid sanctions, while internally producing lively debate and planning."[67] Chávez further explains that "activists use enclaves as the sites to invent rhetorical strategies to publically challenge oppressive rhetoric or to create new imaginaries for the groups and issues they represent and desire to bring into coalition."[68] Enclaves may thus replace a key function of the private by providing the means to generate public subjectivity through the development of alternative logics and modes of relating. However, enclaves are still *public* in the sense that they excise the individual from his or her particular uniqueness.

Throughout these conversations, scholars may scrutinize the characteristics of and relationship between the public and private spheres, but the intrinsic value of the spheres remains constant. However, in working toward reimagining the public sphere to account for its forces on the private, feminist activists may have thrown the balance into a full tilt. Shifting the discussion to a focus on the balance, Berlant warns that "the political public sphere has become an intimate public sphere."[69] In the intimate public sphere, citizenship is conditional, "produced by personal acts and values, especially acts originating in or directed toward the family sphere."[70] Where it was once necessary for minority groups to convince the wider public of the political nature of their personal experiences, the public has become hyperpersonalized as we turn to valuing the individual over the collective. This neoliberal ideal valorizes individualism as long as it progresses the values of the traditional family. One's choices, therefore, are *political*, but the consequences of those choices are *personal*.

Warner similarly warns that the mantra of twentieth-century feminist movements has metastasized because "'the personal is political' means not [only] that personal life could be transformed by political action but that politics should be personalized."[71] This reversal of the feminist dictum "has resulted in an anti-political nationalist politics of sexuality whose concern is

no longer what sex reveals about unethical power but what 'abnormal' sex/
reproduction/intimacy forms reveal about threats to the nation proper/the
proper nation."[72] In this sense, the public and private have become conflated. In the intimate public sphere, private values become the grounds to
legitimate public arguments, while personal choices become a hallmark of
privacy. As symbolic of their private values, or virtue, women's bodies have
become a critical issue for public deliberation and political legislation. To
secure the moral health of the nation, women's bodies must be prescribed
and punished. As a result, women's sexuality has been incorporated into
public debates about healthcare, welfare, education, poverty, and even the
national debt. Conversely, women's *choices* about their bodies and sexuality
have become radically individualized. Because they have choices, and the
freedom to choose, *they* are responsible for any consequences that result
from their choices.

McCarver similarly points out that, by politicizing the personal, oppression and choice have been wrongly perceived as being mutually exclusive.[73]
Building from Hirschman's identification of "choice feminism" in 2005,
McCarver explains that women's liberation has been reduced to the expansion of personal choice. However, the expansion of choice does not indicate the absence of oppression because choice always exists in a larger cultural context. Public culture shapes personal choices and the consequences
and discourse that result from those choices. In terms of rape culture, individuals have the choice on whether or not they wish to transgress gendered norms through dress, speech, or sexual behavior, but certain individuals will be held responsible for the consequences of those acts. For all
but heterosexual white men, these consequences fall on a continuum from
moral devaluation to rape. The mere threat of consequence serves as a cultural regulation.

This turn toward an intimate public sphere provides a framework for
understanding why SlutWalkers' messages deviate from previous trends in
feminist advocacy. In the move to politicize the personal, women's right to
privacy (what little right they held) has been seemingly abolished. Rape
may now be recognized as a crime, but it is women's sexuality standing trial.
It is at this juncture that SlutWalks intervene.

Counterpublicity of SlutWalks

SlutWalkers work to revise the public nature of sexual violence by dividing rape and sex into mutually exclusive categories. But rather than expanding the public sphere, SlutWalkers advocate the conditions of the pri-

vate sphere be transformed. Importantly, SlutWalkers do not simply call for women's right to privacy be recognized, for this would not address those private values that inform the resource disparities that shape the social and material conditions of women's lives; it might even cement those values by protecting them with a veil of privacy (as was previously the case, for instance, with spousal rape). Instead, SlutWalkers advance a vision of the private sphere that rejects the economic logic of the body as property. By recognizing the body as person, SlutWalkers characterize sexual desire as self-expression, which in turn, refines the public nature of rape as an act of violence on one's person, rather than property.

SlutWalks' advocacy of women's sexuality challenges those gender norms that have functioned to marginalize, subordinate, and justify the resource disparities that make up rape culture. Importantly, iterations of rape culture are diverse in both form and function. While SlutWalks embody coalitional politics, indicating a common constituency, walks contest both the local forms of oppression and the superstructure of patriarchy, evidencing a system of multiple, overlapping counterpublics. To narrow my analysis, I focus on the SlutWalk that took place at Monmouth College on April 6, 2013. As with any analysis of counterpublic(s), conclusions are offered tentatively and not meant for generalization. This bears particular import for an analysis of SlutWalks; the conclusions reached are not meant to be applied to SlutWalks as a transnational movement, nor reflect the dynamics of those walks that take place outside the United States.

While not all participants of the SlutWalk had prior knowledge of Constable Sanguietti's remarks correlating dress with assault, all had personally experienced the logic of choice implicit in his claims. Except for the recent influx of policies in education or private business that prohibit some styles of clothing, women are free to dress as they wish without direct legal consequence. Yet, as discussed earlier, choice does not indicate the absence of oppression. By centering choice, victims are held responsible for any negative consequences while systems of oppression remain overlooked. Thus, the rhetoric of choice invokes victim blaming; individuals are responsible for the consequences of *their* choices.

The SlutWalk protested rape culture through parodic performances of slut identities. Both women and men appropriated forms of dress that have been typically associated with promiscuity but intensified the norms' arbitrary nature through a combination of excess and irony. For example, at the start of the walk, four women stood topless, their nipples hidden by Xs created with opaque tape. Their appearance did not conform to traditional norms of feminine beauty: three wore glasses, one's hair was shorn, while another sported a short, "boyish" cut. By alluding to pasties, the tape Xs drew attention more to their purpose (to cover nipples) than "normal" function (to induce sexual desire, as in a striptease). However, not all SlutWalkers dressed provocatively. A man walked with his infant son as the baby held a sign reading "SLUTS UNITE." Both were conservatively dressed in fleece outerwear. The ironic juxtaposition of the baby boy and the sign evoked humor and questioned the tendency to evaluate some sexual intercourse as more acceptable, or even moral, than others.

Protesters also used emotive language combined with irony, such as "FUCK RAPE," or rhetorical questions: "This is what I was wearing, was I asking for it?" The rhetorical question aggressively prompted bystanders to come to terms with victim blaming by bearing witness to the assault. The placards carried by walkers further directed how bystanders should interpret the walker's dress, which ranged from everyday street clothes, like jeans and a T-shirt, or more conservative attire, producing incongruity between the myth that rape is the result of a woman seducing a man through her dress and the reality that a woman's appearance has nothing to do with why she was raped.

The combination of language and performance demonstrates how the protesters used their bodies as a medium. While some protesters used signage to frame observer's interpretation of their dress, others used their bodies as the sign. One walker, wearing a short shirt and bright red bra had marked her midsection, "If you want me, just ask! It doesn't ruin the mood . . . it turns me on!!!" By using their bodies, the protesters incited communicative intimacy. Bystanders were *required* to look, to gaze, to read, and respond. In this "Midwest nice" culture, bystanders may not only have felt exposed, and thus uneasy, but incapable of blaming the victim when face to face with a survivor.

In their protest, the SlutWalkers rendered explicit how the destructive force of rape culture is enforced by an ideology of choice and materialized through slut shaming and victim blaming. Slut shaming and victim blaming assume a woman's body is *property*. Decisional autonomy grants the freedom for individuals to own property, to do with their property as they please, and face the consequences for any damages incurred when the property is put at risk. The body as property is similarly reflected in Habermas's description of the private sphere as being composed of both the intimate and economic. By aligning the body with economic and consumption practices, the body becomes an object one has the right to own and is free to use as they please. This creates the illusion that one's *person*, or subjectivity, is separate and distinct from their body; the body is prosthetic. The body as property reflects a neoliberal ideology that emphasizes individualism and consumptive practices. Warner argues that this *disembodied subjectivity* empowers those whose particular identities align with the heteronormative ideal because their bodies have the capacity to be subtracted in entirety *without* impairing their civic subjectivity.[74] In contrast, the Monmouth SlutWalk empowered women as agents capable of consenting to sex but not responsible for bringing rape upon themselves, as the neoliberal intimate public sphere would have.

The SlutWalkers' parody of female sexuality called bystanders to recognize that women's lack of decisional autonomy has impaired their civic subjectivity *because* the body is associated as property. By using a possessive pronoun, a placard reading "MY PUSSY; MY CHOICE" relied on the bystander to assume the body is an object, a piece of property; but by coupling body with voice, the SlutWalker called the bystander to recognize the body as *person* rather than *property*. "MY PUSSY; MY CHOICE; MY BODY; MY VOICE" uses both parallel form and rhyme to fracture the belief that sex is a commodity. While the phrasing mimics possession, by juxtaposing the materiality of the body and "pussy" with that of action (choice, voice), sex is not something that one takes or gives, so much as an action performed, even a relation between people.[75]

In this argumentative twist, "slut" becomes an enacted, avowed persona. The private body is no longer a thing but evidence of what Cohen terms "inviolate personality." With this logical shift, privacy "protect[s] the processes of self-development and self-realization that go into identity formation."[76] By excising the economic from the private, the body can be reunited with the mind and reflect the whole person, instead of a relationship of causation—I am what I do with my body. This move attempts to redefine privacy from outside the neoliberal ideal. By rejecting the economic, the private is a realm of personal development, ever-mindful of how culture, economy, and institution may impact one's private or public life.

The SlutWalkers build from previous feminist advocacy that focuses on the unequal distribution of resources due to sex difference. Their nuanced argument imagines a private sphere that values individual difference and recognizes that difference in the development of the person, but as mentioned above, it elides the economic, which serves to trap the body in a culture of consumption. According to Cohen: "Reproductive freedom is fundamental also because what is at stake is a woman's ability to have control over her identity: her embodiment, her reformative processes, her life projects and her self-understandings are all at stake or would be if she were denied reproductive freedom."[77] As further emphasized by Cornell, the body and the literal space that the body occupies cannot be conflated with the psychic space of the person.[78] This is to say that the body, particularly a woman's body, is not a direct reflection of woman's virtue, as characterized by those heteronormative forces of the public sphere. Instead, a woman's person, and her public persona or civic subjectivity, should be that which *she* imagines. From this private space a woman may conjure up and express her person in a way that may recognize or rely on public culture but be free from the public scrutiny and evaluation warranted by neoliberalism.

SlutWalks' projection of positive sexuality reflects this nuanced valuation of the private. In so doing, an alternative relationality is imagined—one that recognizes and respects sexual difference and understands that difference as having no relationship to one's virtue. Under this new framework, privacy is issued to protect what Cornell refers to as the "imaginary domain": "The moral and psychic space we all need in order to come to terms with who we are as sexual beings and to have the chance to claim our own person as a sexuate being."[79] This new private sphere values the individual and recognizes the necessity of personal development for public subjectivity but rejects the pitfalls of neoliberalism by rejecting the economic: the body as person, not property.

Conclusion

As described above, counterpublic studies have emphasized the value of inclusion in the public sphere. This study of SlutWalks is not meant to invert this emphasis, but instead disturb our scholarly bias toward the value of inclusivity and public deliberation—particularly in relation to social change and "poetic world making" within an intimate public sphere. SlutWalks' emancipatory potential relies on transforming the conditions of the private sphere in a way that elides the pitfalls of neoliberalism. Particularly, SlutWalks expose how economic and moral characterizations of the private sphere continue to justify women's oppression, even after the "personal" was made "political." Expanding McCarver's observation to rape culture, women are granted the power of choice as long as they make the "right" choice—to control their sexuality, dress, and voices, without fundamentally disturbing men's ability to keep them in their places.

In this neoliberal era, where the personal has indeed become political, it is important to attend to privacy as much as publicity. In particular, scholars may focus on the force that the economic has had on civic subjectivities—a move that could further elucidate arguments posed by counterpublics like the SlutWalk. By conflating the body with property, the body is put at risk, and women's bodies too easily become the means to "moral" ends. The theoretical framework of counterpublic studies provides a useful tool to unpacking the force behind the public and the private, in its philosophical, theoretical, and material forms.

This turn suggests that scholars must remain vigilant in interrogating the relationship between the public and the private, inclusivity and exclusivity in their study of counterpublics. In the case study above, I explored how SlutWalkers responded to rape culture within a neoliberal context that emphasizes personal choice yet ignores the cultural and institutional forces that shape the consequences resulting from choice. As the private is in *relation* to the public, it is valuable for scholars to attend to the role that the private may have in progressing toward a more just and democratic society. Yet we should also be attentive to the neoliberal pitfalls that shade any discussion of the private. As SlutWalks demonstrate, publicity is not always an indication of progress, and inclusion may not always condition equality.

Notes

1. I am thankful for the feedback from my coeditors, Christina and Amy, and the reviewers from the University of Alabama Press. An earlier draft of this essay was presented at the 2013 ACA/AFA Summer Conference on Argumentation in Alta, Utah, and published as "The Personal Is Not Political: A Public Argument for Privatizing Women's Sexuality," in *Disturbing Argument*, ed. Catherine Palczewski (New York: Taylor and Francis, 2015), 123–28.

2. Knowing about my current research on SlutWalks, students in the Women's Studies senior capstone class (the event planners) asked me to provide a brief presentation on the history and purpose of SlutWalks.

3. Heather Jarvis and Sonya JF Barnett, "The Spread of Infected Language," TED video, 19:13, April 27, 2013, accessed August 10, 2016, www.youtube.com/watch?v=gifXXSGtPl8. Heather Jarvis and Sonya JF Barnett designed and coordinated the first SlutWalk that took place in Toronto, Canada, in April 2011.

4. See "The No More Project," www.nomore.org; and White House Council for Women and Girls, *Rape and Sexual Assault: A Renewed Call for Action* (January 2014): 5–6, accessed July 8, 2014, www.whitehouse.gov/sites/default/files/docs/sexual_assault_report_1–21–14.pdf pg 5–6.

5. Jessica Valenti, "Slutwalks and the Future of Feminism," *Washington Post*, last modified June 3, 2011, accessed August 10, 2016, www.washingtonpost.com/opinions/SlutWalks-and-the-future-of-feminism/2011/06/01/AGjB9LIH_story.html.

6. Robert Asen and Daniel C. Brouwer, introduction to *Counterpublics and the State*, ed. Asen and Brouwer (Albany: State University of New York Press, 2001), 10.

7. Ed Pilkington, "Slutwalking Gets Rolling after Cop's Loose Talk about Provocative Clothing: Lecture to Toronto Students Ignites Protests across

Canada and US at Culture of Blaming Rape Victims," *Guardian*, last modified May 6, 2011, accessed August 10, 2016, www.theguardian.com/world/2011/may/06/slutwalking-policeman-talk-clothing.

8. Laura Stampler, "SlutWalks Sweep the Nation," *Huffington Post*, last updated June 20, 2011, accessed August 10, 2016, www.huffingtonpost.com/2011/04/20/SlutWalk-united-states-city_n_851725.html.

9. "Take Back the Night," accessed July 8, 2014, www.takebackthenight.org.

10. Kendall Bitonte, "SlutWalk and Take Back the Night: Polar Opposites Same Cause," *USA Today*, last updated October 14, 2011, accessed August 10, 2016, college.usatoday.com/2011/10/14/slutwalk-and-take-back-the-night-polar-opposites-same-cause/.

11. Deborarah Tuerkeimer, "Slutwalking in the Shadow of the Law," *Minnesota Law Review* 4 (April 2014): 1456.

12. Allie Grasgreen, "'SlutWalks' Attract Attention, Controversy Internationally," *USA Today*, last updated October 5, 2011, accessed August 10, 2016, usatoday30.usatoday.com/news/education/story/2011–10–05/slutwalk/50670972/1.

13. Ann Burnett, Jody L. Mattern, Liliana L. Herakova, David H. Kahl, Jr., Cloy Tobola, and Susan E. Bornsen, "Communicating/muting Date Rape: A Co-cultural Theoretical Anaylsis of Communication Factors Related to Rape Culture on a College Campus," *Journal of Applied Communication Research* 37 (2009): 466.

14. Kathryn Westcott, "Why Is the Word 'Slut' So Powerful?" BBC, last updated May 9, 2011, accessed August 10, 2016, www.bbc.co.uk/news/magazine-13333013.

15. Joetta L. Carr, "The SlutWalk Movement: A Study in Transnational Feminist Activism," *Journal of Feminist Scholarship* 4 (Spring 2013): 26.

16. LiJia Gong and Alina Hoffman, "Sexting and Slutshaming: Why Prosecution of Teen Self-Sexters Harms Women," *Georgetown Journal of Gender and Law* 2 (2012): 580.

17. Judith Butler, *Gender Trouble* (New York: Routledge, 1999), 179.

18. Kathleen Torrens, "Fashion as Argument: Nineteenth Century Dress Reform," *Argumentation and Advocacy* 36, no. 2 (1999): 78.

19. Ibid., 79.

20. Angela G. Ray, "The Rhetorical Ritual of Citizenship: Women's Voting as Public Performance, 1868–1875," *Quarterly Journal Of Speech* 93, no. 1 (February 2007): 1–26.

21. Kate Zittlow Rogness and Christina R. Foust, "Beyond Rights and Virtues as Foundation for Women's Agency: Emma Goldman's Rhetoric of Free Love," *Western Journal of Communication Studies* 75, no. 2 (March/April 2011): 153.

22. Rachel Griffin, "Gender Violence and the Black Female Body: The Enduring Significance of 'Crazy' Mike Tyson," *Howard Journal of Communications* 24, no. 1 (January–March 2013): 71–94.

23. Ibid., 77–78.

24. For a more thorough historical account of how and why women have

been punished for how they use their voice, see Kathleen Hall Jamison, *Beyond the Double Bind: Women and Leadership* (Oxford: Oxford University Press, 1995).

25. Michael Warner, *Publics and Counterpublics* (New York: Zone Books: 2002). For how these norms have influenced women's speech styles in the United States, see Karlyn Kohrs Campbell, *Man Cannot Speak for Her: A Critical Study of Early Feminist Rhetoric*, vol. 1 (Westport, CT: Praeger, 1989).

26. Susan Zaeske, "The 'Promiscuous Audience' Controversy and the Emergence of the Early Woman's Rights Movement," *Quarterly Journal of Speech* 81, no. 2 (1995): 197.

27. Tameka Gillum, "Exploring the Link between Stereotypic Images and Intimate Partner Violence in the African American Community," *Violence against Women* 8 (2002): 64–86.

28. Gong and Hoffman, "Sexting and Slut Shaming," 581.

29. John Wilson, "Rush's 53 Smears against Sandra Fluke," Daily Kos, last updated March 4, 2012, accessed August 10, 2016, www.dailykos.com/story/2012/03/04/1070884/-Rush-s-52-Smears-Against-Sandra-Fluke#.

30. Gong and Hoffman, "Sexting and Slut Shaming."

31. Zhana Vrangalova, Rachel Bukburg, Gerulf Rieger, "Birds of a Feather? Not When It Comes to Sexual Permissiveness," *Journal of Social and Personal Relationahips* 31, no. 1 (February 2014): 93–113.

32. William Ryan, *Blaming the Victim* (New York: Vintage Books, 1976).

33. Ruth Marcus, "In Navy Rape Case, Defense Lawyers Go Wild," *Washington Post*, last updated September 5, 2013, accessed August 10, 2016, www.washingtonpost.com/opinions/ruth-marcus-in-navy-rape-case-defense-lawyers-go-wild/2013/09/05/2c729520-1647-11e3-a2ec-b47e45e6f8ef_story.html.

34. Robert Connell, *Masculinities*, (Berkeley: University of California Press, 1995); Patricia Martin and Robert Hummer, "Fraternities and Rape on Campus," *Gender and Society* 3 (1989): 457–73; Peggy Sanday, *Fraternity Gang Rape* (New York: New York University Press, 1990); Martin D. Schwartz and Walter DeKeseredy, *Sexual Assault on the College Campus* (Thousand Oaks, CA: SAGE Publications, 1997); Diana Scully, *Understanding Sexual Violence* (Boston: Unwin Hymin, 1990).

35. Charlene Muehlenhard and L. C. Hollabaugh, "Do Women Sometimes Say No When They Mean Yes?" *Journal of Personality and Social Psychology* 54, no. 5 (1988): 872–79.

36. Jessica Chasmar, "Ex-Montana Teacher Gets 30 Days for Rape of Student Who Later Killed Herself," *Washinton Times*, last updated August 28, 2013, accessed August 10, 2016, www.washingtontimes.com/news/2013/aug/28former-montana-teacher-gets-30-days-rape-student-w/.

37. Juliet Macur and Nate Schweber, "Rape Case Unfolds on Web and Splits City," *New York Times*, last updated December 16, 2012, accessed August 10, 2016, www.nytimes.com/2012/12/17/sports/high-school-football-rape-case-unfolds-online-and-divides-steubenville-ohio.html.

38. Stephen Rodrick, "Serena Williams: The Great One" *Rolling Stone*, last

updated June 18, 2013, accessed August 10, 2016, www.rollingstone.com/culture/news/serena-williams-the-great-one-20130618?page=4.

39. Jessica Valenti, "In Rape Tragedies, the Shame Is Ours," *Nation*, last updated April 17, 2013, accessed August 10, 2016, www.thenation.com/article/173911/rape-tragedies-shame-ours.

40. It is worth noting that norms of masculine and feminine sexuality create the illusion that women cannot be the perpetrators of sexual violence and men cannot be the victims of sexual violence. This has devastating effects for the GLBTQI community. To report a same-sex rape may serve to reinforce the image of the hypersexual male homosexual or be excused outright with the assumption that women do not rape, and men cannot be raped.

41. Shana Maier, "The Complexity of Victim-Questioning Attitudes by Rape Victim Advocates: Exploring Some Gray Areas," *Violence against Women* 18 (2012): 1415.

42. Griffin, "Gender Violence."

43. Griswold v. Connecticut, 381 U.S. 479 (1965).

44. Jean Cohen, "Democracy, Difference, and the Right of Privacy," in *Democracy and Difference*, ed. Seyla Benhabib (Princeton, NJ: Princeton University Press, 1996), 198.

45. Cohen, "Democracy, Difference," 196.

46. Consciousness-raising groups fortified women's recognition that their experiences were not unique to them but rather part of a collective experience.

47. Linda Horwitz, Donna Kowal, and Catherine H. Palczewski, "Women Anarchists and the Feminine Ideal: Voltairine de Cleyre, Emma Goldman, and Lucy Parsons," in *The Rhetoric of the Nineteenth Century Reform*, ed. Martha Soloman Watson and Thomas Burkholder (East Lansing: Michigan State University Press, 2008); Rogness and Foust, "Beyond Rights and Virtues."

48. Patricia Hill Collins, *Black Feminist Thought* (New York: Routledge, 2000); Combahee River Collective, "A Black Feminist Statement," in *This Bridge Called My Back*, ed. Cherie Moraga and Gloria Anzaldua (Berkeley: Third Woman Press, 2002).

49. Nancy Fraser, "Rethinking The Public Sphere: A Contribution to the Critique of Actually Existing Democracy" in *Habermas and the Public Sphere*, ed. Craig Calhoun (Cambridge: Massachusetts Institute of Technology Press, 1993), 123.

50. Daniel C. Brouwer, "Communication as Counterpublic," in *Communication as . . . Perspectives on Theory*, ed. G. J. Shepherd, J. St. John, and T. Striphas (Thousand Oaks, CA: SAGE Publications, 2006); Fraser, "Rethinking the Public Sphere"; Warner, *Publics and Counterpublics*.

51. Fraser, "Rethinking the Public Sphere."

52. Daniel C. Brouwer, "Counterpublicity and Corporeality in HIV/AIDS Zines," *Critical Studies in Media Communication* 22, no. 5 (2005): 351–71; Pheadra C. Pezzullo, "Resisting 'National Breast Cancer Awareness Month': The Rhe-

toric of Counterpublics and Their Cultural Performances," *Quarterly Journal of Speech* 89, no. 4 (2003): 345–65.

53. Kyle Bella, "Bodies in Alliance: Gender Theorist Judith Butler on the Occupy and SlutWalk Movements," *truth-out.org*, last updated December 15, 2011, www.truth-out.org/news/item/5588:bodies-in-alliance-gender-theorist-judith -butler-on-the-occupy-and-SlutWalk-movements.

54. Seyla Benhabib, "Models of Public Space: Hannah Arendt, the Liberal Tradition, and Jurgen Habermas," in *Habermas and the Public Sphere*, ed. Craig Calhoun (Cambridge: Massachusetts Institute of Technology Press, 1991): 84.

55. Fraser, "Rethinking the Public Sphere."

56. Rober Asen, "Ideology, Materiality, and Counterpublicity: William E. Simon and the Rise of a Conservative Counterintelligentsia," *Quarterly Journal of Speech* 95, no.3 (2009): 282.

57. Jürgen Habermas, *The Structural Transformation of the Public Sphere: An Inquiry into a Category of Bourgeois Society*, trans. Thomas Burger and Frederick Lawrence (Cambridge: Massachusetts Institute of Technology Press, 1989).

58. Ibid., 49.

59. Ibid., 131.

60. Nancy Fraser, "Sex, Lies, and the Public Sphere: Some Reflections on the Confirmation of Clarence Thomas," *Critical Inquiry* 18, no. 3 (1992): 599.

61. Fraser, "Rethinking the Public Sphere."

62. Mary F. Rogers, "Clarence Thomas, Patriarchal Discourse and Public/ Private Spheres," *Sociological Quarterly* 38, no. 2 (1998): 289–308.

63. Warner, *Publics and Counterpublics*, 52.

64. Ibid., 23.

65. Ibid., 24–25.

66. Drucilla Cornell, *At the Heart of Freedom: Feminism, Sex, and Equality* (Princeton, NJ: Princeton University Press, 1998), 234.

67. Catherine R. Squires, "Rethinking the Black Public Sphere: An Alternative Vocabulary for Multiple Public Spheres," *Communication Theory* 12, no. 4 (2002): 448.

68. Karma R. Chávez, "Counter-public Enclaves and Understanding the Function of Rhetoric in Social Movement Coalition-Building," *Communication Quarterly* 59, no. 1 (2011): 3.

69. Lauren Berlant, *The Queen of America Goes to Washington City: Essays on Sex and Citizenship* (Durham, NC: Duke University Press, 1997): 4.

70. Ibid., 5.

71. Warner, *Publics and Counterpublics*, 34.

72. Berlant, *The Queen of America*, 178.

73. Virginia McCarver, "The Rhetoric of Choice and 21st Century Feminism: Online Conversations about Work, Family, and Sarah Palin," *Women's Studies in Communication* 34, no. 1 (2011): 20–41.

74. Michael Warner, "The Mass Public and the Mass Subject," in *Habermas*

and the Public Sphere, ed. Craig Calhoun (Cambridge: Massachusetts Institute of Technology Press, 1993), 377–401.

75. Thomas M. Miller, "Toward a Performance Model of Sex," in *Yes Means Yes*, ed. Jaclyn Friedman and Jessica Valenti (Berkeley: Seal Press, 2008), 29–42.

76. Cohen, "Democracy, Difference," 202.

77. Ibid., 207.

78. Drucilla Cornell, *The Imaginary Domain: Abortion, Pornography, and Sexual Harassment* (New York: Routledge, 1995), 8.

79. Cornell, *At the Heart of Freedom*, 230.

7

Against Equality

*Finding the Movement in Rhetorical Criticism
of Social Movements*

Karma R. Chávez with Yasmin Nair and Ryan Conrad

Against Equality (AE) is a publishing and arts collective and digital archive designed to "reinvigorate the queer political imagination with fantastic possibility."[1] Started in 2009, Ryan Conrad and Yasmin Nair created the collective and archive to challenge the mainstream gay and lesbian rights movement. As a longtime critic of the politics of leading and mainstream gay and lesbian rights organizations such as the Human Rights Campaign (HRC) and the National Gay and Lesbian Taskforce (NGLTF), after meeting Conrad during a campus visit I organized for him in April 2011, I asked to join the AE collective later that year. I have since been an active collective member by archiving materials, writing and presenting original critique from the perspective of the collective, engaging in dialogue and debate as a collective representative, and giving interviews to media outlets.

As a queer Chicana feminist rhetorical critic of social activism and protest, this relationship bridges my academic training and interests with my political commitments. Joining AE also helped me to develop my own answer to Mitchell's important question: "Where is the social movement in rhetorical criticism of social movements?"[2] Mitchell's response advocates for what he calls "public argument action research" (PAAR), which puts reflexivity front and center, as scholars are called to reflect upon the status of their scholarship in relation to the movements about which they write. In so doing, scholars are asked to enter into engagement with those involved in movement activity outside the academy, moving between analysis and action. Mitchell centers the work of one media critic who uses his knowledge to engage in direct activism on behalf of the cause about which he also writes as an academic. In Mitchell's depiction, the academic critic is the primary agent of activism who intervenes in the social and political dynamic single-handedly.

This chapter provides an additional answer to Mitchell's question and

builds upon the broader "activist turn" identified in communication studies.[3] Namely, another way to locate the *movement* in the study of social
movement is to enter existing *collective* spaces—whether the spaces are counterpublics, part of movement, or something defined differently—in order
to contribute to a shared political mission using the skills of a rhetorical
critic to collaboratively create rhetoric.[4] This kind of engagement differs
from what Mitchell describes as it decenters the agency of the individual
scholar by emphasizing coalitional agency and blurs the lines between the
"everyday" and professional critic and vernacular and institutional rhetoric.[5]
In the specific case of my involvement with AE, it also challenges the way
queer rhetorical scholars have characterized queer movement, confronting
the status of this scholarship in relation to movement. Thus, such engagement encourages scholars of movement to allow their scholarly position
and their studies of a particular social movement to be challenged, shaped,
and reconfigured through an intimate and sustained connection with activist collectives.

Importantly, I do not study AE and this is not a study of AE. I am a
queer rhetorical critic of social movement who is a part of a queer activist
collective that understands itself as a part of a long lineage of queer social
movement and agitation. Being a part of AE has greatly informed how I
understand movement activity and also the role of the scholar who studies queer movement and activism. In this chapter, I begin with some background information on the AE collective. Next, I describe my role in relation to the collective and academia within the context of the "activist turn."
I then delineate how my engagement with AE provides one answer to the
question of how to find the movement in the rhetorical criticism of queer
social movement.

Against Equality

The name "Against Equality" is meant to jar you when you hear it. The
name calls attention to how the contemporary gay and lesbian rights movement has positioned "equality" in the most narrow, normative, and liberal
terms: equality is gays and lesbians being able to be included in or protected by the institutions of marriage, military, and the prison industrial
complex (through hate crime legislation) just like straight people. If this
is what equality is, then the AE collective is against it. Although Nair and
Conrad, along with other radical queer activists, had long loathed the focus
and power of the mainstream movement, the specific catalyst for AE occurred in mid-2009 after Maine's governor John Baldacci signed into law
the right to same-sex marriage. Opponents almost immediately petitioned

to put a referendum, Question 1, on the November ballot in order to over-turn the law. Despite that most LGBT-identified people in Maine, a very poor and rural state, cited economic concerns and health care as priorities above marriage, the national marriage equality movement saw Maine as an important fight.[6] Over the next several months, more than $5 million was poured into the battle to defeat Question 1. Meanwhile, as Conrad experi-enced firsthand due to his work at a homeless youth shelter, money for ser-vices like the one his organization provided was scarce. If marriage equality was designed to help all LGBT people, why was it seemingly taking vital services from the most vulnerable in the community?

Conrad vented his anger in a blog he titled "Against Equality." He ex-plained in concrete terms the devastating impacts of the mainstream move-ment's agenda for most queer people, using the situation in Maine as his case study. Shortly thereafter, Nair, a Chicago-based writer, discovered Con-rad's blog, and the two began communicating online. They realized that even as so many queer people despised the mainstream "equality" agenda, there seemed to be few other options. Many LGBT people and allies simply accept that issues such as achieving marriage rights, military inclusion, and stronger hate crime laws create equality for LGBT people. The two decided that AE should become something more than a blog. Building on a long history of radical queer activism in the United States, they saw AE as a way to directly and playfully revitalize the queer political imagination.[7] Since that time, AE has developed into a digital archive and a publishing and arts collective committed to providing an important response to the main-stream gay and lesbian rights movement and also to cultivating a viable po-litical alternative to it.

At the time of this writing, five people, currently spread across the United States and Canada, comprise the Against Equality collective. We are not a 501(c)3 nonprofit organization, so as not to be required to craft our agenda according to the objectives of foundation funders.[8] We have never all been at the same physical place at the same time, and we have not all met each other face to face. The way we found each other is fairly mundane, with Conrad and Nair at the center of our different introductions. Conrad and Alexandra Silverthorne went to college together, Deena Loeffler met Con-rad at an Against Equality presentation, and she and Silverthorne happen to be neighbors. I encountered Nair during a phone interview for my dis-sertation research at the insistence of my professor, H. L. T. Quan, and years later we met in person. And as stated above, Nair and Conrad met through online politics. The five of us play different roles with Conrad, Nair, and me comprising the more public face of the collective—doing media interviews, giving public presentations, and writing essays and commen-

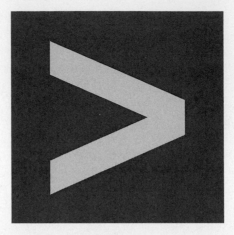

Figure 7.1. "Against Equality Logo"; by
Ryan Conrad; used with permission of
Against Equality

Figure 7.2. "Against Equality Button"; by
Ryan Conrad; used with permission of
Against Equality

taries; and Loeffler and Silverthorne dealing with the behind-the-scenes
work—copy editing, web spinning, and accounting. We make all decisions
collaboratively.

AE produces intellectual and artistic work and archives a rich history of
queer critique of the politics of inclusion and normalization. The original
critique can be found in our various forms of cultural production, perhaps

Figure 7.3. "Against Equality Button"; by Ryan
Conrad; used with permission of Against Equality

most notably Conrad's spoof design of the HRC's blue and yellow equal
sign logo—the blue and yellow "greater than" sign logo (fig. 7.1).

Additionally, AE held two postcard contests, inviting artists to submit
designs that critique the mainstream gay and lesbian movement in creative
ways. AE then mass-produced the postcards. AE also developed a collection of buttons: one with the greater than sign, another that is a citation of
Gran Fury's poster with the pink triangle that proclaims "Silence = Death,"
and declares "Marriage = Death" (fig. 7.2), and a third which is a citation of
the logo Nancy Reagan used while declaring "Just Say No to Drugs," which
says, "Just Say No to Marriage" (fig. 7.3). We have also put the last logo onto
reusable tote bags. The choice to make these particular objects builds on a
history of activist art—branding objects that are easy to carry, distribute,
and exchange. These objects easily draw attention by citing previous images
that may be familiar to viewers or interlocutors, further provoking conversations about the politics informing them.

Additionally, using AE's self-created publisher, Against Equality Press,
Conrad edited three pocket-sized books. Each of these books contains archival material housed in the AE digital archive accompanied by an original introduction by an invited thinker/activist. The books pertain to the
three themes AE critiques in the mainstream movement and feature the
cover art of artist Chris Vargas. The titles include *Against Equality: Queer
Critiques of Gay Marriage*, a book that argues against the gay and lesbian

rights movement's emphasis on marriage. This book suggests, among other things, that marriage is an exclusionary and conservative capitalist institution of the state, one that contends people should only achieve benefits like health care and social security through this institution. The argument in this book also emerges from a feminist critique of the power imbalances imbedded in the institution of marriage, noting that relationships of dependence create the conditions for the person with more power to take advantage of the other. *Against Equality: Don't Ask to Fight their Wars!* is a critique of the liberal politics of inclusion surrounding gays' and lesbians' ability to openly serve in the military. AE maintains that the push for open service functions to justify US imperialism abroad, as well as the racism, sexism, homophobia, and transphobia that plague, and will continue to plague, the military. The third in the trilogy, *Against Equality: Prisons Will Not Protect You*, critiques the mainstream movement's emphasis on hate crime legislation as a means for protecting LGBT populations. Hate crime legislation not only props up the prison industrial complex by adding tougher penalties to sentences, but queer people, especially queer people of color and poor people, are among those most likely to be targeted by law enforcement for arrest and harassment. Prisons are places where queer people are very likely to be subjected to violence. Supporting these institutions then does not protect queer people. While it is possible that an academic or popular press would have picked up these books (the anarchist press, AK Press published a volume of the collections with an original introduction in 2014 called *Against Equality: Queer Revolution, Not Mere Inclusion*), the decision to initially self-publish was a strategic one, both to speed up the process of publication and also to have more control over form and content. The primary reason for publishing books, even though they are almost entirely made up of already published and available material, was also strategic, as a way to create access for rural and incarcerated audiences who have no access to the Internet (we provide the books free to any prisoner who asks).

We actively look for materials to include in our digital archive such as blog posts, commentaries, interviews, debates, or digital art forms. Occasionally, people also send us materials to consider. Many of these materials are contemporary, but we also include older materials that we digitize. The archive functions to preserve materials that demonstrate that an alternative to normative and inclusionary politics exists and has always existed within queer communities. Each object included in the archive is reviewed by the entire collective, discussed, and then added. As suggested above, the last part of our project involves public commentary and presentations, including writing for various academic and activist outlets, giving interviews for publications and radio programs, and presenting our perspectives at universities and an array of community venues. These writings and presentations are sometimes extemporaneous and other times scripted, depending on the audience, and regard our critiques of marriage, military, and hate crime legislation.[9]

The Queer Rhetorical Critic as Activist

Studies of LGBT and queer movement in the United States have increasingly emerged in the field of rhetoric since the 1990s.[10] For the most part, these studies have been conducted from the perspective of the scholar as an observer and critic, in the approach similar to most other studies of the rhetoric of social movement. In other words, while the authors may be participants in the movement or protest they write about, their scholarship is not explicitly activist in orientation. Most queer movement studies are not examples of PAAR. Similarly, very little queer rhetorical scholarship has taken up what Frey and Carregee call "communication activism," where the scholar as activist is first a communication scholar who then uses the tools of the scholarly discipline of communication in the service of various activist pursuits. In this kind of communication activism, scholars immerse "themselves in the stream of human life, taking direct vigorous action in support of or opposition to a controversial issue for the purpose of promoting social change and justice."[11] Frey and others including rhetoric and cultural studies scholars like Dana Cloud, Robert Cox, Danielle Endres, Stephen Hartnett, Shane Moreman, Phaedra Pezzullo, Michelle Rodino-Colocino, and Omar Swartz have been at the forefront of advocating for the necessity of connecting activism, research, and written/performance scholarship.[12] The approaches to research activism vary but often involve either scholars using their research skills to help a community achieve a shared goal or scholars who research in a particular area (e.g., labor activism or prison activism) also participating in actions about those issues.

This type of scholarship, like PAAR, often characterizes the scholar, who is also an activist, as the most agentic person in the narrative. Meanwhile any nonacademic actors who may have been laboring alongside the academic, challenging her/him, or simply doing parallel work in a completely separate sphere, are relegated to the background. Also, as Frey and Carragee write in their introduction to the first volume of *Communication Activism*, there is a distinction between "third-person-perspective studies," where scholars study communication activism, and "first-person-perspective studies," where "researchers want to get in the stream and affect it in some significant ways."[13] Even the phrase "first person" suggests a singular agent who is the subject initiating action. Certainly, the three volumes of *Communication Activism* reveal that a single scholar, or in some instances groups of scholars, are in fact the agents of change within this approach. I do not intend to dismiss or minimize the importance of this sort of work. The work I have done with AE simply does not conform to this paradigm.

Instead of entering this activist space as academic-expert with my own objectives to accomplish, or writing only from a third-person perspective, my work with AE is collaborative in a different way. I have a valuable skill set as researcher and a rhetorical critic, but I am no more equipped (and often far less equipped) than my activist colleagues to make decisions and address our shared concerns. Queer and feminist theories necessarily emerge from dialogue among activists and academics and are least relevant to social justice projects when developed from the top down. For this reason as a queer rhetorical critic who is also a queer activist, I have chosen to shed as much of the jacket of expert as I can in order to share as an equal partner, learn, and use my specific skill set only as needed. This privileging of coalitional agency actively works against the perspective of many non- or marginally academic activists (marginally because they may have advanced degrees or do adjunct teaching but are not full-time, tenured, or tenure-track faculty) who perceive academics as arrogant and unwilling to genuinely collaborate. It also displaces academia and academics as the primary site and producer of knowledge.

Finding the Movement in the Rhetorical Criticism of Queer Social Movement

I turn my attention to how collaborating as a part of a queer activist collective has helped me to locate the movement in the rhetorical criticism of social movement. The movement speaks back to the critic. This speaking back is important.

As a publishing collective and archive, AE does not map easily onto existing understandings of queer movements or counterpublics in rhetorical scholarship. Both Slagle and McCann contend that an ideological rift exists within what McCann terms the LGBTQ rights movement.[14] Writing about the status of gay and lesbian liberation and queer movement in the 1980s and 1990s, Slagle contends that there are two factions: the gay and lesbian movement, which champions identity politics and inclusion, and the queer movement, which advocates a politics of difference. Writing about twenty-first-century movements, McCann updates Slagle's thesis, noting that what distinguishes a queer counterpublic from a mainstream LGBT one is that the former represents "a corporeal politics of desire," while the latter reflects "corporate politics of prudence."[15] Further, McCann contends that whereas the mainstream prefers traditional political channels, queer activists favor agitational politics. However, both McCann and Slagle suggest that ultimately both queer and mainstream movements or counterpublics can be encapsulated, at least in part, by a politics of inclusion. Rather than showing how Queer Nation strategically used the concept of the nation to challenge the idea of nationalism, Slagle suggests that Queer Nation "has re-conceptualized the notion of nationalism to *include* queerness" (emphasis mine).[16] Similarly, McCann claims that both the groups advocating for inclusionary politics using conventional political channels *and* the radical queer activists, who challenge the mainstream by using embodied, agitational politics, can be included within something called "the LGBTQ rights movement," a designation that in itself suggests a politics of inclusion through emphasizing rights (over say, justice). AE rejects such theses and is indiscernible within these characterizations.

The kind of queer critique that AE makes and the kind of activism it seeks are not easily located within the framework of a LGBTQ social movement or counterpublic as conceived by McCann and Slagle, given that they, and other scholars in the field of rhetoric including myself,[17] have regarded these movements in relation to nation-states or other state actors alone. The assumption that queer activism can be collapsed into rights-based struggle is dubious. Rights and the imagined human who possesses said rights are a part of the structural formations that AE critiques. For example, AE's strong stance against the military industrial complex and Western imperialism led AE to a position against the repeal of the Don't Ask, Don't Tell (DADT) military policy. Many advocates of the repeal argued that the question of US imperialism and the question of open service should be addressed separately as both are matters of human or equal rights. Such advocates maintained that anyone who wants to serve should have the right to do so openly at the same time that one can be against US military interventions in places around the globe. In 2012, AE wrote:

> We understand this as a liberal perspective which suggests that any move in the direction of inclusion is a positive one, and we realize the profound affective (and for members of the military, the material) impulse for espousing it. We vehemently disagree with this position. The DADT repeal, the activism before it, and the celebration after it, reflect mainstream gay and lesbian people's acceptance and active

promotion of militarism as a mechanism for national belonging. Not only does this then put gay and lesbian people in the position of accepting state violence as the conduit for their belonging, but it also reinforces the ways in which certain gay and queer subjectivities are taken up in the name of imperialisms, as countries like the U.S. now apply foreign policy pressure in the name of "gay rights."[18]

In this statement, it is clear that AE does not advocate through a discourse of rights nor is it promoting this kind of national inclusion for queers. AE's work exceeds the boundaries that have been placed on queer activism by scholars who write about them when we (scholars) locate this work within a rights-based and nation-based framework. My involvement with AE has shifted my own characterizations in my scholarship as I have built new forms of queer analysis alongside the collective that account for expanded understanding of queer movements and counterpublics.[19] AE's critique has further challenged binary oppositions and normativities that inform the rhetorical criticism of social movement and counterpublics more generally.

The Critique of Binaries and Academic Norms

Concerns over rhetoric's status in relation to other discourse genres have often placed rhetoric scholars in a defensive position. We often feel compelled to legitimate our scholarly work against the likes of philosophy and literature.[20] Ingraham asks: "What would it mean, then, to resolve the status tensions of rhetorical studies or other disciplines burdened with accommodating both their marginality and the authority of their pervasiveness? How can intellectuals . . . become more public, and how can the public become more intellectual? How can vernacular and specialized language effectively coexist in the same voice?"[21] Ingraham's question is akin to Mitchell's call for PAAR, and both intervene in two of the legitimating distinctions upheld in much rhetorical criticism, including within studies of social movements and counterpublics: everyday versus professional criticism and institutionalized/specialized versus vernacular rhetoric.

AE's "modality," or manner for "crafting publicity," strategically intercedes in a number of these binary logics and norms.[22] As Conrad notes in an interview for the journal *American Quarterly*, "the separation between intellectual production and political organizing seems dubious at best—most folks I met on tour were critically engaged with both."[23] Nair insists "'action' is a form of analysis—that action is always ideological."[24] AE believes that the distinctions between the different domains of action or even expertise are mostly fictional. At a philosophical level, AE insists on challenging these distinctions that are upheld in both academic and activist communities by regarding its work as both academic and activist, its critique as both practical and theoretical. The manner in which AE has also chosen to publish work is also part of this intervention. Even though our books are comprised of works mostly available online, the existence of a printed collection adds credibility not offered to disparate blog entries, a move that gives AE access to spaces like libraries and university classrooms. AE's books have been taught in university classrooms, including my own, and activists and thinkers outside of universities also read them. Moreover, some of the contributors to AE's books are academics inside of universities while others are activists or community intellectuals.

The interventionist modality comes from AE's uniquely queer politics. Morris claims that the project of queer criticism is not to recover evidence of gay and lesbian rhetoric or history; rather, queer critique unearths ruptures in normative assumptions and itself, ruptures normativities—archival, disciplinary, and intellectual.[25] For many queer theorists and activists, the queer critique is about challenging larger normativities that uphold hegemonic structures of power. AE's critique, akin to what Ferguson calls queer of color critique,[26] or what women of color feminists have described as intersectionality,[27] is concerned with how capitalism and structures like nation-states enact violence through racialized, gendered, abled, and sexualized norms. Interceding only in the singular issue of heteronormativity without understanding and acknowledging how heteronormativity colludes with capitalism, imperialism, racism, sexism, cissexism, and ableism is not much of an intervention. Such fragmenting logics are the tools of hegemonic power structures (the master's tools, to quote Audre Lorde). As I argue below, the binaries of everyday versus professional critics and vernacular versus specialized rhetoric that greatly inform understanding of movement and counterpublics are similar fragmenting constructions that reinforce status quo power relations. A radical queer critique that embraces AE's modality seeks to subvert those logics in order to make worlds where such normativities can no longer wage violence.

Everyday versus Professional Critics

We learn from both McGee and McKerrow that criticism is a vehicle for doing rhetoric.[28] Criticism can come in many forms, but scholars often erect a binary between two types. McGee claims that so-called everyday critics make snap judgments about rhetoric they encounter, and one of those judgments is action.[29] For McGee, everyday critics' snap judgments and action differ from the work of the professional. McGee claims, "The everyday critic *may* create discourse in response to discourse; but the professional critic *always* creates formal discourse in response to discourse." This distinction is important for McGee as he continues: "Professional critics must thus be sensitive to rhetoric in two dimensions: With regard to the object of criticism, they will be perceived as respondents and interpreters responsible for providing in a formal way the missing fragments of the object of criticism, its influence. With regard to their own formal writing, they will function as advocates or adversaries of 'the text' who invent, arrange, style, remember, and deliver arguments in favor of particular judgments of salience, attitude, belief, and action."[30] Consequently, unlike everyday critics, the job is much larger for the professional critic who is foremost tasked with "*inventing a text suitable for criticism.*"[31] The professional critic then cannot simply accept a text on face value and respond to it in a snap fashion. The professional critic constructs from contextual fragments something that might be called text, which can be interpreted, evaluated, and introduced into broader discourse.

AE and my involvement in it pose several potential dilemmas for rhetorical critics who study social movement or counterpublics and might hold close to a distinction such as McGee's. For example, it is not a far stretch to understand much of AE's writing as rhetorical criticism. Conrad, Nair, and I do most of the collective's writing, and all three of us hold advanced degrees in the arts or humanities. Our critiques engage directly with the logics of publicly available political documents, and our purpose is to encourage different judgments in audiences. AE's writing extends well beyond the work of McGee's "everyday critics." Elucidating this point, in the introduction to the new AK Press anthology, we write:

> Since our inception, we have been criticized for our critiques and accused of not providing alternatives. Our continued response is that the structures of assimilation are so tenacious that they need, first and foremost, hard and insistent critiques in order to dismantle the authority and power they have accrued over the years. . . . Contrary to what our progressive/left critics proclaim, action can be and is a form of analysis. When gay marriage supporters publicly trot out weeping children clinging to their gay or lesbian parents or insist that their lives are more "real" than ours, they obfuscate the ways that such strategies are necessarily born out of their own analysis: an analysis that deter-

mines, for instance, the manipulative extent to which the public can be wooed by such melodramatic and homonormative affect.[32]

While the writing style may not pass in a scholarly journal, the level of analysis obviously reveals creating a text from the material of the mainstream movement in order to interpret it. Likewise, and as we put it, critique is not something we do in snap judgment: "We critique like our lives depend upon it." Working with AE has compelled me to challenge my own complicity with such distinctions, especially since the critique of radical queer activists can sometimes be more sophisticated and rigorous than that of professional critics.

Vernacular versus Institutional Rhetoric

Despite our lack of institutional affiliation, AE's work cannot be easily cast as vernacular rhetoric.[33] As Howard contends, within communication theory, there have been two primary ways that vernacular discourse has been conceptualized: the subaltern and the common vernacular. Howard suggests that "both perspectives conceive the vernacular as an agency alternate to dominant power, and both assume a strict division between the vernacular and institutional."[34] Such a binary is evident in Ono and Sloop's original conceptualization of vernacular discourse when they note, "critics of vernacular discourse would look at discourse that resonates within and from historically oppressed communities."[35] While Ono and Sloop note that the vernacular is characterized at least in part by pastiche, the distinction between the powerful and the oppressed seems relatively clear, and the idea of institutional rhetoric is equally fixed. Moreover, in a slightly different vein, Hauser explains the vernacular as "mundane transactions of words and gestures that allow us to negotiate our way through quotidian encounters. They are not formal exchanges of the podium."[36] While Hauser is less concerned with oppressed groups, his distinction between the podium and the quotidian lends to a similar bifurcation between kinds of rhetoric.

When AE gives public presentations, we intentionally seek to subvert this binary. When invited to a university or college, we deliver a presentation from a manuscript alongside a formal slide show. We cite radical queer and trans activists alongside prominent queer theorists. On these visits, we regularly ask to give presentations to individual classes so we are brought inside the space designed to legitimate knowledge: classrooms. We do this usually while wearing jeans and T-shirts or other street wear. The importance of rupturing epistemic expectations in these ways is calculated and an important part of what we envision as our intellectual and activist project, which addresses different audiences from a somewhat ambiguous location between the vernacular and the institutional.

Rethinking Notions of Agency

Questions regarding rhetorical subjectivity and agency are among the most hotly contested within rhetorical theory.[37] Although studies of counterpublics have been more diverse in the kinds of rhetoric studied, studies of social movement rhetoric, including some queer studies, have been dominated by leader-based studies.[38] Further, just as PAAR emphasizes a single scholar as primary agent, such scholarship stresses the rhetoric "of the streets," while neglecting other types of movement rhetoric.[39] These studies have contributed valuable insight to our understanding of mobilization within social movement and counterpublics. My work with AE works on and against these notions of rhetorical agency. For example, even as Conrad, Nair, and I function as the "public faces" of AE, with the exception of the edited books, which feature only Conrad's name (he acquired the personal debt to produce them), all of our works are collaboratively written. With each essay, we change the order of authorship, and we usually follow our names with the phrase "for Against Equality." In this way, we actively challenge leader-centered approaches and a notion of individual agency. Even in this chapter written for my academic discipline, I have included the phrase "with Yasmin Nair and Ryan Conrad" to indicate that this essay is written in coalition.

Building on the writings of Carrillo Rowe and Keating, Chávez and Griffin write, "A coalitional agency implies that our ability to affect social change, to empower others and ourselves necessitates seeing people, history and culture as inextricably bound to one another."[40] I might revise that thesis to indicate not just that we must *see* these interconnections but that we must realize as Butler does: "Let's face it, we're undone by each other."[41] And furthermore, that as Carrillo Rowe insists, we need to be longing for politics of relation that help us to build the alliances that will lead to coalitional subjectivities and a richer understanding of power and oppression, as well as the possibilities for social change.[42] This is a point I have long reiterated in my own scholarship, and one actively fostered by AE.

Understanding one's subjectivity and agency as coalitional does not require one to seek political coalitions with everyone. A person can realize the nature of her subjectivity and agency as inextricably bound to another without seeking political coalition with that person, as the divides between them may be too deep or damaging. Moreover, espousing a belief in coalitional agency does not suggest that one does not believe in agency or authorship at all. AE members are among those activists who have chastised academics for pilfering the work of activists without giving them credit, while simultaneously adopting and advocating alternative forms of agency outside leader-centered models that are premised upon notions of Western subjectivity and agency that emphasize "great men, speaking well."[43] Collective agency is still agency. AE is committed to the process and the product when it comes to activist rhetoric, which is also why the archiving component of AE's work is so central. AE members insist that our analysis is built on a long tradition of principled, radical queer thought that has existed through the ages. In our public presentation on marriage, we begin the conversation with a discussion of Emma Goldman and other free loving feminists' rhetoric regarding the problems of marriage for women from the late nineteenth and early twentieth centuries.[44] Highlighting the work that comes before us and the ways that that work informs AE's contemporary critique challenges the centrality of one group or one rhetor within movement.

I have also written extensively about the activism of fellow collective member Yasmin Nair, which further reveals the blurry lines around rhetorical agency. In my book, *Queer Migration Politics*, I devote an entire chapter to Nair's activist writing about queer immigrant struggles. In the chapter, I delineate Nair's rhetorical strategies and offer insight into where they function exceptionally well and where they also include possible shortcomings. Since my interactions with Nair are not only within the roles of studied and studier but also friends and activist colleagues, writing about Nair while writing with her raises potential ethical dilemmas about agency and subjectivity. For example, one of the original reasons I wanted to write about Nair's work was because I found it so compelling and original. In writing about her in a scholarly venue, however, I have tried very hard to be clear about which ideas are hers and which are my interpretations so that I do not unfairly get credit for her original thought. This tension between featuring the ideas of very important activists and providing scholarly analysis is fraught in my writing about Nair. It is further complicated due to our personal relationship. AE has taught me that this kind of discomfort is important in creating accountability in academic work and in refusing to think of scholarly or rhetorical agency in clear and facile terms.

A last way AE actively challenges notions of activist agency is in our refusal to rely upon narrative structures to advocate our principles. Burke's concept of identification and Fisher's insistence that humans are narrative beings have become important to the ways to understand rhetorical agency.[45] Similarly, in activist communities, particularly LGBT activism,

telling the stories of loving couples, good soldiers, and victimized but innocent gays has been a central strategy for arguing for inclusion. AE refuses
to engage in those methods, believing as Nair has suggested, that it is very
hard to use narrative in a way that does not put the personal and the affective before the political, and that does not play into a politics of abjection.[46]
This is not to say that AE does not rely on the use of stories to convey political points, but realizing that in contemporary times, narrative has regularly been used as a means for affecting a very narrow kind of change, AE
insists on reimagining agency. Warner similarly points out that agency exists in publics by articulating in relation to the maintenance of existing and
dominant lifeworlds.[47] Since the lifeworld is profoundly heteronormative,
as well as embedded in particular race, class, gender, ability, and national
norms, the most successful narrative approaches to world making are ones
that promote and maintain the status quo like marriage.

All narrative should not be the baby thrown out with the lukewarm bath
water, but for AE, locating or creating agency outside of the maintenance
of existing norms is vital. This requires not necessarily limiting who can tell
a story or when but in modeling ways to tell different stories that actively
refuse liberal politics of inclusion, which maintain the status quo. When
people ask about our personal stories in interviews, we regularly refuse such
lines of questioning, intending to keep focus on the issues at hand in a more
abstract sense, so that those issues cannot be obscured or ignored due to
our stories becoming center. Denying our own personal rhetorical agency
in order to relocate the agency of ideas and analysis, then, is at the core of
AE's activist project. Though such a move risks disembodying subjectivity,
we would rather risk privileging abstraction, as sentimental (normative)
narrative identifications may distract attention from queer lives. With this
tactic, AE operates very much like a counterpublic, even if AE would not
and does not advance a notion of a public to define our work. The charge
that I have had to heed as a rhetorical critic then is to rethink how identification operates, what can and does constitute identification, and what non-
narrative or alternative-narrative forms of identification may exist. It is also
a charge to reconsider which forms of narrative we can and should use in
our own work and whether in the construction of a complete text, we too,
reinscribe norms that contradict our critical and political values.

Queer theory and activism have long been concerned with what Yep calls
queer "worldmaking."[48] This has manifested in theoretical turns to utopia
and also in activist turns to concepts like "fabulosity" and making missions
like AE's "reinvigorating the queer political imagination."[49] Reconceptualizing agency in these various ways emerges from a commitment to queer

politics, which while often committed to projects like self-determination that could be said to reinscribe a stable subject with agency, is equally committed to playing with and refusing conventional notions of authorship, subjectivity and narrative. Thus, the new understandings of agency I have developed in concordance with AE's activism are uniquely queer.

Conclusions

In this chapter, I have tried to demonstrate an additional answer to Mitchell's question about the location of movement in rhetorical criticism of social movement. Speaking in relation to the broader activist turn in communication studies and also writing from my position as a queer rhetorical critic of social movement, I have shown how working closely with the radical queer collective, Against Equality, has both challenged taken-for-granted binaries in rhetorical studies and compelled a rethinking of the notion of agency. In the remaining paragraphs, I suggest some implications for rhetorical theory and studies of social movement and counterpublics.

I am not *necessarily* implying that there is no place for distinctions among professional and everyday critics, institutional and vernacular rhetoric. I am suggesting that working closely with an activist community like AE throws all of these taken-for-granted assumptions into crisis, a crisis that, I believe, is productive. In looking at vernacular rhetoric within participatory social media contexts, Howard finds that the lines between institutional and vernacular are not clear in such contexts. In proposing what he calls the "dialectical vernacular," Howard writes that it "resists a romanticizing or essentializing identification. It imagines agents as individuals or groups of individuals who in any given case may be acting through some institutional and/or some vernacular agency. Further, it imagines the locations of discourse made possible by institutional forces as harboring some vernacularity."[50] Working with AE has compelled me to push Howard's findings even further. While a dialectic still implies separation between two distinct poles, activism like AE requires rethinking the institutional and vernacular altogether in certain contexts. A similar rethinking of the everyday and the professional critic seems warranted, and further, binaries that continue to greatly inform the study of social movement such as in-group/out-group and counterpublic studies such as public/private also need to be placed under the theoretical microscope in light of this project. AE's queer modality of engagement emerges from a queer commitment to challenging all binaries and the normativities they uphold, reinforce, and police. Rethinking these binaries does not mean we must discard them entirely, as if that would ever be possible. Instead, this rethinking suggests a need to keep present and fraught that which is usually taken for granted and imagined in the background. This queering of theoretical assumptions has been very productive for me in my work.

One way to read this paper would be to hear that I am implying that all academics should become activists. Much to the relief of my activist colleagues, this is not what I am suggesting. This paper does point to the need for more experiential understanding of social movements, whether through fieldwork or through ongoing participation in movements. An increasing number of rhetoric scholars have been taking the plunge into using methods such as interviews, focus groups, and participant observation to enrich the quality of their rhetorical analyses.[51] Importantly, as Middleton, Senda-Cook and Endres note, while there are many opportunities involved in what they describe as "rhetorical field methods," many possible risks and concerns also arise when rhetoricians intervene directly in people's everyday lives.[52] The risks cannot be understated, yet as the scholarship of Conquergood and Pezzullo have aptly revealed, ongoing presence in the movements and other arenas about which we write supplies the kind of nuanced understanding that is very hard to obtain without interacting with people in their lived environments. I certainly want to be cautious in suggesting the need for more experiential research; for me, it comes quite easily as I have always been involved in the communities about which I write in some form. I also do not intend to issue a normative claim that only research into the rhetoric of social movements that includes an experiential component is valid.

There are also great ethical risks and potentially problematic normative claims that could ensue from not just passively participating in a movement or counterpublic but actively laboring in one, growing to care about the other activists, and putting your fingerprint on the work. Still, I assume, like Jakobsen, that a relationship between academics and activism is a good thing.[53] And for now, AE has helped me to find one very compelling answer to Mitchell's question. Collective engagement can push scholars of movement to be transformed through that engagement. The participatory approach does not need to be everyone's approach, but it seems very worthwhile to me that all scholars of the rhetoric of social movement, counterpublics, or perhaps social justice more generally, engage in some form of the reflective process that this approach mandates.

Notes

1. Karma would like to thank the editors of this volume for incredible feedback as well as Yasmin Nair, Ryan Conrad, Deena Loeffler, Alexandra Silver-

thorne, Sara McKinnon, Chuck Morris, and an audience from the Education Studies Department at the University of Oregon who saw a version of this presented.

2. Gordon R. Mitchell, "Public Argument Action Research and the Learning Curve of New Social Movements," *Argumentation and Advocacy* 40, no. 4 (2004): 213, 217.

3. Peter A. Andersen, "Beyond Criticism: The Activist Turn in the Ideological Debate," *Western Journal of Speech Communication* 57 (1993): 247–56; Benjamin J. Broome, Christopher Carey, Sarah Amira De la Garza, Judith N. Martin, and Richard Morris, "'In the Thick of Things': A Dialogue about an Activist Turn in Intercultural Communication," *International and Intercultural Communication Annual* 28 (2005): 145–75; Lawrence R. Frey and Kevin M. Carragee, eds., *Communication Activism: Communication for Social Change*, vol. 1 (Cresskill, NJ: Hampton Press, 2007).

4. I recognize that, as Cox and Foust reveal, there is a different lineage within rhetorical studies of what might be characterized as "social movement studies," which began in the mid-twentieth century, and "counterpublic studies," which began in the mid-1990s. As this edited volume clearly evidences, these are distinct though often overlapping bodies of scholarship that offer different conceptual tools and frameworks for understanding. For reasons too expansive to fully explicate in this endnote, I have always struggled with the very idea of a "counterpublic," even as I have used it within my scholarship. By definition, counterpublic reifies the idea of the "public"—even if that public is said to be multiple—to which it is counter. As Asen puts it, counterpublics develop as "explicitly articulated alternatives to wider publics that exclude the interests of potential participants" ("Seeking the 'Counter' in Counterpublics." *Communication Theory* 10, no. 4 [2000]: 425). The notion of the counterpublic is premised on a binary between exclusion and inclusion; a defining characteristic of a counterpublic is "recognition of exclusion from wider public spheres" (427). The counterpublic seems, to me, to be embedded in liberal logics, logics that do not even begin to capture the movement activity of many radical activists. Moreover, and perhaps more to the point, in more than a decade of personal and scholarly time in vast and varied activist communities I have never once heard anyone use the term "counterpublic" to describe their movement work or their relationship to the forces they challenge. Therefore, in the spirit of the argument I am trying to make in this chapter about the impacts that collective movement work should have on how scholars understand themselves in their work, I do not describe AE as a counterpublic entity nor do I locate myself in the lineage of counterpublic sphere studies. I do draw on this scholarship as it is relevant in explicating theoretical points. Asen, "Seeking the 'Counter' in Counterpublics"; Robert Cox and Christina R. Foust, "Social Movement Rhetoric," in *The SAGE Handbook of Rhetorical Studies*, ed. Andrea A. Lunsford, Kirt H. Wilson, and Rosa A. Eberly (Thousand Oaks, CA: SAGE Publications, 2009).

5. "Coalitional agency" is a term Cindy Griffin and I developed. Karma R. Chávez and Cindy L. Griffin, "Power, Feminisms, and Coalitional Agency: Inviting and Enacting Difficult Dialogues," *Women's Studies in Communication* 32, no. 1 (2009).

6. Ryan Conrad, "Against Equality, in Maine and Everywhere," in *Against Equality: Queer Critiques of Gay Marriage*, ed. Ryan Conrad (Lewiston, ME: Against Equality Press, 2010).

7. See www.againstequality.org.

8. INCITE! Women of Color against Violence, ed. *The Revolution Will Not Be Funded: Beyond the Non-Profit Industrial Complex* (Cambridge, MA: South End Press 2007).

9. To access some of these interviews and reports on these presentations, visit www.againstequality.org/press/.

10. A very truncated list: James Darsey, "From 'Commies' and 'Queers' to 'Gay Is Good,'" in *Gayspeak: Gay Male and Lesbian Communication*, ed. James W. Chesebro (New York: Pilgrim Press, 1981); "From 'Gay Is Good' to the Scourge of AIDS: The Evolution of Gay Liberation Rhetoric," *Communication Studies* 42, no. 1 (1991); R. Anthony. Slagle, "In Defense of Queer Nation: From Identity Politics to a Politics of Difference," *Western Journal of Communication* 59, no. 2 (1995); Bryan J. McCann, "Queering Expertise: Counterpublics, Social Change, and the Corporeal Dilemmas of LGBTQ Equality," *Social Epistemology: A Journal of Knowledge, Culture and Policy* 25, no. 3 (2011); Charles E. Morris III, "Forum: Remembering AIDS Coalition to Unleash Power (ACT UP), 1987–2012 and Beyond," *Quarterly Journal of Speech* 98 (2012); Mary L. Gray, "'Queer Nation Is Dead/Long Live Queer Nation': The Politics and Poetics of Social Movement and Media Representation," *Critical Studies in Media Communication* 26, no. 3 (2009); Erin J. Rand, "An Inflammatory Fag and a Queer Form: Larry Kramer, Polemics, and Rhetorical Agency," *Quarterly Journal of Speech* 94, no. 3 (2008); C. Riley Snorton, "Marriage Mimesis," *Journal of International and Intercultural Communication* 6, no. 2 (2013); Davin Allen Grindstaff, *Rhetorical Secrets: Mapping Gay Identity and Queer Resistance in Contemporary America* (Tuscaloosa: University of Alabama Press, 2006).

11. Lawrence R. Frey and Kevin M. Carragee, "Communication Activism as Engaged Scholarship," in *Communication Activism*, 10.

12. Dana L. Cloud, "The Only Conceivable Thing to Do: Reflections on Academics and Activism," in *Activism and Rhetoric: Theories and Contexts for Political Engagement*, ed. Seth Kahn and Jonghwa Lee (New York: Routledge, 2011); Stephen John Hartnett, Jennifer K. Wood, and Bryan J. McCann, "Turning Silence into Speech and Action: Prison Activism and the Pedagogy of Empowered Citizenship," *Communication and Critical/Cultural Studies* 8, no. 4 (2011); Shane T. Moreman and Persona Non Grata, "Learning from and Mentoring the Undocumented Ab540 Student: Hearing an Unheard Voice," *Text and Performance Quarterly* 31, no. 3 (2011); Phaedra C. Pezzullo, "Perform-

ing Critical Interruptions: Stories, Rhetorical Invention, and the Environmental Justice Movement," *Western Journal of Communication* 65, no. 1 (2001); Michelle Rodino-Colocino, "Getting to 'Not Especially Strange': Embracing Participatory-Advocacy Communication Research for Social Justice," *International Journal of Communication* 5 (2011); Omar Swartz, *In Defense of Partisan Criticism: Communication Studies, Law, and Social Analysis* (New York: Peter Lang, 2005).

13. Frey and Carragee, "Communication Activism as Engaged Scholarship," 6.

14. McCann, "Queering Expertise"; Slagle, "In Defense."

15. McCann, "Queering Expertise," 250.

16. Slagle, "In Defense," 91.

17. Karma R. Chávez, "Beyond Complicity: Coherence, Queer Theory, and the Rhetoric of the 'Gay Christian Movement,'" *Text and Performance Quarterly* 24, no. 3/4 (2004), "Border (in)Securities: Normative and Differential Belonging in LGBTQ and Immigrant Rights Discourse," *Communication and Critical/Cultural Studies* 7, no. 2 (2010).

18. Yasmin Nair, Ryan Conrad, and Karma R. Chávez for Against Equality, "Against Equality: Don't Ask to Fight Their Wars!" *Fifth Estate* (2012): 9–10.

19. See Karma R. Chávez, *Queer Migration Politics: Activist Rhetoric and Coalitional Possibilities* (Urbana: University of Illinois Press, 2013).

20. Robert Hariman, "Status, Marginality, and Rhetorical Theory," *Quarterly Journal of Speech* 72, no. 1 (1986).

21. Chris Ingraham, "Talking (about) the Elite and Mass: Vernacular Rhetoric and Discursive Status," *Philosophy and Rhetoric* 46, no. 1 (2013): 16.

22. Daniel C. Brouwer and Robert Asen, "Introduction: Public Modalities, or the Metaphors We Theorize By," in *Public Modalities: Rhetoric, Culture, Media, and the Shape of Public Life*, ed. Daniel C. Brouwer and Robert Asen (Tuscaloosa: University of Alabama Press, 2010).

23. Margot Weiss, "'Reinvigorating the Queer Political Imagination': A Roundtable with Ryan Conrad, Yasmin Nair, and Karma Chávez," *American Quarterly* 64, no. 4 (2012): 845.

24. Ibid., 847.

25. Charles E. Morris III, "Archival Queer," *Rhetoric and Public Affairs* 9, no. 1 (2006); Charles E. Morris III, "Introduction: Portrait of a Queer Rhetorical/Historical Critic," in *Queering Public Address: Sexualities in American Historical Discourse*, ed. Charles E. Morris III (Columbia: University of South Carolina, 2007).

26. Chandan Reddy coined this term. See Roderick A. Ferguson, *Aberrations in Black: Toward a Queer of Color Critique* (Minneapolis: University of Minnesota Press, 2004).

27. Karma R. Chávez and Cindy L. Griffin, eds., *Standing in the Intersection: Feminist Voices, Feminist Practices in Communication Studies* (Albany: State University of New York Press, 2012); Kimberle Crenshaw, "Mapping the Mar-

gins: Intersectionality, Identity Politics and Violence against Women of Color," *Stanford Law Review* 43 (1991).

28. Raymie E. McKerrow, "Critical Rhetoric: Theory and Praxis," *Communication Monographs* 56, no. 2 (1989); Michael Calvin McGee, "Text, Context, and the Fragmentation of Contemporary Culture," *Western Journal of Speech Communication* 54 (1990).

29. McGee, "Text, Context," 282.

30. Ibid.

31. Ibid., 288.

32. Ryan Conrad, Karma Chávez, Yasmin Nair, and Deena Loeffler for Against Equality, "Against Equality: Queer Revolution, Not Mere Inclusion," introduction to *Against Equality: Queer Revolution, Not Mere Inclusion*, ed. Ryan Conrad (Oakland, CA: AK Press, 2014), 5.

33. Kent A. Ono and John M. Sloop, "The Critique of Vernacular Discourse," *Communication Monographs* 62, no. 1 (1995).

34. Robert Glenn Howard, "The Vernacular Web of Participatory Media," *Critical Studies in Media Communication* 25, no. 5 (2008): 491.

35. Ono and Sloop, "The Critique of Vernacular Discourse," 20.

36. Gerard A. Hauser, *Vernacular Voices: The Rhetoric of Publics and Public Spheres* (Columbia: University of South Carolina Press, 1999), 11.

37. For instance, this back and forth: Cheryl Geisler, "How Ought We to Understand the Concept of Rhetorical Agency? Report from the ARS," *Rhetoric Society Quarterly* 34, no. 3 (2004), "Teaching the Post-Modern Rhetor: Continuing the Conversation on Rhetorical Agency," *Rhetoric Society Quarterly* 35, no. 4 (2005); Christian Lundberg and Joshua Gunn, "'Ouija Board, Are There Any Communications?' Agency, Ontotheology, and the Death of the Humanist Subject, or, Continuing the Ars Conversation," *Rhetoric Society Quarterly* 35, no. 4 (2005).

38. A short list of examples: John C. Hammerback and Richard J. Jensen, *The Rhetorical Career of César Chávez* (College Station: Texas A&M University Press, 1998); Rand, "An Inflammatory Fag;" Stacey K. Sowards, "Rhetorical Functions of Letter Writing: Dialogic Collaboration, Affirmation, and Catharsis in Dolores Huerta's Letters," *Communication Quarterly* 60, no. 2 (2012); Charles J. Stewart, "The Evolution of a Revolution: Stokely Carmichael and the Rhetoric of Black Power," *Quarterly Journal of Speech* 83 (1997); Robert Terrill, "Protest, Prophecy, and Prudence in the Rhetoric of Malcolm X," *Rhetoric and Public Affairs* 4, no. 1 (2001); Kirt H. Wilson, "Interpreting the Discursive Field of the Montgomery Bus Boycott: Martin Luther King Jr.'s Holt Street Address," *Rhetoric and Public Affairs* 8, no. 2 (2005).

39. Franklyn S. Haiman, "The Rhetoric of the Streets: Some Legal and Ethical Considerations," *Quarterly Journal of Speech* 53, no. 2 (1967).

40. Chávez and Griffin, "Power, Feminisms," 8.

41. Judith Butler, *Undoing Gender* (New York: Routledge, 2004).

42. Aimee Carrillo Rowe, *Power Lines: On the Subject of Feminist Alliances* (Durham, NC: Duke University Press, 2008).

43. We certainly offer that critique here: Weiss, "'Reinvigorating the Queer.'"

44. For an excellent discussion of the free love movement in rhetorical studies, see Kate Zittlow Rogness, "The Intersectional Style of Free Love Rhetoric," in *Standing in the Intersection: Feminist Voices, Feminist Practices in Communication Studies*, ed. Karma R. Chávez and Cindy L. Griffin (Albany: State University of New York Press, 2012).

45. Kenneth Burke, *A Rhetoric of Motives* (Berkeley: University of California Press, 1950); Walter R. Fisher, "Narration as a Human Communication Paradigm," *Communication Monographs* 51 (1984).

46. Yasmin Nair, "What's Left of Queer?: Immigration, Sexuality and Affect in a Neoliberal World," Immigrant City Chicago, accessed January 4, 2013, www.uic.edu/jaddams/hull/immigrantcitychicago/essays/nair_leftofqueer. html; on the question of the problems of affect and sentimentality in politics, see also: Lauren Berlant, *The Female Complaint: The Unfinished Business of Sentimentality in American Culture* (Durham, NC: Duke University Press, 2008).

47. Michael Warner, *Publics and Counterpublics* (New York: Zone Books, 2002).

48. Gust A. Yep, "The Violence of Heteronormativity in Communication Studies: Notes on Injury, Healing and Queer World-Making," *Journal of Homosexuality* 45, no. 2/3/4 (2003).

49. On utopia, see José Esteban Muñoz, *Cruising Utopia: The Then and There of Queer Futurity* (New York: New York University Press, 2009). "Fabulosity" is a term created by San Francisco Pride at Work in their zine *Undoing Borders*. HAVOQ, "Undoing Borders: A Queer Manifesto," https://undoingborders .wordpress.com/undoing-borders/.

50. Howard, "The Vernacular Web," 497.

51. E.g., Danielle Endres and Samantha Senda-Cook, "Location Matters: The Rhetoric of Place in Protest," *Quarterly Journal of Speech* 97, no. 3 (2011); Aaron Hess, "Critical-Rhetorical Ethnography: Rethnking the Place and Process of Rhetoric," *Communication Studies* 62, no. 2 (2011); Phaedra C. Pezzullo, "Resisting 'National Breast Cancer Awareness Month': The Rhetoric of Counterpublics and Their Cultural Performances," *Quarterly Journal of Speech* 89, no. 4 (2003).

52. Michael K. Middleton, Samantha Senda-Cook, and Danielle Endres, "Articulating Rhetorical Field Methods: Challenges and Tensions," *Western Journal of Communication* 75, no. 4 (2011).

53. Janet R. Jakobsen, "Collaborations," *American Quarterly* 64, no. 4 (2012).

III

New Directions for Studying Social Movements and Counterpublics Rhetorically

8

Latina/o Vernacular Discourse

Theorizing Performative Dimensions
of an Other Counterpublic

Bernadette Marie Calafell and Dawn Marie D. McIntosh

A pure white wall offers only a shadow as Guillermo Gómez Peña walks toward the camera. He walks toward you in a black cowboy hat and black leather vest. His long, grey hair sways on his open vest. We voyeuristically examine his brown body. His large tattoo on his chest makes momentary appearances. In his deep voice, he begins to speak Spanish while subtitles run below the screen. "I have a surprise for you. . . .

> Last night at the bar, you asked me . . .
> What performance art was;
> I answered
> It was pure presence,
> in real time,
> without artifice,
> taking necessary risks."[1]

Gómez Peña's words resonate so eloquently with counterpublic practices and articulations. He demonstrates both through his body and performance how Latina/o bodies simultaneously serve as public and counterpublic enactments. Latina/o performance reveals how racial minorities must publicly enact survival, resistance, and empowering tactics that fluidly work as counterpublic enactments. Squires argues for a fluid understanding of public sphere and counterpublics, noting "even if access to public arenas is theoretically guaranteed to all, all will not necessarily be equal within those spaces."[2] She draws attention to how black public spheres are often misidentified, overlooked, and misrepresented.[3] The simultaneous nature of people of color's actions work within public life but also serve as counterpublics. We follow Squires's call for a fluid definition of counterpublic in order to not reduce counterpublics only to specificities of particular identities. We build upon her articulations of counterpublics through performance theories that center themselves with the ways bodies, specifically Latina/o bodies, denote the complex fluidity of public/private, public/counterpublic, and disenfranchised/empowered. Our vehicle for exploring this complex fluidity is Latina/o vernacular discourse.

Drawing on existing work in Latina/o communication studies that employs a vernacular discourse perspective, Holling and Calafell[4] theorize three key aspects of Latina/o vernacular discourse (LVD): the tensions of identities, a decolonial aim, and the critic/al role. Building on their work, we theorize the performative aspects of LVD through a metatheoretical analysis of work that uses a performance-centered perspective to understand Latina/o vernaculars. More specifically, this work contributes to understanding the connection of performative LVD to public sphere and counterpublic theories, particularly as they relate to historically marginalized communities. We press scholars to acknowledge performing bodies in their everyday enactments as terms of studying social change. Too often the everyday acts of survival, resistance, and empowerment are overlooked for their powerful contributions as social movements. These "mundane" lived experiences are quite possibly the pivotal future of studying social change. They demand a departure from Eurocentric ways of knowing, logics, and registers and reveal the ability to exist in contradiction and ambiguity. Theorizing across the work of Latina/o vernaculars and performance illustrates some of the ways LVD performances disrupt the public sphere. These disruptions emerge in three dimensions: embodiments of resistance that disrupt the public/private divide, the role of performers as tricksters and cultural translators, and the use of the body in disrupting or queering temporality. We begin by explicating where LVD meets public and counterpublic theories.

The "Counter" Body: Latina/o Vernacular Discourse As/Is Counterpublics

Ono and Sloop theorize vernacular discourse as discourse emanating from historically marginalized communities.[5] Unlike Hauser, whose use of the vernacular is related to communities organizing around ideas,[6] Ono and Sloop ground the vernacular in identities. We are not suggesting here that ideas never grow out of identities or visa versa. But the distinction Ono and Sloop begin to draw out is the fact that the politics of the body necessitate marginalized communities to negotiate their own (vernacular) discourses. Felski refers to this distinction of ideas from identities in her articulation of "the feminist counter-ideology"[7] arguing "like the original bourgeois public sphere constitutes a discursive space which defines itself in terms of a common identity; here is the shared experience of gender-based oppression which provides the mediating factor intended to unite all participants beyond their specific differences."[8] Marginalized identities unite discursively through identity not ideas. Embodied rhetoric derives from the materiality of the body and its negotiations in relation to hegemonic rhetorical discourses. Communities may organize around "ideas" as in Hauser's use of vernacular, but vernaculars of the body are carved out by marginalized bodies intrinsic to their difference. These embodied vernaculars create community built not solely on ideas but on their embodied differences.

These embodied rhetorics can happen everywhere and take multiple forms. Performance informs our understanding of everyday rhetorics.[9] The manner of dress, the politics of silence, mannerisms of speaking/listening, the politics of which bodies congregate, and where they meet are all performative examples of vernacular discourses. Feminists of color point to the fact that vernaculars are rhetorics of the body, specifically marginalized bodies. Drawing on the work of Anzaldúa[10] and Hill Collins,[11] Calafell argues for understanding the importance of oral or performative rhetorics by women of color as alternative forms of theorizing.[12] "Theories in the flesh" drive feminists of color toward a theoretical understanding of the everyday ways we theorize through experience, especially as related to the reverberations and everyday encounters with racism. Since theoretical articulations of white patriarchal discourse are the only reputable theorizing, Othered bodies become theoretically removed from historical definitions of "publics." Theories of the flesh or performative rhetorics of women of color denote a different picture of theorizing, a vernacular rhetoric, an embodied praxis.

This form of theorizing is not only a practice of survival but, we posit, a cornerstone to counterpublic articulations, understandings, and theorizing. This argument is similarly advanced by performance scholar Madison in her study of black women's oral history, personal narrative, and performance.[13] Calafell articulates the importance of understanding how power frames performances of resistance by women of color through Scott's framework of public and hidden transcripts,[14] which describe the performances that take place both in front of powerholders and behind the scenes.[15] These public transcripts or performances may appear to be complicit with powers of domination, but Scott asks us to think differently about the ways resistance and power function.[16] Scott challenges that resistive practices of subordinate groups are more complex, perhaps even deceptive. We challenge the conceptualization of "power" that sees resistance organized as the powerless "publicly" resisting the powerful. LVDs are perfect examples of counterpublic practices that resist dominance through everyday acts of being. These counterpublic performances exist amongst the "public" and quietly (re)negotiate dominant-hegemonic relations inflicted on their bodies, displaying embodied practices that emanate social change from a nonnormative, nonelite public understanding.

What distinguishes LVD from other marginalized vernacular discourses is the profound correlations to performance and performing bodies. Holling's retrospective essay on the emergence of Latina/o communication studies points to the increasing number of works published from a performance studies perspective, demonstrating the important role performance should play in LVD and also counterpublic theorizing.[17] When studying acts of resistance that emerge from historically marginalized groups, performance offers researchers new ways to think about the body as/is rhetoric/al.[18] Performance offers Other perspectives to understanding rhetorics of the body in the study of resistance, particularly as emerging from historically marginalized communities that do not have the privilege of invisibility. In this chapter we work to connect Latina/o communication performance work explicitly to LVD in order to picture what performance studies offers counterpublic theorizing. In doing this, we place ourselves in conversation with public sphere and counterpublic theories.

Habermas theorizes that the public sphere is a space of political participation and deliberation.[19] Challenging Habermas's conceptualization of the public sphere, Fraser argues that marginalized people are excluded from *the* public sphere, instead forming subaltern counterpublics that "formulate oppositional interpretations of their identities, interests, and needs."[20] Fraser elaborates, "The view that women were excluded from the public sphere turns out to be ideological; it rests on a class and gender-biased notion of publicity, one which accepts at face value the bourgeois public's claim to be *the* public."[21] Fraser also notes the function of hegemony in this conception, as "the official public sphere . . . is the prime institutional site for the construction of the consent that defines the new, hegemonic mode of domination."[22] Fraser's critiques of Habermas's public/private divide point to how public sphere and counterpublic theories are theoretically grounded in a disembodied understanding of the politics of identities in relation to articulations of what constitutes "the" public. Integrating performance theory into this conversation calls us to see the natures of "publics," "counterpublics," and even social movement rhetorics in relation to the material realities of bodies organized within these groups. Certainly publics, counterpublics, and social movements rhetorically function around and within purposes emanating from identities. But these groups become reduced to specific "ideas."

Warner acknowledges the complexity of "the dialectic of embodiment" that subjects marginalized bodies to consumption or objectification, while the privileged are offered "a utopian self-abstraction," or the privilege to not need access to publicness but to simply be "the public sphere."[23] Warner offers us categorical explanations of counterpublics as "far more than the expression of subaltern culture"; he asks us to see the poetic functions of public discourse outside of stringent framings of "public discourse."[24] Warner provides us an avenue to explicate counterpublics as performative in nature. Brouwer's study of self-stigmatization in the case of HIV/AIDS tattoos demonstrates the ways counterpublics can be organized around ideas *and* intricate embodied ways of being.[25] Warner argues that within specific counterpublics, identities are not ignored because some counterpublics are sensitive to the discourses and ideologies of the individuals that constitute them.[26] In recognizing that counterpublics are constituted by the identities that manifest their policies and ideas, we begin to locate the intrinsic connection between LVDs and counterpublics. Warner's articulation that identities are always in service to negotiations of heternormative framings of the public sphere organizes how Latina/o vernaculars offer particularities to understand workings of counterpublics that press against white counterpublics. We press against Warner's claim that "minoritized subjects had few strategies open to them, but one was to carry their unrecuperated positivity into consumption."[27] LVD demonstrates that the embodied practices of resistance and strategies oppressed people have employed are acts of empowerment. Our chapter teases out how the "mundane" everyday enactments of Latina/o performances are strategic to both resist white dominant-hegemonic marginalization while at the same time empower Other enactments.

LVDs stand as examples of counterpublic discursive entities that "disclose relations of power that obliquely inform public discourse and reveal potentially emancipatory practice that participants nevertheless undertake."[28] LVDs serve as counterpublic discourses. However, this chapter stretches articulations of what is the "counter" in counterpublic by pushing counterpublic scholars to acknowledge that Latina/o *bodies* are always and already reduced to *only* counterpublic discourses. This framework of Latina/o bodies as counterpublic discourses speaks to Asen's claim that "social inequality is pervasive and adversely affects the lives of citizens simply because others perceive them as belonging to a particular group. Such belonging, however, which oftentimes cannot be disavowed, is by itself an insufficient and sometimes unnecessary marker of counterpublic status."[29]

We are not suggesting that all bodies that are collapsed under specific identities believe or act similarly; however, are there histories of racialization and colonialism that interpellate these bodies into preexisting ideologies that locate them as counter to normative ideologies? Holling and Calafell gesture to Latina/o bodies as counter to dominant ideologies through their performances as decolonial in relation to the colonialism of Latin America and the United States.[30] For example, the genesis of Chicana/o and Mexican cultures is continually tied back to the narrative of Hernán Cortés and Malintzin Tenepal (the native woman who served as his translator). Through the birth of their mestizo child, Martin Cortés, a new race was both figuratively and literally born. What would ensue would continue elaborate racial charts marking the levels of Otherness in relationship to whiteness in how mixed-race people should be understood. Thus, the birth of mestiza/os created identities that were continually contrasted against and with whiteness.[31] We see this positing of Latina/o (colonized bodies) as less than white in the continued popularity of skin-lightening creams and the absence of dark-skinned Latina/os in the media. When they are present they are often referred to as black or African American, rather than Afro-Latina/o. Additionally, people of color historically have been not invited to public discourse or even to share the same spaces as those in power—whites.

Similarly, Brouwer suggests that we think of counterpublics as "the workings of marginal peoples."[32] Calafell defines vernacular texts and knowledges as "texts that may not be so *public* and that may take Other rhetorical forms."[33] LVDs are primary examples of the "workings of marginal peoples" betwixt the public and counterpublic spheres. LVD performatives may take place within the public sphere without intention of counterpublic movement but are always separated from the dominant public sphere, due to the politics of racialized marginalized bodies. This differentiates LVD performatives from other work on counterpublics focused on bodies, such as Brouwer's work on HIV/AIDS tattoos and HIV/AIDS zines.[34] The bodies in Brouwer's studies make the choice to be visible or out themselves, while most Latina/os do not have the choice or privilege of racial invisibility. Brouwer acknowledges this privilege: "Regarding zines, generally, White middle-class people who compromise the majority of zine creators might perceive themselves as marginalized and alternative, and so their zines might constitute counterpublics. However, such people generally benefit from race and class privileges; failing to recognize this, they might fail to interrogate more tragic systems of domination that do not seem to involve them directly."[35]

Similar to Warner's critique of the public sphere,[36] marginalized bodies cannot simply disembody their difference in order to actively engage as citizens in the public sphere. As Asen explains, "representations grant social values and in turn, communicate and perpetuate social values."[37] For example, the Latina body is represented in particular ways in the majoritarian public sphere. In turn, these representations position the social values of Latina/o bodies as inferior in the public sphere.[38] LVD is one form of counterpublic discourse that points to the ways marginalized bodies work to resist and regain power, especially in regard to their understandings of identities from dominant social politics. These performances act similarly to Gregg's ego-function rhetoric as they are both continually in the process of creating and maintaining identities/egos.[39] However, whereas Gregg's ego-function rhetoric comes from a need for visibility or revision that may come from a position of deficit, the LVD performances are more dynamic, speaking to and revising already existing scripts and movements through the use of pastiche and cultural syncretism.

The emancipatory potential of counterpublics located within everyday acts makes it imperative to see the correlation of performance with counterpublic rhetorics. Foust lays a foundation of understanding performative acts of resistance as public movements of transgression.[40] She reveals the performative nature of the body as a pivotal tool within social movements' discourse. The aesthetic qualities of performance disrupt representational politics and jar connections between the politics of the body and discourse. Foust's argument outlines the aesthetic intricacies of transgression through a detailed analysis of different anarchist social movements.[41] Building on this work, we challenge scholars to view the aesthetic and disruptive power located in the performative acts of resistance embodied within the everyday. These are the performative qualities located within and through Latina/o vernacular performances.

Performance theory sees the body as a site of knowing and doing. This grounds rhetorical conceptualizations of counterpublic research in the materiality of the body. Centering the body as "counter" in the counterpublics exposes qualities of counterpublics that move beyond explanations of how they become counterpublics, or why there are counterpublics. Instead it becomes a matter of exploring the performative qualities of "counter" bodies in relation to normative framings of "the" public sphere. Approaching counterpublics from this perspective redirects our attention to how the public sphere operationalizes race, sexuality, gender, class, and ability in and through the discursive framings of embodied discourses. Pezzullo has argued for examining cultural performances through the lens of counterpublics.[42] Wanzer builds on this work in his study of the Young Lords Garbage offensive.[43] Performance studies points us to the mundane aspects of our everyday lives as theoretically significant.[44] We challenge scholars to move the "counter" in counterpublics toward articulations of the everyday. We do not discount the importance of research grounded in the study of organized actions of dissent. But we do question the notion that "perhaps the most recognizable way in which counterpublics approach the state (at least in relatively democratic states) is in the form of protest groups or social movements."[45]

Latina/o communication research presses this theoretical significance by challenging scholars to understand how Latina/o bodies are continually re-performing both within and against dominant ideologies through disidentificatory performances.[46] An example of this includes Pedro Zamora's activist performance of his experience as a queer Latino living with AIDS on the *Real World: San Francisco*.[47] In this case, choosing to live an already surveilled life through the lens of hypersurveillence, Zamora disrupted the disjuncture between queerness and Latinidad while putting a face on AIDS. Our aim is to consider how performances of resistance from historically marginalized racial or ethnic groups, such as Latina/os, are more localized and manifest differently from dominant conceptions of resistance. Rather than focusing on collective group performances as counterpublics, we are concerned with how individuals in their everyday lived experiences can press us to think in new ways about counterpublic performances.

Counterpublic scholarship has ignored the everyday lived experiences and performances of culturally nuanced resistance of historically marginalized raced and colonized bodies in favor of more generalized (meaning white) focus on resistance. Squires argues: "Focusing on traditional political protest actions, such as boycotts or marches, may cause us to overlook important developments in inter- or intrapublic discourse as well as publicity."[48] Warner elaborates upon the assumption of reason and rationality as guiding the form of discourse in the public sphere, which fails to see the potential poetic discourses of Others. This echoes Fraser who argues that "participation means being able to speak 'in one's own voice,' thereby simultaneously constructing and expressing in one's cultural identity through idiom and style."[49] Additionally Deem asserts, "The abstract(ed) body of the bourgeois white male, imbued with rational speech, came to stand in for the representativeness of the political. Logics of abstraction account for the invisibility of the male body and the simultaneous visibility of those groups (racial and ethnic minorities and women) traditionally associated with the body, affect, and desire."[50] Certainly, performance and the poetic go hand in hand, and this reciprocal relationship should not be undervalued in understanding performance of resistance. Furthermore, performance theories' intrinsic tie with the body impels us to acknowledge the everyday embodied acts of marginalized bodies, not simply public discursive accounts but as powerful vernacular discourses. In considering this, we narrow our focus to Latina/o vernaculars as they intersect with performance, and specifically Latina/o performativities. We explore three themes: challenging the public/private divide, tricking and translating the public sphere, and blurring temporalities. It is our hope that these themes will offer new insights for theories of counterpublics and resistance.

Challenging the Public and the Private

The first characteristic of a performance-centered LVD is an embodiment of resistance that disrupts the public/private divide. This argument aligns with feminist scholars, such as Fraser, who argue against the divide in public sphere scholarship. Many white male heterosexual middle-class able bodies can live their lives relatively unnoticed or not surveilled until they *choose* to participate in "actions of dissent." The lived realities of marked bodies of color demonstrate the blurring of these "public"/"private" spheres. hooks notes that these bodies are for dominant culture's consumption.[51] Similarly, Muñoz terms this the "burden of liveness" in that the bodies of people of color are called to "be live" for the purpose of entertaining elites: "This 'burden of liveness' is a cultural imperative within the majoritarian public sphere that denies subalterns access to larger channels of representation, while calling the minoritarian subject to the stage, performing her or his alterity as a consumable local spectacle."[52] We look to everyday movements of marginalized bodies as counterpublic acts of survival. Muñoz terms these survival methods "disidentifications."[53] Muñoz explains, "Disidentification is meant to be descriptive of the survival strategies the minority subject practices in order to negotiate a phobic majoritarian public sphere that continuously elides or punishes the existence of subjects who do not conform to the phantasm of normative citizenship."[54] He further argues that other times a conformist path is necessary to survive a hostile public sphere. Disidentification explicates how queer bodies of color are constantly negotiating the "permeable boundaries" of public and private spheres. Muñoz claims disidentification is a survival strategy that "works within and outside the dominant public sphere simultaneously."[55] Disidentification as a theory of the body points to the intentional performances of marginalized bodies that function as "counter" doings within the dominant public sphere. Arrizón defines these survival actions as "queering mestizaje" as they "open a space for the articulations of bodies and desires that emanate from subjective experiences at the borderlines of race, gender, and sexuality."[56] Arrizón returns us to the body as politically charged; that it is not just our actions but within the Othered body itself that emanates counterpublic discourses. She expands understandings of "counter" public knowledge as not only survival methods but actions of agency. What their work teaches us is that LVD acts performatively because their knowings and doings begin within a body that is already and always marked as Other.

Many Latina/os do not have the privilege of invisibility because of their racial embodiments and racist ideologies associated with these embodiments.[57] Whiteness, as the hegemony, allows for the safety of cultural invisibility, creating the privilege of not having to claim a cultural identity. While there are certainly Latina/os that can pass and perform in ways consistent with whiteness, this is not an option available to everyone. Thus, it is important to consider how the Otherness of Latina/o bodies is subjected to surveillance and policing. Theoretical explanations of surveillance teach us how the politics of the body are always on display even when in "private" spaces. Our work urges counterpublic theory to account for the ways Othered bodies are always "public" or on display. Thus, the mundane or everyday lived experiences of these bodies are constantly operating in conjunction with public sphere framings.

We learn to reconceptualize resistance through these spaces. Small acts of resistance come through the politics of the body simply living within and through the public sphere. For example, Calafell examines how Mario, a Chicano transplant to North Carolina, performs against black and white racial discourses that negate his identity.[58] His performance transforms the space, affectively enabling the possibility for Chicana/o identifications as he disidentifies against the black/white dichotomy. Similarly, Chávez explores narratives of her family in Nebraska to consider their disidentificatory practices against the space's whiteness, practices that also go against dominant narratives of Latinidad.[59] Pineda's work highlights the intimate yet politically/publicly discussed narrative of the journey from Mexico to the United States that many migrants face through his critical examination of the work of the musical group *Los Lobos*.[60] Additionally, Calvente discusses her border crossing experiences as a Puerto Rican who is read through lenses of "illegality" when crossing the US/Mexico border.[61] Similar themes of creating space for Latina/o identities, points of connections and rearticulation, are also seen in the work of Moreman[62] and McIntosh.[63] The negotiation of surveillance and public/private negotiations of intimacy and power is probably the most pronounced in Calafell's discussion of the required performances of citizenship needed to ensure one's ability to act as a responsible sponsor for immigration.[64] Calafell demonstrates how a narrative of desired US citizenship, heterosexuality, and "non-threatening" racial performances of intimacy are performed visually through photographs and in the actual immigration interview.[65] This Latina/o performative scholarship demonstrates how everyday performances of resistance embodied by Latina/o bodies disrupt normative understandings of the public/private divide.

Tricking and Translating the Public Sphere

The second characteristic of a performance-centered LVD is the role of the performer as a trickster or cultural translator. This characteristic can be traced to Chicana feminist theories, particularly informed by Anzaldúa.[66] A central component of Anzaldúa's conceptualization of mestiza identities is the ability to "continually walk out of one culture and into another" because the mestiza is "in all cultures, at the same time."[67] With a cultural lineage tied to the Spanish colonialism of Latin America, mestiza identities are based in mixed-race identities. Anzaldúa's mestiza performs as a product of multiple cultures, having a tolerance for ambiguity. This tolerance for ambiguity allows for the bridging position, which permits Chicana feminists to create spaces that connect with others across difference.[68] Through Chicanas the opportunity to act as bridges creates spaces of empowerment and agency. Augmenting this perspective, Muñoz argues, "The importance of such public and semipublic enactments of the hybrid self cannot be undervalued in relation to the formation of counterpublics that contest the hegemonic supremacy of the majoritarian public sphere."[69] These performances "offer the minoritarian subject a space to situate itself in history and thus seize social agency."[70] Calafell demonstrates such power in her examination of pop star Ricky Martin, who draws on both racial and sexual ambiguity as strategies that simultaneously grant him agency, empowerment, and protection.[71]

In examining trickster performances, we can understand how performances by people of color that may seem consistent with hegemonies may in fact be imbued with hidden transcripts or performative means of disidentification, such as excess, camp, or kitsch that work in resistance to these ideologies, operating as counterpublics. Thus, many people of color perform in a trickster position as an act of resistance and livelihood, such as in the case of Ricky Martin prior to his coming out of the closet. It is within contradiction (even with the theme of the public/private) that possibility exists. Martin was viewed through the lens of hypersurvellience because of his celebrity. Martin embodied and performed the desired Latin Lover archetype through his movement, marketing, and music. He performed the desired Other or "dark" sexuality for mainstream consumption, while he also drew upon gay archetypes such as Dyer's sad gay young man in other promotional materials. As we argue in the previous section of this chapter, the public and private split is false in the case of LVD performances. Here, we see how Martin recognizes and performs within the constraints. For example, through the referencing of hegemonic archetypes and queering them subversively, Martin is able to create spaces of possibility within surveillance. In some ways Martin's performance "spectacle" could mirror Deem's argument about how women's transgressive practices "can dislodge constraints on female speech. By putting the male body on the line, both Bobbitt and SCUM render the male body visible and displace the logics of witnessing and testimony."[72] Through Martin's tongue in cheek hyperheterosexual performance, he is able to gesture toward the absurdity of heteronormativity, specifically the Latin lover image.

In his resistance to naming his sexuality and through his embodied performance of racial ambiguity, Martin disrupted dominant racial and sexual logics. He used the trickster position to challenge racist and homophobic discourses and create a space of safety and possibility for himself. These trickster performances often rely on creativity, which Anzaldúa argues is connected to resistance. She states, "For many of us the acts of writing, painting, performing, and filming are acts of deliberate and desperate determination to subvert the status quo. Creative acts are forms of political activism employing definite aesthetic strategies for resisting dominant cultural norms and are not merely aesthetic exercises."[73] This trickster position is similar to Muñoz's theorization of performances of disidentification, which simultaneously work on and against dominant ideologies.[74] This strategy of disidentification also mirrors key principles of vernacular discourse, pastiche and cultural syncretism, as in many cases elements are torn out of popular culture and reconstituted with different meanings for the rhetor.[75]

Within a LVD performance perspective the cultural translator or trickster plays a key role in educating others about Latina/o worldviews, working against hegemonic representations and archetypes, and bridging.[76] For example, part of a Chicana feminist project has been the reappropriation and rearticulation of cultural archetypes such as the Virgin of Guadalupe and La Malinche, through which patriarchal definitions have contributed to the oppressive virgin/whore dichotomy.[77] This critical project manifests itself in LVD performances through the reexaminations and reimaginings of the stories of La Malinche/Malintzin Tenepal (translator, lover of Hernán Cortés, and symbolic mother of mestiza/os)[78] and her son Martín,[79] as well narratives that disrupt dominant discourses about Latina/o immigrants in performances by *Los Lobos*[80] and *El Vez*.[81]

Through these acts of reinterpretation or revision, performance-centered LVD creates spaces of possibility for a bridging position with other communities in which they are invited to partake in and with these discourses.[82] This bridging position can manifest itself in multiple forms of mestizaje, including performances by individuals who perform biculturality or racial hybridity.[83] When performed at the level of popular culture these bridging positions can manifest themselves through the lens of the trickster who plays with discourses of racial or sexual ambiguity.[84] The trickster relishes in ambiguity, which creates middle spaces that enable both resistance and connection, mirroring Anzaldúa's borderlands, where the mestiza lives.[85] They mirror what Madison terms a performance of possibilities centering on "the principles of transformation and transgression, dialogue and interrogation, as well as acceptance and imagination to build worlds that are *possible*."[86] Connecting Madison's work to LVD, Moreman and McIntosh expose possibilities that lay in wait through performance.[87] Their research uncovers the intersectional complexities between bodies and performance, specifically through the performative embodiment of queer mestiza performance. Within the liminal space between Latina drag queen performer and Latina audience members, performative possibilities lay in wait, "offering insights into how these negotiations intricately work through the body and show how these performances politically de-center hegemonic identity norms."[88] The possibilities of these performances manifest solely due to the politics of the Latina/o body.

The role of trickster or cultural translator as a key aspect of performative LVD offers us a mode by which to understand how these performances operate as counterpublics. Though initially the trickster theme may seem in contraction with the theme of the disruption of the private/public split, we embrace this potential contradiction as a space of possibility and invitation for readers to look closely at the cultural nuances and referents to consider the subversive potentials of trickster performances. An already highly surveilled body works to create spaces of possibility and resistance through disidentifications that both work on and against dominant discourses and serve as bridges, inviting connections across difference. The trickster's positionality operates in a manner similar to Scott's hidden transcripts. Tricksters' acts of resistance draw upon cultural nuances and signifiers that are understood within their communities[89] (i.e., Ricky Martin's coding of his queerness,[90] Gomez-Peña's tools and acts of exorcism,[91] or references used in Culture Clash's "Chicanos on the Storm"); while in their role as cultural translators they create spaces where connection across difference is possible. In this cultural translator position, performers work to counter oppressive ideologies about race, class, gender, sexuality, nationality, and ability, offering an Other view to audiences who they hope will accept the invitation for dialogue. Thus, the counterpublic offered by these performances is resistive, based in education *and* extends the possibility for alliance building. This potential for alliance building mirrors Squires's discussion of goals for the definition of counterpublic within her rethinking of the black public sphere. Whereas enclavement and satellite performances are more focused within or through the theme of retreat, the specificity Squires offers in defining counterpublics includes fostering resistance, creating alliances, and working to persuade "outsiders to change their views."[92]

Blurring Temporalities

A final important aspect of LVD performances is the queering of temporality, which blurs lines between past, present, and future. This queering or blurring of temporality works within Muñoz's "burden of liveness,"[93] which often forces postcolonial subjects to perform in the present for dominant cultures. Calafell describes queer temporality as relating to the backward glance, the desire in the present for the past that never was (i.e., a noncolonized past), which conversely affects the potentials for performances in the future.[94] Calafell writes:

> My intention is not to use this framework as if to suggest that those who employ a queer temporality have no history of their own, thus they must create history; rather I argue that dominant discourses do in fact include them in narratives, but in ways that marginalize them, do not privilege their experiences, or allow them to define those experiences. Thus, they employ disidentificatory strategies such as memory and queer temporality to challenge these constructions and power interests, offer counter narratives, and create communities based upon these feelings of difference and excess.[95]

This desire to "look back," to blur the line between the past, present, and future is a key aspect of LVD performances and is in many ways tied to histories of colonialism, and the desire to perform against or reinterpret these histories.[96]

This "looking back" performance acts as a form of disidentification; as it "transports us across symbolic space, it also inserts us in a coterminous time where we witness a new formation within the present and the future."[97] The violence of colonialism written on the Latina/o body is a constant reminder of this history. Thus, the backward glance is not unusual as understandings of temporality are based in the legacy written on and through the feeling body. These legacies have the potential to be remade through performance. This backward glance manifests itself through rearticulation of key colonial figures, as in Calafell's performative pilgrimage in honor of Malintzin Tenépal,[98] or Calafell and Moreman's examination of the narrative of Martín Cortés,[99] the symbolic first mestizo, as they revisit his story to consider what implications it has for contemporary Chicana/os. The backward glance also manifests itself in the exorcism of the ills of colonialism or psychic trauma as seen in performances by Guillermo Gomez-Peña and Culture Clash.[100] These symbolic exorcisms allow Latina/o subjects to imagine a future imbued with possibilities. We also see the mixing of temporalities in the late Celia Cruz exhibit at the Smithsonian as her life is represented for audience members who engage her visually and aurally as she sings.[101] These performances mirror what Warner argues—that "counterpublics are spaces of circulation in which it is hoped that the poesis of scene making will be transformative, not replicative merely."[102] Furthermore, each of these performances considers how the past reverberates in the present and into the future, and gestures to how the backward glance might not simply be a symptom of postcolonial identities but in some cases is tied to diasporic subjectivities as individuals are removed from homelands.

In revisiting the past through queering temporality, there is also a move to revisit the meanings located in mestiza/o or hybrid identities.[103] For example, Calafell pushes understandings of Latina/o mestizaje by asking how we might also tie our mixed-race identities to the Moors in Spain as we consider the Arab influences that might be in the shadow of our Latina/o identities.[104] These kinds of connections have been erased by discourses of racial purity that drove elaborate racial categorizations after colonialism. They have also been ignored because of the use of strategic essentialism in social movement discourses, such as in the Chicana/o movement, which was driven by discourses of indigenism. However, it might benefit us to ask how these past neglected connections might enable new performances and coalitions in the present and the future. An example more traditionally centered in stage performance, Robert Lopez performs as a Chicano Elvis

Presley "translator," *El Vez*. He uses his hybrid/mestizo body to further jux-
tapose layers of cultural hybridity through his embodiment of a mix of Che
Guevarra and Elvis Presley.[105] Not only does Lopez wear the cultural signifiers of each on his mestizo body but he also blurs the narratives of each in
politically charged songs that change "Suspicious Minds" to "Immigration
Time."[106] The juxtaposition of these symbols and their respective narratives
on his mixed-race body and in his music further challenges colonial hegemonies about race and their contemporary manifestations in stereotype.

The reinterpretation of cultural archetypes continues to have meanings
for Latina/o bodies across the past, present, and future in a sense blurring
temporality. In addition, Latina/o vernacular performances have the possibility to play with racial hybridity against dominant racial logics, offering powerful counterpublics. In thinking about the blurring or queering of
temporality we must remember, as Muñoz argues, "queerness is also a performative because it is not simply a being but a doing for and toward the
future. Queerness is essentially about the rejection of a here and now and
an insistence on potentiality or concrete possibility for another world."[107]
This embodied hybridity and the blurring of temporality work as counterpublics against dominant "postracial" logics in the public sphere that insist
we are living in a society that is free of racism and sexism. Hybridity and
queer temporality demonstrate that the violence of colonialism must never
be forgotten as it is written on the body.

Additionally, through the reinterpretation of mythic or archetypal colonial figures, LVD performances present new meanings that counter oppressive systems of representation, which in turn creates new possibilities
for future generations. The backward glance adds another dimension to
counterpublics by building upon traditional social movement studies focused on Chicana/o communities such as those written by Hammerback,
Jensen, and Gutiérrez.[108] While these scholars consider the use of Aztec or
indigenous imagery in the rhetoric of Rodolfo "Corky" Gonzales, which
manifested in the rhetoric of Chicanismo, the effects of the postcolonial
condition has not yet been fully explored. Additionally, their understandings of Aztlán, the Chicana/o homeland, are not framed through the lens
of diaspora as more recently argued by Calafell.[109] Thus, by offering the
queering of temporality or the backward glance as a central aspect of LVD
performances we extend counterpublic and social movement studies to
consider how colonialism may alter the form and content of resistance.

In a similar vein, work by Enck-Wanzer and Cisneros respectively pushes
social movement studies to view resistance through a more performative,
active, or processual frame.[110] Though each of these studies might not call

themselves LVD, they mirror properties we outline here as central to LVD, namely a performative element that undergirds embodied action and decolonial critique through hybridity. While the early studies of Chicana/o movement discourse certainly grounded themselves in the work of social movements, they also grounded themselves in many ways in identity formations that were static and sometimes essentialist because they were connected to specific historical movements. However, we might consider that more recent studies of Latina/o discourse appear to be driven by more dynamic performances of identities that are undergirded by a performance and performativity relationship. Furthermore, it could be that traditional social movement studies often focus on the ironically hegemonic voices of the movement, as in the case of Chicana/o movement rhetorics that focused on the discourses espoused by the straight male leaders. Within counterpublics we find more subaltern voices (such as those Chicanas in the movement who were silenced), and in the study of vernaculars we find those that happen everyday (i.e., murals, song, and performance). These LVD performances denote the queering of temporality and thus the blurring of lines between past, present, and future.

Conclusions

In this chapter we have demonstrated the ways LVD performances challenge counterpublic theories in new directions, asking us to consider how the bodies of people of color are always and already "counter" to dominant ideologies that govern the public sphere. Specifically, informed by Holling and Calafell's work,[111] we have considered how colonialism and everyday acts of performance offer Other dimensions to counterpublic theory. LVD performances disrupt the public-private divide, offer trickster and translator performances, and blur or queer temporalities. This work demands that scholars come to LVD on its own terms. Latina/os often dwell in spaces of contradiction, borderlands, and duality. We ask that scholars move from Eurocentric ways of knowing and understanding to take an Other perspective and logics.

We surveyed the small, but growing body of work in Latina/o communication studies that operates from a performance perspective. As this body of scholarship further develops, we are curious to see the forms it takes and how it might continue to enhance and nuance our understanding of counterpublic performances by "minority" groups. Counterpublics must be understood as an embodied process of the everyday. The "counter" body moves within and through "the" public sphere, tricking, blurring, and bridging counterpublics and publics alike. LVDs remake "the" public sphere each and everyday.

Gómez Peña stands before you in an iron, spiked headdress and shell-lined vest.[112] The lighting darkens his brown body against a cream back-drop. His intense eyes look from his right shoulder to you. He lifts his right hand and begins to open and snap close kitchen shears in front and around his face. A young girl begins to speak. She repeats the same line, but un-like prior performances, her words are not translated into English subtitles. As her voice lingers into silence, Gómez Peña brings the shears to his ear. He begins to open and close the shears around his left ear. We watch as his ear begins to fold under the pressure. He repeats this movement, while his eyes grimace in pain. You hear him groaning and feel a visceral response.

The young girl breaks the silence and repeats her words, again no trans-lations offered. Gómez Peña slowly moves the shears to his nose. He snaps the shears closed at the base of his nose. The repeated pressure bulges the tip of his nose. We experience his pain through his twitching eyes, his la-bored breathing, his flinching neck and shoulders. The young girl's voice returns, saying something different now. She repeats this new line. Gómez Peña pauses and moves the shears to his tongue. His hand begins to move quickly as the young girl repeats the same words. The shears pinch his flesh as he grunts and strains. His face becomes disfigured as the shears bind his lips.

Silence

Gómez Peña slowly releases his lips and lowers his hand. The young girl speaks one last time and he lifts his head high and holds his shoulders broadly. As her voice trails off, he turns his face from the camera to his left shoulder. The performance ends, as it began, with his body on display. But his eyes do not meet yours.

"The Museum of Fetishized Identities" is visually abrasive. Gómez Peña's performance succinctly denotes how Latina/o bodies are simultaneously public and counterpublic. This performance stages that which is experienced by bodies of color on a daily basis. In turn, it moved me deeply. I engage with his pain and simultaneously feel convicted for his pain. I also deeply desire to know, "What is the young girl saying?" The translation frustration nags at me. I feel as though I am missing a critical piece of the puzzle. I feel cheated. I watch the video multiple times. The more I watch the more painful it is. My ears and tongue begin to sting as the shears clasp closed.

Eventually, I play the video with my eyes closed focusing on her voice only. There is nothing I can pick out or recognize. She is not speaking Spanish. I do not know what she is speaking. Gómez Peña demonstrates the public consumption of bodies of color and their negotiations within and through the hegemonic public. His performance bleeds into my lived experience of it. He tricks me with his blurring of "Brown" languages. And in the end, he stages the bridging Latina/o bodies conjure through the hegemonic public as counterpublics. His staged performance poignantly enacts the everyday lived realities of Latina/os, denoting the complex fluidity of public/private, public/counterpublic, and disenfranchised/empowered. Gómez Peña demonstrates how dominant discursives cannot fully consume, absorb, or appropriate the complex fluidity of embodied performances of "Others." I still wonder, what is she saying . . .

Notes

1. See Guillermo Gómez Peña, "Guillermo Gómez Peña in Performance," YouTube video, 2:53. posted September 6, 2009, accessed August 5, 2016, www.youtube.com/watch?v=TZMlbpoYnGI&list=FLIwymFG6Wb8r6oxwLvAu13Q.

2. Catherine R. Squires, "Rethinking the Black Public Sphere: An Alternative Vocabulary for Multiple Public Spheres," *Communication Theory* 12, no. 4 (2002): 450.

3. Ibid., 465.

4. Michelle A. Holling and Bernadette Marie Calafell, "Tracing the Emergence of Latina/o Vernaculars in Studies of Latin@ Communication," in *Latina/o Discourse in Vernacular Spaces: Somos de Una Voz?* ed. Michelle A. Holling and Bernadette M. Calafell (Lanham, MD: Lexington Press, 2011), 17–29.

5. Kent A. Ono and John M. Sloop. "The Critique of Vernacular Discourse," *Communication Monographs* 62, no. 1 (1995): 19–46.

6. Gerard Hauser, *Vernacular Voices: The Rhetoric of Publics and Public Spheres* (Columbia: University of South Carolina Press, 1999).

7. Rita Felski, *Beyond Feminist Aesthetics: Feminist Literature and Social Change* (Cambridge, MA: Harvard University Press, 1989), 166.

8. Ibid.

9. For more on what performance offers the study of rhetoric see E. Patrick Johnson, ed., *Dwight Conquergood: Performance, Ethnography, Praxis* (Ann Arbor: University of Michigan Press, 2013).

10. Gloria Anzaldúa, *Borderlands/La Frontera: The New Mestiza* (San Francisco: Aunt Lute Books, 1987).

11. Patricia Hill Collins, *Black Feminist Thought: Knowledge, Consciousness, and the Politics of Empowerment* (New York: Routledge, 1990).

12. Calafell, "Rhetorics of Possibility," in *Rhetorica in Motion: Feminist Rhetorical Methods and Methodologies*, ed. Eileen Schell and K. J. Rawson (Pittsburgh: University of Pittsburgh Press, 2010), 104–17.

13. D. Soyini Madison, "That Was My Occupation," *Text and Performance Quarterly* 13, no. 3 (1993): 213–32.

14. James C. Scott, *Domination and the Arts of Resistance: Hidden Transcripts* (New Haven, CT: Yale University Press, 1991).

15. Calafell, "Rhetorics of Possibility."

16. Scott, *Domination and the Arts of Resistance*.

17. Michelle Holling, "Retrospective on Latin@ Rhetorical-Performance Scholarship," *Communication Review* 11, no. 4 (2008): 293–322.

18. For examples of this work reference see Calafell, "Rhetorics of Possibility"; Michelle Holling and Bernadette Marie Calafell, "Identities on Stage and Staging Identities," *Text and Performance Quarterly* 27, no. 1 (2007): 58–83.

19. Jürgen Habermas, *The Structural Transformation of the Public Sphere: An Inquiry into a Category of Bourgeois Society*, trans. T. Burger and F. Lawrence (Cambridge: Massachusetts Institute of Technology Press, 1991).

20. Nancy Fraser, "Rethinking the Public Sphere," *Social Text* 25/26 (1990): 67.

21. Ibid., 61.

22. Ibid., 62.

23. Michael Warner, "The Mass Public and the Mass Subject," in *Habermas and the Public Sphere*, ed. Craig J. Calhoun (Cambridge: Massachusetts Institute of Technology Press, 1993), 384.

24. Michael Warner, *Publics and Counterpublics* (New York: Zone Books, 2002), 114.

25. Daniel Brouwer, "The Precarious Visibility Politics of Self-Stigmatization: The Case of HIV/AIDS Tattoos," *Text and Performance Quarterly* 18, no. 2 (1998): 114–36.

26. Michael Warner, "Publics and Counterpublics," *Public Culture* 14, no. 1 (2002): 49–90.

27. Warner, "The Mass Public and the Mass Subject," 384.

28. Robert Asen, "Seeking the 'Counter' in Counterpublics," *Communication Theory* 10, no. 4 (2000): 444.

29. Ibid, 432.

30. For further explanation see Holling and Calafell, "Tracing the Emergence," and Holling and Calafell, "Identities on Stage."

31. For further discussion of mestiza/o identities, colonialism, and present-day reverberations see Bernadette Marie Calafell and Shane Moreman, "Iterative Hesitancies and *Latinidad*: The Reverberances of Raciality," in *Handbook of Critical Intercultural Communication*, ed. Rona Halualani and Thomas K. Nakayama (Malden, MA: Wiley-Blackwell, 2010), 400–16.

32. Daniel C. Brouwer, "ACT-ing up in Congressional Hearings," in *Counter-*

publics and the State, ed. Robert Asen and Daniel C. Brouwer (Albany: State University of New York Press, 2001), 89.

33. Calafell, "Rhetorics of Possibility," 106 (our emphasis).

34. Brouwer, "The Precarious Visibility" and "Counterpublicity and Corporeality in HIV/AIDS Zines," *Critical Studies in Media Communication* 22, no. 5 (2005): 351–71.

35. Brouwer, "Counterpublicity and Corporeality," 364.

36. Warner, "Publics and Counterpublics."

37. Robert Asen, "Representing the State in South Central Los Angeles," in *Counterpublics and the State*, ed. Robert Asen and Daniel C. Brouwer (Albany: State University of New York Press, Albany, 2001), 139.

38. Angharad Valdivia, *A Latina in the Land of Hollywood* (Tucson: University of Arizona Press, 2000).

39. Richard Gregg, "The Ego-Function of the Rhetoric of Social Protest," in *Readings in the Rhetoric of Social Protest*, 3rd ed., ed. Charles E. Morris III and Stephen Howard Browne (State College, PA: Strata Publishing, 2013), 45–47.

40. Christina Foust, *Transgression as a Mode of Resistance: Rethinking Social Movement in an Era of Corporate Globalization* (Lanham, MD: Lexington Books, 2010).

41. Ibid.

42. Phaedra C. Pezzullo, "Resisting 'National Breast Cancer Awareness Month': The Rhetorics of Counterpublics and Their Cultural Performances," *Quarterly Journal of Speech* 89, no. 4 (2003): 345–65.

43. Darrel Enck-Wanzer, "Trashing the System: Social Movement, Intersectional Rhetoric, and Collective Agency in the Young Lords Organization's Garbage Offensive," *Quarterly Journal of Speech* 92, no. 2 (2006): 174–201.

44. Elizabeth Bell, *Performance Theories* (Thousand Oaks, CA: SAGE Publications, 2008).

45. Robert Asen and Daniel Brouwer, "Reconfigurations of the Public Sphere," in *Counterpublics and the State*, ed. Robert Asen and Daniel C. Brouwer (Albany: State University of New York Press, 2001), 20.

46. José Esteban Muñoz, *Disidentifications: Queers of Color and the Performance of Politics* (Minneapolis: University of Minnesota Press, 1999).

47. Ibid.

48. Squires, "Rethinking the Black Public Sphere," 447.

49. Fraser, "Rethinking the Public Sphere," 69.

50. Melissa D. Deem, "From Bobbitt to SCUM: Re-memberment, Scatological Rhetorics, and Feminist Strategies in the Contemporary United States," *Public Culture* 8, no. 3 (1998): 511–37.

51. bell hooks, "Eating the Other," in *Black Looks: Race and Representation* (Boston: South End Press, 1992), 29.

52. Muñoz, *Disidentifications*, 182.

53. Ibid.

54. Ibid., 4.

55. Ibid., 5.

56. Alicia Arrizón, *Queering Mestizaje: Transculturation and Performance* (Ann Arbor: University of Michigan, 2006), 183.

57. Jonathan Inda, "Performativity, Materiality, and the Racial Body," *Latino Studies Journal* 11, no. 3 (2000): 74–99.

58. Bernadette Calafell, "Disrupting the Dichotomy: Yo Soy Chicana/o in the New Latina/o South," *Communication Review* 7, no. 2 (2004): 175–204.

59. Karma Chávez, "Remapping Latinidad: A Performance Cartography of Latina/o Identity in Rural Nebraska," *Text and Performance Quarterly* 29, no. 2 (2009): 165–82.

60. Richard Pineda, "Will They See Me Coming? Do They Know I'm Running?" *Text and Performance Quarterly* 29, no. 2 (2009): 183–200.

61. Lisa Calvente, "'This Is One Line You Won't Have to Worry about Crossing': Crossing Borders and Becoming," in *Latina/o Discourse in Vernacular Spaces: Somos de Una Voz?* ed. Michelle A. Holling and Bernadette M. Calafell (Lanham, MD: Lexington Press, 2011): 185–201.

62. Shane T. Moreman, "Hybrid Performativity, South and North of the Border," in *Latina/o Communication Studies Today*, ed. Angharad Valdivia (New York: Peter Lang, 2008), 91–111; "Memoir as Performance," *Text and Performance Quarterly* 29, no. 4 (2009): 346–66.

63. Dawn Marie McIntosh, "Staging the Critical Functions of Identity: An Ethnography of Latina Drag Queens," master's thesis, California State University Fresno, 2007.

64. Bernadette Calafell, "Performing the Responsible Sponsor," in *Latina/o Communication Studies Today*, ed. Angharad Valdivia (New York: Peter Lang, 2008), 69–89.

65. Ibid.

66. Anzaldúa, *Borderlands*; Gloria Anzaldúa, "Haciendo caras: una entrada," in *The Gloria Anzaldúa Reader*, ed. Ana Louise Keating (Durham, NC: Duke University Press, 2009): 124–40.

67. Anzaldúa, *Borderlands*, 91.

68. Lisa A. Flores, "Creating Discursive Space through a Rhetoric of Difference: Chicana Feminists Craft a Homeland," *Quarterly Journal of Speech* 82 (1996): 142–56.

69. Muñoz, *Disidentifications*, 1.

70. Ibid. 2.

71. Calafell, *Latina/o Communication Studies* (New York: Peter Lang, 2007).

72. Deem, "From Bobbitt to SCUM," 515.

73. Anzaldúa, "Haciendo Caras," 135.

74. Muñoz, *Disidentifications*.

75. Ono and Sloop, "Critique of Vernacular Discourse," 19–46.

76. Work that exemplifies this role of the trickster or translator are as fol-

lows: Calafell, *Latina/o Communication Studies*; Calafell and Moreman, "Iterative Hesitancies"; Holling and Calafell, "Identities on Stage"; Moreman, "Hybrid Performativity," "Memoirs," and "Qualitative Interviews of Racial Fluctuations," *Communication Theory* 21, no. 2 (2011): 197–216; Shane Moreman and Dawn Marie McIntosh, "Brown Scriptings and Rescriptings," *Communication and Critical/Cultural Studies* 7, no. 2 (2010): 115–35; Pineda, "Will They See Me Coming"; and Shane T. Moreman and Bernadette Marie Calafell, *"Buscando Para Nuestros Hijos*: Utilizing *La Llorona* for Cultural Critique," *Journal of International and Intercultural Communication* 1, no. 4 (2008): 309–26.

77. Calafell, *Latina/o Communication Studies*.

78. Bernadette Marie Calafell, "Pro(re-)claiming Loss: A Performative Pilgrimage in Search of Malintzin Tenépal," *Text and Performance Quarterly* 25, no. 1 (2005): 43-56.

79. Calafell and Moreman, "Iterative Hesitancies."

80. Pineda, "Will They See Me Coming."

81. Calafell, *Latina/o Communication Studies*.

82. Works that demonstrates this bridged position and spaces of possibilities are as follows: Calafell, *Latina/o Communication Studies*; Calafell and Moreman, "Iterative Hesitancies"; Moreman and McIntosh, "Brown Scriptings and Rescriptings"; Holling and Calafell, "Identities on Stage"; Moreman "Hybrid Performativity," "Memoirs," and "Qualitative Interviews;" and Pineda, "Will They See Me Coming."

83. Works that denote our framing of performing biculturality or racial hybridity are as follows: Holling and Calafell, "Identities on Stage"; Moreman, "Memoirs" and "Qualitative Interviews."

84. For further examples of tricksters see: Calafell, *Latina/o Communication Studies*; Holling and Calafell, "Identities on Stage"; Moreman, "Hybrid Performativity"; and McIntosh, "Staging the Critical Functions."

85. Anzaldùa, *Borderlands*.

86. Soyini Madison, "Performance, Personal Narratives, and the Politics of Possibility," in *The Future of Performance Studies: Visions and Revisions*, ed. Sheron J. Dailey (Annandale, VA: National Communication Association, 1998), 278.

87. Moreman and McIntosh, "Brown Scriptings and Rescriptings."

88. Ibid., 130.

89. Scott, *Domination and the Arts of Resistance*.

90. Calafell, *Latina/o Communication Studies*; see Squires, "Rethinking the Black Public Sphere," for a discussion of how public and hidden transcripts work in conjunction with enclavement in the black public sphere.

91. Holling and Calafell, "Identities on Stage."

92. Squires, "Rethinking the Black Public Sphere," 460.

93. Muñoz, *Disidentifications*.

94. Calafell, "Pro(re)claiming Loss."

95. Ibid., 52.

96. Calafell, "Rhetorics of Possibility."

97. Muñoz, *Disidentifications*, 198.

98. Calafell, "Pro(re)claiming Loss."

99. Calafell and Moreman, "Iterative Hesitancies."

100. Holling and Calafell, "Identities on Stage."

101. Ramon Rivera-Servera, "Exhibiting Voice/ Narrating Migration," *Text and Performance Quarterly* 29, no. 2 (2009): 131–48.

102. Warner, "Publics and Counterpublics," 88.

103. For work that establishes the move to revisit the meanings in mestiza/o or hybrid identities, see Calafell, "Performing the Responsible Sponsor" and "Love, Loss, and Immigration," in *Border Rhetorics: Citizenship and Identity on the U.S. Mexico Frontier*, ed. Robert DeChaine (Tuscaloosa: University of Alabama Press, 2012), 151–62; and Calafell and Moreman, "Iterative Hesitancies."

104. Calafell, "Performing Responsible Sponsor" and "Love, Loss, and Immigration."

105. Calafell, *Latina/o Communication Studies*.

106. Ibid.

107. José Esteban Muñoz, *Cruising Utopia: The Then and There of Queer Futurity* (New York: New York University Press, 2009), 1.

108. John C. Hammerback, Richard J. Jensen, and José Angel Gutiérrez, *A War of Words: Chicano Protest in the 1960s and 1970s* (Westport, CT: Greenwood Press, 1985).

109. Calafell, "Disrupting the Dichotomy."

110. Enck-Wanzer, "Trashing the System"; and Josue David Cisneros, "(Re) Bordering the Civic Imaginary: Rhetoric, Hybridity, and Citizenship in *La Gran Marcha*," *Quarterly Journal of Speech* 97, no. 1 (2011): 26–49.

111. Holling and Calafell, "Tracing the Emergence."

112. Guillermo Gòmez Peña, "Museum of Fetishized Identities 'Guillermo Gómez-Peña,'" YouTube video, 1:30, January 25, 2008, accessed August 5, 2016, www.youtube.com/watch?v=UHWKXdeC6Vg&list=FLIwymFG6Wb8r6ox wLvAu13Q.

9

Activism in the Wake of the Events of China and Social Media

Abandoning the Domesticated Rituals of Democracy
to Explore the Dangers of Wild Public Screens

Kevin Michael DeLuca and Elizabeth Brunner

The world is changing.[1] The twin irruptions of *China*[2] and social media force scholars and citizens across the globe to think of new possibilities beyond our stunted imaginations. The challenge: to think these changes. The point will not be to contemplate China and social media and then tweak our thinking appropriately. Instead, the challenge is to think with and in these changes. What we mean by this will become clearer in the course of this chapter. First, back to our opening statement. The world is changing. Of course, the world is always changing, but not all changes matter. China and social media are momentous changes, what we will term *events*.[3]

The reawakening of China is an event that ruptures the world as it is and forces us to think everything anew, to conceptualize the truths of this emerging world. China's reemergence forces us to resist falling back upon old ways of seeing. It forces us to disrupt the strict hierarchies we imagine governing China with proliferating resistance, to replace singular subjects with networked assemblages, and to develop new tools by which to chart this ever-changing terrain. China, as an event, is opening up a new world, apparent in myriad areas from the economic to the environmental to the social and cultural and political. The emergence of social media is also an event. Panmediation made possible by smartphones—public screens in people's pockets—has altered media practices, political practices, and social practices. Before panmediation and smartphones, institutions and authorities defined the world and what mattered. As the *New York Times* still anachronistically loves to claim, they select "all the news that's fit to print." Now, every single day exposes the lie of that slogan. We live in new worlds. People deploying social media become decentered knots of world making that disrupt the architectures of mass media.[4]

So what does this mean for social change scholarship? It means we must rethink our assumptions of Democracy, the public sphere, and activism that underlie current social change scholarship. To do so, we turn to China and social media because, with tens of thousands of protests each year, China is a hotbed of social movement. These social movements are fundamentally altering China's governance in a way that complicates Western notions of Democracy. Our case studies thwart traditional notions of democracy, especially as they relate to public sphere theory. We introduce *wild public screens*, a concept that builds on the notion of *public screens* put forward by DeLuca and Peeples,[5] by thoroughly engaging the notion of *wildness* in the form of transgressions, shifting networks, speeds, and disruptive creativities.

Since we are making a claim to being theorists of social movement, that is, of change, we must examine the grounds of our own thinking and be open to changes following encounters with events. We will then provide evidence for our claims that China and social media are events opening spaces for emerging worlds, beyond current portrayals of China as either somber and sedated or as a terrifying hegemon in the making.

Beginning: Deleuze's *Détournement* of Thinking

So, how do we think an encounter with the events of China and social media? This is a difficult issue since the reflexive reaction is to retreat to old habits of thinking, comforting yet hackneyed ideas, chronic concepts that cripple our contemplations, well-worn ruts that damage our brains. How to think the new is an especially vexing problem for social movement scholars, since that is purportedly our mission. Yet we oscillate between encounters with the new and rhetorical notions of the subject, text, persuasion, and the public chained to the fossilized fumblings of Ancient Athens.[6] We turn to Deleuze because, in short, his confrontation with China forced him to do the very thing we are attempting in this essay—a rethinking of concepts so familiar they have morphed into commonsense assumptions. He (along with Guattari) asks us throughout his oeuvre to question all presuppositions, to make space for new ways of being, and to use new concepts (including the rhizome, the war machine, and the assemblage) to *think*, to map, and to explore.

Though not as celebrated as other works, Deleuze's *Difference and Repetition* provides an ungrounded grounding of his thinking. "The Image of Thought" is the vital core of that book. Deleuze starts off this chapter with what he understands to be the problem at the heart of Western thinking, "where to begin in philosophy has always—rightly—been regarded as a very delicate problem, for beginning means eliminating all presuppositions."[7] Deleuze spends the rest of the chapter performing this task. Deleuze insists that we must start with abandoning what "everybody knows" through common sense.[8] As scholars of social movements, we must unravel the pre-suppositions that ground the nonthinking of common sense: the image of the Human (the "I think" of *Homo sapiens*) and the image of Democracy (equal and rational beings using good reasons and civil discourse to make informed decisions). In a climate where "belief in progress is contemporary common sense," how can we enact new ways of thinking?[9] The new "calls forth forces in thought which are not the forces of recognition, today or to-morrow, but the powers of a completely other model, from an unrecognized and unrecognizable *terra incognita*."[10]

Now, to think. For Deleuze, "thought is primarily trespass and violence. . . . The contingency of an encounter with that which forces thought to raise up, . . . Something in the world forces us to think. This something is an object not of recognition but of a fundamental *encounter*."[11] For us at this world historical moment, it is the encounters with the events of China and social media that force us to think.

The West through the Looking Glass of China: A Shattered Vision

China is the place where hyper-urbanization/industrialization, postmodern panmediation, and a rabidly optimistic environmentalism collide at speeds and scales that create new worlds. As Campanella explains, "in terms of speed and scale as sheer audacity, China's Urban Revolution is off the charts of Western or even global experience. . . . The dull blue-gray world of Mao suits and rationed goods is long gone; China today is a 24/7 frenzy of con-sumerism and construction."[12] These changes are, in some ways, beyond un-derstanding; yet the China erupting, awakening, reemerging today warrants a closer look. We cannot overstate the size and scale of the changes cur-rently taking place in China. In order to undermine deeply embedded as-sumptions about China as "backward,"[13] allow us to elaborate on the sheer magnitude of the changes occurring.

Campanella offers some shocking figures that evidence the unprece-dented pace at which China is urbanizing. Between 1970 and the early 2000s, the number of cities in China more than tripled. As of 2012, China had over 160 cities with populations that exceed 1 million people, mak-ing over half of China's almost 1.4 billion plus people urban.[14] This rise of urban culture has brought with it the need for an extraordinary expansion of infrastructure including roads, public transit, and bridges. In 1980, China had 180 miles of highway, but today has over 30,000 miles and is expected to have 53,000 miles of modern highway roads by 2020, which exceeds the US highway system by 7,000 miles. China's public transit system is unparalleled. In 2008 alone, China spent $100 billion to establish and expand public transit systems in cities and across the country, linking urban centers such as Beijing and Shanghai by high-speed train and, in 2014, completed another set of expansions giving China more high-speed train tracks than the rest of the world combined.

Concomitant with its growth has also come a movement toward more sustainable energy practices. Today, China is the world's leader in the production of both wind turbines and solar panels and is working to build nuclear reactors as well as more efficient coal power plants.[15] In some small towns such as Rizhao, solar power is in at least 95 percent of all the buildings.[16] China must innovate, especially in regard to energy, to support its urbanizing population. As of 2011, China took the lead in the number of patent applications according to research conducted by Thomson Reuters. In 2012, Chinese scientists published the second-highest number of articles in the world, with about 80 percent of them in international journals.[17]

At the same time, Chinese environmental nongovernment organizations (ENGOs) are feverishly working to increase awareness and incite change in the wake of urbanization. To do so, they are melding and bending the Internet in creative ways. For example, the Institute of Public and Environmental Engagement created a China Water Pollution Map detailing where pollution is happening and offering links to pollution reports. Larger ENGOs such as Greenpeace have also become increasingly involved in identifying industrial facilities that are dumping hazardous waste into water supplies and, with heightened awareness, villagers have gathered, using their bodies to protest.

New media has become an essential tool to organize protests for groups and individuals. In the words of one interviewee, "social movements in China would be impossible without social media."[18] Chinese Internet users represent a significant and growing portion of the virtual universe. They are the world's largest Internet nation. In 2000, China had only 22.5 million Internet users, but as of the end of January 2014, the number of Chinese Internet users exceeded 618 million, which surpasses the 279 million Internet users in the United States two times over.[19] Of the 618 million Internet users in China, upwards of 355 million use WeChat, a microblogging and personal messaging service.

Sina Weibo is just one form of many new media in China. As Google debated its presence in China, Baidu, a comparable China-based search engine, skyrocketed in popularity and is now the most-used search engine in China. Similarly, QQ and renren fill the roles of instant messaging and Facebook (respectively), Youku offers users many of the same abilities as Youtube, and, of course, Weibo and Weixin offer users functionalities similar to Twitter. China is the most socially engaged country in the world with three-quarters of the population regularly active on some type of social media platform.[20]

Collectively, China's technological, structural, physical, political, and economic changes constitute an event that obliterates the image of an oppressed and repressed country and introduces a cacophonous frenzy of activity, new connections, and new ways of seeing and becoming. In the space left by this rupture lies room for many responses, and in this chapter rather than turn back to outdated Cold War notions of China, we advocate for a new mapping of the political terrain being constructed by hundreds of thousands of individuals marching down city streets, toting banners, and insisting that their government listen.

Responses to China as Event

To date, media portrayals of China have been steeped in Cold War and "yellow peril" discourses that constitute a China unilaterally oppressed by a harsh dictatorship. However, the China that has been so neatly drawn in the Western imaginary is exploding and challenging the confines placed around it. The rise of social media in China threatens the entire Western framework constructed around this *other* country. China's success rebukes the Western idea that democracy is the *only* means by which a country can be successful under global capitalism. This contests Western exceptionalism and has the potential to open an "infinity of worlds."[21] In the Western imagination, a governmental system outside of democracy is simply unthinkable for many. Badiou sees "genuine change" as "an *exit from the West*, a 'de-Westernization;, and it would take the form of an *exclusion*. A daydream, you will say. But it could be that it is right there, in front of our eyes."[22] China's rise is challenging the hegemony of the West and changing the order of the world.

There are two dominant ways to respond: 1) by disfiguring the event so that it fits into the old discourses of the world as it is and 2) to think through the truths of the event that disrupts the world as it is. In the United States, not surprisingly, the first strategy predominates and can be seen in a variety of discourses. For instance, scholarship that attempts to impose the public sphere model onto China in order to find proof of the emergence of democracy[23] becomes so encumbered with caveats and addenda that the public sphere as Habermas envisioned it is barely recognizable. For us, and scholars like Xin, the public sphere is being "insufficiently operationalized" then applied to "the Chinese case," with little to no explanatory power.[24] As such, we "run the risk of getting involved in an ideological or teleological exercise in which the Western model of development is merely projected onto China," instead of seeing China anew.[25]

We need to look outside Habermas to understand what is happening in China. The insistence that a turn to Western-style democracy is the best option for China is a persistent problem,[26] not to mention deeply problematic, seeing as Western-style democracy is currently in shambles (e.g., having been infiltrated by widespread government surveillance of the US's own people and other countries and corruption by corporate "free speech.").[27]

Today, in the age of the glance[28]—a time when the studious gaze has all but become extinct—Westerners are bombarded with negative framings of China as they search for books, skim the front page of the *New York Times*, or listen to the rhetoric of US political leaders. The repetition of this negative framing via hundreds of glances from different directions ensures that the rutted ways of thinking about China as a threat, creatively inept, and inherently inferior to the United States persist. To mimic the glance, we first turn to popular book titles about China, before moving on to journalistic reductions and political portraits. These popular book titles echo how social theorists treat China as the other, including: *Playing Our Game: Why China's Rise Doesn't Threaten the West*;[29] *China's Trapped Transition: The Limits of Developmental Autocracy*;[30] and *China Shakes the World: A Titan's Rise and Troubled Future—and the Challenge for America*.[31] Several important themes can be distilled from the book titles that populate bookshelves and search engine results. First, China is posited as a threat to US standing in the world order. Second, this threat is a challenge for the United States, but one that can be overcome. Third, China is constructed as playing unfairly as it threatens to overtake the United States. These types of discourses shoehorn China back into old patterns rather than thinking China anew.

The US mass media has also been largely negative about China, which forecloses rather than opens possible discussions and collaborations. Research has shown that news about China is laced with Sinophobic discourse and outdated conceptions that frame the country as backward, totalitarian, and the enemy.[32] The *Los Angeles Times* provides one anachronistic example, which positions Barack Obama as the opposite of "China's gray, staid Communist chiefs."[33] More significantly, the *New York Times* has provided saturation coverage of China while consistently framing China as a threat. Their front-page headlines, which offer glimpses into the China of the Western imaginary, provide ample evidence; examples of this include "Pollution from Chinese Coal Casts Shadow around the Globe,"[34] "As

China Roars, Pollution Reaches Deadly Extremes,"[35] and "China Grabs West's Smoke-Spewing Factories."[36]

This pervasive framing of China as a threat is echoed and amplified in the sound bytes and catch phrases that populate the political arena. During the 2012 presidential debates, China was a frequent topic. Governor Romney labeled the Chinese as thieves of America's intellectual property and counterfeiters of American goods, and President Obama promised to crack down on China. Chinese citizens took note of this, and, as one CNN story stated, "Obama, Romney's 'China Bashing' Grates Chinese Netizens."[37] Such US responses relegate China to Cold War discourses. *China as threat* simply replaces the *Soviet Union as threat*.

The second strategy available is to take the emergence of China as an event that opens up the world to new possibilities. It is to take seriously a very simple fact that Ailun Yang of Greenpeace China points out: "It's a very simplistic way of thinking of China as just one singular thing. It is a place where you have 1.3 billion people and there are huge differences from region to region, and economic structures are different, education levels are different. So it's actually a country with huge diversity."[38] It is time to start thinking from the ground of China instead of the vantage point of the West. As Jacques starkly concludes, "having been hegemonic for so long, the West has become imprisoned within its own assumptions, unable to see the world other than in terms of itself. . . . By seeing China in terms of the West, it refuses to recognize or acknowledge China's own originality and, furthermore, how China's difference might change the nature of the world in which we live."[39]

Our task, then, is to think the differences that the event of China introduces into the world. What worlds are now emerging? What new knowledges are being created? We consider this amid the twilight of Democracy and the emergence of social media and wild public screens.

Delusional Axioms of Activism and Outrageous Possibilities

> "Democracy—rule by the people—sounds like a fine thing; we should try it sometime in America."
>
> —Edward Abbey

China's reemergence is a call to think anew and use this vantage point to examine Democracy as a system that acutely constricts activism. An idealized image of Democracy that revolves around transcendental concepts of the public and the public sphere has hampered activism and social change.

The "axioms of activism"—Democracy, rationality, civility, the public sphere, and freedom of speech and assembly—not only are *not* essential to activism and social change but are often impediments.

Recent research has made clear that the United States is not a democracy but an oligarchy, where large corporations advance policy with far more success than any individual.[40] The democracy we now inhabit is a disfigured totem of the democracy of which we may have once dreamed.[41] This is true in both theory and praxis. As Rancière explains, "we do not live in democracies. Every State is oligarchic. Strictly speaking, democracy is not a form of State. It is always beneath and beyond these forms."[42] Nancy elaborates this position by arguing that *democracy* is not a property of the State, it is not only not a form of government but the very opposite of the State: "Democracy is not a regime but an uprising against the regime. . . .The democratic *kratein*, the power of the people, is first of all the power to foil the *arche* and then to take responsibility, all together and each individually, for the infinite opening that is thereby brought to light."[43]

Thinking using an idealized activism is limited by axiomatic tendencies with respect to Democracy. This is evident in Habermas's theorizing: "Citizens act as a public when they deal with matters of general interest without being subject to coercion; thus with the guarantee that they may assemble and unite freely, and express and publicize their opinions freely."[44] In naively idealizing "freely," Habermas's point becomes suspect in his own writing, for in the same paragraph he writes of "public discussions that are institutionally protected."[45] As Foust argues, transgression involves "true risk" by moving outside the confines of the existing systems and their promises of protected protest.[46] Institutional protection suggests not so much freedom as taming, a domestication.

To be blunt, Democracy and its *accoutrements* hamper activism and social change. In practice in the United States, over time, institutional protection has produced domesticated public spheres and tamed free speech, until now we have chain-linked free speech and protest zones. For example, the 2004 Democratic National Convention in Boston created a "free speech zone" underneath a highway overpass out of sight of the convention. This practice was repeated in 2008 and 2012. Far from Democracy being the condition for activism, institutional protection tames it and produces a domesticated activism as mere ritual. The shutdown of Occupy Wall Street across the United States was a stunning example of what has become the Architecture of Oppression, the nefarious combination of free speech zones, the Patriot Act, Internet surveillance with the cooperation of corporations such as Facebook, Google, and AT&T, privatized public spaces, and the use of local zoning laws to violate the First Amendment right to assemble.

Linking Democracy, the public sphere, and activism becomes even more problematic when trying to internationalize the concept. For starters, America's imperialism has rendered Democracy a terrifying and violent export, as the hundreds of thousands of corpses littering the globe mutely testify. In *Polemics*, Badiou rails against the current international manifestation of Democracy when he writes: "Ours is not a world of democracy but a world of imperial conservatism using democratic phraseology. . . . A solitary power, whose army single-handedly terrorizes the entire planet, dictates its law to the circulation of capital and images."[47]

By contrast, we want to proffer a proliferation of *wild public screens*, public screens full of risk, without First Amendment guarantees. China is a vibrant example of wild public screens, of spreading democratic activist practices with no guarantees of domesticating protection, wherein the decrepit delusions of the public sphere are absent, but there are "true risks" and powerful images and conversations and protests. From the giant public screens overlooking Beijing Olympics Bird's Nest to Shanghai's Nanjing Road, to ancient hutongs glowing with TVs and computers, to Yantai's middle classes absorbed by iPhones and iPads, public screens are as ubiquitous in China as they are around the globe. In comparison to the rationality, detachment, embodied conversations, and compulsory civility of the public sphere, public screens highlight images, glances, speed, panmediation, spectacular publicity, cacophony, immersion, distraction, and dissent.[48]

The phrase "wild public screen" points to another manifestation. The spread of public screen technologies, especially smartphones, forces all contemporary actors to engage and deploy public screens, including corporations, governments, and politicians as well as citizens and activists, thereby creating a very complex moving topography. As a consequence, powerful actors such as Facebook or Google are able to set technological, commercial, and cultural norms that domesticate public screens in stultifying ways tilted in favor of industrial corporate capitalism.

So, for example, the public screens of Times Square or Facebook are difficult spaces for imagining and enacting different worlds. And yet, certain Internet platforms make possible unruly spaces for thinking differently—wild public screens. Twitter or Weibo combined with smartphones have proven especially wild, from the Arab Spring to Occupy Wall Street to multiple environmental protests across China as citizens armed with smartphones and social media platforms become decentered knots of world making able to transform the world as it is. As the case studies below highlight, creativity, speed, and networks coalesce to form an arena in which netizens enact guerilla-style warfare.

For us "wild" suggests not something alternative or entirely other but an unruly and dangerous supplement.[49] The emergence of China combined with a mediascape transformed through the advent of social media gives birth to new conditions of possibility for activism and social change. We abandon the fossilized metaphor of the public sphere to engage the excessive proliferation of wild public screens characterized by *arrangiasti* (making do by any means necessary in the myriad places of the world). *democracy* lives in practices not institutional protections.

In highlighting the transformative impacts of public screens and social media, we are taking the strong stance that technologies transform conditions of possibilities. In doing so, we reject the inane and infantile wish that in a technologically driven world that transforms everything from love to work to the landscape of the Earth itself, some mystical human essence remains magically untouched. Humans becoming in an oral culture differ from humans becoming in a print culture and both differ from humans becoming in our mobile panmediated culture of myriad media.[50] McLuhan, author of the phrase "the medium is the message," argues that "the personal and social consequences of any medium results from the new scale that is introduced into our affairs by each extension of ourselves. . . . For the 'message' of any medium or technology is the change of scale or pace or pattern that it introduces into human affairs."[51] There are two key points that we want to emphasize here. First, following Innis, McLuhan is explaining how a medium/technology works on scale, pattern, and pace, thus transforming structures of space, time, and speed in which we are immersed.[52] Quite simply, reality is transformed, for far from being static, reality is always in processes of becoming.[53] Second, McLuhan explodes the human beyond its sack of skin—media are extensions of ourselves. In Deleuzian terms, we are always an assemblage, in this case an assemblage of our bodies and the media we engage and live amid. These new assemblages make possible new ways of being—including new ways of enacting democracy across social media platforms.

Deleuze thinks through the famous example of the stirrup from the perspective of assemblage: "Taking the feudal assemblage as an example, we would have to consider the interminglings of bodies defining feudalism: the body of the earth and the social body; the body of the overlord, vassal, and serf; the body of the knight and the horse and their new relation to the stirrup; the weapons and tools assuring a symbiosis of bodies—a whole machinic assemblage."[54] Deleuze sounds prescient in his description of the transformative impacts of new media on the human, the emergence of new assemblages: "Is it not commonplace nowadays to say that the forces of man have already entered into a relation with the forces of information technology and their third-generation machines which together create something other than man, indivisible 'man-machine' systems? Is this a union with silicon instead of carbon?"[55] Deleuze offers digital becoming in place of analog Being.

As the Internet becomes the central organizing principle of posthuman societies, social theorists have reimagined society literally and metaphorically as a network.[56] Benkler compellingly demonstrates how the Internet, as "the move to a communications environment built on cheap processors with high computation capabilities, interconnected in a pervasive network," has enabled the transformation of the industrial economy into a "networked information economy" that "has made human creativity and the economics of information itself the core structuring facts."[57] Technology is central. Internet platforms enable individuals to reach millions of others and to engage in "effective, large-scale cooperative efforts—peer production of information, knowledge, and culture."[58] As Benkler, Castells, and others note, this radical decentralization puts individuals outside of easy institutional control, enabling efforts that bypass political and corporate authorities. Benkler, throughout his magnum opus, celebrates how Internet platforms make it possible for individuals to operate outside of commercial markets and proprietary models.

Almost accidentally, the complex of technologies we call the Internet have transformed the structure of society and created possibilities for new forms of social relations, economic practices, knowledge production, and sharing that threaten the assumptions and practices of capitalism. In describing the Arab Spring, Spain's *Indignadas*, and Occupy Wall Street, Castells champions the role of "Internet social networks, as these are spaces of autonomy, largely beyond the control of governments and corporations that had monopolized the channels of communication as the foundation of their power, throughout history."[59] Benkler and Castells are not simplistic optimists. They, along with dark pessimist Morozov, provide somber reminders that governments and corporations will not yield control willingly, will not go gently into the good night, yet . . .[60]

Despite the layered levels of censorship imposed globally and by the Chinese government, censorship-circumventing technologies have been developed by Chinese netizen engineers that can outsmart the government's most highly developed Internet–filtering schemes. The gridded labyrinthine foundation laid by Web 2.0 means that "the porousness and decentralization that are basic to the Internet's design make it hard to come up with a firewall that works 100 percent of the time."[61] People will always be able to use creative technological devices and software to render obstacles placed by the government defunct.

Similar to the United States, China has its own complex architecture of oppression. In fact, the structure created by the Chinese government "has adopted a very similar language of cyber-security [from the U.S.] to justify its Internet control structures and procedures."[62] The similarities of surveillance have become ever more evident with Edward Snowden's release of thousands of confidential National Security Administration (NSA) documents via Glen Greenwald that reveal the expansive network of domestic and international surveillance conducted by the United States. China also has competing interests, with corporations and local governments (motivated by industrial growth bonuses and corporate bribes) at odds with local publics and often the national government, seeking to promote harmony and quell unrest. Yet, this complicated configuration of censoring devices has yet to silence voices, for "the Internet first helped to propel certain political happenings into the media despite resistance from censors," and in so doing, "Internet activity effectively set the agenda for public discourse."[63] Even within this claustrophobic climate of surveillance, the creative use of new media to circumvent censors, which can be seen proliferating across screens in China, provides grounds for hope.

The Wild Public Screens of China

We turn to environmental activism in China to elaborate on wild public screens because it offers a way to think outside Western Democracy. Within China's changing governmental system, illegal protests are erupting across the country and social media is playing no small part. In this section we discuss several environmental protests in China and the role of wild public screens.

Waves of protests centering on polluting factories have spread across cities such as Xiamen, Dalian, Shifang, and Qidong. These protests mark an expansion of environmental activism from committed activists to ordinary citizens, from green issues to social justice issues, and from civil disobedience to activism by any means necessary. As professor and columnist Tang Hao comments, "no longer is green campaigning solely the work of a small elite. Ordinary people, whose interests are at stake, are also taking to the streets."[64] Such wild activism also reveals the complicated political terrain of China and the promise of social media.

The myriad social media activities in China echo and inspire and enable social activism at large. Through wild public screens and risky practices, the people are manifesting the Chinese expression that warns about the power of the people: "水能載舟亦能覆舟" (*shui neng zai zhou, yi neng fu zhou*), which translates as "the water carries the boat but can also capsize it."

China has long been a society that utilizes strikes to defend the rights of its citizens.[65] In 2004, China experienced at least 74,000 protests, riots, and mass petitions, compared to a mere 10,000 such cases a decade earlier.[66] This number continues to grow. According to a leaked report, an estimated 127,000 protests occurred in 2008 and, in 2010, the number reported had risen to 180,000.[67] The rise in activism cannot be ignored by the official state-sanctioned media because the prevalence of these issues on social media demands mass media coverage—even on government-run CCTV.[68]

Within this dramatic rise in activism, environmentalism is currently the main source of social unrest.[69] In 2007, new media helped garner a critical mass of citizen support to stop the construction of a $1.6 billion chemical plant in Xiamen. Opposition to the construction of the plant was, in part, fueled by a prominent writer and blogger in the area who posted a report generated by academic Zhao Yufen explaining the highly toxic nature of the chemical proposed to be processed—paraxylene (PX). According to Zhao, PX has been linked to birth defects, nervous system damage, and cancer, and the location of the plant near a residential area would endanger Xiamen citizens. Though Zhao filed a case in local courts, the government did not take much notice. The plant was anticipated to almost double the local revenue of the city. Through blogs and Bulletin Board Systems, discourse and accompanying outrage was ignited not just locally but across the nation. When the debate landed in Beijing, officials became alarmed at the possibility of a mass uprising.

In response to online unrest and protests in the streets, the deputy environment minister initiated an environmental impact statement that was then conducted in concert with an assessment of Xiamen's plans for urban development. In June, 2007, an estimated eight thousand to ten thousand citizens organized an anti-PX march. Participants used their cell phones to text message updates about the protests to bloggers in other cities to insure authorities did not cover up the event. Soon, the story was also picked up by mass media including *People's Daily* and *Guangming Daily*. The central government pressured the local Xiamen government to reconsider. Local officials were publicly condemned in *People's Daily*, which ran a front-page editorial admonishing local officials for disregarding President Hu's edict to preserve the environment.[70] Opposition to the plant was obvious. In an online poll set up to measure attitudes about the plant postprotest, 55,376 of 58,454 voters opposed the plant.[71] Construction halted.

In 2012, the protests located in the city of Shifang against the construction of a $1.65 billion molybdenum-copper plant proved to be both large and bloody. In the early summer months, citizens concerned about the environmental and health impacts of the proposed plant took to the online avenues of Sina Weibo in an attempt to organize opposition protests. Users posted lists detailing the side effects of a molybdenum overdose. One user asserted that the molybdenum-copper plant would produce pollution that exceeded the amount of pollution released by the Fukushima nuclear plant after the 2011 earthquake. Regardless of accuracy, this proved to be a powerful comparison. People also posted signs around town to rally support, which were then captured by social media users with camera phones and disseminated on Sina Weibo.

On July 1, students organized protests using QQ and Baidu Tieba. Messages spread quickly and large numbers of student protestors gathered to sign petitions and make their voices heard. Their presence was felt and recorded. A larger protest erupted early the next day, during which protestors stormed government buildings and turned over police cars. Local Shifang government authorities responded to on-the-ground protests with police, tear gas, and grenades. They replied on Sina Weibo as well, announcing that they were concerned about citizen rights, stability, and harmony and sent out a text message to every local resident announcing that the plant would be well supervised to avoid deleterious health and environmental effects. Yet, the online presence of local authorities was no match for the mass of citizens determined to shut down the factory and expose police brutality. During the protests, Shifang became the most talked about subject on Sina Weibo, with in excess of 100 million entries.[72] Pictures of bloody protestors peppered user feeds. Top blogger, Hanhan, drew further attention to the events in Shifang by posting criticisms of the Chinese government's violent response. His wide user base rallied support. Responses rapidly ran across platforms, joining people across China. Police brutality was captured and the offenders called out for the violence they inflicted. By the late afternoon, local officials felt the pressure of the protestors and announced that further construction on the plant would be delayed. Throughout the entirety of this intense event, Sina Weibo did not censor Shifang related searches.

In July 2012, citizens ransacked government offices and seized and displayed material bribes in the city of Qidong during protests against a planned wastewater pipeline. They smashed computers and overturned cars and sartorially assaulted the mayor and Qidong's party secretary.[73] Within one day the citizens succeeded in canceling plans for the pipeline by mobilizing the assemblage of social media and bodies. Decentralized news sharing via Weibo challenged government- and corporate-controlled news media.

Chinese citizens have demonstrated repeatedly that their voices will be heard. Thus, local governments that decide that a new factory or plant is in the best interest of the people without consulting the people run the risk of mass uprisings—especially when the environment is in question, as all social groups are affected. What these protests make evident is that "government officials have begun to recognize that the Internet has set an irreversible trend toward a society that is more transparent, a citizenry that is more eager to participate in public life, and a public whose opinion carries more weight."[74]

Although Chinese governmental rules too often favor secrecy over transparency, social media provide improvised forms of transparency, as networks of citizens are enabled to share information and organize outrage. Today, "we are witnessing how these new electronic meeting places on the Internet have influenced the verdicts of court judges, Party officials and the news agenda in traditional media types."[75] Organizing via social media beyond effective government control and blocked from ritualized and domesticating forms of participation, Chinese citizens deploy protests by any means necessary. The wildness of the public screens in China stems from the risk users are taking when they operationalize social media screens for political purposes. Free speech rights do not ensure free speech, nor are they necessary for free speech to occur, as is clear in the case of *China*. The censors in China simply cannot keep pace with the "dense cluster of Chinese netizens," whose ability to spread controversial information quickly and widely flits past censors and rapidly "become public knowledge—a state of affairs that has huge political implications. When a *huo* [the Chinese word for *fire*] phenomena occurs, the Internet plays the role of a massive distribution platform that denies the government its agenda-setting power."[76] This fire spills onto the streets of cities across China and forces action. *democratic* practices proliferate in a nondemocratic country via the potential of panmediation that breaks out of the striated spaces of Western Democratic rituals. Public screens are networked flows of information that, in China, have allowed for wild forms of protest that are not shackled to fenced-in protest zones laced with barbed wire.

As Benkler, Castells, and others describe, the Internet's decentralizing technologies create opportunities for politics and activism that exceed the control of any centralized government, including China. Though academic analyses of China tend to concentrate on the "stale debate between digital-activism and cyber-censorship—the good versus evil struggle between the liberating potential and the Chinese party-state's ongoing efforts at thought control," the discussion must push beyond these boundaries.[77] Such a polarized debate obfuscates and obliterates what is happening outside of these binaristic discourses—a cacophony of voices interacting across vast expanses to reshape public conversations and what it means to be a citizen in China. Though, as Leibold points out, much of the Internet bandwidth in China is laden with banal chatter about entertainment, news, messaging, and gaming, the portion of the population that is using online forums to start movements and protest environmental and human rights abuses is an important sector engaging in online guerrilla warfare amid the cover of the mundane.[78]

Wild Hopes beyond Reason

In performing unruly activism on wild public screens outside the confines of institutionally protected/permitted protests and free speech zones, Chinese environmentalists enact a radical democracy beyond the ossified Democracy of the West. In inventing new forms of activism and democracy with the help of diverse social media platforms, the people make leaders follow. In the recently concluded eighteenth National Congress of the Communist Party of China, President Hu established ecological progress as one of the five pillars of progress: "Faced with increasing resource constraints, severe environmental pollution and a deteriorating ecosystem, we must raise our ecological awareness of the need to respect, accommodate and protect nature."[79]

Our encounters with the events of China and social media require us to drop all of our presuppositions and start thinking again. Institutionalized Democracy may guarantee only docile citizens. Social media platforms displace the privileged rhetor, the coherent text, and the resourced organization, instead creating panmediated people who are decentered sources of information and inspiration. People freed from institutional protection and armed with smartphones can race and rage across wild public screens and enact changes on local and global scales.

The world is balancing on a knife's edge. Seeing the work and the impact of Chinese people and ENGOs give us hope. In deploying both bodies and social media, they are changing conceptions of the "space of possibilities" and the "space of impossibilities," the very thinking enabling social change. As analyst Elizabeth Economy notes, "China's greatest environmental achievement over the past decade has been the growth of environmental activism among the Chinese people. They have pushed the boundaries of environmental protection well beyond anything imaginable a decade ago."[80] As Democracy fades, democracies and activisms emerge. People becoming decentered knots of social media form cacophonous networks across vast arrays of millions of wild public screens that transform the tenor of the earth.

Notes

1. A version of this chapter was presented at the 2013 Conference on Communication and the Environment in Uppsala, Sweden. The argument advanced in this chapter complements a larger body of work dedicated to exploring the use of social media in environmental activism in China that includes "Weibo, WeChat, and the Transformative Events of Environmental Activism on China's Wild Public Screens," a piece coauthored with Ye Sun that appeared in the *International Journal of Communication* in 2016.

2. Gilles Deleuze and Félix Guattari, *A Thousand Plateaus: Capitalism and Schizophrenia* (Minneapolis: University of Minnesota Press, 1987). In this chapter, we have chosen to conceptualize China as an assemblage, a multiplicity, a *process* of subjectification. Therefore, when we talk about China, we are talking about China as a people, government, economy, five thousand years of history, Han majorities, ethnic tensions, and relationships with the West.

3. Alain Badiou, *Ethics: An Essay on the Understanding of Evil*, trans. Peter Hallward, (New York: Verso, 2002), and *Logics of Worlds*, trans. Alberto Toscano (New York: Continuum Pub Group, 2008); Gilles Deleuze, *The Logic of Sense*, ed. Constantin V. Boundas, trans. Mark Lester and Charles Stivale (New York: Columbia University Press, 1990).

4. Kevin M. DeLuca, Sean Lawson, and Ye Sun, "Occupy Wall Street on the Public Screens of Social Media: The Many Framings of the Birth of a Protest Movement," *Communication, Culture and Critique* 5, no. 4 (2012): 483–509.

5. Kevin M. DeLuca and Jennifer Peeples, "From Public Sphere to Public Screen: Democracy, Activism, and the 'Violence' of Seattle," *Critical Studies in Media Communication* 19, no. 2 (2002): 125–51.

6. Gilles Deleuze, *Difference and Repetition* (New York: Columbia University Press, 1994).

7. Ibid, 125.

8. Ibid, 129–30.

9. Kevin M. DeLuca, *Image Politics: The New Rhetoric of Environmental Activism* (New York: Guilford Press, 1999), 46.

10. Deleuze, *Difference and Repetition*, 136.

11. Ibid.

12. Thomas J. Campanella, *The Concrete Dragon* (Princeton, NJ: Architectural Press, 2011), 15.

13. Michael Adas, *Machines as the Measure of Men: Science, Technology, and Ideologies of Western Dominance* (Ithica, NY: Cornell University Press, 1990).

14. Peter Simpson, "China's Urban Population Exceeds Rural for First Time Ever," *Telegraph*, January 17, 2012, accessed April 24, 2013, www.telegraph.co.uk/news/worldnews/asia/china/9020486/Chinas-urban-population-exceeds-rural-for-first-time-ever.html.

15. Keith Bradsher, "China Is Leading the Race to Make Renewable Energy," *New York Times*, January 30, 2010, accessed December 13, 2012, www.nytimes

.com/2010/01/31/business/energy-environment/31renew.html; Greenpeace East Asia, "China's Wind Power Market Remained the World No. 1, with Developing Pattern Diversified, Says Report," September 18, 2012, accessed April 24, 2013, www.greenpeace.org/eastasia/press/releases/climate-energy/2012/wind -energy-report-2012/.

16. Bill McKibben, "Can China Go Green?," *National Geographic*, June 2011, accessed April 24, 2013, ngm.nationalgeographic.com/2011/06/green-china/ mckibben-text.

17. Shengli Ren, Hong Yang, Adrian Stanley, Philippa Benson, and Weiguo Xu, "China's Scientific Journals in a Transforming Period: Present Situation and Developing Strategies," *Scholarly and Research Communication* 4, no. 1 (April 10, 2013): 16.

18. Hui Li, author interview with Li Hui, September 11, 2014.

19. Internet Live Statistics, "Number of Internet Users (2015)—Internet Live Stats," accessed March 24, 2015, www.internetlivestats.com/internet-users/.

20. "Social Engagement Benchmark // GlobalWebIndex // October 2012," GlobalWebIndex, October 24, 2012, accessed December 2, 2012, www.slideshare .net/globalwebindex/social-engagement-benchmark-global-webindex-october -2012; Simon Kemp, "Understanding Social Media in China in 2014," *Social Media Today*, April 14, 2014, accessed March 24, 2015, www.socialmediatoday .com/content/understanding-social-media-china-2014.

21. Badiou, *Logics of Worlds*.

22. Alain Badiou, *The Rebirth of History: Times of Riots and Uprisings*, trans. Gregory Elliott (New York: Verso, 2012), 52–53.

23. Goubin Yang and Craig Calhoun, "Media, Civil Society, and the Rise of a Green Public Sphere in China," *China Information* 21, no. 2 (2007): 211–36.

24. Gu Xin, "Review Article: A Civil Society and Public Sphere in Post-Mao China?: An Overview of Western Publications," *China Information* 8, no. 3 (1993): 51–52.

25. Ibid., 52.

26. Stephen J. Hartnett, "To 'Dance with Lost Souls': Liu Xiaobo, Charter 08, and the Contested Rhetorics of Democracy and Human Rights in China," *Rhetoric and Public Affairs* 16, no. 2 (2013): 223–74.

27. Glenn Greenwald, Laura Poitras, and Ewen MacAskill, "Edward Snowden: US Surveillance 'Not Something I'm Willing to Live Under,'" *Guardian*, July 8, 2013, accessed July 15, 2013, www.guardian.co.uk/world/2013/jul/08/ edward-snowden-surveillance-excess-interview; Zachary Davies Boren, "The US Is an Oligarchy, Study Concludes," April 16, 2014, accessed February 4, 2015, www.telegraph.co.uk/news/worldnews/northamerica/usa/10769041/The -US-is-an-oligarchy-study-concludes.html.

28. Edward S. Casey, *The World at a Glance* (Bloomington: Indiana University Press, 2007).

29. Edward S. Steinfeld, *Playing Our Game: Why China's Rise Doesn't Threaten the West* (Oxford: Oxford University Press, 2010).

30. Minxin Pei, *China's Trapped Transition: The Limits of Developmental Autocracy* (Boston: Harvard University Press, 2009).

31. James Kynge, *China Shakes the World: A Titan's Rise and Troubled Future—and the Challenge for America* (Boston: Mariner Books, 2007).

32. Chin-Chuan Lee, Hongtao Li, and F. L. F. Lee, "Symbolic Use of Decisive Events: Tiananmen as a News Icon in the Editorials of the Elite U.S. Press," *International Journal of Press/Politics* 16, no. 3 (2011): 335–56; Chin-Chuan Lee, "Established Pluralism: US Elite Media Discourse about China Policy," *Journalism Studies* 3, no. 3 (2002): 343–57; Kent Ono and Joy Yang Jiao, "China in the US Imaginary: Tibet, the Olympics, and the 2008 Earthquake," *Communication and Critical/Cultural Studies* 5, no. 4 (2008): 406–10.

33. Barbara Demick, "Chinese Await an Obama so Unlike Their Own Leaders," *Los Angeles Times*, November 14, 2009, accessed September 12, 2014, articles.latimes.com/2009/nov/14/world/fg-obama-china14.

34. Keith Bradsher and David Barboza, "Pollution From Chinese Coal Casts a Global Shadow," *New York Times*, June 11, 2006, accessed August 7, 2013, www.nytimes.com/2006/06/11/business/worldbusiness/11chinacoal.html.

35. Joseph Kahn and Jim Yardley, "As China Roars, Pollution Reaches Deadly Extremes," *New York Times*, August 26, 2007, accessed April 14, 2013, www.nytimes.com/2007/08/26/world/asia/26china.html.

36. Joseph Kahn and Mark Landler, "China Grabs West's Smoke-Spewing Factories," *New York Times*, December 21, 2007, accessed April 14, 2013, www.nytimes.com/2007/12/21/world/asia/21transfer.html.

37. Madison Park, "Obama, Romney's 'China Bashing' Grates Chinese Netizens," CNN, October 22, 2012, accessed April 14, 2013, www.cnn.com/2012/10/22/world/asia/china-us-debates-comments/index.html.

38. Interview with Ailun Yang, Greenpeace China, 2008.

39. Martin Jacques, *When China Rules the World: The End of the Western World and the Birth of a New Global Order*, 2nd ed. (New York: Penguin Books, 2012), 12, 416.

40. Boren, "The US Is an Oligarchy, Study Concludes."

41. We will capitalize "Democracy" when referring to the institutionalized, state form. We will write "democracy" when referring to noninstitutionalized practices.

42. Jacques Rancière, *Hatred of Democracy*, trans. Steve Corcoran, 2nd ed. (New York: Verso, 2009).

43. Jean-Luc Nancy, *The Truth of Democracy*, trans. Pascale-Anne Brault and Michael Naas (Bronx: Fordham University Press, 2010), 31.

44. Jürgen Habermas, *The Structural Transformation of the Public Sphere: An Inquiry into a Category of Bourgeois Society*, trans. by Thomas Burger and Frederick Lawrence (Cambridge: Massachusetts Institute of Technology Press, 1991), 23.

45. Ibid.

46. Christina R. Foust, *Transgression as a Mode of Resistance: Rethinking So-*

cial Movement in an Era of Corporate Globalization (Lanham, MD: Lexington Books, 2010), 5.

47. Alain Badiou, *Polemics*, trans. Steve Corcoran, Bruno Bosteels, Ray Brassier, and Peter Hallward (New York: Verso, 2012).

48. DeLuca and Peeples, "From Public Sphere to Public Screen."

49. Jacques Derrida, *Of Grammatology*, trans. Gayatri Chakravorty Spivak (Baltimore: Johns Hopkins University Press, 1998).

50. Ian Angus, *Primal Scenes of Communication: Communication, Consumerism, and Social Movements* (Albany: State University of New York Press, 2000); DeLuca, Lawson, and Sun, "OWS on the Public Screen"; Walter J. Ong, *Orality and Literacy* (New York: Routledge, 2002).

51. Marshall McLuhan, *Understanding Media: The Extensions of Man* (Berkeley: Gingko Press, 1964), 23, 24.

52. Harold A. Innis, *The Bias of Communication*, 2nd ed. (Toronto: University of Toronto Press, Scholarly Publishing Division, 2008).

53. Alfred North Whitehead, *Process and Reality*, 2nd ed. (New York: Free Press, 1979).

54. Deleuze and Guattari, *A Thousand Plateaus*, 98.

55. Gilles Deleuze, *Foucault*, trans. Sean Hand, 1st ed. (Minneapolis: University of Minnesota Press, 1988), 74.

56. Yochai Benkler, *The Wealth of Networks: How Social Production Transforms Markets and Freedom* (New Haven, CT: Yale University Press, 2007); Manuel Castells, *Networks of Outrage and Hope: Social Movements in the Internet Age*, 1st ed. (Malden: Polity, 2012); Manuel DeLanda, *A New Philosophy of Society: Assemblage Theory and Social Complexity*, 1st ed. (New York: Continuum, 2006).

57. Benkler, *The Wealth of Networks*, 3.

58. Ibid., 5.

59. Castells, *Networks of Outrage and Hope*, 2.

60. Evgeny Morozov, *The Net Delusion: The Dark Side of Internet Freedom* (New York: PublicAffairs, 2012).

61. Evgeny Morozov, "Whither Internet Control?," *Journal of Democracy* 22, no. 2 (2011): 65.

62. Rebecca MacKinnon, "China's 'Networked Authoritarianism,'" *Journal of Democracy* 22, no. 2 (2011): 90.

63. Xiao Qiang, "The Battle for the Chinese Internet," *Journal of Democracy* 22, no. 2 (2011), 63.

64. Tang Hao, "Shifang: A Crisis of Local Rule," *ChinaDialogue*, July 18, 2012, accessed July 18, 2012, www.chinadialogue.net/article/show/single/en/5049 -Shifang-a-crisis-of-local-rule.

65. Elizabeth Perry, *Shanghai on Strike: The Politics of Chinese Labor*, 1st ed. (Stanford, CA: Stanford University Press, 1995).

66. Howard W. French, "Land of 74,000 Protests (but Little Is Ever Fixed)," *New York Times*, August 24, 2005, accessed August 24, 2013, www.nytimes.com/ 2005/08/24/international/asia/24letter.html.

67. Bloomberg News, "China's Wukan Village Elects New Leader After Land Protests," March 3, 2012, accessed April 15, 2013, www.bloomberg.com/news/2012-03–03/china-s-wukan-village-votes-for-new-leaders-after-protests-1-.html; Bloomberg News, "Chinese Anger over Pollution Becomes Main Cause of Social Unrest," March 6, 2013, accessed January 15, 2014, www.bloomberg.com/news/2013–03–06/pollution-passes-land-grievances-as-main-spark-of-china-protests.html.

68. Xiao Qiang, "The Battle for the Chinese Internet," in *Will China Democratize*, ed. Andrew J. Nathan, Larry Diamond, and Mark F. Plattner (Baltimore: Johns Hopkins University Press, 2013).

69. Bloomberg News, "Chinese Anger over Pollution."

70. Ibid.

71. Joel Martinsen, "Citizens Air Opinions on the Xiamen PX Project," *Danwei*, December 14, 2007, accessed April 21, 2013, www.danwei.org/environmental_problems/citizens_opinions_on_the_xiame.php.

72. *Al Jazeera*, "Chinese Citizen Journalism Succeeds," July 5, 2012, accessed April 21, 2013, http://blogs.aljazeera.com/blog/asia/chinese-citizen-journalism-succeeds.

73. Nan Xu, "Qidong Protest: Another Polluting Project Cancelled," January 8, 2012, accessed April 15, 2013, www.chinadialogue.net/article/show/single/en/5076-Qidong-protest-another-polluting-project-cancelled.

74. Larry Diamond, "Liberation Technology," *Journal of Democracy* 21, no. 3 (2010): 74.

75. Johan Lagerkvist, "The Rise of Online Public Opinion in the People's Republic of China" *China: An International Journal*, 3, no. 1 (2005): 128.

76. Qiang, "The Battle for the Chinese Internet," 240.

77. James Leibold, "Blogging Alone: China, the Internet, and the Democratic Illusion?," *Journal of Asian Studies* 1, no. 1 (2011): 1–19.

78. Ibid.

79. Lina Yang, trans., "Full Text of Hu Jintao's Report at 18th Party Congress," *Xinhua*, November 17, 2011, accessed April 28, 2014, news.xinhuanet.com/english/special/18cpcnc/2012–11/17/c_131981259_9.htm.

80. Elizabeth C. Economy, "The Great Leap Backward?," *Foreign Affairs*, September 1, 2007, accessed August 24, 2013, www.foreignaffairs.com/articles/62827/elizabeth-c-economy/the-great-leap-backward.

WikiLeaks and Its Production of the Common

An Exploration of Rhetorical Agency in the Neoliberal Era

Catherine Chaput and Joshua S. Hanan

The Battle of Algiers, directed by Gillo Pontecorvo, problematizes the normative binaries of social struggle.[1] The film offers a particular challenge to the leader/follower dichotomy represented through the Hobbesian metaphor of the head and the body. Charged with ending the Algerian rebellion, French colonel Mathieu mistakenly declares that the only way to squelch the uprising is to cut off its head by assassinating its top three leaders, the so-called executive bureau. Contrary to the leader/follower structure, he goes on to describe the resistance as an infinite pyramid in which one person identifies two others, and the three function as an independent unit. Each of the two initiates repeats this process by securing a new pair of members. The structure ensures its continued reproduction by weaving itself throughout the entire social fabric: an individual corresponds only with the two members of the triangular section into which he or she was recruited and with the two recruits he or she solicits. This nonhierarchical model of resistance transforms ordinary civilians into a loosely organized, and ultimately victorious, counterinsurgency—one that requires, says Colonel Mathieu, constant policing and surveillance. Renowned worldwide for its complex exploration of urban warfare and anticolonial struggle, this film reflects the difficulties of theorizing social movement rhetoric and counterpublic theory in a historical moment wherein the traditional friend-enemy binary and the political borders between state and civil society have become increasingly indistinguishable and overlapping.[2]

WikiLeaks, for instance, reflects the nonhierarchical model of power and resistance depicted by Pontecorvo and illustrates the extent to which this historical condition has become part and parcel of everyday experiences within a civil sphere organized through digital technologies designed to exchange, store, and share information on a vast scale as well as to maintain smooth trails of surveillance.[3] An online organization for the collection and dissemination of information, WikiLeaks quietly launched its Internet presence in 2007. A project of the Sunshine Press, whose editor-in-chief is the now famous Julian Assange, the purpose of WikiLeaks was twofold: to create digital apparatuses for the safe transfer of national and corporate leaks and to facilitate the reporting of those leaks. Assange and the WikiLeaks project were catapulted onto the world scene through their central involvement in the 2010 "Cablegate" controversy, an event organized around the release of classified US military intelligence, first from the Afghanistan War and then the Iraq War. Prior to that, WikiLeaks helped uncover the discrepancy between the external financial ratings of Kaupthing Bank, one of Iceland's largest lending institutions, and its internally fraudulent monetary practices. These revelations were of immense interest to the Icelandic people because the bank's 2008 collapse led to a nationwide financial crisis and subsequent reorganization of public governance.[4]

As these benchmark cases illustrate, WikiLeaks is fundamentally decentered. It exists in the ether world of virtual space and operates through collaboration with voluntary whistleblowers, whose grievances are not bound by any clear friend-enemy divide. Even a cursory glance through its website suggests that its truth-telling and transparency goals are not focused on any one particular national target. Its archive exposes classified documents from the United States, Canada, and Europe, but it also reveals corruption in African, Asian, and Middle Eastern countries.

Like *The Battle of Algiers*, WikiLeaks's resistant practices challenge the traditional shibboleths of social movement rhetoric and publics theory, especially the in-group/out-group structure, its collective identification practices, and its strategic, goal-oriented conception of rhetorical agency. Illustrative of the recent work of Foust, who outlines what she calls "transgressive alternatives to friend-enemy agents and metaphorical representations" through "companion subjects and a politics of enactment," WikiLeaks requires a rhetorical perspective that goes beyond a logic of identification.[5] As Foust carefully illustrates, working within the traditional boundaries of identification and disidentification enables individuals and groups to establish shared political antagonisms but tends to reproduce a hegemonic analysis that elides more subtle and everyday practices of rhetorical resistance. In her words, "traditional theories ignore the potential that rhetoric has an immediate (though not directly causal) impact on witnesses and surroundings, which may translate into further impacts."[6] This notion of witness to the everyday is crucial to WikiLeaks, which functions as a clearinghouse for individuals who may or may not identify with a particular social movement, but whose rhetorical agency derives from the discrepancies between information as it appears in public and the more informal and colloquial forms of information to which they have exposure. It is precisely this asymmetry in information that WikiLeaks seeks to share with the public.

The 2010 Cablegate controversy indicates just how outmoded traditional models of social movement rhetoric are within the decentered structure and more open-ended agenda of many contemporary movements. Cablegate materialized as a political event largely because one individual, Pvt. Chelsea Manning,[7] acting on her own accord, chose to upload more than 250,000 classified US Embassy cables to the WikiLeaks website. Manning, an individual potentially ill-suited for military service who nonetheless enlisted in an effort to help pay for college, never articulated underlying motivations nor specific friend-enemy identifications. Indeed, neither Manning nor WikiLeaks self-identify as an avowed enemy of the United States. Although her reasons for these leaks remain unclear, what is known is that Manning felt persecuted for her effeminate nature both before and during her enlistment in the US Army. These everyday experiences may have contributed to Manning's empathy toward the civilian casualties and commonplace horrors of war, which in turn may have compelled her to leak a record-breaking number of documents, parts of which were printed in leading newspapers—the *Guardian*, the *New York Times*, *Der Spiegel*, and *Le Monde*—throughout the Western world. No doubt, this is entirely speculative. Yet we can say with certainty that traditional notions of rhetorical agency do not fully explain this and other actions taken by WikiLeaks, nor their indeterminable political outcomes.

Even though the rhetorical import of these publicity efforts is difficult to tack within the dichotomous power grids of twentieth-century rhetorical criticism, it becomes clearer, we contend, if understood within the political rationality of neoliberalism. A buzzword of scholarship since at least the 1990s, neoliberalism signifies a cartography of power that breaks down the imagined modernist boundaries between the private and the public, the state and civil society, the economic and the political.[8] Neoliberalism has come to be framed as a heterogeneous assemblage irreducible to any unified center of sovereign power through public policies that dismantle social welfare programs and deregulate corporate oversight; through economic structures that foster international financial speculation and borderless trade; and through cultural practices that valorize individual responsibility and self-discipline as the source of personal, political, and economic freedom. Rather, by promoting an image of sovereignty that governs its population recursively—as a strategic relationship among individuals, collective social institutions, and the "free-market"—neoliberalism functions through a logic of global "exceptionalism" that produces a borderless vision of the world in which the nationalist logics of collective identification and friend/enemy antagonisms appear increasingly obsolete.[9]

This porous cartography notwithstanding, neoliberalism maintains a privileged position for global capitalism. As the truth of the marketplace comes to define the way all public and private problems are understood and acted upon, neoliberalism maintains dominant power hierarchies by rationalizing economic exclusion as a problem of individual choice and poor community decision making. We thus anchor our rhetorical analysis in the language of Marxist autonomous critique, which attempts to theorize resistance to capitalism immanently.[10] Like Foust's theory of transgression, autonomous Marxism teaches scholars of social movement rhetoric that the immediate deviance from capitalist production might be more important than the political and ideological identifications attached to that form of deviation. In other words, to resist capitalism today, one need not identify with the working class or against the owning class because even the minutest aspects of our private lives are pulled into the governing logics of capital, as we will later detail.

Deploying WikiLeaks as its primary example, this chapter explores the changing structure of rhetorical agency from within the political rationality of neoliberalism. To do this, we first survey two dominant modalities of rhetorical agency and illustrate their inadequacies for understanding how the WikiLeaks project mobilizes rhetoric to affect change against the neoliberal order. We then turn to Foucault, excavating his late lectures on biopolitics and *parrhesia*, to develop a theory of rhetorical agency more appropriate to the contemporary scene. For us, Foucault's analysis of biopolitics (the emergence of individual and everyday behavior as the crucial site of political economic production) and parrhesia (the ways in which such criticism becomes first a problem and second socially regulated) are crucial to understanding WikiLeaks as a form of rhetorical agency that evolves within the economic landscape of neoliberalism. We end by advocating exodus and the common—practices derived from Foucault's genealogy and forged in the autonomist tradition—as rhetorical resources that better illuminate some of the crucial aspects of WikiLeaks and other contemporary social movement projects.

Traditional Models of Rhetorical Agency and Their Limitations

One of the most important debates to emerge in social movement rhetoric and publics theory over the past thirty-five years centers on the question of rhetorical agency. This debate has historically privileged two divergent theoretical camps: the functionalists, on the one hand, and the discursivists, on the other. As the original pioneers of social movement rhetoric in the field of communication studies, functionalist scholars—such as Griffin, Simons, and Stewart[11]—define rhetorical "agency [as the means] through which social movements perform essential functions."[12] For these thinkers, rhetorical agency must pursue the pathways offered by dominant organizational structures and the political subjectivities they subsequently create. For instance, Griffin divides rhetoric into "*pro* movements," which advocate for a new or existing idea, and "*anti* movements," which advocate against such ideas. Both types of movements, he says, "employ all, or nearly all, the available channels of propagation" in their attempt "to move the public to [their] desired action."[13] Consequently, rhetorical agency is bound to forms of "resistance generated by the larger structure" of society.[14] By conceptualizing rhetoric as a strategic means to a concrete end that uses available modalities of public address, functionalist articulations of rhetorical agency align with what Biesecker terms a "logic of influence" model.[15] Under this conceptual schema, sociopolitical and economic structures preexist the movement and determine both its identity and its norms of rhetorical engagement, even if its efforts are directed toward changing those normative structures. This is equally the case among foundational publics theorists. Habermas sees the bourgeois public sphere as asserting its political economic interests against the receding aristocratic structure and Fraser contends multiple counterpublics manage their goals vis-à-vis rhetorical deliberation. In either conception, a group identity precedes the rhetorical work of asserting that identity's needs through preestablished venues.

The discursivists, by contrast, tend to approach rhetorical agency from a constitutive lens.[16] A theoretical perspective originating from the writings of McGee, Sillars, and Cathcart, discursivism describes movement rhetoric as a process that entails the construction and transformation of identity rather than simply its mobilization.[17] Whereas functionalists conceptualize rhetorical agency as a stable property or essence that precedes the practice of rhetorical criticism, discursivists understand rhetorical agency "more [as] an argumentative claim than an operational definition."[18] For this reason, discursivists believe that a social movement should be studied as an ongoing symbolic performance. There exists an analogous trend toward subject constitution within publics theory. For instance, Warner argues that counterpublics are not only defined by their performances they actually cease to exist once they exchange such performativity for the "rational critical discourse" of instrumental goals.[19] For Warner, there is no role for practical rhetorical work within this *poietic* space of theatrical production, tying agency exclusively to the ends of subject formation.

Although scholarship from the 1990s onward became increasingly interested in conceptualizing social movement rhetoric as an agentive means of discursive self-fashioning, an analysis of WikiLeaks's rhetorical agency from within the disciplinary vocabulary of either functionalism or discursivism suggests that neither critical methodology offers the movement interpretative justice. As a nonprofit media institution whose primary aim is to "bring important news and information to the public," WikiLeaks's rhetorical agency resonates with a number of functionalist practices.[20] From raising private capital to maintaining its public legitimacy, WikiLeaks works within the organizational framework of modern society to accomplish its political objectives. In fact, it must engage preconstituted national news organs in order to reach its desired audience. Even as WikiLeaks makes use of these traditional media infrastructures, it simultaneously subverts them because, as it asserts, these modalities of public address have become "far less willing to ask the hard questions of government, corporations and other institutions."[21] WikiLeaks is thus in excess of the hegemonic-counterhegemonic power structures imagined by the functionalist model at the same time that it requires such infrastructural logics for its ongoing rhetorical production. It does not pit itself antagonistically against the institutional norms of the establishment; instead, WikiLeaks reinvents such organization by transforming the conditions of possibility in which public discourse can be imagined and disseminated. In this regard, WikiLeaks is more commensurate with DeLuca's new social movements and Asen and Brouwer's theorization of counterpublics than with an old-fashioned campaign for social change.[22] Insofar as WikiLeaks is a social movement that "cannot be delimited to a formal sphere of politics," its rhetoric aims at nothing less than constitutively transforming the very political structures governing our world.[23] Yet, because WikiLeaks reinvents the meaning of publicity and counterpublicity at the same time that it depends on these infrastructural conditions for situating its rhetorical practices, a discursivist model also fails to explain the transformative function of WikiLeaks's social movement rhetoric.

Not fully comprehensible within either framework, WikiLeaks illustrates the need for a different conceptualization of rhetorical agency—one that captures how both rhetorical forms operate within the fluid and indeterminate governing logics of neoliberalism. The critical task of social movement rhetoric and counterpublics theory is thus to rethink the meaning of functionalism in an era of neoliberalism, an intellectual inquiry for which Foucault offers useful entryways.

Biopolitics, Parrhesia, and the Rhetorical Agency of WikiLeaks

Publics theory since Dewey has relied on a publicity approach that utilizes both the notion of good citizenship and artistic production to advocate issues of civic importance. The problem with this extensive tradition, according to Greene, is that such "aesthetic-moral theories of communication are more likely to be implicated in new forms of bio-political power in postmodern capitalism" than to produce social change.[24] For Greene, the deliberating publics, as well as the performative social movements that make possible such theories, fail to enact their desired outcomes precisely because their communicative acts are subsumed within the machinations of capitalism. Because there is no longer anything beyond its reaches, capitalism absorbs communication practices and "disables the Habermasian distinction between the instrumental rationality of the economy and the communicative rationality of the life world."[25] Economic instrumentalism—the imperative to make profit—has so saturated our lives that not only our consumer activities but also our communicative activities take place in for-profit mediums such as YouTube, Twitter, and Facebook; or, they are co-opted by for-profit mechanisms (the sale of protest masks, signs, and bumper stickers, for example). Activities like blogging, texting, and contributing to online protests enable identification and may initiate change, but they are also recorded, repackaged, and sold to high-tech surveillance companies.[26]

To resist this contemporary confluence between communication and capitalism, Greene argues it is necessary to "abandon the view of the eloquent citizen as a moral solution to the crisis of democracy."[27] Only by deploying a materialist perspective, he argues, is it possible to develop a logic of resistance that can destabilize capitalism from within its own immanent and intensive terrain of social production. This commitment to radically reconceiving the rhetorical agent, a materialist logic Greene develops more concretely in two later essays, offers a way to rethink the inventional potential of social movement rhetoric.[28] Working from within the same underlying assumptions as Greene, we now turn to Foucault's scholarship on biopolitics as a way to further understand the capture of communication by capitalism and, inversely, his scholarship on parrhesia as a way to begin rethinking rhetorical resistance in line with the dispersed and distributed agency of Wikileaks.

During Foucault's last fourteen years of his life, he held a chair in the History of Systems of Thought at the Collège de France. This position required that he conduct one public seminar each year. Accordingly, he delivered an open lecture, once a week, over the course of several months during each academic year. Some of this lecture material became published in his *History of Sexuality* series, but the later lectures, which dealt with biopolitics and parrhesia, have become available only recently as the recorded seminars have been transcribed, translated into English, and published in book form. Although several rhetorical scholars have addressed biopolitics and others have explored his lectures on parrhesia, we believe a rhetorical understanding of social movement rhetoric and counterpublics is best illuminated by a critical lens that combines these discrete topics as both are central to contemporary governing practices.[29]

Whether developing a genealogy of the modern state or of parrhesiastic speech, Foucault relies on an analysis of what he calls governmentality. As Lemke emphasizes, "the concept of governmentality demonstrates Foucault's working hypothesis on the reciprocal constitution of power techniques and forms of knowledge."[30] More specifically, governmentality presumes that techniques for asserting or challenging power are embroiled within individual and collective discourses about institutions, individuals, and normative rules of behavior. Both producing and regulating a web of interrelated relations, governmentality includes specific political structures, but also individual behaviors, cultural practices for cultivating those behaviors, and the rules of speech that facilitate particular activities. Given the obvious imbrications between political and cultural practices and speech acts within Foucault's methodology generally, and his discussion of neoliberal governmentality more particularly, it makes sense to combine his discussion of biopolitics with his analysis of parrhesia. It makes even more sense in a study of social movement rhetoric and counterpublics, which is founded on the assertion of agency through discursive practices designed to mediate within as well as between normative political, economic, and cultural structures.

Using the theoretical lens of governmentality, Foucault dedicates an entire course—the 1978–79 lectures published as *The Birth of Biopolitics*—to distinguishing contemporary neoliberalism from classical liberalism, a distinction that hinges on their divergent governing rationalities. Whereas classical liberalism argues that government should not intervene in the marketplace, separating the sphere of politics from that of economics, German and Austrian Ordoliberalism, which arose after World War II and from which contemporary neoliberalism emerged, argues that the role of government is to clear and maintain a fertile terrain for free market competition. Framing itself in opposition to popular postwar Keynesianism, Ordoliberalism requires "a state under the supervision of the market rather than a market supervised by the state."[31] Among its foundational principles is the tenant that capitalism goes off the rails—as indicated by such things as high unemployment, bank insolvencies, and inflation—not because of its internal contradictions but because the necessary terrain of free competition has been compromised through Keynesian policies and/or corporate monopolies. This conception of the state as the necessary apparatus by which to forge a clearer path to "free market" capitalism becomes, under neoliberalism, a "regime of truth" to which all governing practices align themselves. Such governing rationality not only must fuel the political and economic spheres but also must organize our everyday sensibility and behavior.

Foucault identifies the Chicago School of Economics and its behaviorist thread as crucial to the extension of neoliberalism into this broader sphere of everyday life where it begins to subsume resistant processes in accordance with Greene's earlier critique of the Deweyian public sphere. For instance, Foucault cites Becker's theory of human capital as the pivotal formulation of neoliberalism within biopolitics, a move that facilitates the regulation of one's life activities according to a rationality that places economics at the heart of individual, cultural, and political decision making. Influenced by Ordoliberalism, Becker's theory of human capital develops the logic of neoliberal governmentality independent from the juridical and political structures of the nation-state. For Becker, the crux of this shift centers on reformulating economics as an anthropological explanation of all human behavior. Put simply, he conceptualizes a new political subject, *Homo oeconomicus*, whose decision-making processes are based less on a "repressive" relationship to the law and more on an ever shifting productive relationship to the economic "norm." From career choices and reproductive decisions to whether one will or will not break the rule of law, Becker argues that every important human decision can be calculated instrumentally.

Becker's theory of neoliberalism thus arrives at a logic of biopolitics in which the political/public and economic/private domains of life no longer need to be conceptualized antagonistically. By promoting institutional policies that encourage all citizens to conduct their behavior through the normative organizational grid of cost/benefit analysis, the subject of human capital is trained to locate political antagonism inside oneself. Rather than identify with the oppositional interests of some collective group against a particular law or social injustice, the subject of human capital is constituted as a self-contained enterprise, or "ability-machine," capable of self-government and internal differentiation from power. According to this formulation, individuals internalize the logic of capitalism and habituate their actions accordingly, in an instinctive, embodied way prior to conscious reflection.

As human capital theory illustrates, biopolitics is a way of governing conduct without antagonistic debate by collapsing the distinction between political and economic life. To accomplish this, biopolitics first folds the political into the economic sphere, which from the classical age through the early twentieth-century were imagined as separate, and then regulates the civil sphere and its nonstate activities according to its economic rationality. Such organization of life activities, says Foucault, calibrates with fluctuating social norms and political values because, under neoliberalism, "exchange determines the true value of things."[32] Insofar as neoliberalism governs all practices, including oppositional conduct, according to its economic rationality, Foucauldian biopolitics offers a diagram of power that captures the inventional possibilities of many counterpublics and new social movement models.

Exploring social movements and counterpublics from Foucault's formulation thus offers an important insight into the question of rhetorical agency in the contemporary world. As neoliberalism transforms individuals from rhetorical agents who resist repressive forms of power into rhetorical agencies that institutionalize economic power in relation to a fluctuating norm, the antagonistic possibility to resist the status quo becomes the very "apparatus of capture" that secures capitalism's ongoing survival. As rhetorical agencies, individuals often reproduce the power structures of neoliberalism even as they attempt to invent new political and social subjectivities in opposition to the cold, hard cash nexus. Although neoliberalism incorporates a range of practices—the deregulation of corporate and financial institutions, the privatization of state-owned industries (ranging from health care and education services to military operations), and the individualization of financial risk (replacing state pensions with market-based retirement funds, for instance)—the most important one for rhetoricians has to do with the everyday habits of individuals that have become captured by a market logic that masquerades as commonsense self-responsibility.

There exists a paradox inherent to this articulation of power and resistance. If, under neoliberalism, rhetorical agency can no longer be understood as mediating the political antagonisms that emerge in the gap between the liberal state and civil society, then the democratic rationale of social movement rhetoric, the negotiation of power through language or the cultivation of new subjects of power, becomes, as Greene says, obsolete. Importantly, this is only a defeatist position if scholars of social movement rhetoric remain wedded to a traditional notion of protestor as agent and discourse as the agency of rhetorical invention; if, however, they reimagine the categories of agent and agency, in step with the structural transformations brought about by neoliberalism, a counterpublic or social movement positionality can be reinvigorated.

Given that neoliberalism requires a rethinking of traditional categories that ground liberal articulations of rhetorical agency, it is not surprising that on the heels of his lectures on biopolitics, Foucault turned his attention to parrhesia or frank speech. These investigations, which intersect substantively with rhetoric, occupied Foucault's lectures until his untimely death in 1984.[33] Like his genealogy of liberalism, Foucault's study of parrhesia offers the history of an answer or "a reply to some concrete and specific aspect of the world."[34] The historical phenomenon precipitating the evolution of parrhesia is the function of criticism—speech that interrogates power—within the Greco-Roman world. While parrhesia emerged as "a guideline for democracy," grounded in the notion of the good citizen, it also carried within itself its own negation—the bad parrhesia of those uneducated and generally undisciplined individuals of questionable origins. In this way, truth telling, which begins unproblematically, comes into crisis over "recognizing who is capable of speaking the truth."[35] What we find interesting, from a contemporary perspective, is that this anxiety over the agent of criticism resolves itself by reorienting rhetorical agency away from the state and toward what Foucault elsewhere calls the "cultivation of the self."[36] The extension and multiplication of types of parrhesia under neoliberalism, originally located within the good citizen who risks angering those in power by frankly speaking an unpleasant truth, prompts the redirection of truth from the public sphere to the private individual.

Foucault chronicles this shift in both the agent and agency of truth, concluding that it results in two different parrhesiastic forms. The new form of "*parrhesia* is no longer an institutional right or privilege—as in the democratic city—but is much more a personal attribute, a choice of *bios*."[37] Truth telling is a *techne* for the administration of the self, coordinating one's conduct with the normative rules of behavior and their underlying rationality. As Foucault explains, self-accounting and self-criticism serve as "a kind of administrative scrutiny which enables [the individual] to reactivate various rules and maxims in order to make them more vivid, permanent, and effective for future behavior."[38] In short, as parrhesia becomes increasingly directed toward oneself, its truth tellers embody a life practice that primes their capacity to engage opportunities for social change wherever and whenever they might emerge. This is the form of parrhesia we wish to explore.

According to Foucault's survey of antiquity, the power of truth telling moves in two distinct trajectories. The first, which he calls the critical tradition, facilitates the disruption and possible redirection of reality. The second, which he calls the analytical tradition, maintains or governs the historically contingent *nomos*. Obviously, advocates of social movement rhetoric and counterpublics theory attempt to situate themselves within a critical genealogy of parrhesia, even as they cannot fully extricate themselves from the latter tradition. WikiLeaks, for example, exposes what it believes to be unethical practices of global power even as those leaks get repackaged for the maintenance of such power as Fox News commentator Bill O'Reilly did when he said, in his "Talking Points Memo," that whoever gave classified US documents to the website is "a traitor and should be executed or put in prison for life."[39] Indeed, it is precisely the collapse of these two forms of parrhesia that constitute the paradox of our neoliberal historical moment. If, as we have argued, the very power of neoliberalism lies in its capacity to rationalize all dimensions of public and political life as if they were private and economic, then parrhesia must be theorized in excess of both trajectories laid out by Foucault and the divergent conceptions of rhetorical agency that they support.

It is for this reason that we believe the recent uptake of Foucault's account of parrhesia in rhetorical studies is so important. If neoliberalism calls into question the very opposition between the critical and the normative, the truthful and persuasive, and the economic and political, then a new rhetorical perspective is needed that resists giving logical priority to one term or the other and instead, following Foucault, approaches parrhesia as a figure "without any figure."[40] Contemporary scholars are no doubt right to highlight the limitations of Foucault's work on parrhesia in that it appears to endorse philosophical truth as opposed to rhetorical dissimulation as well as to construct the parrahesiaste as a hero figure; yet we are intrigued by a different aspect of parrhesia, one that Vivian describes as "neither philosophy nor rhetoric, but something else."[41] Conceived outside this traditional binary, parrhesia aligns with a range of other work that questions the foundational categories that give rise to our disciplinary conception of rhetorical agents and agencies. In other words, although it is certainly reasonable to push back against Foucault's limited understanding, and indeed general dismissal, of rhetoric, as Walzer does, or against his seemingly noncritical endorsement of parrhesia among canonical philosophers, as Jarratt does, there seems to be something useful in Foucault's conception of parrhesia as a form of extrarhetorical rhetoric that exceeds all traditional categories (e.g., tropes, publicity, agency, etc.) for measuring the effects of rhetorical agency. As a mode of rhetorical invention that destabilizes the categories of truth and persuasion even as it works within the givenness of those categories, we believe Foucault's account of parrhesia points to a logic of rhetorical invention that provides new ways to imagine social movements and counterpublics trapped within a logic that Aune describes as neoliberalism's "realist rhetorical style."[42] From our perspective, parrhesia does not confront ideology with a more foundational reality, but asserts itself as a form of rhetoric that can neither be suppressed by conscious desires nor manufactured by those desires. Such speech does not happen when we self-consciously attempt to persuade an audience according to the rules of a pregiven situation but when we are compelled by some force to address power beyond the rules of the situation. So conceived, parrhesia represents the embodied desire to act and not the artful construction of the act.

This almost impulsive desire to speak truth to power is, it seems to us, precisely the modality of rhetorical agency made possible by WikiLeaks. Private Manning, for instance, simply downloaded information to the website with no artful reconstruction of that material, and Julian Assange passed this information in full onto the news media, which then sifted through the data, chose specific cables, and framed them within particular narratives. By circulating public information prior to its private commodification and capture by capital, WikiLeaks enables a new definition of rhetorical agency that attempts to embrace paradox and contradiction. Put differently, WikiLeaks offers what Biesecker calls an "evental rhetoric," one that facilitates the circulation of discourse prior to its stylization and capture by neoliberalism.[43]

Of course, Foucault's discussion of parrhesia as unadorned truth takes place within a larger network of relations and so this speech is never "outside" power structures. The speaker of truth has to take a risk by passing along unwelcome advice to a superior. Often the parrhesiaste was an advisor to the sovereign, positioning the truth teller within official apparatuses of power. Although WikiLeaks and its whistleblowers certainly take risks by exposing classified information, they do not do so in any official capacity. The truth delivered through WikiLeaks circulates outside and beyond formal institutional spaces. It is not the sage counsel of a trusted friend nor is it an attack by one's enemy. In its original expression, before it gets captured by the corporate-state apparatus and its official organs of public address, WikiLeaks enacts a less mediated form of parrhesia than any form of its subsequent mediations and thus its truth tellers occupy a more embodied and fluid tradition of parrhesia than one dictated by dominant power structures. The force of such rhetoric lies in the new conditions of possibility it opens up and not in the way it presents its parrhesiastic rhetoric.

From this vantage, the WikiLeaks project renews the possibility for rhetorical agents by positioning them as parrhesiastes, whose power lies in their ability to forge a space and provide content for future rhetorical events, which may, in turn, open up a host of other possibilities. Like Foust's transgressive rhetoric, this logic of resistance places the rhetorical agent in "the role of witness, attuned to the subtleties of everyday politics."[44] In such an arrangement, rhetorical agency gets redefined as an ongoing process of articulation and rearticulation, leaving the functionalist concern with effectivity open to democratic contestation and experimentation.

To that end, we now suggest two specific concepts—exodus and the common—as ways to reconceptualize rhetorical agents and their mode of agency. These concepts, utilized by autonomist Marxists such as Hardt and Negri as well as rhetorical critics like Greene, owe their theoretical filiation to Foucault's engagement with neoliberalism and biopolitics; they, therefore, keep good company with parrhesia.[45] Representing new possibilities for rhetorical intervention, these critical concepts recognize the collapse of rigid antagonisms and identifications at the same time they assert their power within a sociopolitical and economic structure that, although complex, can nevertheless be mapped and resisted. To illuminate how these new resources help reinvigorate our understanding of social movement rhetoric and counterpublics, we end with an analysis of WikiLeaks's Cablegate leak from the perspective of exodus and the common.

Exodus and the Common: Transgressive Tactics for the Neoliberal Era

WikiLeaks's 2010 release of over 250,000 secret US Embassy cables has become one of the most widely discussed examples of social movement rhetoric in recent years. Referred to colloquially as the Cablegate leak, the rhetorical effects of this (h)ac(k)tivist project have been nothing short of global in scope and reach. Without Cablegate, and a number of more moderated leaks that preceded it, one could argue that the unprecedented social unrest of 2011—ranging from Occupy Wall Street to the Arab Spring—might have looked significantly different. From inspiring in Tunisia what has been dubbed the "first WikiLeaks revolution," to fomenting international out-rage at the United States with the release of its (in)famous "Collateral Murder" video, the rhetorical agency of Cablegate was a central node in the political network that gave rise to *Time*'s 2011 person of the year—"the protestor."[46] As we have illustrated, this influence does not stem from any clear friend/enemy antagonism, nor from a desire to identify with a single group or collective political project. On the contrary, its influence derives from a parrhesiastic strategy that positions itself outside of traditional an-tagonisms (the exodus) and from agents who conceptualize themselves in transindividualistic terms (the common).

To fully understand the rhetorical effectivity of WikiLeaks requires that critics theorize social change less along the lines of friend-enemy identifi-cation and more as a process of democratic subtraction, or exodus. As de-fined by Hardt and Negri, exodus is a mode of resistance to power that self-consciously and continuously opts out of the governmental limits placed on rhetorical agency. It refuses to participate in the power structures of neoliberalism, which impose a colonizing market logic that defines resis-tant practices in terms of economic compensation. Instead, exodus inhab-its the nonidentity of the refugee, a figure of "bare life" that stands in an oblique and nonconforming relationship with the nation-state in which s/he resides.[47] Exodus thus abandons stale modernist categories, such as the citizen-nation couplet, in favor of new articulations of sovereignty that have yet to be invented.

For example, WikiLeaks, through its 2010 release of US Embassy cables, uses exodus as a tactic to undermine the very reasoning behind economic and national antipathies. These cables do not simply criticize the US gov-ernment and its military but attune a critical eye on nation-states across the globe. They criticize the troubled regimes in Egypt, Tunisia, and Libya without asserting a clash of civilizations thesis; they reveal a struggle be-tween the United States and Russia for political influence over former So-viet states without returning to Cold War antagonisms; and, they highlight the economic dependency of the United States on China, reinventing a po-litical enemy as an economic competitor.[48] The range of implicit criticisms as well as the sheer volume of leaked cables speaks to the inherent exodus strategy of WikiLeaks, one that develops a mobile rhetorical infrastructure that is heterogeneous, internationally dispersed, and nonunified.

Rather than advocating specific material ends, the rhetorical resistance perpetuated by exodus aims at the production of a democratic common, one that unites people and resources prior to their axiomatic capture and division by capital. Whereas neoliberalism encourages conceptualizing rhetorical agents in an insular economic language of privatization, risk calculation, and individual choice, the common is defined through the emergent possibilities of collective labor power within a socially shared and valued material ecology. As a direct challenge to what Barad terms "the metaphysics of individualism,"[49] the common attempts to make public "not only the earth we share but also the languages we create, the social practices we establish, [and] the modes of sociality that define our relationships."[50] Not a preconstituted rhetorical subject, as advocated by the friend/enemy logics of identification, but an irreducibly heterogeneous and evolving space of shared cultural values, the common reinvents the meaning of liberal democracy and its presupposition that "the rationality of the governed must serve as the regulating principle for the rationality of government."[51]

Consider, for example, one of the most memorable leaks of Cablegate: the so-called Collateral Murder video provided to WikiLeaks by Private Manning.[52] Released on April 5, 2010, to various news agencies, Collateral Murder can be conceptualized as an "image event" that rhetorically translates the reality of war into the language of the common.[53] As a "classified U.S. military video depicting the indiscriminate slaying of over a dozen people in the Iraqi suburb of New Baghdad,"[54] Collateral Murder animates war casualties within an interwoven narrative of a Western reporter doing his job, a parent dutifully taking his children to school, and a passerby who felt compelled to help these innocent victims. Including the workforce, families, education, and the Good Samaritan, this narrative is neither unified nor caught up in political antinomy. By deploying an institutional logic of counterpublicity to illuminate a series of lives that otherwise have neither political nor economic meaning within the discursive apparatuses of dominant Western powers, Collateral Murder reveals the power of the common trapped within the decontextualizing logic of neoliberal statistics. The dead and those resurrecting them become rendered intelligible as rhetorical agents, gesturing at an as yet unknown democratic future.

Strikingly, this video can be interpreted in this as well as other ways only because it was first made available to the public vis-à-vis WikiLeaks. One such YouTube version of this video, titled "Collateral Murder" and contextualized through quotes and commentary, has been viewed over 14.7 million times, indicating a significant public interest in the everyday practices of US military operations. This exigency must have certainly contributed to Private Manning's decision to filter the video through the WikiLeaks site. Both the narratives that frame the redistribution of the video once it became available as well as the narratives that individual viewers bring with them are fraught with problems for critical analysis, but the impulse to circulate unaltered information outside of its official structures does not participate in this rhetorical narration. WikiLeaks and other such practices simply present larger audiences with a host of information, compelling an engagement with details prior to any kind of policy discussion. In so doing, it forces the deliberating public to grapple with the complexities of our contemporary political economic world.

Going beyond the representational limits of neoliberal governmentality, the dual tactics of exodus and commoning align with Foust's politics of transgression. Defined as an attempt "to free human individuality from the bonds of representation that would contain it,"[55] transgression also promotes the decomposition of identity categories rather than their continued commodity production for global capitalism. Exodus and the common highlight the need for transgressive articulations of rhetorical agency that can resist "the disciplining mediations of institutions (notably, the state, school, family, and work)."[56] Moreover, exodus and the common emphasize how a logic of transgression should not be read as an attempt to remove "the 'social' from the social movement model" but instead as a struggle to reclaim rhetorical agency before it becomes instrumentalized within the structures of neoliberalism.[57] The primary communicative goal of WikiLeaks is to increase transparency by circulating previously unavailable information. Although it does this without commenting extensively on that information it nonetheless retains the skeletal structure of a communicative act—agent, text, and audience—and therefore is irreducibly social. By understanding exodus as the rhetorical agency of transgression and the common as its decentered rhetorical agents, new materialist strategies emerge for rethinking social movement rhetoric in the present.

Conclusion

Returning to *The Battle of Algiers*, in which Colonel Mathieu ventriloquizes neoliberalism's shift in tactics from a military state to a surveillance state, we can now see how WikiLeaks is emblematic of resistance in a historical moment wherein friend/enemy antagonisms no longer constitute the proper logic for critiquing sovereign power. Like the Algerian National Liberation Front depicted in the film, as well as other more recent social movements such as Occupy Wall Street and Anonymous, WikiLeaks illustrates the new face of social movements and counterpublics as a network of autonomous relations that will not crumble without centralized leadership and collective political identifications. Attempting to create, in the language of *Time* columnist Kurt Anderson, "a new social contract" that can respond to "the failure of hell-bent megascaled crony hypercapitalism," these movements partake in a transgressive mode of resistance that is best understood as a reaction to the political rationality of neoliberalism.[58]

Perhaps the most recent example of such a rhetorical approach took place in 2013 when Edward Snowden forwarded thousands of classified US documents directly to the news media. Without the mediation of a second party like WikiLeaks, Snowden adopted a rhetorical tactic of exodus by making information available about the National Security Agency (NSA) that was previously excluded from the domain of public knowledge. Revelatory of his independent but shared relationship to WikiLeaks, Snowden's documents included evidence that the NSA monitors not only the WikiLeaks site but all those who frequent the site.[59] In fact, the NSA designated the WikiLeaks site as a malicious foreign actor, which means that anyone who views it (as we did in the course of our research) is considered to be communicating with a foreign enemy target and thus is fair game for surveillance. The NSA simply collects the IP address of visitors to the WikiLeaks website, which identifies a particular computer, and then cross-references that computer with the person who pays for its Internet connection. According to Julian Sanchez, a research fellow at the Cato Institute, the NSA's assurance that it does not conduct domestic spying rings "hollow" once "you realize that the 'foreign target' can be an entire Web site or online forum used by thousands if not millions of Americans."[60] This is not, of course, to suggest that the new enemy is the NSA. Instead, what we want to point out is the NSA, intended to protect the United States and its worldwide interests, perceives the common and its mass exodus as threatening.

These transgressive tactics highlight a historical moment wherein rhetorical agency lies less in its leadership and centralized organization and more in people's desire to destabilize the divisive structural conditions that secure the democratic fantasy of liberal individualism in the first place. Although the parrhesiastic rhetorical acts of individuals such Julian Assange, Private Manning, and Edward Snowden have played a key role in making this new terrain of social struggle possible, it is ultimately an over-determined network of conscious and the unconscious practices activated by such individuals that maintain and carry forward the struggle for social transformation. Indeed, Julian Assange remains self-exiled in a single room of the Ecuadorian embassy in London, Private Manning has been sentenced to thirty-five years in prison for her role in exposing classified US intelligence, and Edward Snowden has taken residence in Russia to escape US extradition. And yet this prosecution of high-profile (h)ac(k)tivists does little to stop the circulation of information that has emboldened a worldwide commons capable of rethinking democracy in its own terms. Hence, by conceptualizing contemporary movements as a constitutive end in themselves, rather than as a form of political mediation between friend/ enemy antagonisms, social movement rhetoric can maintain its commitment to a transgressive mode of truth telling that even the fluid and flexible logic of neoliberalism cannot contain and manage.

Notes

1. The two authors would like to acknowledge the equal labor they invested in this essay.

2. See Michael Hardt, "The Withering of Civil Society," *Social Text* 45 (1995): 27–44.

3. See Mark Andrejevic, *iSpy: Surveillance and Power in the Interactive Era* (Lawrence: University Press of Kansas, 2009).

4. See Manuel Castells, *Networks of Outrage and Hope: Social Movements in the Internet Age* (Malden, MA: Polity, 2012).

5. Christina R. Foust, *Transgression as a Mode of Resistance: Rethinking Social Movement in an Era of Corporate Globalization* (Lanham, MD: Lexington Books, 2010), 73.

6. Ibid., 22.

7. Having subsequently undertaken a gender transition, Pvt. Chelsea Manning was then Pvt. Bradley Manning.

8. For social imaginaries in modern thought see Charles Taylor, *Modern Social Imaginaries* (Durham, NC: Duke University Press, 2004). For neoliberalism, see David Harvey, *A Brief History of Neoliberalism* (New York: Oxford University Press, 2005).

9. See Aihwa Ong, *Neoliberalism as Exception: Mutations in Citizenship and Sovereignty* (Durham, NC: Duke University Press, 2006).

10. The founding essay for the autonomist movement is often cited as Mario Tronti's "Strategy of Refusal," published originally in 1966. See Mario Tronti, "The Strategy of Refusal," in *Autonomia: Post-political Politics*, ed. Sylvere Lotringer and Christian Marazzi (Cambridge, MA: Semiotext, 2007). For a general historical discussion of autonomous Marxism see Roberto Esposito, *Living Thought: The Origins and Actuality of Italian Philosophy* (Stanford, CA: Stanford University Press, 2012).

11. Leland Griffin, "The Rhetoric of Historical Movements," *Quarterly Journal of Speech* 38, no. 2 (1952): 184–88; Herbert Simons, "Requirements, Problems, and Strategies: A Theory of Persuasion for Social Movements," *Quarterly Journal of Speech* 56, no. 1 (1970): 1–11; and Charles Stewart, "A Functional Approach to the Rhetoric of Social Movements," *Central States Speech Journal* 31, no. 4 (1980): 298–305.

12. Stewart, "A Functional Approach."

13. Griffin, "The Rhetoric of Historical Movement," 186.

14. Simons, "Requirements, Problems, and Strategies," 4.

15. See Barbara Biesecker, "Rethinking the Rhetorical Situation from within the Thematic of 'Différance,'" *Philosophy and Rhetoric* 22, no. 2 (1989): 110–30.

16. See Maurice Charland, "Constitutive Rhetoric: The Case of the *People Quebecois*," *Quarterly Journal of Speech* 73, no. 2 (1987): 133–50.

17. Michael Calvin McGee, "'Social Movement': Phenomenon or Meaning?" *Central States Speech Journal* 31, no.4 (1980): 233–44; Malcolm Sillars, "Defining Movements Rhetorically: Casting the Widest Net," *Southern Speech Communication Journal* 46, no.1 (1980): 17–32; Robert Cathcart, "Movements: Confrontation as Rhetorical Form," *Southern Speech Communication Journal* 43, no.3 (1978): 233–47.

18. McGee, "'Social Movement,'" 237.

19. Michael Warner, "Publics and Counterpublics," *Public Culture* 14, no. 1 (2002): 49–90.

20. Wikileaks, "About: What Is Wikileaks," last modified May 7, 2011, accessed January 28, 2016, http://wikileaks.org/About.html.

21. Ibid.

22. See Kevin Michael DeLuca, *Image Politics: The New Rhetoric of Environmental Activism* (New York: Guildford Press, 1999); and Robert Asen and Daniel C. Brouwer, eds. *Counterpublics and the State* (Albany: State University of New York Press, 2001).

23. DeLuca, *Image Politics*, 60.

24. Ronald Walter Greene, "John Dewey's Eloquent Citizen: Communication, Judgment, and Postmodern Capitalism," *Argumentation and Advocacy* 39 (2003): 196.

25. Ibid., 198.

26. See Jodi Dean, "Communicative Capitalism: Circulation and the Foreclosure of Politics," *Cultural Politics* 1, no. 1 (2005): 51–74.

27. Greene, "John Dewey's Eloquent Citizen," 199.

28. Ronald Walter Greene, "Rhetoric and Capitalism: Rhetorical Agency as Communicative Labor," *Philosophy and Rhetoric* 37, no. 3 (2004): 188–206; and "Orator Communist," *Philosophy and Rhetoric* 39, no. 1 (2006): 85–95.

29. For discussions of biopower and rhetoric see Catherine Chaput, "Rhetorical Circulation in Late Capitalism: Neoliberalism and the Overdetermination of Affective Energy," *Philosophy and Rhetoric* 43, no. 1 (2010): 1–25; and Joshua S. Hanan, "Home Is Where the Capital Is: The Culture of Real Estate in an Era of Control Societies," *Communication and Critical/Cultural Studies* 7, no. 2 (2010): 176–201; for discussions of parrhesia and rhetoric see Arthur E. Walzer, "Parrēsia, Foucault, and the Classical Rhetorical Tradition," *Rhetoric Society Quarterly* 43, no. 1 (2013): 1–21; and Susan C. Jarratt, "Untimely Historiography? Foucault's 'Greco-Latin Trip,'" *Rhetoric Society Quarterly* 44, no. 3 (2014):220–33; for a combined analysis, see Kelley Happe, "Parrhēsia, Biopolitics, and Occupy" *Philosophy and Rhetoric* 48, no. 2 (2015): 211–23.

30. Thomas Lemke, "'The Birth of Bio-politics': Michel Foucault's Lecture at the Collège de France on Neo-Liberal Governmentality," *Economy and Society* 30, no. 2 (2001): 190–207, 191.

31. Foucault, *Birth of Biopolitics*, trans. Graham Burchell (New York: Palgrave Macmillan, 2008), 116.

32. Ibid., 46.

33. Foucault explores parrhesia in his public seminars from 1981 to 1984, which are published in three distinct books: *The Hermeneutics of the Subject* (New York: Picador, 2005); *The Government of Self and Others* (New York: Picador, 2010); and *The Courage of Truth* (New York: Picador, 2011). He also discussed this in a short lecture series delivered in English at the University of California, Berkeley, in 1983, which is published as *Fearless Speech*.

34. Michel Foucault, *Fearless Speech*, ed. Joseph Pearson (Los Angeles: Semiotext(e), 2001), 173.

35. Ibid., 73.

36. Michel Foucault, *The Care of the Self: The History of Sexuality*, vol. 3, trans. Robert Hurley (New York: Random House, 1986), 43.

37. Foucault, *Fearless Speech*, 86.

38. Ibid., 149–50.

39. Bill O'Reilly, "There Are Traitors in America," Fox News, November 20, 2010, accessed January 28, 2016, www.foxnews.com/on-air/oreilly/transcript/there-are-traitors-america.

40. Foucault, *Fearless Speech*, 21.

41. Specifically, Vivian connects this aspect of Foucault's parrhesia to his own work as well as that of Barbara Biesecker, Diane Davis, Joshua Gunn, Christian Lundberg, John Muckelbauer, and Thomas Rickert, all of whom are interested in the embodied work of persuasion that happens prior to or separate from conscious deliberation. See Pat J. Gerke, Susan C. Jarratt, Bradford Vivian, and Arthur E. Walzer, "Forum on Arthur Walzer's 'Parrēsia, Foucault, and the Classical Rhetorical Tradition,'" *Rhetoric Society Quarterly* 43, no. 4 (2013): 372.

42. See Robert Hariman, *Political Style: The Artistry of Power* (Chicago: University of Chicago Press, 1995), and James Arnt Aune, *Selling the Free Market: The Rhetoric of Economic Correctness* (New York: Guilford, 2001).

43. According to Biesecker, evental rhetoric requires no critical interpretation; such rhetoric exerts its effect in the moment and not in a later effect. See "Prospects of Rhetoric for the Twenty-First Century: Speculations on Evental Rhetoric Ending with a Note on Barack Obama and a Benediction by Jacques Lacan," in *Reengaging the Prospects of Rhetoric: Current Conversations and Contemporary Challenges*, ed. Mark J. Porrovecchio (New York: Routledge, 2010), 16–36.

44. Foust, *Transgression*, 217.

45. Exodus is a concept taken from the critical tradition of autonomous

Marxism, particularly the work of Hardt and Negri. See Michael Hardt and Antonio Negri, *Empire* (Cambridge, MA: Harvard University Press, 2000); Michael Hardt and Antonio Negri, *Multitude* (Cambridge, MA: Harvard University Press, 2004); Michael Hardt and Antonio Negri, *Commonwealth* (Cambridge, MA: Harvard University Press, 2011). For a discussion of exodus in the context of social movement rhetoric see Greene, "Rhetoric and Capitalism" and "Orator Communist."

46. See Kurt Anderson, "The Protester," *Time*, December 14, 2011, accessed December 31, 2011, http://content.time.com/time/specials/packages/article/0,28804,2101745_2102132,00.html.

47. See Giorgio Agamben, *Homo Sacer: Sovereign Power and Bare Life*, trans. Daniel Heller Rosen (Stanford, CA: Stanford University Press, 1998).

48. For a general discussion and analysis of these cables, see the BBC documentary *Wikileaks: The Secret Life of a Superpower* (March 21, 2012).

49. Karen Barad, *Meeting the Universe Halfway: Quantum Physics and the Entanglement of Matter and Meaning* (Durham, NC: Duke University Press, 2007).

50. Hardt and Negri, *Commonwealth*, 350.

51. Foucault, *Birth of Biopolitics*, 312.

52. Wikileaks, "Collateral Murder," accessed January 28, 2016, www.collateralmurder.com/.

53. See DeLuca, *Image Politics*.

54. Wikileaks, "Collateral Murder."

55. Foust, *Transgression*, 209.

56. Ibid., 104.

57. See Brian L. Ott, "Review Essay: Assessing Rhetorics of Social Resistance," *Quarterly Journal of Speech* 97 no. 3 (2011): 341.

58. Anderson, "The Protester."

59. Glenn Greenwald and Ryan Gallagher, "Snowden Documents Reveal Covert Surveillance and Pressure Tactics Aimed at WikiLeaks and Its Supporters," *Intercept*, February 18, 2014, accessed January 28, 2016, https://theintercept.com/2014/02/18/snowden-docs-reveal-covert-surveillance-and-pressure-tactics-aimed-at-wikileaks-and-its-supporters/.

60. Ibid., 3.

Selected Bibliography

Alinsky, Saul. *Rules for Radicals: A Pragmatic Primer for Realistic Radicals*. New York: Vintage Books, 1971.

Andrews, James R. "History and Theory in the Study of the Rhetoric of Social Movements." *Central States Speech Journal* 31, no. 4 (1980): 274–81.

Asen, Robert. "Ideology, Materiality, and Counterpublicity: William E. Simon and the Rise of a Conservative Counterintelligentsia." *Quarterly Journal of Speech* 95, no. 3 (2009): 263–88.

———. "Seeking the 'Counter' in Counterpublics." *Communication Theory* 10, no. 4 (2000): 424–46.

Asen, Robert, and Daniel C. Brouwer, eds. *Counterpublics and the State*. Albany: State University of New York Press, 2001.

Berlant, Lauren. *The Queen of America Goes to Washington City: Essays on Sex and Citizenship*. Durham, NC: Duke University Press, 1997.

Bevington, Douglas, and Chris Dixon. "Movement-relevant Theory: Rethinking Social Movement Scholarship and Activism." *Social Movement Studies* 4, no. 3 (2005): 185–208.

Bowers, John W., Donovan J. Ochs, Richard J. Jensen, and David P. Shulz. *The Rhetoric of Agitation and Control*. 3rd ed. Long Grove, IL: Waveland Press, 2009.

Brouwer, Daniel C. "Communication as Counterpublic." In *Communication as . . . Perspectives on Theory*, edited by Gregory Shepherd, Jeffrey St. John, and Ted Striphas, 195–208 . Thousand Oaks, CA: SAGE Publications, 2006.

———. "Counterpublicity and Corporeality in HIV/AIDS Zines." *Critical Studies in Media Communication* 22, no. 5 (2005): 351–71.

Brouwer, Daniel C., and Robert Asen, eds. *Public Modalities: Rhetoric, Culture, Media, and the Shape of Public Life*. Tuscaloosa: University of Alabama Press, 2010.

Bruner, M. Lane. "Carnivalesque Protest and the Humorless State." *Text and Performance Quarterly* 25, no. 2 (2005): 136–55.

Buechler, Steven M. *Social Movements in Advanced Capitalism: The Political*

Economy and Cultural Construction of Social Activism. New York: Oxford University Press, 2000.

Campbell, Karlyn Kohrs. "The Rhetoric of Women's Liberation: An Oxymoron." *Quarterly Journal of Speech* 59, no. 1 (1973): 74–86.

Castells, Manuel. *Networks of Outrage and Hope: Social Movements in the Internet Age.* Malden, MA: Polity, 2012.

Cathcart, Robert S. "Defining Social Movements by Their Rhetorical Form." *Central States Speech Journal* 31, no. 4 (1980): 267–73.

———. "Movements: Confrontation as Rhetorical Form." *Southern Speech Communication Journal* 43, no. 3 (1978): 233–47.

———. "New Approaches to the Study of Movements: Defining Movements Rhetorically." *Western Speech* 36, no. 2 (1972): 82–88.

Chaput, Catherine. "Rhetorical Circulation in Late Capitalism: Neoliberalism and the Overdetermination of Affective Energy." *Philosophy and Rhetoric* 43, no.1 (2010): 1–25.

Charland, Maurice. "Constitutive Rhetoric: The Case of the *Peuple Quebecois.*" *Quarterly Journal of Speech* 73, no. 2 (1987): 133–51.

Chávez, Karma R. "Counter-public Enclaves and Understanding the Function of Rhetoric in Social Movement Coalition-Building." *Communication Quarterly* 59, no. 1 (January–March 2011): 1–18.

Cisneros, Josue David. "(Re)Bordering the Civic Imaginary: Rhetoric, Hybridity, and Citizenship in *La Gran Marcha.*" *Quarterly Journal of Speech* 97, no. 1 (2011): 26–49.

Cloud, Dana L. "The Null Persona: Race and the Rhetoric of Silence in the Uprising of '34." *Rhetoric and Public Affairs* 2, no. 2 (1999): 177–209.

Cox, J. Robert. "Beyond Frames: Recovering the Strategic in Climate Communication." *Environmental Communication* 4, no. 1 (2010): 122–33.

Cox, Robert, and Christina R. Foust. "Social Movement Rhetoric." In *The SAGE Handbook of Rhetorical Studies,* edited by Andrea A. Lunsford, Kirt H. Wilson, and Rosa A. Eberly, 605–27. Thousand Oaks, CA: SAGE Publications, 2009.

Day, Richard J. F. "From Hegemony to Affinity: The Political Logic of the Newest Social Movements." *Cultural Studies* 18, no. 5 (2004): 717–48.

Deem, Melissa. "Stranger Sociability, Public Hope, and the Limits of Political Transformation." *Quarterly Journal of Speech* 88, no. 4 (2002): 444–54.

Del Gandio, Jason. *Rhetoric for Radicals: A Handbook for 21st Century Activists.* Gabriola Island, BC, Canada: New Society Publishers, 2008.

DeLuca, Kevin Michael. *Image Politics: The New Rhetoric of Environmental Activism.* New York: Guilford Press, 1999.

———. "Unruly Arguments: The Body Rhetoric of Earth First!, ACT UP and Queer Nation." *Argumentation and Advocacy* 36, no. 1 (1999): 9–21.

DeLuca, Kevin Michael, Sean Lawson, and Ye Sun. "Occupy Wall Street on the

Public Screens of Social Media: The Many Framings of the Birth of a Protest Movement." *Communication, Culture and Critique* 5, no. 4 (2012): 483–509.

DeLuca, Kevin Michael, and Jennifer Peeples. "From Public Sphere to Public Screen: Democracy, Activism, and the 'Violence' of Seattle." *Critical Studies in Media Communication* 19, no. 2 (2002): 125–51.

Diani, Mario. "The Concept of Social Movement." *Sociological Review* 40, no. 1 (1992): 1–25.

———. "Introduction: Social Movements, Contentious Actions, and Social Networks: 'From Metaphor to Substance.'" In *Social Movements and Networks: Relational Approaches to Collective Action*, edited by Mario Diani and Doug McAdam, 1–20. New York: Oxford University Press, 2003.

Dubriwny, Tasha N. "Consciousness-Raising as Collective Rhetoric: The Articulation of Experience in the Redstockings' Abortion Speak-Out of 1969." *Quarterly Journal of Speech* 91, no.4 (2005): 395–422.

Dutta, Mohan J. *Communicating Social Change: Structure, Culture, and Agency*. New York: Routledge, 2011.

Enck-Wanzer, Darrel. "Trashing the System: Social Movement, Intersectional Rhetoric, and Collective Agency in the Young Lords Organization's Garbage Offensive." *Quarterly Journal of Speech* 92, no. 2 (2006): 174–201.

Endres, Danielle, and Samantha Senda-Cook. "Location Matters: The Rhetoric of Place in Protest." *Quarterly Journal of Speech* 97, no. 3 (2011): 257–82.

Felski, Rita. *Beyond Feminist Aesthetics: Feminist Literature and Social Change*. Cambridge, MA: Harvard University Press, 1989.

Foust, Christina R. *Transgression as a Mode of Resistance: Rethinking Social Movement in an Era of Corporate Globalization*. Lanham, MD: Lexington Books, 2010.

Foust, Christina R., and Jenni Marie Simon. "Memories of Movement in a Postfeminist Context: Conservative Fusion in the Rhetoric of Tammy Bruce and 'Dr. Laura' Schlessinger." *Western Journal of Communication* 79, no. 1 (2015): 1–21.

Fox, Rebekah L., and Joshua J. Frye. "Tensions of Praxis: A New Taxonomy for Social Movements." *Environmental Communication: A Journal of Nature and Culture* 4, no. 4 (2010): 422–40.

Fox Piven, Frances. "The Structuring of Protest." In *Who's Afraid of Frances Fox Piven: The Essential Writings of the Professor Glenn Beck Loves to Hate*, 67–102. New York: New Press, 2011.

Fraser, Nancy. "Rethinking the Public Sphere: A Contribution to the Critique of Actually Existing Democracy." In *Habermas and the Public Sphere*, edited by Craig Calhoun, 109–42. Cambridge: Massachusetts Institute of Technology Press, 1992.

Frey, Lawrence R., and Kevin M. Carragee, eds. *Communication Activism: Communication for Social Change*. Vol. 1. Cresskill, NJ: Hampton Press, 2007.

Fuchs, Christian. "The Self-Organization of Social Movements." *Systemic Practice and Action Research* 19, no. 1 (2006): 101–37.

Gaonkar, Dilip Parameshwar. "The Forum: Publics and Counterpublics." *Quarterly Journal of Speech* 88, no. 4 (2002): 410–12.

Greene, Ronald Walter. "Rhetorical Pedagogy as a Postal System: Circulating Subjects through Michael Warner's 'Publics and Counterpublics.'" *Quarterly Journal of Speech* 88, no. 4 (2002): 434–43.

Greene, Ronald Walter, and Kevin Douglas Kuswa. "'From the Arab Spring to Athens, from Occupy Wall Street to Moscow': Regional Accents and the Cartography of Power." *Rhetoric Society Quarterly* 42, no. 3 (2012): 271–88.

Gregg, Richard B. "The Ego-Function of the Rhetoric of Protest." *Philosophy and Rhetoric* 4, no. 2 (1971): 71–91.

Griffin, Charles J. G. "Movement as Memory: Significant Form in *Eyes on the Prize.*" *Communication Studies* 54, no. 2 (2003): 196–210.

Griffin, Leland M. "On Studying Movements." *Central States Speech Journal* 31, no. 4 (1980): 225–32.

———. "The Rhetoric of Historical Movements." *Quarterly Journal of Speech* 38, no. 2 (1952): 184–88.

Habermas, Jürgen. *The Structural Transformation of the Public Sphere: An Inquiry into a Category of Bourgeois Society.* Translated by Thomas Burger and Frederick Lawrence. Cambridge: Massachusetts Institute of Technology Press, 1991.

Hahn, Dan F., and Ruth M. Gonchar. "Social Movement Theory: A Dead End," *Communication Quarterly* 28, no. 1 (1980): 60–64.

Haiman, Franklyn S. "The Rhetoric of the Streets: Some Legal and Ethical Considerations." *Quarterly Journal of Speech* 53, no. 2 (1967): 99–114.

Hammerback, John C., Richard J. Jensen, and José Angel Gutiérrez. *A War of Words: Chicano Protest in the 1960s and 1970s.* Westport, CT: Greenwood Press, 1985.

Hardt, Michael, and Antonio Negri. *Commonwealth.* Cambridge, MA: Harvard University Press, 2011.

———. *Empire.* Cambridge, MA: Harvard University Press, 2000.

———. *Multitude.* Cambridge, MA: Harvard University Press, 2004.

Harold, Christine. "Pranking Rhetoric: 'Culture Jamming' as Media Activism." *Critical Studies in Media Communication* 21, no. 3 (2004): 189–211.

Harold, Christine, and Kevin Michael DeLuca. "Behold the Corpse: Violent Images and the Case of Emmett Till." *Rhetoric and Public Affairs* 8, no. 2 (2005): 263–86.

Hauser, Gerard. *Vernacular Voices: The Rhetoric of Publics and Public Spheres.* Colombia: University of South Carolina Press, 1999.

Hirschkind, Charles. *The Ethical Soundscape: Cassette Sermons and Islamic Counterpublics.* New York: Columbia University Press, 2006.

Hoerl, Kristen. "Burning Mississippi into Memory? Cinematic Amnesia as a

Resource for Remembering Civil Rights." *Critical Studies in Media Communication* 26, no. 1 (2009): 54–79.

Huesca, Robert. "Conceptual Contributions of New Social Movements to Development Communication Research." *Communication Theory* 11, no. 4 (2006): 415–33.

Jablonski, Carole J. "Promoting Radical Change in the Roman Catholic Church: Rhetorical Requirements, Problems and Strategies of the American Bishops." *Central States Speech Journal* 31, no. 4 (1980): 282–89.

Jensen, Richard. "Evolving Protest Rhetoric: From the 1960s to the 1990s." *Rhetoric Review* 20, no. 1/2 (2001): 28–32.

———. "Interdisciplinary Perspectives on Rhetorical Criticism: Analyzing Social Movement Rhetoric." *Rhetoric Review* 25, no. 4 (2006): 372–75.

Kahn, Seth, and Jonghwa Lee, eds. *Activism and Rhetoric: Theories and Contexts for Political Engagement*. New York: Routledge, 2011.

Kurzman, Charles. "Meaning-Making in Social Movements." *Anthropological Quarterly* 81, no. 1 (2008): 5–15.

Laraña, Enrique, Hank Johnston, and Joseph R. Gusfield, eds. *New Social Movements: From Ideology to Identity*. Philadelphia: Temple University Press, 1994.

Loehwing, Melanie, and Jeff Motter. "Publics, Counterpublics, and the Promise of Democracy." *Philosophy and Rhetoric* 42, no.3 (2009): 220–41.

Lucas, Stephen E. "Coming to Terms with Movement Studies." *Central States Speech Journal* 31, no. 4 (1980): 255–66.

Maddux, Kristy. "When Patriots Protest: The Anti-suffrage Discursive Transformation of 1917." *Rhetoric and Public Affairs* 7, no. 3 (2004): 283–310.

McGee, Michael Calvin. "'Social Movement': Phenomenon or Meaning?" *Central States Speech Journal* 31, no. 4 (1980): 233–44.

McKerrow, Raymie E. "Critical Rhetoric: Theory and Praxis." *Communication Monographs* 56, no. 2 (1989): 91–111.

Melucci, Alberto. "The New Social Movements: A Theoretical Approach." *Social Science Information* 19, no. 2 (1980): 199–226.

———. "The Symbolic Challenge of Contemporary Movements." *Social Research* 52 no. 4 (1985): 789–816.

Mitchell, Gordon R. "Public Argument Action Research and the Learning Curve of New Social Movements." *Argumentation and Advocacy* 40, no. 4 (2004): 209–25.

Morris, Charles E., III, and Stephen H. Browne, eds. *Readings on the Rhetoric of Social Protest*. 3rd ed. State College, PA: Strata Publishing, 2013.

Murphy, John M. "Domesticating Dissent: The Kennedys and the Freedom Rides." *Communication Monographs* 59, no.1 (1992): 61–78.

Negt, Oskar, and Alexander Kluge. *Public Sphere and Experience: Toward an Analysis of the Bourgeois and Proletarian Public Sphere*. Translated by Peter Labanyi, Jamie Owen Daniel, and Assenka Oksiloff. Minneapolis: University of Minnesota Press, 1993.

Olson, Kathryn M., and G. Thomas Goodnight. "Entanglements of Consumption, Cruelty, Privacy, and Fashion: The Social Controversy over Fur." *Quarterly Journal of Speech* 80, no. 3 (1994): 249–76.

Ono, Kent A., and John M. Sloop. "The Critique of Vernacular Discourse." *Communication Monographs* 62, no. 1 (1995): 19–46.

Palczewski, Catherine H. "The Male Madonna and the Feminine Uncle Sam: Visual Argument, Icons, and Ideographs in 1909 Anti-woman Suffrage Postcards." *Quarterly Journal of Speech* 91, no. 4 (2005): 365–94.

Peeples, Jennifer A. "Downwind: Articulation and Appropriation of Social Movement Discourse." *Southern Communication Journal* 76, no. 3 (2011): 248–63.

Pezzullo, Phaedra C. "Contextualizing Boycotts and Buycotts: The Impure Politics of Consumer-Based Advocacy in an Age of Global Ecological Crises." *Communication andCritical/Cultural Studies* 8, no. 2 (2011): 124–45.

———. "Performing Critical Interruptions: Stories, Rhetorical Invention, and the Environmental Justice Movement." *Western Journal of Communication* 65, no. 1 (2001): 1–25.

———. "Resisting 'National Breast Cancer Awareness Month': The Rhetoric of Counterpublics and Their Cultural Performances." *Quarterly Journal of Speech* 89, no. 4 (2003): 345–65.

Polletta, Francesca. "Culture Is Not Just in Your Head." In *Rethinking Social Movements: Structure, Meaning, and Emotion*, edited by Jeff Goodwin and James Jasper, 97–110. Lanham, MA: Rowman and Littlefield, 2004.

———. *It Was Like a Fever: Storytelling in Protest and Politics*. Chicago: University of Chicago Press, 2006.

Polletta, Francesca, and James M. Jasper. "Collective Identity and Social Movements." *Annual Review of Sociology* 27, no. 1 (2001): 283–305.

Reed, T. V. *The Art of Protest: Culture and Activism from the Civil Rights Movement to the Streets of Seattle*. Minneapolis: University of Minnesota, 2005.

Scott, James C. *Domination and the Arts of Resistance: Hidden Transcripts*. New Haven, CT: Yale University Press, 1990.

Scott, Robert L., and Donald K. Smith. "The Rhetoric of Confrontation." *Quarterly Journal of Speech* 55, no. 1 (1969): 1–8.

Sillars, Malcolm O. "Defining Movements Rhetorically: Casting the Widest Net." *Southern Speech Communication Journal* 46, no. 1 (1980): 17–32.

Simons, Herbert W. "Changing Notions about Social Movements." *Quarterly Journal of Speech* 62, no. 4 (1976): 425–30.

———. "On Terms, Definitions and Theoretical Distinctiveness: Comments on Papers by McGee and Zarefsky." *Central States Speech Journal* 31, no. 4 (1980): 306–15.

———. "On the Rhetoric of Social Movements, Historical Movements, and 'Top-Down' Movements: A Commentary." *Communication Studies* 42, no. 1 (1991): 94–101.

———. "Requirements, Problems, and Strategies: A Theory of Persuasion for Social Movements." *Quarterly Journal of Speech* 56, no. 1 (1970): 1–11.

Smith, Ralph R. "The Historical Criticism of Social Movements." *Central States Speech Journal* 31, no. 4 (1980): 290–97.

Sowards, Stacey K., and Valerie Renegar. "Reconceptualizing Rhetorical Activism in Contemporary Feminist Contexts." *Howard Journal of Communications* 17, no. 1 (2006): 57–74.

Squires, Catherine R. "Rethinking the Black Public Sphere: An Alternative Vocabulary for Multiple Public Spheres." *Communication Theory* 12, no. 4 (2002): 446–68.

Stevens, Sharon McKenzie, and Patricia Malesh, eds. *Active Voices: Composing a Rhetoric of Social Movements*. New York: State University of New York Press, 2010.

Stewart, Charles J. "Championing the Rights of Others and Challenging Evil: The Ego Function in the Rhetoric of Other-Directed Social Movements." *Southern Communication Journal* 64, no. 2 (1999): 91–105.

———. "A Functional Approach to the Rhetoric of Social Movements." *Central States Speech Journal* 31, no. 4 (1980): 298–305.

———. "A Functional Perspective on the Study of Social Movements." *Central States Speech Journal* 34, no. 1 (1983): 77–80.

Stewart, Charles, Craig Allen Smith, and Robert E. Denton. *Persuasion and Social Movements*. 6th ed. Long Grove, IL: Waveland Press, 2012.

Tarrow, Sydney G. *Power in Movement: Social Movements and Contentious Politics*. New York: Cambridge University Press, 2011.

Virno, Paolo. *A Grammar of the Multitude: For an Analysis of Contemporary Forms of Life*. Translated by Isabella Bertoletti, James Cascaito, and Andrea Casson. Los Angeles: Semiotext(e), 2004.

Voss, Cary R. W., and Robert C. Rowland. "Pre-inception Rhetoric in the Creation of a Social Movement: The Case of Frances Wright." *Communication Studies* 51, no. 1 (2000): 1–14.

Warner, Michael. *Publics and Counterpublics*. New York: Zone Books, 2002.

Wilson, Kirt H. "Interpreting the Discursive Field of the Montgomery Bus Boycott: Martin Luther King Jr.'s Holt Street Address." *Rhetoric and Public Affairs* 8, no. 2 (2005): 299–326.

Zarefsky, David. "President Johnson's War on Poverty: The Rhetoric of Three 'Establishment' Movements." *Communication Monographs* 44, no. 4 (1977): 352–73.

———. "A Skeptical View of Movement Studies." *Central States Speech Journal* 31, no. 4 (1980): 245–54.

Zittlow Rogness, Kate, and Christina R. Foust. "Beyond Rights and Virtues as Foundation for Women's Agency: Emma Goldman's Rhetoric of Free Love." *Western Journal of Communication* 75, no. 2 (2011): 148–67.

Contributors

Daniel C. Brouwer is an associate professor in the School of Human Communication at Arizona State University. His contributions to theorizing and analyzing publics, counterpublics, and social movements appear in his coedited books, *Counterpublics and the State* and *Public Modalities: Rhetoric, Culture, Media, and the Shape of Public Life*, and in the journals *Rhetoric and Public Affairs* and *Critical Studies in Media Communication*.

Elizabeth Brunner is an assistant professor at Idaho State University. Her scholarship focuses on the use of social media in environmental activism in China. She has published essays on visual rhetoric, new media, civic engagement, and transnational social movements.

Bernadette Marie Calafell is a full professor of communication studies at the University of Denver. She is author of *Latina/o Communication Studies: Theorizing Performance* and *Monstrosity, Performance, and Race in Contemporary Culture*. She is coeditor (with Michelle Holling) of *Latina/o Discourse in Vernacular Spaces: Somos de Una Voz?*

Catherine Chaput is an associate professor of rhetoric in the English department at the University of Nevada. She teaches courses in social movement rhetoric and publics theory at the graduate level and rhetorical criticism at the undergraduate level. Her research focuses on rhetoric, political economy, affect, and social change.

Karma R. Chávez is an associate professor in the Department of Mexican American and Latino/a Studies at the University of Texas, Austin. She is the author of *Queer Migration Politics: Activist Rhetoric and Coalitional Possibilities*.

Kevin Michael DeLuca is a professor of communication at the University of Utah. His scholarship explores how humanity's relations to nature are mediated by technology. Besides the book *Image Politics*, DeLuca has published dozens of essays on media, activism, social theory, images, events, and force. His current work engages environmental activism and social media in China.

Christina R. Foust is an associate professor and chair of communication studies at the University of Denver. Her teaching and scholarship engage rhetoric, power, and social change in many contexts. Her book, *Transgression as a Mode of Resistance* explores anarchistic activism in global justice protests. Her essays on conservatism, feminism, and environmentalism appear in such outlets as *Southern Communication Journal, Western Journal of Communication*, and *Environmental Communication: A Journal of Nature and Culture*.

Joshua S. Hanan is an assistant professor of rhetoric and communication ethics at the University of Denver. His work critiquing the rhetoric neoliberalism has been published in journals such as *Communication and Critical/Cultural Studies, Quarterly Journal of Speech*, and *Environmental Communication*.

Kelsey Harr-Lagin is a lecturer of communication at Kennesaw State University. Her work focuses primarily on critical pedagogy, rhetoric, public advocacy, intercollegiate forensics, and social justice.

Dawn Marie D. McIntosh is an adjunct professor of communication studies at the University of Denver. Her work has appeared in *Communication and Critical/Cultural Studies, Liminalities: A Journal of Performance Studies*, and *QED: A Journal in GLBTQ Worldmaking*.

Raymie E. McKerrow is professor emeritus, School of Communication Studies, Ohio University. His early research focused on the work of Richard Whately and argumentation theory. His more recent focus has been on contemporary rhetoric and criticism, with essays on critical rhetoric as an orientation toward criticism and historical reviews of rhetoric's theoretical development (including the nature and scope of social movement analysis).

Catherine Helen Palczewski is a professor of communication studies and affiliate faculty in women's and gender studies at the University of Northern Iowa. She coauthored *Gender in Communication* and *Rhetoric in Civic Life*, and edited *Disturbing Argument*. Her essays on social protest over woman suffrage, pornography, abortion, and Native American genocide have appeared in *Quarterly Journal of Speech, Argumentation and Advocacy*, and other journals and books.

Amy Pason is an assistant professor at the University of Nevada. Her teaching and scholarship engages with rhetoric and persuasion, including dissent by social movements and counterpublics. Her scholarship tends to focus on contemporary struggles exploring the limits and possibility of advocacy in the given context, and she has published on academic labor, student movements, peace movements, and most recently Occupy Wall Street in *ephemera*, *International Journal of Communication*, and other rhetorical collections.

Marie-Louise Paulesc teaches in the School of Human Communication at Arizona State University, including special topics courses on "Unlocking the Secrets of the Public" and "The Rhetoric of Everyday Life." Her master's thesis explored conditions of public discourse in Communist central and eastern Europe, and her doctoral dissertation featured rhetorical ethnography of practices of remembering Communism in contemporary Romania.

Kate Zittlow Rogness is a visiting assistant professor at the University of St. Thomas. Her work focuses on critical approaches to rhetoric and argumentation, with a particular emphasis on the intersections of gender, sexuality, race, class, and citizenship. Her work has appeared in *First Amendment Studies* and the *Western Journal of Communication*.

Index

abortion, state laws over, 136. See also *Roe v. Wade*; US Supreme Court
action, direct, 122, 136. *See also* activism; Occupy Wall Street movement; protests
action research, public argument, 175
activism, 11, 61, 113, 175, 183, 190–91, 225–40; American Indian, 13, 54; anarchist, 39–40; antiabortion, 129, 138, 141–43, 145, 147n25; in China, 223, 229; civil rights, 139; communication as, 19, 181; culture jamming, 55–56; digital, 239; environmental, 236; feminist, 89; forms of political, 212; gay and lesbian rights, 176; labor, 181; prison, 181; queer, 183; radical, 21n9; recent configurations of, 14; Serbian, 52; situationist, 55; student, 37–8; prochoice, 129, 132, 139, 141, 144, 145n1, 167, 254; of United Farmworkers, 69n36; of Zapatistas, 135. *See also* action, direct; protests; resistance
ACT UP, 134
aesthetics, 11, 13–14, 81, 207
affinity groups, 11, 51
afrocentric methods, 54
Against Equality, 175–92
agency, 8, 9, 41, 50, 58, 109, 111, 188–91; actions of, 210; coalitional, 19, 176, 182, 188; collective, 189; in network, 38; personal, 61; rhetorical, 246–64; women's, 60, 154. *See also* subjectivity
agent, 31, 33, 182; collective, 3, 33, 49, 58; friend-enemy, 247; goal-driven, 15;

preexistent, 62; protestor as, 256; rhetorical, 41, 255, 261; singular, 182; social movement as, 53, 59; text as, 111
agonistics, public, 82, 132
Alinsky, Saul, 116
anarchist, 11, 39, 56, 132, 149. *See also* activism
Anonymous, 262
antagonism, 7, 8, 10, 14–15, 23n47, 25n77, 49, 66, 259; political, 247, 254; traditional, 260
Anzaldúa, Gloria, 203, 211–13. *See also* women of color feminism
Arab Spring, 78, 233, 235, 259. *See also* protests; public sphere
Asen, Robert, 3, 4, 60, 111, 134, 136, 153, 161, 193n4, 205, 207, 251

Badiou, Alain, 229, 233
Benhabib, Seyla, 161
Berlant, Lauren, 163
Biesecker, Barbara, 250, 258, 266n41, 266n43
biopolitics, 249, 252–53. *See also* Foucault, Michael
blog/blogging, 38, 177, 185, 237, 252
bodies, 166, 209; assemblage of, 234; bodies of color, marked 209; bodies of color, queer, 209; body rhetoric, 53; hybrid/mestizo, 216; Latina/o, 201–19; othered, 203; and performance, 53, 213; politics of racialized marginalized, 206; as property, 19, 154, 165–67; racialized, 83; women's, 164, 168
border crossing, 19, 210–11